J.K. LASSER'S™

YEAR-ROUND TAX STRATEGIES

2004

J.K. LASSER'S™

YEAR-ROUND TAX STRATEGIES

2004

David S. De Jong, Esq., CPA, &
Ann Gray Jakabcin, Esq.

WILEY

John Wiley & Sons, Inc.

Look for these and other titles from J. K. Lasser™—Practical Guides for All Your Financial Needs.

J. K. Lasser's Pick Winning Stocks by Edward F. Mrkvika Jr.

J. K. Lasser's Invest Online by Laura Maery Gold and Dan Post

J. K. Lasser's Year-Round Tax Strategies by David S. De Jong and Ann Gray Jakabcin

J. K. Lasser's Taxes Made Easy for Your Home-Based Business by Gary W. Carter

J. K. Lasser's Finance and Tax for Your Family Business by Barbara Weltman

J. K. Lasser's Pick Winning Mutual Funds by Jerry Tweddell with Jack Pierce

J. K. Lasser's Your Winning Retirement Plan by Henry K. Hebeler

J. K. Lasser's Winning with Your 401(K) by Grace Weinstein

J. K. Lasser's Winning with Your 403(b) by Pam Horowitz

J. K. Lasser's Strategic Investing After 50 by Julie Jason

J. K. Lasser's Winning Financial Strategies for Women by Rhonda Ecker and Denise Gustin-Piazza

J. K. Lasser's Online Taxes by Barbara Weltman

J. K. Lasser's Pick Stocks Like Warren Buffett by Warren Boroson

J. K. Lasser's The New Tax Law Simplified

J. K. Lasser's New Rules for Retirement and Tax by Paul Westbrook

J. K. Lasser's New Rules for Small Business Taxes by Barbara Weltman

J. K. Lasser's Investor's Tax Guide by Elaine Floyd

J. K. Lasser's Choosing the Right Long Term Care Insurance by Ben Lipson

J. K. Lasser's Winning Ways to Save for College by Barbara Wagener

J. K. Lasser's Financial Basics for Business Managers by John Tracy

Published by John Wiley & Sons, Inc.
Published simultaneously in Canada.

For general information on our other products and services, or technical support, please contact our Customer Care Department within the United States at (800) 762-2974, outside the United States at (317) 572-3993 or fax (317) 572-4002.

Wiley also publishes its books in a variety of electronic formats. Some content that appears in print may not be available in electronic books.

ISBN 0-471-45469-9

Printed in the United States of America.

10 9 8 7 6 5 4 3 2 1

About the Authors

David S. De Jong is an attorney, certified public accountant, and certified valuation analyst. A principal of the law firm of Stein, Sperling, Bennett, De Jong, Driscoll & Greenfeig, P.C., with three offices in the Washington, D.C. area, he received his law degree from Washington & Lee University and his Master of Laws in Taxation degree from Georgetown University Law Center. Mr. De Jong has taught at four Washington, D.C., area universities, most recently for 20 years as an adjunct professor at American University. He is President of the American Association of Attorney-Certified Public Accountants for 2003–2004. Mr. De Jong is listed in *Who's Who in American Law*.

Ann Gray Jakabcin is a principal of Stein, Sperling, Bennett, De Jong, Driscoll & Greenfeig, P.C. She received her law degree from Temple University and her Master of Laws in Taxation degree from Georgetown University Law Center.

Both Mr. De Jong and Ms. Jakabcin are frequent speakers on various tax and estate planning topics.

For more than 50 years, the J.K. Lasser Tax Institute has specialized in writing tax and business publications for both nonprofessionals and professionals. The Institute is an editorial organization composed of tax attorneys, accountants, financial analysts, and writers—all experienced in presenting complicated tax, investment, and business material to the public and to professionals in related fields. J.K. Lasser's best-selling annual guide, *Your Income Tax*, has helped more than 25 million taxpayers reduce their taxes and make informed financial decisions.

Contents

Acknowledgments

The authors would like to thank Susan E. Anderson, CPA, for her continuing major substantive contributions and Zhiavictoria Hall for her substantial assistance in preparing the 2004 edition. Additionally, the authors want to acknowledge the following individuals who contributed their time, ideas, and support:

Alan Bergamini, CPA
Edward A. Bortnick, CPA
Donald W. Burton, CDP
Karen Carolan, Esquire
Frank W. Dunham III, Esquire
Eugene C. Fisher, Esquire, CPA
Robert C. Hammond, CPA
Roland W. Johnson, CPA
Robert J. Kopera, CPA
Philip Meade, Jr., CPA
Michael Muntner
Douglas A. Rausch, CPA
Isaac Reitberger, CPA
Jeffrey B. Rosenbloom, CPA
T. Theodore Schultz
Silvija A. Strikis, Esquire, CPA
Peter Wilhelm, CFP, EA
Alan Zipp, Esquire, CPA
Fred A. Balkin, Esquire
Millard S. Bennett, Esquire
Jolie S. Deutschman, Esquire
David C. Driscoll, Jr., Esquire
Stuart S. Greenfeig, Esquire
Jeffrey M. Schwaber, Esquire
Darcy A. Shoop, Esquire
Donald N. Sperling, Esquire
Paul T. Stein, Esquire
Susan E. Webb
Tracy Barger De Jong, Esquire
George J. Jakabcin

Summary of Year-End Tax Strategies

Tax planning is a year-round concern. However, it is a fact that most Americans neglect their tax planning until late in the year. As you will see, this can cost you in lost opportunities to save tax dollars. Still, you can make certain moves during the last few months of the year to save money. In fact, you can take steps right up to December 31 (or even up to April 15) that may save you hundreds of dollars in taxes.

J. K. Lasser's™ *Year-Round Tax Strategies 2004* tells you about special tax strategies that you can use to cut your tax bill and increase your personal wealth. You may be facing a specific tax problem right now. The following table lists various year-end tax problems and possible steps you can take to cut your tax bill:

PROBLEM	POSSIBLE SOLUTION	EXPLAINED IN
You support someone but do not claim the person as a dependent.	Provide additional support for possible dependent.	Chapter 1
You face a penalty for not having paid enough taxes during the year.	Increase your income tax withholding to avoid penalty.	Chapter 1
You have homes in two states and want to pay as little in state taxes as possible.	Watch time spent in the two states if you have more than one home and you seek to claim residence in the state with the lower tax rates.	Chapter 1
You face payment of an alternative minimum tax.	Preference items may be delayed to reduce tax.	Chapter 1

PROBLEM	POSSIBLE SOLUTION	EXPLAINED IN
You face a high tax bill; you want to defer taxes to a later year.	Minimize December collections of income accounts.	Chapter 1
	Purchase a CD maturing next year; sell assets on an installment basis.	Chapter 2
	Use deferred compensation arrangement to postpone receipt of salary.	Chapter 2
	Prepay next year's courses beginning before April 1 for an educational tax credit or deduction in the earlier year.	Chapter 3
	Use an escrow to delay closing until conditions are satisfied.	Chapter 5
You have passive losses, but cannot use them because you do not have passive income.	Increase hours devoted to an activity to cause "material participation" against which to use them.	Chapter 2
You are in a higher-than-average tax bracket this year (or will be next year).	Consider timing of election of stock options.	Chapter 2
	Determine whether stock, real estate, and other transactions should be closed in current year or next year.	Chapter 4
Your income is low, and you may not be able to use the full child credit.	Accelerate income to the extent needed and possible.	Chapter 3
You need to boost your itemized deductions.	Accelerate the payment of medical bills.	Chapter 4
	Make all planned cash charitable contributions.	Chapter 4
	Donate used clothes and other property to a charity.	Chapter 4
	Pay unescrowed property taxes.	Chapter 4
	Pay educational expenses for the upcoming term if the courses will be deductible by you.	Chapter 4
	Pay all anticipated state tax liability by December 31.	Chapter 4
	Close on your new home to get deduction for points.	Chapter 4

PROBLEM	POSSIBLE SOLUTION	EXPLAINED IN
	Make next payment on mortgages and other obligations that bear interest.	Chapter 4
	Pay professional and investment expenses if they will be deductible to you.	Chapter 4
You have capital gains you want to shelter.	Sell securities at a loss (or at a gain if you would otherwise have unused capital losses).	Chapter 5
You want to buy mutual fund shares but are concerned about capital gains.	Avoid purchase of shares before a distribution, which is often in December.	Chapter 5
You want to sell securities, but you want to delay taxes.	Buy a "put" to protect your position.	Chapter 5
You have securities that are possibly worthless.	Sell the instrument for a small amount.	Chapter 5
You own a vacation home.	Increase or decrease use of vacation home for best tax results.	Chapter 6
You have rental property income that you want to shelter.	Pay all bills related to rental properties and consider needed repairs unless you will have unusable losses.	Chapter 6
	Demonstrate active participation in rental property management and limit AGI.	Chapter 6
You are planning to get married.	Accelerate marriage if it will reduce taxes.	Chapter 8
You are planning to get divorced.	Attempt to finalize divorce or legal separation if taxes will be lower filing as unmarried.	Chapter 8
You are obligated to pay alimony to your ex-spouse.	Make year-end alimony payment.	Chapter 8
You need to shelter income.	Set up qualified retirement plan or SEP for your business (the latter until extended due date of return in the following year).	Chapter 9
	Open up IRA (until April 15 of following year).	Chapter 9
	Make elective deferrals to your employer's 401(k) or Simple plan.	Chapter 9

PROBLEM	POSSIBLE SOLUTION	EXPLAINED IN
You are considering purchasing equipment for your business.	Make needed capital expenditures for your business assets.	Chapter 10
You fear that a business activity may be deemed a hobby.	Delay payment of bills to create a profit (if a cash basis taxpayer).	Chapter 10
You expect to sell your residence next year.	Discontinue business or rental use of any portion of home.	Chapter 10
You want to shift income to other relatives.	Consider gifts of up to $11,000 to any family member.	Chapter 12

J.K. LASSER'S™

YEAR-ROUND TAX STRATEGIES

2004

CHAPTER 1

Introduction to Personal Tax Planning

Paying Tax May Be Inevitable—Paying Too Much Is Not

The word **tax** is derived from the Latin *tangere*; it means "to touch." Taxes touch us all as one of the absolute certainties in life.

Studies indicate that you, as the typical American, work until April 19 to pay your taxes for the year and then you work for yourself. The average Connecticut resident feels the greatest tax burden, needing to work until May 9 to cover taxes. Despite the universal tax burden, numerous tax strategies remain for satisfying your tax obligation before April Fools' Day.

Changes to the Tax Law Are Also Inevitable

Louis XIV's finance minister once stated that "the art of taxation consists in so plucking the goose as to obtain the largest amount of feathers with the least amount of hissing." In the last four decades, the way in which the goose is plucked has changed almost annually. Hardly a year or two has passed since 1954 without tax law changes for one or more of these purported reasons:

- Tax reduction
- Budget reconciliation
- Equity
- Revenue enhancement
- Tax simplification

- Economic recovery
- Fairness
- Jobs and growth
- Restructuring and reform

The year 1996 was particularly busy, with four important laws enacted only days apart, each with significant tax changes. Even before the ink had dried on these changes, the Taxpayer Relief Act of 1997 caused the largest overhaul of the Internal Revenue Code since 1986. One year later, numerous technical changes to the 1997 legislation were coupled with large numbers of procedural changes. Although major tax legislation in 1999 and 2000 was vetoed by President Clinton as being too costly, the Economic Growth and Tax Relief Reconciliation Act of 2001 slashed personal taxes. The Job Creation and Worker Assistance Act of 2002 was designed to stimulate recovery from the September 11, 2001 terrorist attacks. One year later, the Jobs and Growth Tax Relief Reconciliation Act of 2003 accelerated the 2001 reduction in individual tax brackets and cut the tax rate on dividends and capital gain through 2008.

The law becomes more complicated with each new tax change. The Internal Revenue Code has grown from just more than 400,000 words in 1954 to about 1.4 million words today and is now 500,000 words longer than the Bible. Regulations, which express the Internal Revenue Service's position on how the Code should be interpreted, run about 8 million words.

Individual tax compliance alone requires an estimated $140 billion annually. Then the IRS requires almost 100,000 employees to be sure that everyone has filed and has reported accurately.

The annual "patchwork" to the Internal Revenue Code can be expected to continue in part because all provisions contained in the 2001 tax legislation will expire at the end of 2010 in the absence of new legislation.

Sunrise Sunset

Among tax legislation, the 2001 Act was unique in its time because of its "sunset" language. All of its income tax provisions automatically expire on December 31, 2010. All of its retirement plan provisions automatically expire for plan years beginning after that date. All estate, gift, and generation-skipping tax provisions automatically expire for deaths and other transfers after that date.

At sunset, the law as existed in 2001 will be restored. Tax rates will go back up; deductions and tax credits will be lost; and retirement plan contribution limits will be slashed. Most significantly, the federal estate tax, scheduled to be abolished at the start of 2010 (see Chapter 12, "Estate Planning Strategies") will be reinstated.

Will this really happen? Certainly not, but succeeding Congresses and administrations will need to contend with which provisions of the 2001 Act will live and which provisions will die. Some provisions, such as the scheduled repeal of the federal estate tax, may be killed off before sunrise.

Although your year-round income tax strategies will typically look ahead only a few years (these 2010 sunset provisions are not specifically referenced), your year-round estate planning strategies will look far into the future (these 2010 sunset provisions are specifically referenced). Unfortunately, the cloud cover may remain until shortly before sunset.

The trend to sunset tax legislation may continue. Many of the provisions of the Jobs and Growth Tax Relief Reconciliation Act of 2003 grow dark at various times between 2004 and 2008.

The Basic Tax Structure for Individuals—From Gross Income to Tax Liability

Computation of your tax liability begins with an accounting of your gross income, which essentially constitutes your earnings and your gains. (Income and benefits constituting earnings are discussed in Chapter 2, "Taxable and Tax-Free Income and Benefits"; gains are discussed in Chapter 5, "Gains and Losses.")

From your gross income, certain expenses are deductible if you are eligible, irrespective of whether you itemize. These expenses include, most importantly:

- Alimony paid (discussed in Chapter 8, "Marriage and Divorce")
- Contributions to an individual retirement account (IRA), simplified employee pension plan (SEP), Keogh plan, or Simple plan (discussed in Chapter 9, "Retirement Plans")
- Health insurance costs paid by a sole proprietor, partner, limited-liability company member, or more than 2 percent S corporation shareholder not eligible to participate in a health insurance plan (discussed in "Deductions and Credits—For Itemizers and Nonitemizers")
- Contributions to an Archer Medical Savings Account (MSA) (discussed in Chapter 3)
- Certain education expenses including some student loan interest (discussed in Chapter 3)
- Limited types of moving expenses (discussed in Chapter 3)
- One-half of the self-employment tax paid by a sole proprietor or partner
- Penalties imposed by financial institutions on early withdrawal of savings

When these deductions are subtracted from gross income, the difference is your adjusted gross income (AGI). Many deductions are lost under the law if your AGI is too high. This would seemingly necessitate knowing your AGI to determine your AGI. However, to avoid the need for a degree in higher mathematics to solve this circular problem, the phaseout of deductions is actually based on modified adjusted gross income—which is AGI before computing certain deductions dependent on AGI and, in some contexts, after adding the exclusion for income earned abroad (see Chapter 11, "Special Groups of Taxpayers"). Consequently, modified AGI has a slightly different definition in each context.

From AGI, you subtract itemized deductions (discussed in Chapter 4, "Deductions—For Itemizers Only") or the standard deduction as well as personal exemptions to determine taxable income. Six marginal tax rates are then applied to levels of taxable income to determine your federal tax liability.

Credits reduce your tax liability dollar for dollar, including most importantly:

- The Child Credit (discussed in Chapter 3)
- The Adoption Expense Credit (discussed in Chapter 3)
- The Dependent Care Credit (discussed in Chapter 3)
- The Earned Income Credit (discussed in Chapter 3)
- The Hope Scholarship Credit and the Lifetime Learning Credit (discussed in Chapter 3)
- The Credit for the Elderly or Disabled (discussed in Chapters 3 and 11)
- The Employee Credit for Retirement Plan Contributions (discussed in Chapter 9)
- The Foreign Tax Credit (discussed in Chapter 11)

Itemized Deductions versus the Standard Deduction

AGI is reduced by itemized deductions or the standard deduction. About 35 percent of individual filers itemize; however, an estimated 2.2 million individual filers who claim the standard deduction would save by itemizing.

Itemized deductions are write-offs for certain medical expenses, taxes, interest, charitable contributions, casualty and theft losses, as well as job expenses and other miscellaneous itemized deductions. In lieu of claiming itemized deductions, an individual generally can use the standard deduction, which is a set dollar amount and varies with filing status. However, a nonresident alien, as well as a married individual filing separately whose spouse itemizes, cannot use the standard deduction and must itemize.

For 2003, prior to indexing in 2004 for cost of living, the standard deduction amounts are:

Filing Status	Standard Deduction
Married filing jointly	$9,500
Married filing separately	$4,750
Single	$4,750
Head of household	$7,000

If you are single or file as head of household, the standard deduction is increased by $1,150 if you are 65 years old or blind ($2,300 if you are both age 65 and blind). If you are married, the standard deduction is increased in multiples of $950 to a maximum standard deduction of $13,300, reflecting additional allowances for either or both spouses being over age 65, blind, or both. These increases are subject to indexing in 2004 and later years.

To receive the extra standard deduction, an individual need not be totally blind. For tax purposes, a taxpayer is blind if vision in the better eye does not exceed 20/200 with glasses or if the diameter of the visual field "subtends an angle no greater than 20 degrees."

See the discussion later in this chapter on the "Kiddie" Tax for a special limited standard deduction in the case of an individual who can be claimed as a dependent on another's return.

Individuals with AGI in excess of $139,500 ($69,750 for married individuals filing separately) must reduce the total of their itemized deductions except for medical expenses, casualty, theft, gambling losses (see the restrictions in Chapter 11), and investment interest. The reduction in otherwise allowable itemized deductions is an amount equal to 3 percent of AGI in excess of the threshold amount. However, the itemized deductions subject to the adjustment cannot be reduced by more than 80 percent. The threshold amounts will be indexed for inflation in 2004 and succeeding years. During the phaseout levels, the reduction in itemized deductions for 2004 generally will increase the true marginal tax bracket of affected individuals by between 0.84 and 1.05 percent depending on the tax bracket. The phaseout applied to about 5.7 million individuals in 2001. It is scheduled to be eliminated between 2006 and 2010.

Caution

In the absence of corrective legislation, the standard deduction for married couples filing jointly will drop in 2005 to 174 percent of the amount allowed single individuals. That ratio will climb until 2009 when the standard deduction for married couples filing jointly will once again be twice the amount allowed single individuals. At all times the standard deduction for married individuals filing separately will be one-half the amount allowed married couples filing jointly.

Filing Pointer

If your itemized deductions barely exceed the amount of the standard deduction, you need to consider the effect on state taxes before itemizing. In some states, you must itemize on the state return if you itemize on your federal return. Because state income taxes are not deductible on most state returns, you can have state itemized deductions far less than the state standard deduction when state income taxes constitute your largest federal itemized deduction. The result could be that itemizing on your federal return causes you to pay more to the state than you save with the IRS.

Question: I feel deprived. Each year I fall short of being able to itemize deductions by a few hundred dollars. What can I do to save taxes?

Answer: Attempt to bunch deductions into alternating years. To the extent you can, time your payments of such deductible expenditures as charitable contributions, property taxes, and state income taxes (if you pay estimates) to double up every other calendar year. Then you will be able to itemize once every two years and claim the standard deduction in the other years.

Maximizing Your Personal Exemptions

The final computation needed to determine taxable income is the subtraction of your personal exemptions. The amount of the deduction for each personal exemption, $3,050 in 2003 except for high-income individuals, will be adjusted annually for increases in the cost of living. You are entitled to claim a deduction for your own personal exemption unless you are claimed as a dependent on another's tax return. Consequently, children cannot claim deductions for a personal exemption on their returns when being claimed as dependents on the tax return of a parent.

In addition to your own personal exemption, you are entitled to claim a personal exemption deduction for your spouse if a joint return is filed. If you are married but file a separate return, you can claim a personal exemption for your spouse only if the spouse has no gross income and is not claimed as a dependent on someone else's return.

Additional exemptions are also available for certain dependents. To qualify for the dependency deduction, these requirements must be met:

- The dependent must have one of the following relationships to the taxpayer: child or stepchild; grandchild; parent or stepparent; grandparent; sibling or stepsibling; mother/father-in-law; brother/sister-in-law; son/daughter-in-law; or uncle, aunt, nephew, or niece related by blood. In addition, any other individual who is a member of the taxpayer's household for the entire year will qualify unless the living arrangement is in violation of local law.

- The dependent must have less than the exemption deduction amount of $3,050 (increased in 2004 for cost of living) of gross income or be the taxpayer's child who has not attained the age of 19 or is a full-time student under age 24.
- The dependent must receive more than one-half of his or her support from the taxpayer.
- The dependent must be a U.S. citizen or resident or a resident of Canada or Mexico.
- If the dependent is married, the dependent may not file a joint return with a spouse except for the purpose of getting a tax refund.

If a dependent was born during the year, died during the year, or was born alive but died shortly thereafter, the dependency deduction is available.

The benefit of each personal exemption is phased out based on levels of AGI. In 2003 the phaseout commenced at $209,250 of AGI for married individuals filing jointly, $174,400 for heads of household, $139,500 for single individuals, and $104,625 for married individuals filing separately. Each exemption will be reduced by 2 percent (4 percent in the case of married individuals filing separately) for each $2,500 or fraction by which AGI exceeds the threshold amount. Consequently, the benefit of all personal exemptions will be lost when AGI exceeds $331,750 in the case of married individuals filing jointly, $296,900 in the case of heads of household, $262,000 in the case of single individuals, and $164,625 in the case of married individuals filing separately. During this phaseout, the loss of exemptions for 2004 generally will increase the marginal tax bracket of most affected individuals by between 0.68 and 0.81 percent (double for married individuals filing separately) for each exemption claimed. Thresholds will be indexed for inflation in 2004 and succeeding years. The phaseout is scheduled to be eliminated between 2006 and 2010.

For purposes of satisfying the gross income test, only income that is taxable by the federal government is taken into account. Consequently, nontaxable Social Security benefits and tax exempt interest, for example, are not considered in determining whether the dependent exceeds the $3,050 gross income ceiling.

The most difficult issue usually associated with dependency deductions is whether a taxpayer provided more than one-half of the support of the proposed dependent. Consider the means of support for the potential dependent both from the dependent's sources as well as from those of other parties—who spent what for the support of this individual?

"Support" is interpreted broadly and includes such expenditures as food, clothing, lodging, education, and medical care. Lodging is based on the property's fair rental value. If a dependent lives in the dependent's own home and the taxpayer seeking the exemption does not live with the dependent, the rental value of the home is deemed contributed by the dependent for his or her own support. If the taxpayer pays part of the expenses of the home (such as mortgage interest, taxes, fire insurance premiums, or repairs), the fair rental value is reduced by the taxpayer's payments in determining the dependent's contribution.

Most sources of support, including items that are exempt from tax (if actually used for support), are counted in determining whether the support test has been met. Consequently, even though nontaxable Social Security benefits and tax exempt interest do not count toward the gross income test, they will be counted in determining whether the support test has been met.

Illustration

You provide $3,000 in cash for your father's support during the year. He lives in his own house, which has a fair rental value of $3,600 a year. He uses $800 of the money you give him to pay real estate taxes. Your father's contribution for his own lodging is $2,800 ($3,600 − $800 for taxes). Thus, if the lodging and the $3,000 in cash were the only support items involved for that tax year, you would be able to claim your father as a dependent as long as he satisfied the other dependency requirements, such as the gross income test.

Children can be claimed as dependents regardless of their gross income if they are under the age of 19 (or are under the age of 24 and enrolled as full-time students for at least five months of the year) and receive more than half of their support from their parents. In calculating the support provided to a child, nontaxable scholarships are not taken into account.

When a majority of an individual's support is from public assistance, no one can claim the individual as a dependent (not even that person).

When several family members collectively provide majority support of an individual by each contributing more than 10 percent of the support, but no one person contributes more than one-half of the support, the contributors can enter into a Multiple Support Agreement, in which all but one of the contributors waive the right to claim the individual in question as a dependent. The contributor who will be claiming the individual as a dependent should obtain signed IRS Forms 2120 from each of the other contributors of more than 10 percent. The agreement may be changed annually to allow each contributor a year in which to claim the dependency allowance.

Each dependent's Social Security number must appear on your tax return. The IRS uses this information to determine whether multiple individuals, such as both divorced parents, are claiming the same person as a dependent (see Chapter 8). The IRS has the authority to disallow a dependent personal exemption by summary procedure—without a statutory notice of deficiency (discussed in Chapter 13, "Dealing with the Internal Revenue Service")—when the proper Social Security number is not shown.

The IRS believed that, prior to requiring the listing of Social Security numbers on returns, one in seven purported dependents was improperly claimed. The first year the requirement went into effect, 9 percent fewer individuals (7 million in number)—and probably 100 percent fewer household pets—were claimed as dependents. Nevertheless, the IRS continues to believe that millions of erroneous dependent claims are still filed each year.

Year-End Reminder

A few dollars wisely spent before the end of 2003 could result in a big tax saving. Suppose that your child is a full-time student under age 24 with a part-time job earning, say, $6,000, all of which is spent on rent and food. You spend $5,500 a year for the child's support. Currently, you get no deduction because you provide less than half of your child's support.

Have your child bank $300 and increase your support by $300. Now you get an extra $3,050 exemption because you provide more than half of your child's support—$5,800 compared to $5,700. Although your child loses a $3,050 personal exemption, that exemption is worth only $305. If you are in a higher bracket, the extra exemption, if usable in full, is worth either $763 (25 percent bracket), $854 (28 percent bracket), or $1,007 (33 percent bracket). If your child is under age 17, the extra exemptions may be worth another $1,000 as a result of the Child Credit (discussed in Chapter 3).

Tax Planning

As a result of the phaseout of personal exemptions, an exemption may be worth more to your child than to you. In such a case, help your child claim the exemption by decreasing your support or having the child spend more of his or her earnings.

Question: I live in a large home with my girlfriend. We have a full-time housekeeper who has her own bedroom and bathroom. I provide all of the support for both my girlfriend and my housekeeper. Can I claim them as dependents?

Form **2120** (Rev. December 2002) Department of the Treasury Internal Revenue Service

Multiple Support Declaration

▶ **Attach to Form 1040 or Form 1040A.**

OMB No. 1545-0071

Attachment Sequence No. **114**

Name(s) shown on return | **Your social security number**

During the calendar year ____________________, the eligible persons listed below **each** paid over 10% of the support of:

____

Name of person supported

I have a signed statement from each eligible person waiving his or her right to claim this person as a dependent for any tax year that began in the above calendar year.

Eligible person's name | Social security number

Address (number, street, apt. no., city, state, and ZIP code)

Eligible person's name | Social security number

Address (number, street, apt. no., city, state, and ZIP code)

Eligible person's name | Social security number

Address (number, street, apt. no., city, state, and ZIP code)

Eligible person's name | Social security number

Address (number, street, apt. no., city, state, and ZIP code)

Instructions

A Change to Note

The signature of another eligible person is no longer required on Form 2120. However, you still must obtain a signed statement from each other eligible person. For details, see **Signed Statement** on this page.

Purpose of Form

Use Form 2120 to:

- Identify each other eligible person (see below) who paid over 10% of the support of another person whom you are claiming as a dependent and
- Indicate that you have a signed statement from each other eligible person waiving his or her right to claim that person as a dependent.

An **eligible person** is someone who could have claimed another person as a dependent except that he or she did not pay over half of that person's support.

If there are more than four other eligible persons, attach a statement to your return with the required information.

Who Can Claim the Dependent

Generally, to claim someone as a dependent, you must pay over half of that person's support. However, even if you did not meet this support test, you may be able to claim him or her as a dependent if **all five** of the following apply.

1. You and one or more other eligible person(s) (see above) together paid over half of that person's support.
2. You paid over 10% of the support.
3. No one alone paid over half of that person's support.
4. The other four dependency tests are met. See **Dependents** in the Form 1040 or Form 1040A instructions.
5. Each other eligible person who paid over 10% of the support agrees not to claim that person as a dependent by giving you a signed statement. See **Signed Statement** on this page.

Note: *To find out what is included in support, see* **Pub. 501,** *Exemptions, Standard Deduction, and Filing Information.*

Signed Statement

You must have received, from each other eligible person listed above, a signed statement waiving his or her right to claim the person as a dependent for the calendar year indicated on this form. The statement must include:

- The calendar year the waiver applies to,
- The name of the person the eligible person helped to support, and
- The eligible person's name, address, and social security number.

Do not file the signed statement with your return. **But** you **must** keep it for your records and be prepared to furnish it and any other information necessary to show that you qualify to claim the person as your dependent.

Additional Information

See Pub. 501 for details.

Paperwork Reduction Act Notice. We ask for the information on this form to carry out the Internal Revenue laws of the United States. You are required to give us the information. We need it to ensure that you are complying with these laws and to allow us to figure and collect the right amount of tax.

You are not required to provide the information requested on a form that is subject to the Paperwork Reduction Act unless the form displays a valid OMB control number. Books or records relating to a form or its instructions must be retained as long as their contents may become material in the administration of any Internal Revenue law. Generally, tax returns and return information are confidential, as required by Internal Revenue Code section 6103.

The time needed to complete and file this form will vary depending on individual circumstances. The estimated average time is: **Recordkeeping,** 6 minutes; **Learning about the law or the form,** 4 minutes; **Preparing the form,** 7 minutes; and **Copying, assembling, and sending the form to the IRS,** 13 minutes.

If you have comments concerning the accuracy of these time estimates or suggestions for making this form simpler, we would be happy to hear from you. You can write to the Tax Forms Committee, Western Area Distribution Center, Rancho Cordova, CA 95743-0001. **Do not** send the form to this address. Instead, attach it to your return.

Form **2120** (Rev. 12-2002)

Form 2120, Multiple Support Declaration

Answer: For your girlfriend to be claimed as a dependent, she must have been a member of your household for the entire year, and the relationship between the two of you must not violate state law. Some jurisdictions have criminal statutes prohibiting cohabitation between unmarried individuals, and this would apparently prohibit claiming the dependency exemption, even though such laws may not be enforced. Live-in housekeepers generally will not qualify for the dependency exemption, even though they may have no other means of support, because the room and board furnished by the taxpayer are considered by the courts to have been furnished as compensation and not as items of support.

Question: Last year my 17-year-old daughter had a child out of wedlock. They both live in my home, and I provide all of the support for both of them. I guess that I can claim my daughter again this year, but can I claim my grandchild?

Answer: Sure. It makes no difference whether or not a child or grandchild is born out of wedlock.

Question: My son attended "Chicken College" from January 20 until May 10 and, as a result of this employee training course, became an assistant manager in a fast-food restaurant. Aside from the months that he was away at school, he lived at home. I definitely provided more than one-half of his support for the year. He is 20 years old. Can I claim him as a dependent even though he was only a full-time student for less than four months?

Answer: A student age 19 through 23, inclusive, must be enrolled for some part of five calendar months at an educational institution on a full-time basis to be claimed as a dependent by a parent when the student earns more than $3,050 (adjusted in 2004 and succeeding years for cost of living). Your son was in his training course for parts of five calendar months and would qualify. However, on-the-job training or other employee training programs are not considered as qualifying educational curricula; a regular vocational education program would have qualified.

Question: I was more than eight months pregnant at the end of last year and gave birth to a baby boy on January 8 of this year. Can I claim my son as a dependent last year? I paid more than $2,000 out-of-pocket last year to my obstetrician.

Answer: The U.S. Court of Federal Claims in 1994 backed up the position of the IRS and ruled that taxpayers are not entitled to a dependency exemption for a child unborn at year-end.

Question: My mother is a widow, and to help her make ends meet, I pay the rent on her apartment and all of her utility bills. Can I claim my mother as a dependent on my 2003 tax return? Her annual rent is $7,500, and her utilities are $1,200. My mother spends about $7,000 on food, clothing, and doctor bills and another $2,000 on incidentals. She receives about $5,000 per year in Social Security benefits, $1,000 in interest on her savings account, and $3,000 in interest on municipal bonds.

Answer: Your mother satisfies one crucial requirement for being claimed as a dependent: She will have less than $3,050 of gross income subject to tax.

However, your mother will be deemed to have contributed $9,000 toward her total support, and you have paid only $8,700 of her total bills. If you increase the amount of your support by $151 and decrease the amount your mother provides by the same amount, you can claim your mother as a dependent on your tax return and save between $763 (in a 25 percent bracket) and $1,007 (if the exemption is fully usable in a 33 percent bracket). Do not overlook other items of support you may pay—car insurance, repairs, new clothes, and the like.

Caution

Congress is considering legislation that, if enacted, would establish a uniform definition of "child," affecting some dependency allowances. HR 1308, the All American Tax Relief Act of 2003, containing this provision, was approved by the Senate on June 5, 2003. The House version, passed one week later, omits this provision.

Marginal Tax Rates—From 10 to 35 Percent

After taxable income is calculated, marginal tax rates are applied to determine regular tax liability before any available tax credits. Marginal tax rates reflect the percentage of the next dollar of taxable income that will be lost to taxes.

The 2004 marginal tax rates for various levels of taxable income are set forth in the following table for the four filing status options from which an individual must choose: married filing jointly, married filing separately, single, or head of household. The levels of income to which these rates apply are shown for 2003 prior to indexing in 2004 as the cost of living increases. The income levels of the 10 percent bracket will not be indexed until 2008.

For those who are married and file a joint return, taxable income will be subject to these marginal rates of tax:

Married Filing Jointly

IF TAXABLE INCOME IS	MARGINAL TAX RATE IS
Up to $14,000	10%
$14,001–$56,800	15%
$56,801–$114,650	25%
$114,651–$174,700	28%
$174,701–$311,950	33%
More than $311,950	35%

For those who are married but file separate returns, each spouse's taxable income will be taxed at these rates:

Married Filing Separately

IF TAXABLE INCOME IS	MARGINAL TAX RATE IS
Up to $7,000	10%
$7,001–$28,400	15%
$28,401–$57,325	25%
$57,326–$87,350	28%
$87,351–$155,975	33%
More than $155,975	35%

For single individuals, taxable income will be taxed at these rates:

Single

IF TAXABLE INCOME IS	MARGINAL TAX RATE IS
Up to $7,000	10%
$7,001–$28,400	15%
$28,401–$68,800	25%
$68,801–$143,500	28%
$143,501–$311,950	33%
More than $311,950	35%

For unmarried individuals who qualify as head of household, taxable income will be taxed at these rates:

Head of Household

IF TAXABLE INCOME IS	MARGINAL TAX RATE IS
Up to $10,000	10%
$10,001–$38,050	15%
$38,051–$98,250	25%
$98,251–$159,100	28%
$159,101–$311,950	33%
More than $311,950	35%

Taxpayers in a marginal tax bracket of 25 percent or more are now taxed at a maximum rate of 15 percent on most dividends and long-term capital gains; taxpayers in the 15 percent marginal tax bracket are now taxed at a maximum rate of 10 percent on most dividends and long-term capital gains. See Chapter 2 for a discussion of dividends qualifying for the lower rates and Chapter 5 for a discussion of capital gains qualifying for the lower rates.

Caution

For 2005–2007 the 15 percent bracket will commence at $6,000 of taxable income for single individuals and married individuals filing separately. The 15 percent bracket will then commence at $12,000 of taxable income for married couples filing jointly. It will terminate during these years for married couples at less than the current twice the taxable income level for single filers, commencing in 2005 at 180 percent of the level. The 15 percent bracket always terminiantes for married individuals filing separately at one-half the taxable income level for married couples filing jointly.

Year-End Reminder

To the extent that you can determine the timing of income, deferral of income to a succeeding year can take you out of a higher marginal bracket into a lower one when a decline in income from other sources is anticipated.

Married—Joint versus Separate Returns

Individuals who are married on the last day of the year (or whose spouse died during the year, provided the survivor did not remarry) have the option of filing a joint return or separate returns. You may be legally married without ever taking out a license or having a ceremony. About a quarter of the states and the District of Columbia recognize common-law marriages. Although each such jurisdiction has its own definition, a common-law marriage generally requires cohabitation coupled with public recognition as husband and wife (often for a set number of years). If you meet the criteria of your state of residence for a common-law marriage, the IRS will consider you married, even if you subsequently move to a state that does not recognize common-law marriages. By electing to file a joint return, the husband's and the wife's incomes and deductions are combined in computing the couple's taxable income. If a joint return is filed, the husband and wife generally are jointly and individually liable for the tax liability, regardless of whose income generated the liability. See Chapter 8 for the "innocent spouse" exception.

Electing to file a joint return usually will produce a lower tax liability for a couple, particularly when substantial disparity exists between the levels of taxable income for each spouse.

Illustration

Both John and Mary are wage earners and have some interest income. Both are eligible to contribute to their own IRAs because neither participates in an employer-sponsored retirement plan, and each has itemized deductions of $5,000 from qualified residence interest and taxes. If the couple elected to file a joint return for 2003, their federal tax liability would be $16,845. In contrast, if John and Mary chose to file separate returns, John's federal tax liability would be $3,243, and Mary would owe $14,457, for a combined total of $17,700, an increase of $855 over what would have been owed had they filed a joint return. Itemized deductions claimed do not equal total itemized deductions as a result of the overall reduction for individuals with AGI in excess of $139,500 ($69,750 for married individuals filing separately).

	JOHN	MARY
Wages	$30,000	$75,000
Interest	5,000	5,000
IRA	(3,000)	(3,000)
Adjusted Gross Income (AGI)	$32,000	$77,000
Itemized Deductions	(5,000)	(4,782)
Personal Exemptions	(3,050)	(3,050)
Taxable Income	$23,950	$69,168
Separate Return Tax	$3,243	$14,457

	JOHN AND MARY
Joint AGI	$109,000
Itemized Deductions	(10,000)
Personal Exemptions	(6,100)
Joint Taxable Income	$92,900
Joint Return Tax	$16,845
Savings Filing Jointly	$ 855

About 95.5 percent of married couples file a joint tax return because a joint return generally produces a lower tax liability. However, there are exceptions. For example, suppose that one spouse has substantial medical expenses or unreimbursed employee business expenses. Both types of expenses are permitted as itemized deductions only if the total of the expenses exceeds a percentage of AGI. Filing a separate return may produce a lower tax liability because that spouse can claim a higher medical expense deduction or a higher deduction for the unreimbursed employee business expenses than would have been possible had the couple elected to file a joint return. The joint return produces a higher AGI, and as a result, may eliminate or reduce the ability to claim the medical expenses or unreimbursed employee business expenses as itemized deductions.

Illustration

Assume that in the prior illustration, in addition to the items of income and deduction shown, John had $2,000 of unreimbursed employee business expenses and $8,000 of unreimbursed medical expenses. If the couple opted to file a joint return, they would not be able to claim an itemized deduction for the $2,000 of employee business expenses because they are deductible (subject to the overall reduction by high-income individuals) only to the extent that the total exceeds 2 percent of the couple's AGI ($109,000). Because $2,000 is less than 2 percent of the couple's AGI (2% × $109,000 = $2,180), the deduction for the $2,000 of unreimbursed employee business expenses is lost. Similarly, the couple loses the ability to deduct the $8,000 in medical expenses if they file a joint return. The medical expenses are deductible (subject again to the overall reduction by high-income individuals) only to the extent that they exceed 7.5 percent of AGI (7.5% × $109,000 = $8,175).

However, if John and Mary had chosen to file separate returns in 2003, John would have been entitled to an additional itemized deduction of $1,360, the amount by which his unreimbursed employee business expenses ($2,000) exceed 2 percent of his AGI of $32,000 (2% × $32,000 = $640) and an additional itemized deduction of $5,600, the amount by which the medical expenses ($8,000) exceed 7.5 percent of his AGI (7.5% × $32,000 = $2,400). Consequently, John's itemized deductions have increased by $6,960 (the sum of $1,360 and $5,600), and John's federal tax liability on a separate return is $2,199. Mary's separate tax liability remains at $14,457. Because John can claim the additional itemized deductions for his unreimbursed employee business expenses and for the medical expenses on his separate return, the couple's combined tax liability, if they file separate returns in 2003, is $16,656, as compared to a joint tax liability of $16,845, a savings of $189 as shown next:

Illustration (cont.)

	JOHN	MARY
Wages	$30,000	$75,000
Interest	5,000	5,000
IRA	(3,000)	(3,000)
Adjusted Gross Income (AGI)	$32,000	$77,000
Itemized Deductions	(11,960)	(4,782)
Personal Exemptions	(3,050)	(3,050)
Taxable Income	$16,990	$69,168
Separate Return Tax	$2,199	$14,457

	JOHN AND MARY
Joint Taxable Income (from prior illustration)	$92,900
Joint Return Tax (from prior illustration)	$16,845
Savings Filing Separately	$189

A husband and wife who elect to file separate returns must allocate their itemized deductions between them. Only the spouse who paid the deductible expense is entitled to the write-off and then only if that spouse was legally obligated to make the payment. Thus, for example, when there is joint liability for real estate taxes, both spouses are entitled to claim a deduction on their separate returns for the real estate tax that they actually paid. When there is joint liability for home mortgage interest, the spouse making the mortgage payment is entitled to the home interest expense deduction on a separate return. If one spouse has no obligation for the mortgage debt, however, that spouse's payment of the mortgage interest will result in neither spouse being able to claim a deduction for that interest expense on separate returns; the spouse who paid the interest is not liable for the debt, and the spouse who is liable for the debt did not pay the interest.

In community property states, on separate returns the spouses must generally divide equally all income from wages and self-employment as well as other community income net of allocable deductions. Itemized deductions are also divided equally except to the extent underlying expenses were paid from non-community funds. As a result, it is even more rare for residents of community property states, as opposed to other states, to save taxes by filing separately. However, the IRS will disregard community property laws when one spouse is not notified of the nature and amount of community income or may disregard such laws upon request for equitable relief. (See Chapter 8 for an additional circumstance when community property laws may be disregarded in the case of a marital breakup.)

The community property states are Arizona, California, Idaho, Louisiana, Nevada, New Mexico, Texas, Washington, and Wisconsin.

Question: I said "I do" to my partner of the same sex in a formal ceremony. We live in Vermont, which recognizes these civil unions. Can we file a joint return?

Answer: Federal law denies federal recognition of same sex marriages or civil unions. In a 2000 decision, the Tax Court determined that two such individuals must file as unmarried.

Question: My son got married secretly last year to a girl who was under age at the time. When I found out about it a year later, I sent him to one of those islands where he could get a quick divorce. When he got back, my lawyer told me that my state would not recognize the divorce, but that he could seek to get the marriage annulled. The annulment will be final this year, but my son has asked me whether he can properly file as unmarried for last year.

Answer: Except for "sham" divorces—those filed prior to year-end to save taxes, with a remarriage planned for the following year—the IRS generally recognizes any divorce anywhere in the world unless set aside by a local court. Annulments are trickier. Although an annulment, foreign or domestic, should be recognized by the IRS unless set aside by a local court or unless a sham, applicable law determines whether your son's annulment relates back to the date of the marriage (in which case he files as unmarried for last year) or not (in which case he files as married for last year). In some states an annulment relates back as to rights and obligations of the couple as between themselves but does not relate back as to third parties such as the IRS (in which case your son also files as married for last year).

A married individual suspecting unstated income or overstated deductions on the spouse's part should hesitate to sign a joint return. See Chapter 8 concerning the advisability of separate returns by divorcing individuals.

Filing Pointer

Very often a married couple will have to compute their tax liability under both options to determine which produces the lower tax cost. This is particularly true when either or both spouses have one or more deductions that are restricted based on AGI. Besides medical expenses and miscellaneous itemized deductions, other write-offs that may be more usable on a separate return include capital losses and casualty losses.

Tax Planning

Married individuals who initially file separately may amend to file a joint tax return within a three-year period measured from the later of the original due date of the return or the date when the return was actually filed. Any unpaid tax liability need not be paid with the amended return. Married individuals who file jointly may not amend to file separate tax returns with one narrow exception—when a surviving spouse has signed for a deceased individual prior to the appointment of another as the decedent's personal representative.

Caution

Despite the higher tax liability, separate filings are generally advisable when the tax liability from a joint return is attributable, entirely or primarily, to one spouse and probably can never be paid. As discussed in Chapter 13, separate filings facilitate acceptance of an installment agreement or Offer in Compromise and possibly save one spouse from a future filing for bankruptcy protection.

Unmarried—Filing Status Alternatives

Unmarried individuals generally will file as single taxpayers. However, a widow or widower who has not remarried and who was eligible to file a joint tax return for the year of the spouse's death can use the tax rates (as well as the standard deduction) for married individuals filing jointly for the two years following the death of a spouse, provided that the surviving spouse provides more than one-half of the cost required to maintain a home for a dependent child as defined for head of household purposes.

If certain conditions are met, unmarried individuals can file as head of household. Individuals who qualify as head of household will have more of their income taxed in the lowest four brackets than would individuals filing as single taxpayers. If your 2003 taxable income is $80,000 and you file as a single taxpayer, you will owe $17,146; if you qualify for the head of household rate, you will owe only $15,695—a savings of $1,451.

You will qualify as head of household if you are a citizen or unmarried resident alien on the last day of the year and

- You pay more than one-half of the cost of maintaining your home, which for more than one-half of the year is also the principal residence of your child or any other relative you are entitled to claim as a dependent on your tax return; or

- You pay more than one-half of the cost of maintaining a parent's principal residence (which is not necessarily your home), and you are entitled to claim that parent as a dependent on your tax return.

For the purpose of determining who qualifies for the head of household rates, a married individual will be considered as unmarried for tax purposes if the taxpayer's spouse is a nonresident alien or if the spouse does not live with the taxpayer during the last six months of the year and the taxpayer's household is the principal residence of a child for whom the taxpayer is entitled to claim the dependency deduction—or would have been entitled to claim the dependency deduction had it not been transferred to the noncustodial spouse (see Chapter 8).

Temporary absences from the home due to vacation or schooling, for example, will not prevent the home from qualifying as the principal residence for the purpose of determining head of household status.

Question: I am a single parent. My ex-wife and I have joint custody of our only child. We alternate years claiming the child as a dependent. The child spends Monday through Wednesday at my house. On Thursday morning I take the child to school and after school he returns to his mother's home, where he spends Thursday and Friday nights. Saturday the child returns to my house. Sunday he goes back to his mother's. Can I use the head of household rates?

Answer: Yes. Your home is the child's principal residence (four out of seven days a week).

Controversy

Where the taxpayer seeking to claim head of household status maintains two households, the question may arise as to which home constitutes the principal residence of the child or other related dependent. To qualify for head of household status, the home maintained by the taxpayer must constitute the principal home of the child or other dependent. So long as the taxpayer spends a substantial amount of time at a residence, the Ninth Circuit Court of Appeals, with a Massachusetts federal district court in accord, would allow the head of household rates to apply. The IRS, the Fifth and Seventh Circuit Courts of Appeal, and the Tax Court take a more strict view, holding that a taxpayer cannot have two residences. However, no court will permit head of household status if an individual maintains one home for himself or herself and another where the child lives (at which location the individual is present only on an infrequent basis).

Caution

Congress is considering legislation that, if enacted, would establish a uniform definition of "child," affecting the ability of some individuals to claim head of household status. HR 1308, the All American Tax Relief Act of 2003, containing this provision, was approved by the Senate on June 5, 2003. The House version, passed one week later, omits this provision.

Operating at a Loss—Carryback or Carryforward

Although the right to calculate tax liability in periods of rising income through the use of income averaging has been eliminated, individuals can still level out their tax liabilities over a number of years if they have net operating losses. A net operating loss is created whenever your deductions exceed your gross income. To the extent that this loss is attributable to trade or business deductions, you may elect to carry that loss back to offset up to two prior years of income and, if unused in the carryback years, carry the loss forward as many as 20 years to offset taxable income. Alternatively, you can elect to forgo the entire carryback period and simply carry the net operating loss forward. The election to forgo the carryback years must be made by the return due date, including extensions, for the year in which the net operating loss arises and, once made, the election is irrevocable.

The carryback period is three years for individual casualty and theft losses and for small business losses attributable to disaster areas declared by the President (see Chapter 5), and the carryback period is five years for farming losses (see Chapter 11).

If you had positive taxable income in previous years against which the net operating loss can be used, using a carryback will give you an immediate refund of previously paid taxes. Forgoing the carryback period so that the net operating loss can be used against future income, however, will delay the benefit to be derived from the net operating loss.

It normally is beneficial to use the net operating loss as a carryback when your marginal tax rate in the earlier years was higher than or equal to what is anticipated in the carryforward years.

Question: I expect a net operating loss of about $10,000 in 2003 arising from starting a new business. In 2004 I expect my sole proprietorship to make at least $60,000. I had small amounts of taxable income in prior years but not more than $6,000 in any year. Should I carry the loss back and then use the rest of the loss, if any, in 2005 and future years?

Answer: Although you can get an immediate refund by using the carryback, you will probably be better off to skip the carryback, file the election, and use the net operating loss to offset future income. Your marginal rate of tax in the carryback period was lower than your likely rate in the future.

Avoiding the Alternative Minimum Tax

In addition to the regular income tax, about 2 million individuals each year are required to pay the alternative minimum tax (AMT), an additional tax computed on Form 6251 equal to the tentative minimum tax (determined through a special computation) less the regular income tax liability.

The starting point in computing the AMT is the determination of alternative minimum taxable income. In general terms, this is regular taxable income increased by many deductions used in computing the regular taxable income, but which are disallowed in the computation of alternative minimum taxable income and further increased by certain tax preference items, such as accelerated depreciation on real property acquired before 1987 (see Chapter 5), percentage depletion and intangible drilling costs (see Chapter 7, "Other Tax-Favored Investments"), and the spread between the fair market value of incentive stock options that were exercised during the year and the option price (see Chapter 2). Additionally, a special net operating loss deduction for AMT purposes is substituted for any regular net operating loss deduction.

After alternative minimum taxable income has been computed, married individuals who file a joint return are entitled to an exemption amount of $58,000 ($40,250 for single individuals and $29,000 for those who are married and file separate returns), but the exemption amount is phased out for those on a joint return with alternative minimum taxable income greater than $150,000 ($112,500 for single individuals and $75,000 for married taxpayers filing separately). The exemption amount is completely phased out when the alternative minimum taxable income on a joint return is $382,000 ($273,500 for single taxpayers and $191,000 for married taxpayers who file separately).

A tax rate of 26 percent is applied to the first $175,000 ($87,500 for married taxpayers who file separately) of alternative minimum taxable income less the applicable exemption, if any. A tax rate of 28 percent is applied to the excess. A special foreign tax credit is computed and subtracted if the taxpayer paid any foreign taxes. The result is a tentative minimum tax from which the regular tax liability before all credits, except the foreign tax credit, is subtracted. The difference is the additional tax arising from the AMT.

The number of individuals paying the AMT is increasing dramatically each year and, absent relief legislation, will continue to rise dramatically in coming years. Unlike regular tax liability, the AMT exemption and rates are not indexed for cost of living. In fact, the AMT exemptions are scheduled to be reduced in 2005 by $13,000 ($6,500 for married individuals filing separately) to their pre-2001 Act levels. Additionally, certain tax credits offset regular tax liability but not AMT liability. However, the lower tax rates for most dividends (see Chapter 2) and capital gains (see Chapter 5) are also used in the computation of AMT.

Year-End Reminder

Whenever tax benefits such as accelerated depreciation, incentive stock options, intangible drilling costs, percentage depletion, net operating losses, or passive activity losses are being considered, the impact of the transaction on both regular tax liability and on the AMT must be considered. The refinancing of a principal home or a designated second home may cause or increase AMT as discussed in Chapter 6. Certain preference items (such as the exercise of an incentive stock option) can often be timed in order to avoid AMT.

Caution

You can face AMT liability even if you do not have tax preference items. Individuals with popular deductions not allowable for AMT purposes such as dependency exemptions, state income taxes, and home equity interest are most vulnerable to AMT. (See Chapter 4 for discussions of state income tax and home mortgage interest deductions.) In a 1999 decision, the Tenth Circuit Court of Appeals agreed with the IRS and the Tax Court that a married couple with 10 children and no tax preference items was properly subject to AMT, even though the legislative history of this law did not contemplate that they be charged with this added tax.

Caution

Future tax legislation may modify or eliminate the individual AMT before more and more individuals each year find themselves with unexpected AMT liability, especially because the ability to use nonrefundable credits to offset the AMT is scheduled to lapse after 2003. In its 2001 Annual Report to Congress, the IRS National Taxpayer Advocate recommended repeal of the AMT. Without repeal or modification, tax for taxpayers paying AMT is expected to increase from about 2.4 million in 2003 to at least 30 million by 2010.

No Kidding—You Can Minimize the "Kiddie" Tax

A child under the age of 14 with one or both parents alive at year-end will be taxed on unearned income (interest and dividends, for example) at his or her parents' top marginal tax rate (perhaps as high as 35 percent in 2004) rather than at his or her own marginal tax rate (perhaps as low as 10 percent). The first $750 of the child's unearned income is not taxed because it is offset by a special $750 standard deduction, and the next $750 of unearned income is taxed at the child's own tax rates. However, the child's unearned income in excess of $1,500 will be taxed at the parents' top marginal rate. The special $750 standard deduction and the $750 of unearned income taxed at the child's own rates will be indexed in 2004 and succeeding years. Use IRS Form 8615 to compute the "Kiddie" tax.

A child who is subject to the "Kiddie" tax may be subject to the AMT if his or her parents have to pay AMT. The child's AMT exemption is limited to his or her earned income plus $5,600 indexed in 2004 and succeeding years for cost of living rather than the full $40,250 usually available to single individuals. For 2003 the AMT exemption for a child subject to the "Kiddie" tax was the greater of his or her earned income plus the greater of $1,500 or the parents' unused exemption.

If a child's gross income is more than $750 but less than $7,500, the parents can elect on IRS Form 8814 to include the child's income in excess of $1,500 in their AGI and the child's tax on the first $1,500 of his or her income as part of their tax liability. If the election is made, the child will not be required to file a tax return. The election is available only if the child's income consists solely of interest and dividends and if no estimated tax payments or backup withholding payments have been made on behalf of the child. All dollar figures relating to IRS Form 8814 will be indexed in 2004 and succeeding years for cost of living.

Caution

By making the election to include your child's income on your tax return, you avoid having to file a separate return for your child. However, including the child's income of more than $1,500 on your personal return will increase your AGI and may have an adverse impact on your ability to claim deductions for IRA contributions as well as itemized deductions for medical expenses, casualty losses, and miscellaneous itemized deductions. State tax liability may also increase. In addition, your withholding and estimated tax obligations will rise to cover the increased tax liability.

Caution

Congress is considering legislation which, if enacted, would expand the "Kiddie" tax to children up to age 18.

Question: My son (12 years old) has a paper route this year for which he will probably earn $2,800. He will also receive interest totaling about $2,100. My taxable income will be $65,000. How will the "Kiddie" tax affect us, if at all?

Also, I did not file a tax return for him last year, although he had the same income. Can he be penalized for my mistake?

Answer: The "Kiddie" tax will cost your son $90 in taxes because a portion of his income will be taxed at a 25 percent rate rather than at a 10 percent rate. Of the interest income, $750 will not be taxed because it is sheltered by $750 of your son's $3,050 standard deduction, which is normally $4,750 (prior to indexing in 2004) for unmarried taxpayers but is specifically limited to the greater of $750 or earned income plus $250 for those who can be claimed as dependents. The next $750 is taxed at your son's 10 percent rate, and the remaining amount is taxed at your 25 percent rate. His earned income ($2,800) is sheltered in part by the remaining $2,300 of his $3,050 standard deduction ($3,050 − $750 = $2,300), and the balance is taxed at a 10 percent rate:

$750 interest income × 10%	=	$75
$600 interest income × 25%	=	$150
$500 net earned income × 10%	=	$ 50
		$275

You are not eligible to use Form 8814 to include your son's income on your tax return because your son had some noninvestment income.

As for the penalties, some years ago the Tax Court decided that actress Skye Bassett was liable for penalties when her parents failed to file for her when she was ages 11 through 14. Only if her parents' conduct as her guardians was reasonably justified might she have avoided the penalties. Bassett's father was a college graduate, and the Court determined that he was capable of understanding his responsibility. See a full discussion of penalties in Chapter 13.

Question: Which parent's tax rate is used if the parents are not married? I am in a 15 percent bracket, but I am certain my ex-husband is in a higher bracket. Does it make sense for either of us to transfer funds into an account in the name and Social Security number of our 9-year-old child?

Answer: Use the rate of the parent who has custody. If you were married but filed separate returns, the "Kiddie" tax would have been imposed at the rate used by the parent with the higher income.

Parents often want to make gifts of investment assets to their children, both from a financial planning point of view—providing them with a nest egg to finance college education, business startup costs, and the like—as well as with a view toward shifting the income tax burden of these investment assets to children who are generally in lower tax brackets. However, as a result of the "Kiddie" tax, to the extent that the investment income exceeds $1,500, no income tax savings can be accomplished. The key then is to limit the taxable investment income of any child under the age of 14 to $1,500.

Tax Planning

If a child's investment income might be expected to exceed $1,500, consider purchasing U.S. Series EE Bonds in the child's name. Series EE Bonds mature in 10 years, and no federal taxes need be paid on the interest until the bonds are cashed. If a bond is purchased for a child no earlier than age four, the interest at maturity will be taxed at the child's rate rather than at the parent's marginal tax rate. Other investments that will produce a similar result are growth stocks (those that pay little or no current dividends but are expected to appreciate in value) and municipal bonds, the interest from which is exempt from federal tax. If the child is closer to age 14, consider purchasing certificates of deposit in the child's name that will mature after the child attains the age of 14. The interest on these certificates will be taxed at the child's rate after age 14.

When shifting investment assets from your portfolio to a child's portfolio, keep in mind that no more than an aggregate of $11,000 in gifts ($22,000 for gifts from both parents) indexed in 2004 and succeeding years may be made in any single tax year to each recipient without causing potential adverse estate and gift tax consequences. (See Chapter 12 for a detailed discussion of the tax consequences of gifts.)

Avoid Penalty by Pinpointing Your Tax Prepayment Amount

Wage earners are all required to prepay income tax liabilities by having amounts withheld from each paycheck. If nonwage income exists, such as investment income or income from sole proprietorships or partnerships, prepayments of income tax liabilities through quarterly payments of the estimated tax bill may be required. Correctly calculating both the amount of tax to be withheld from your paycheck as well as correctly calculating the quarterly estimated tax payments are important tasks in year-round tax planning.

Failure to have the correct amount withheld from your paycheck or failure to make the appropriate deposits of estimated tax payments may lead to the imposition of a penalty, normally applicable when 90 percent of the liability has not been prepaid through withholding or estimates. However, the penalty usually can be avoided, even when a substantial liability is due on April 15 because too little has been withheld or too little has been paid in estimated tax payments, provided these prepayments total at least 100 percent of the previous year's tax bill. For example, if your 2002 federal tax obligation (line 61 of the 2002 Form

1040) was $10,000 and your withholding or estimated tax payments during 2003 total at least $10,000, then even though the actual 2003 tax bill turns out to be more, no penalty usually will be imposed for failure to properly prepay this obligation. Of course, the additional liability must still be paid on April 15, 2004.

Individuals with prior year AGI in excess of $150,000 ($75,000 on a married filing separate return) are required to prepay 110 percent of their tax bill as a protective estimate based on prior liability.

Filing Pointer

You should prepay in estimated taxes and withholding only the minimum amount certain to keep you from being penalized so that you, rather than IRS, have the use of your money during the year for cash flow, for earning more money, or for paying down other debt. If you prepay more than that which is needed to avoid penalty, you are, in essence, giving the IRS an interest-free loan. In 2003 about 75 percent of individual filers received average refunds of $1,967—lost opportunities for taxpayers and found money for the IRS. Interestingly, in a 2002 CNBC survey, a majority of individuals receiving a refund indicated that it would be used to curtail other debt.

Caution

Congress is considering legislation which, if enacted, would convert the penalty for insufficient estimated taxes into an interest payment. HR 1528, the Taxpayer Protection and IRS Accountability Act of 2003, containing this provision, was approved by the House on June 19, 2003.

Help with Form 1040-ES

The IRS provides Form 1040-ES to assist taxpayers in computing the appropriate amount of estimated tax payments. This form should be completed each year if it is anticipated that the amount withheld from your paycheck will not be sufficient to pay at least 90 percent of the current year's expected tax bill or at least 100 percent of the preceding year's actual tax bill (upper income individuals substitute the applicable percentage for 100 percent). If it is determined that estimated tax payments are needed, they are due on April 15, June 15, September 15, and January 15 of the following year. No estimated payments are required if the estimated tax liability is less than $1,000.

Here is an example of the completed Form 1040-ES for 2003. Fred and Ethel are married and have one child. Fred is a wage earner and anticipated his 2003 annual salary to be $60,000. Ethel has her own business from which she anticipated a profit of approximately $35,000. The couple will receive about $7,000 in interest income and each will contribute $3,000 to an IRA. Itemized deductions will be $11,000. To enable Fred and Ethel to continue their respective jobs, their child is taken to a day-care center, the cost of which is $5,000 per year.

2003 Estimated Tax Worksheet (keep for your records)

1	Adjusted gross income you expect in 2003 (see instructions above)	1	93,527
2	• If you plan to itemize deductions, enter the estimated total of your itemized deductions. **Caution:** *If line 1 above is over $139,500 ($69,750 if married filing separately), your deduction may be reduced. See Pub. 505 for details.* • If you do not plan to itemize deductions, enter your standard deduction from page 2.	2	11,000
3	Subtract line 2 from line 1	3	82,527
4	Exemptions. Multiply $3,050 by the number of personal exemptions. If you can be claimed as a dependent on another person's 2003 return, your personal exemption is not allowed. **Caution:** *See Pub. 505 to figure the amount to enter if line 1 above is over: $209,250 if married filing jointly or qualifying widow(er); $174,400 if head of household; $139,500 if single; or $104,625 if married filing separately*	4	9,150
5	Subtract line 4 from line 3	5	73,377
6	**Tax.** Figure your tax on the amount on line 5 by using the **2003 Tax Rate Schedules** on page 2. **Caution:** *If you have a net capital gain, see Pub. 505 to figure the tax*	6	11,964
7	Alternative minimum tax from Form 6251	7	-----
8	Add lines 6 and 7. Also include any tax from Forms 4972 and 8814 and any recapture of the education credits (see instructions above)	8	11,964
9	Credits (see instructions above). **Do not** include any income tax withholding on this line	9	1,980
10	Subtract line 9 from line 8. If zero or less, enter -0-	10	9,984
11	Self-employment tax (see instructions above). Estimate of 2003 net earnings from self-employment $................ ; if **$87,000 or less,** multiply the amount by 15.3%; if **more than $87,000,** multiply the amount by 2.9%, add $10,788.00 to the result, and enter the total. **Caution:** *If you also have wages subject to social security tax, see Pub. 505 to figure the amount to enter*	11	4,945
12	Other taxes (see instructions on page 5)	12	-----
13a	Add lines 10 through 12	13a	14,929
b	Earned income credit, additional child tax credit, and credits from **Form 4136** and **Form 8885**	13b	-----
c	**Total 2003 estimated tax.** Subtract line 13b from line 13a. If zero or less, enter -0- ▶	13c	14,929
14a	Multiply line 13c by 90% (66⅔ % for farmers and fishermen) — 14a: 13,436		
b	Enter the tax shown on your 2002 tax return (110% of that amount if you are not a farmer or fisherman and the adjusted gross income shown on line 36 of that return is more than $150,000 or, if married filing separately for 2003, more than $75,000) — 14b: 20,000		
c	**Required annual payment to avoid a penalty.** Enter the **smaller** of line 14a or 14b ▶	14c	13,436
	Caution: *Generally, if you do not prepay (through income tax withholding and estimated tax payments) at least the amount on line 14c, you may owe a penalty for not paying enough estimated tax. To avoid a penalty, make sure your estimate on line 13c is as accurate as possible. Even if you pay the required annual payment, you may still owe tax when you file your return. If you prefer, you may pay the amount shown on line 13c. For details, see Pub. 505.*		
15	Income tax withheld and estimated to be withheld during 2003 (including income tax withholding on pensions, annuities, certain deferred income, etc.)	15	7,920
16	Subtract line 15 from line 14c. (**Note:** *If zero or less or line 13c minus line 15 is less than $1,000, stop here. You are not required to make estimated tax payments.*)	16	5,516
17	If the first payment you are required to make is due April 15, 2003, enter ¼ of line 16 (minus any 2002 overpayment that you are applying to this installment) here, and on your payment voucher(s) if you are paying by check or money order. (**Note:** *Household employers, see instructions on page 5.*)	17	1,379

Page 4

Fred and Ethel's 2003 Estimated Tax Worksheet.

Fred and Ethel completed the 2003 Form 1040-ES when they finished their 2002 income tax return, which showed a tax liability of $20,000. Based on the information available to them at that time, the couple decided that estimated tax payments for 2003 were in order. The minimum amount of quarterly payments needed to be made by the couple was $1,379. Assuming that their estimates of salary, self-employment income, interest income, and itemized deductions were accurate, Fred and Ethel's 2003 tax bill will be $14,929, including $4,945 of self-employment tax arising from Ethel's profitable sole proprietorship. If the amounts of tax to be withheld from Fred's salary checks were as predicted and the couple makes the four quarterly payments of $1,379, they will owe the Internal Revenue Service $1,493 on April 15, 2004.

The computation of Ethel's self-employment tax reflects a reduction in the self-employment tax base equal to 7.65 percent of the business profit. The computation of AGI reflects a deduction for one-half of the self-employment tax.

Caution

Unless your expected tax liability for a year will decline significantly from the previous year, it is often best to ensure that you will not be penalized by prepaying for the current year based on 100 percent or, for higher income taxpayers, 110 percent of the previous year's liability (whichever is applicable). This guarantees that you will not be penalized if you miscalculate 90 percent of the current year's liability. In our example, Fred and Ethel would protect against a miscalculation of 2003 liability by increasing estimated payments by $6,564 ($1,641 per quarter). Their total prepayment would then be $20,000, equaling the previous year's liability. Of course, Fred must still monitor his withholding so that it is not less than projected.

Caution

Congress is considering legislation which, if enacted, would require estimated tax payments only if anticipated tax liability were greater than $1,600 (up from $1,000). HR 1528, the Taxpayer Protection and IRS Accountability Act of 2003, containing this provision, was approved by the House on June 19, 2003.

Help with Form W-4

Every employee fills out IRS Form W-4 to determine how much of each paycheck will be withheld and paid to the IRS by the employer. Proper completion of Form W-4 should pinpoint the proper prepayment of taxes through withholdings.

Here is an example of the completed Form W-4. Assume the same facts about Fred and Ethel as previously described, except that Ethel gave up her own business on December 31, 2002, and now has a salaried position that will pay her $35,000 in 2003. Based on these assumptions, Fred and Ethel want to compute their withholding allowances on one Form W-4 worksheet. After the withholding allowances for the couple have been calculated, they can divide the withholding allowances between them and file their own separate Forms W-4 with their respective employers. The employers then determine the appropriate amount of withholding from tables prepared by the IRS.

Form W-4 (2003)

Purpose. Complete Form W-4 so that your employer can withhold the correct Federal income tax from your pay. Because your tax situation may change, you may want to refigure your withholding each year.

Exemption from withholding. If you are exempt, complete only lines 1, 2, 3, 4, and 7 and sign the form to validate it. Your exemption for 2003 expires February 16, 2004. See **Pub. 505,** Tax Withholding and Estimated Tax.

Note: *You cannot claim exemption from withholding if: (a) your income exceeds $750 and includes more than $250 of unearned income (e.g., interest and dividends) and (b) another person can claim you as a dependent on their tax return.*

Basic instructions. If you are not exempt, complete the **Personal Allowances Worksheet** below. The worksheets on page 2 adjust your withholding allowances based on itemized deductions, certain credits, adjustments to income, or two-earner/two-job situations. Complete all worksheets that apply. **However, you may claim fewer (or zero) allowances.**

Head of household. Generally, you may claim head of household filing status on your tax return only if you are unmarried and pay more than 50% of the costs of keeping up a home for yourself and your dependent(s) or other qualifying individuals. See line **E** below.

Tax credits. You can take projected tax credits into account in figuring your allowable number of withholding allowances. Credits for child or dependent care expenses and the child tax credit may be claimed using the **Personal Allowances Worksheet** below. See **Pub. 919,** How Do I Adjust My Tax Withholding? for information on converting your other credits into withholding allowances.

Nonwage income. If you have a large amount of nonwage income, such as interest or dividends, consider making estimated tax payments using **Form 1040-ES,** Estimated Tax for Individuals. Otherwise, you may owe additional tax.

Two earners/two jobs. If you have a working spouse or more than one job, figure the total number of allowances you are entitled to claim on all jobs using worksheets from only one Form W-4. Your withholding usually will be most accurate when all allowances are claimed on the Form W-4 for the highest paying job and zero allowances are claimed on the others.

Nonresident alien. If you are a nonresident alien, see the **Instructions for Form 8233** before completing this Form W-4.

Check your withholding. After your Form W-4 takes effect, use Pub. 919 to see how the dollar amount you are having withheld compares to your projected total tax for 2003. See Pub. 919, especially if your earnings exceed $125,000 (Single) or $175,000 (Married).

Recent name change? If your name on line 1 differs from that shown on your social security card, call 1-800-772-1213 for a new social security card.

Personal Allowances Worksheet (Keep for your records.)

A Enter "1" for **yourself** if no one else can claim you as a dependent .... A 1

B Enter "1" if:
- You are single and have only one job; or
- You are married, have only one job, and your spouse does not work; or
- Your wages from a second job or your spouse's wages (or the total of both) are $1,000 or less.

.... B ____

C Enter "1" for your **spouse.** But, you may choose to enter "-0-" if you are married and have either a working spouse or more than one job. (Entering "-0-" may help you avoid having too little tax withheld.) .... C 1

D Enter number of **dependents** (other than your spouse or yourself) you will claim on your tax return .... D 1

E Enter "1" if you will file as **head of household** on your tax return (see conditions under **Head of household** above) .... E ____

F Enter "1" if you have at least $1,500 of **child or dependent care expenses** for which you plan to claim a credit .... F 0
(**Note:** *Do **not** include child support payments. See **Pub. 503,** Child and Dependent Care Expenses, for details.*)

G **Child Tax Credit** (including additional child tax credit):
- If your total income will be between $15,000 and $42,000 ($20,000 and $65,000 if married), enter "1" for each eligible child plus **1 additional** if you have three to five eligible children or **2 additional** if you have six or more eligible children.
- If your total income will be between $42,000 and $80,000 ($65,000 and $115,000 if married), enter "1" if you have one or two eligible children, "2" if you have three eligible children, "3" if you have four eligible children, or "4" if you have five or more eligible children. .... G 0

H Add lines A through G and enter total here. **Note:** *This may be different from the number of exemptions you claim on your return.* ..... ▶ H 3

For accuracy, complete all worksheets that apply.
- If you plan to **itemize or claim adjustments to income** and want to reduce your withholding, see the **Deductions and Adjustments Worksheet** on page 2.
- If you have **more than one job** or are **married and you and your spouse both work** and the combined earnings from all jobs exceed $35,000, see the **Two-Earner/Two-Job Worksheet** on page 2 to avoid having too little tax withheld.
- If **neither** of the above situations applies, **stop here** and enter the number from line H on line 5 of Form W-4 below.

STF FED6105F.1

Cut here and give Form W-4 to your employer. Keep the top part for your records.

Form **W-4**
Department of the Treasury
Internal Revenue Service

Employee's Withholding Allowance Certificate

▶ **For Privacy Act and Paperwork Reduction Act Notice, see page 2.**

OMB No. 1545-0010
2003

1 Type or print your first name and middle initial	Last name	2 Your social security number
Fred	Mertz	000-00-0000

Home address (number and street or rural route): 518 Crestview Drive

3 ☐ Single ☒ Married ☐ Married, but withhold at higher Single rate.
Note: If married, but legally separated, or spouse is a nonresident alien, check the "Single" box.

City or town, state, and ZIP code: Mayfield, OH 99999

4 **If your last name differs from that shown on your social security card, check here. You must call 1-800-772-1213 for a new card.** ..... ▶ ☐

5 Total number of allowances you are claiming (from line H above **or** from the applicable worksheet on page 2) .... 5 | 0

6 Additional amount, if any, you want withheld from each paycheck .... 6 | $ 33

7 I claim exemption from withholding for 2003, and I certify that I meet **both** of the following conditions for exemption:
- Last year I had a right to a refund of **all** Federal income tax withheld because I had **no** tax liability **and**
- This year I expect a refund of **all** Federal income tax withheld because I expect to have **no** tax liability.

If you meet both conditions, write "Exempt" here .... ▶ 7 ____

Under penalties of perjury, I certify that I am entitled to the number of withholding allowances claimed on this certificate, or I am entitled to claim exempt status.

Employee's signature
(Form is not valid unless you sign it.) ▶ **Date ▶**

8 Employer's name and address (Employer: Complete lines 8 and 10 only if sending to the IRS.)	9 Office code (optional)	10 Employer identification number

ISA

Fred's Form W-4 (page 1).

If the form is properly completed by the couple and then each properly files his or her own W-4 with their respective employers, Fred and Ethel will each claim 0 allowances, and Fred will have $330 withheld from each of his semi-monthly paychecks (including an additional $33 over the amount determined from the IRS tables) for a total of $7,920 withheld for the year. Ethel will have

Form W-4 (2003) Page 2

Deductions and Adjustments Worksheet

Note: *Use this worksheet **only** if you plan to itemize deductions, claim certain credits, or claim adjustments to income on your 2003 tax return.*

1	Enter an estimate of your 2003 itemized deductions. These include qualifying home mortgage interest, charitable contributions, state and local taxes, medical expenses in excess of 7.5% of your income, and miscellaneous deductions. (For 2003, you may have to reduce your itemized deductions if your income is over $139,500 ($69,750 if married filing separately). See **Worksheet 3** in Pub. 919 for details.)	1	$ 11,000
2	Enter: $7,950 if married filing jointly or qualifying widow(er); $7,000 if head of household; $4,750 if single; $3,975 if married filing separately	2	$ 9,500
3	**Subtract** line 2 from line 1. If line 2 is greater than line 1, enter "-0-"	3	$ 1,500
4	Enter an estimate of your 2003 adjustments to income, including alimony, deductible IRA contributions, and student loan interest	4	$ 6,000
5	**Add** lines 3 and 4 and enter the total. Include any amount for credits from **Worksheet 7** in Pub. 919.	5	$ 14,826
6	Enter an estimate of your 2003 nonwage income (such as dividends or interest)	6	$ 7,000
7	**Subtract** line 6 from line 5. Enter the result, but not less than "-0-"	7	$ 7,826
8	**Divide** the amount on line 7 by $3,000 and enter the result here. Drop any fraction	8	2
9	Enter the number from the **Personal Allowances Worksheet**, line H, page 1	9	3
10	**Add** lines 8 and 9 and enter the total here. If you plan to use the **Two-Earner/Two-Job Worksheet**, also enter this total on line 1 below. Otherwise, **stop here** and enter this total on Form W-4, line 5, page 1	10	5

Two-Earner/Two-Job Worksheet

Note: *Use this worksheet **only** if the instructions under line H on page 1 direct you here.*

1	Enter the number from line H, page 1 (or from line 10 above if you used the **Deductions and Adjustments Worksheet**)	1	5
2	Find the number in **Table 1** below that applies to the **lowest** paying job and enter it here	2	6
3	If line 1 is **more than or equal to** line 2, subtract line 2 from line 1. Enter the result here (if zero, enter "-0-") and on Form W-4, line 5, page 1. **Do not** use the rest of this worksheet	3	0

Note: *If line 1 is **less than** line 2, enter "-0-" on Form W-4, line 5, page 1. Complete lines 4 - 9 below to calculate the additional withholding amount necessary to avoid a year-end tax bill.*

4	Enter the number from line 2 of this worksheet — 4: 6		
5	Enter the number from line 1 of this worksheet — 5: 5		
6	**Subtract** line 5 from line 4	6	1
7	Find the amount in **Table 2** below that applies to the **highest** paying job and enter it here	7	$ 800
8	**Multiply** line 7 by line 6 and enter the result here. This is the additional annual withholding needed	8	$ 800
9	Divide line 8 by the number of pay periods remaining in 2003. For example, divide by 26 if you are paid every two weeks and you complete this form in December 2002. Enter the result here and on Form W-4, line 6, page 1. This is the additional amount to be withheld from each paycheck	9	$ 33

Table 1: Two-Earner/Two-Job Worksheet

Married Filing Jointly				All Others			
If wages from **LOWEST** paying job are —	Enter on line 2 above	If wages from **LOWEST** paying job are —	Enter on line 2 above	If wages from **LOWEST** paying job are —	Enter on line 2 above	If wages from **LOWEST** paying job are —	Enter on line 2 above
$0 - $4,000	0	44,001 - 50,000	8	$0 - $6,000	0	75,001 - 100,000	8
4,001 - 9,000	1	50,001 - 60,000	9	6,001 - 11,000	1	100,001 - 110,000	9
9,001 - 15,000	2	60,001 - 70,000	10	11,001 - 18,000	2	110,001 and over	10
15,001 - 20,000	3	70,001 - 90,000	11	18,001 - 25,000	3		
20,001 - 25,000	4	90,001 - 100,000	12	25,001 - 29,000	4		
25,001 - 33,000	5	100,001 - 115,000	13	29,001 - 40,000	5		
33,001 - 38,000	6	115,001 - 125,000	14	40,001 - 55,000	6		
38,001 - 44,000	7	125,001 and over	15	55,001 - 75,000	7		

Table 2: Two-Earner/Two-Job Worksheet

Married Filing Jointly		All Others	
If wages from **HIGHEST** paying job are —	Enter on line 7 above	If wages from **HIGHEST** paying job are —	Enter on line 7 above
$0 - $50,000	$450	$0 - $30,000	$450
50,001 - 100,000	800	30,001 - 70,000	800
100,001 - 150,000	900	70,001 - 140,000	900
150,001 - 270,000	1,050	140,001 - 300,000	1,050
270,001 and over	1,200	300,001 and over	1,200

Privacy Act and Paperwork Reduction Act Notice. We ask for the information on this form to carry out the Internal Revenue laws of the United States. The Internal Revenue Code requires this information under sections 3402(f)(2)(A) and 6109 and their regulations. **Failure to provide a properly completed form will result in your being treated as a single person who claims no withholding allowances; providing fraudulent information may also subject you to penalties.** Routine uses of this information include giving it to the Department of Justice for civil and criminal litigation, to cities, states, and the District of Columbia for use in administering their tax laws, and using it in the National Directory of New Hires. We may also disclose this information to Federal and state agencies to enforce Federal nontax criminal laws and to combat terrorism.

You are not required to provide the information requested on a form that is subject to the Paperwork Reduction Act unless the form displays a valid OMB control number. Books or records relating to a form or its instructions must be retained as long as their contents may become material in the administration of any Internal Revenue law. Generally, tax returns and return information are confidential, as required by Code section 6103.

The time needed to complete this form will vary depending on individual circumstances. The estimated average time is: **Recordkeeping,** 46 min.; **Learning about the law or the form,** 13 min.; **Preparing the form,** 59 min. If you have comments concerning the accuracy of these time estimates or suggestions for making this form simpler, we would be happy to hear from you. You can write to the Tax Forms Committee, Western Area Distribution Center, Rancho Cordova, CA 95743-0001. **Do not** send the tax form to this address. Instead, give it to your employer.

STF FED8105F.2

Fred's Form W-4 (page 2).

$138 withheld from each of her semimonthly paychecks for a total withholding of $3,312. The couple's combined withholding for 2003 will be $11,232. Assuming that the estimates of the couple's income were exact, their 2003 federal income tax liability will be $10,603. Thus, the couple will receive a refund of $629.

Caution

Even careful completion of Form W-4 may cause overwithholding in certain instances. Wage earners should monitor their expected tax liability versus withholding throughout the year and make adjustments as needed.

Changing Your Tax Prepayment Amount

What do you do if circumstances change after you have completed the Form 1040-ES or Form W-4? For example, assume that on October 1, 2003, Fred and Ethel unexpectedly sell some stock that generates a long-term capital gain of $20,000. Obviously, their tax liability will be substantially increased.

The couple has several available options. They can make a fourth-quarter estimated tax payment due January 15, 2004, or they can have additional amounts withheld from either or both of their remaining 2003 wages to cover the increased liability. Alternatively, no additional amount of withholding or estimated taxes need be paid under these facts, despite the unexpected increase in taxable income in 2003 if the current rate of withholding and/or estimated tax payments will at least equal their 2002 tax liability. In our example, we had assumed that the couple's 2002 tax liability was $20,000 so this alternative will be unavailable to Fred and Ethel.

Consequently, Fred and Ethel should calculate what the additional $20,000 of capital gain will cost them in taxes. Given the 15 percent maximum applicable tax rate (see Chapter 5), the capital gain will increase their tax liability by $3,000. To cover this additional liability, Fred and Ethel can either have an additional amount withheld from their remaining 12 paychecks (six each) or pay the $3,000 by January 15, 2004, as an estimated tax payment.

Year-End Reminder

Estimated payments must be made pro rata for the four calendar quarters unless changed circumstances cause a modification. Taxpayers are credited with prepayment when estimated taxes are paid. In contrast, withholding is presumed to be divided equally among the four calendar quarters unless the taxpayer demonstrates to the contrary. Consequently, increasing your withholding at the end of the year can help you avoid the penalty for being underwithheld earlier in the year. Suppose that, in November, you realize that you have been drastically underwithheld during the year and that you will not only owe tax to Uncle Sam, but will also be liable for the penalty. Here is a way out.

Year-End Reminder (cont.)

File a new W-4 and increase your withholding to a level that will bring your total within 90 percent of this year's or, depending on AGI, 100 percent or 110 percent of last year's tax liability. You do not even have to have a job to use this loophole; you can have your spouse hike his or her withholding. Many people do not realize that they may have as much withheld from their pay as they want, up to the full amount of their salary. It may mean tightening the belt through the Christmas season, but this beats paying an underpayment penalty come filing time the next Easter. This loophole also works for taxpayers who have fallen behind in their estimated tax payments. The only catch is that you or your spouse must earn enough money from employment to be able to have enough money withheld to avoid the penalty.

Tax Planning

Effective tax planning and the prepayment of one's federal tax liability will involve careful computations of withholding allowances and estimated tax obligations. These computations will have to be reviewed whenever there is a change in marital status, a change in the number of dependents, or an increase or decrease in the amount of estimated nonwage income or in deductible expenses. Household employers should see Chapter 11 concerning additional prepayments needed to cover employee payroll taxes.

Your Home State and Its Impact on Your Tax Liability

Regardless of your home state, the federal tax laws will apply to you in the same manner that they apply to your friend who lives across the state line. However, the two of you will likely be subject to two different state tax structures. A few jurisdictions (the largest being Texas and Florida) do not impose any income taxes on individuals. Other jurisdictions, such as California and New York, impose heavy tax burdens.

In many situations, there is no choice in selecting a home or place of employment. However, retirees in particular may have flexibility, and locating in a state without an income tax can save thousands of dollars.

Year-End Reminder

Many retirees enjoy spending part of the year in Florida. For individuals who divide time between two homes, one of which is in a state such as Florida that does not have an individual income tax, it is important to become familiar with the law of the taxing state and possibly to limit time there as year-end approaches. By restricting time in the taxing state, usually just under one-half of the year, you typically avoid being considered a resident of that state. You must also avoid being treated as a domicile of the taxing state. This test is subjective and is based on what you consider your home state as shown by voting records, automobile registration, driver's license, and other indicia.

CHAPTER 2

Taxable and Tax-Free Income and Benefits

Income Classifications: Portfolio, Active, and Passive

Depending on its source, income falls into one of three categories, which are not always easily distinguishable: portfolio (also known as investment) income, active income, and passive income. Your ability to claim certain types of deductions will hinge on the existence of a particular type of income.

Portfolio income or *investment income* is generated by an activity that is not considered a trade or business. Portfolio income consists primarily of interest (even interest paid by the IRS, according to an IRS letter ruling) and dividends, although self-charged interest income related to an individual and a pass-through entity (partnership or S corporation) in which he or she owns an interest as a passive investment may be recharacterized as passive in order to prevent inequity. (See Chapters 6, "Real Estate—The Most Tax-Favored Investment," and 10, "Business Tax Planning," for discussions of the various types of business entities, including multimember limited liability companies that are generally taxed as partnerships and single-member limited liability companies that are generally treated for tax purposes as an "alter ego" of the member.)

The amount of portfolio income is significant in that individuals can claim a deduction for investment interest expense only to the extent of net investment income (investment income less expenses) for the year.

Active income or *business income* is salary, income derived from a sole proprietorship business in which the individual materially participates, and income from partnerships and S corporations in which the partner or shareholder materially participates in business operations.

Passive income is generated by a business operation in which the taxpayer does not materially participate, whether that business activity is conducted in the form of a sole proprietorship, a partnership, or a corporation. Except for nonrecurring casualties or thefts, losses from passive business enterprises can be used only to offset passive income. Any losses that are not deductible as a result of the passive loss rule can be carried forward indefinitely and deducted against passive income generated in a subsequent year or any income generated by disposition of the passive activity.

The distinction between active income and passive income depends on the extent of the individual's participation in the business operations. Participation on a regular and continuous basis is considered material, and any income or loss generated by such a business enterprise is active in nature with any loss being fully deductible.

If the individual's participation in the business enterprise does not meet the standards for material participation, any income or loss generated by the business generally will be considered passive. See Chapter 7, "Other Tax-Favored Investments," concerning how income, otherwise passive in nature, will be recharacterized as nonpassive when material participation standards are not met but the lesser standards for significant participation are satisfied.

Except for certain real estate-related businesses (see Chapter 11, "Special Groups of Taxpayers"), income from real estate rentals is automatically considered passive. However, income from short-term rentals (those of seven days or less or 30 days or less if services are provided) are not automatically passive according to a Temporary Regulation but will be classified as absent material participation.

Temporary Regulations define material participation in terms of the number of hours devoted to the activity. If you work more than 500 hours a year, or if you work more than 100 hours during the year and no one else works more than 100 hours, you meet the definition of material participation, and any loss generated will be deductible. Other tests are available for meeting the material participation standard. They include situations when

- The individual's work constitutes substantially all of the work in the activity.
- The individual satisfied a material participation standard in at least five of the last 10 years.
- With respect to personal service activities such as medicine, law, accounting, engineering, architecture, or performing arts, the individual satisfied a material participation standard in at least three years.

To determine your degree of participation in an activity, you are permitted to include your spouse's participation in the activity. However, according to a 1993 Tax Court decision, activities in an individual's capacity as an investor do not count toward satisfying the requisite number of hours for material participation.

Gains and losses on dispositions of income-producing assets are generally classified in an identical manner as the income produced (that is, investment, active, or passive). However, the rules on the use of suspended passive losses on disposition of an investment are complex. When you sell the passive investment, the losses that have been carried forward will be used to offset income in this order:

1. Current year income or gain from the passive activity, including any gain recognized on the sale
2. Net income or gain from all other passive activities
3. Any other nonpassive income or gain, including wages and investment income

If the gain on the sale of the passive investment is reported on the installment method (see Chapter 5, "Gains and Losses"), then the losses can be used only as your buyer makes payments.

If you sell your passive investment to certain related parties—for example, your family or your closely held corporation—the losses that have been carried forward cannot be used. Rather, you continue to carry forward the losses against other passive income until the related party sells the passive investment to an unrelated party. Then you can claim any remaining losses from the particular investment.

To be eligible to use the suspended passive losses, your disposition of the passive activity usually must be a taxable transaction. If you make a gift of the passive investment, you are not entitled to use the losses. Instead, the recipient of your gift adds your losses to his or her basis in the investment.

Any suspended losses that may remain at the time of your death may be claimed only to the extent that they are greater than the difference between the value of the investment and your basis in the investment just prior to your death. For example, if you have $18,000 of suspended losses and your passive investment is worth $15,000 against a basis of $7,000, $10,000 of the suspended losses are usable to offset both passive and nonpassive income. The remaining $8,000 of losses are wasted. If the amount of the suspended losses had been $8,000 or less, nothing would have been deductible on your final tax return.

Question: I am receiving payments under a covenant not to compete with the person to whom I sold my business. Are these payments passive in nature because I get paid for doing nothing?

Answer: Although your payments appear to be the exact opposite of active income, the Tax Court in 1995 upheld a Regulation that designates payments under a covenant not to compete as active income. The Court observed that restraint from work traditionally has been considered akin to work itself.

Question: I own an arts and crafts business. I operate only during the summer weekends, and I have no employees. Do I materially participate in my business?

Answer: Yes. Even if you do not work 100 hours a year, you are considered materially participating in the business because no one else is helping out, and you are doing all of the work. This meets the definition of material participation even when the total hours of work are fewer than 100.

Question: I invested in a restaurant that opened on October 1. I worked 200 hours on evenings and weekends. There is a full-time staff. If the restaurant had been open for the entire year, I would have worked well over 500 hours. We lost some money in the first three months, and I need to be considered as materially participating to claim the loss. Do I have a problem?

Answer: According to a 2000 decision of an Oregon federal district court, you may not "annualize" your hours spent in the activity. Only next year would you be considered as materially participating.

Question: I have been a general partner in a retail clothing firm since 1976. I retired on New Year's Eve of 1999, but I continue to be a partner. Is my share of the profit active or passive income?

Answer: Through 2004, you will be treated as a material participant in this business under the five-out-of-ten-year rule. However, any profit that you receive in 2005 and subsequent years will be passive income.

Year-End Reminder

As year-end approaches, watch the number of hours you have devoted to an activity if losses are expected. Increase the number of hours that you work in order to ensure material participation. Your record keeping with respect to the type of work done and the amount of time spent is critical. When you want to show material participation in an activity, you must maintain time records, appointment books, or other written documentation detailing the amount of time devoted to an activity.

Reporting Income Properly Against the IRS Match

The IRS has a sophisticated program by which it can match, using the Social Security number or other taxpayer identification number, data on information returns against that reported on the tax return. Any discrepancy usually will trigger IRS correspondence. When income-producing property is owned by two or more persons, the income derived from the property must be reported in accordance with the type of co-ownership involved. On the federal return, if the only co-owners are husband and wife and they file a joint income tax return, it makes no difference whose income it is or whether the property is jointly owned or owned in individual names. However, when the co-owners are other than husband and wife, each co-owner should report his or her share of the income. That share generally is determined by state law. This requires the reporting of income proportionate to ownership interests, but in some cases, each co-owner will include on his or her return the same proportion of income as contributed to the acquisition of the asset.

The payer of income to these co-owners, such as a bank or brokerage firm, will usually issue only one IRS Form 1099 to the party whose taxpayer identification number it was given. Even though a bank account or brokerage account may have been opened in joint names, only one taxpayer identification number will be accepted by the institution. The co-owners are entitled to split the income in accordance with their entitlement to the property under state law, but because only one of the co-owners will receive the information return, he or she will have to report all of that income and then issue the other co-owner(s) their own 1099s. The co-owner who received the 1099 from the institution then will reduce his or her income by the portion of the income for which he or she is a nominee.

Illustration

If two sisters, Cathy and Chris, have a joint bank account to which they made equal contributions, each should report one-half of the interest earned on that account annually. If Cathy's Social Security number was given to the bank at the time the account was opened, Cathy will receive a 1099 for all of the interest. If the account generated $1,000 of income in 2003, Cathy will receive a 1099 for $1,000. Cathy must report the $1,000 on her Schedule B for 2003. Because her sister, Chris, is the true owner of one-half of the account, Cathy should issue her sister a Form 1099 in the amount of $500. On Cathy's 2003 income tax return, she reports the entire interest on Schedule B and then subtracts the nominee distribution of $500 from her other interest income. Chris, having received the 1099 from her sister, will include the $500 reported on that information return on her Form 1040, Schedule B.

When tax preparation time rolls around, you should check data reported on information returns (Form 1099, 1099B, W-2, W-2P, K-1, and so on) against the records received during the year from the payer of the income, whether it is your employer, bank, credit union, or brokerage firm. If the records do not confirm the information received on the 1099 or similar form, you should obtain clarification from the payer. If the original information return is incorrect, you must request a corrected tax form.

Caution

The IRS is attempting to match flowthrough income reported on forms K-1 with that shown by partners, S corporation shareholders (see Chapter 10), and beneficiaries on their respective returns. See Chapter 13 for a further discussion.

Tax Planning

In an effort to tax income at the lowest possible marginal rate, income splitting may be undertaken. Family members can title bank accounts, or other property in joint names in an effort to divide the total tax burden among the family members. (With a maximum tax rate of 15 percent on qualifying dividends through 2008, the benefit of retitling securities is currently limited.) However, as a result of the creation of the "Kiddie" tax, this technique has been substantially limited when a co-owner is a child under the age of 14. This approach is still available between parents and older children or between siblings, but caution must be exercised so as to prevent the loss of the dependency exemption for that child. Otherwise, the tax savings generated by the shifting of income will be reduced.

Illustration

Assume that you have a 16-year-old son and are considering making a gift to him of $22,000, the maximum which can be given by a couple each year using the gift tax annual exclusion (see Chapter 12). He can earn $700 in interest on the Funds. You are in the 25 percent tax bracket. You will lose $175 (25% × $700) of the interest income in federal taxes.

If you give the funds to your son, he will be subject to tax on $700. If this is his only taxable income, there will be no tax and a savings of $175.

Do not lose a dependency exemption through income shifting; in 2004 it could cost you as much as $1,763 even prior to indexing the exemption (25 percent × $3,050 exemption + $1,000 child credit) and save only $175—a net loss of $1,588! See Chapter 3, "Deductions and Credits—For Itemizers and Nonitemizers," for a discussion of the child credit.

Illustration (cont.)

Be careful of potential issues in the estate tax area discussed in Chapter 12, "Estate Planning Strategies," if the value of your gift to any beneficiary is more than $11,000 in any single year; the threshold is indexed in 2004 and succeeding years for cost of living.

Using the Tax Benefit Rule to Avoid Income

If you claimed a deduction in an earlier year (such as for state and local taxes) and you receive a refund or reimbursement of the deducted amount in a later year, you generally have taxable income in that later year. However, under the Tax Benefit Rule, you have taxable income only to the extent of your tax benefit in the prior year.

For example, suppose that your itemized deductions in the earlier year, excluding the state tax deduction, exceeded your AGI. Under these circumstances, claiming an additional deduction for state taxes provided you with no tax benefit because your other itemized deductions more than offset your AGI resulting in no tax liability. A refund of state taxes in the subsequent year will, therefore, be excludable from your income.

Individuals who claimed the standard deduction in the prior year are never required to report any attributable state tax refund as income in the subsequent year.

Illustration

In 2003 Kevin's AGI was $15,000 and his itemized deductions totaled $18,000, including $1,900 of state income taxes withheld from his paycheck. In 2004, after filing his 2003 state income tax return, Kevin will receive a refund of all $1,900 in state taxes paid during 2003. The $1,900 refund will not be taxable in 2004 because Kevin received no tax benefit when he filed his 2003 return and claimed a deduction for the withholding from his paycheck.

Question: Last year I lost out on $2,500 of $22,500 of itemized deductions shown on my return because high AGI got me caught in the phaseout. My deduction for state income taxes would have been $7,200. The remaining $15,300 was from mortgage interest and property taxes. This year I received a $3,000 refund from the IRS. Do I have to report the entire refund as income even if I could not use one-ninth of the deduction, or can I report eight-ninths of the refund as income?

Answer: The IRS position is that an individual caught in the phaseout of itemized deductions must recompute what prior-year itemized deductions would have totaled after the phaseout if the taxes paid had been netted with the subsequent-year refund. If, as in most situations, the recomputation would have caused a reduction in allowable deductions equal to the tax refund, the IRS says that the individual received a benefit from the entire deduction of state taxes and must consequently report the entire tax refund as income.

To illustrate, in your case, if your prior year allowable itemized deductions after the phaseout were recomputed at $17,000, the IRS says you must report the full $3,000 state tax refund as income. Your reduction in itemized deductions on the recomputation is equal to the amount of the tax refund.

Upon recomputation, some individuals will find their deductions reduced by less than the amount of their tax refunds. These individuals may limit their income from the refund to the amount by which their deductions are reduced. They include taxpayers whose reductions would have caused them to claim the standard deduction and those affected by the maximum 80 percent phaseout of itemized deductions scheduled to be phased out between 2006 and 2010 (see Chapter 1, "Introduction to Personal Tax Planning").

Lower Yield Tax-Exempt Bonds May Give You a High Yield

One significant way to reduce your taxable investment income is to invest in state and local bonds. The interest earned on most state and local bonds will be exempt from federal income tax and, if the bonds that you purchase are issued by your state of residence or a locality within that state, they usually will be exempt from state taxes as well.

The yields on state and local bonds usually will be lower than the yields on corporate bonds and other investments, but you will want to compare the after-tax yield of the investments. For example, if you are in a 35 percent marginal federal tax bracket and in a state marginal tax bracket of 8 percent and you invest $1,000 in a corporate bond yielding 7 percent, you will earn $70 of interest annually. However, you will lose $30.10 in federal and state taxes (ignoring the state tax benefit on the federal return, $24.50 to the federal government, and $5.60 to your state of residence). Thus, from that $70 of interest income, you will net only $39.90. If you invested $1,000 in a tax-exempt municipal bond of your state yielding 5 percent, the same $1,000 investment produces only $50 of income per year but will cost you nothing in taxes.

Although most state and local bond interest is exempt from federal taxes, the exemption will be lost if the bond was issued after August 15, 1986, in an unregistered form; that is, if the bond is a bearer bond. Also, no tax exemption is given for state and local bonds when the proceeds are used for private business purposes rather than for governmental business purposes unless the proceeds are used for particular kinds of private activities sanctioned by the

Internal Revenue Code, such as building residential rental projects, sewage facilities, airports, or hazardous waste disposal facilities; financing student loans; or investing in empowerment zones (see Chapter 7).

Caution

Before investing in any state or local bond, it is important to have your investment adviser check into the tax-exempt status of the bond as well as the financial stability of the issuing jurisdiction. The bond will be rated based on that financial stability. If a greater risk of default by the jurisdiction issuing the bond exists, the bond may have a lower rating but a higher yield to attract investors. The two primary rating services are Standard and Poor's and Moody's. Standard and Poor's top-rated bonds receive an AAA rating, although a bond in default receives a D rating. If you want a higher rate of return and are willing to take a greater degree of risk, look into state and local bonds that receive less than the AAA rating. If you are a conservative investor, look only for the highest rated bonds for your investments.

Federal Obligations May Give You an Even Higher Yield

Lending money to the federal government by purchasing Treasury bills, Treasury notes, or Treasury bonds will yield interest income that is exempt from state and local taxes but is taxed by the federal government. Treasury bills have short maturity dates of one to 12 months. Treasury notes mature within two to 10 years, and Treasury bonds are long-term investments of 10 to 30 years.

The purchase of certain federal government obligations can result in a deferment of taxes. The interest from Treasury bills with a maturity of one year or less is taxed only at maturity. Thus, if in December 2003, you purchase a three-month Treasury bill, the interest will not be taxed until April 15, 2005, when you pay your 2004 federal tax bill.

Additionally, the interest on the Series EE bonds is not taxable until the bond is cashed, unless you elect to report the interest currently. Because the Series EE bonds do not pay interest until the bond is cashed, rarely does anyone choose to report income as it accrues. If the bond is disposed of prior to maturity, for example, by gift, the donor must include the accrued interest prior to the date of the gift as income.

Although Treasury bills, notes, and bonds are exempt from state and local tax, other types of federal obligations may not be exempt from tax at the state or local level. Each jurisdiction must be consulted to determine whether or not other particular federal government investments are exempt.

Tax Planning

Individuals over age 24 who purchase Series EE bonds may use IRS Form 8815 to exclude some or all of the Series EE bond interest from their income if, in the same year that the bond is redeemed, the bond owner pays tuition and other fees so that the bond owner, spouse, or dependent is able to attend college. If the bond redemption proceeds exceed the total tuition and fees paid during the year, only the ratio of expenses to redemption proceeds multiplied by the bond interest received is exempt.

Furthermore, the amount that can be excluded from income in 2003 is phased out if the bond owner's modified AGI exceeds the threshold amount of $58,500 ($87,750 in the case of a joint return) and is completely phased out at AGI of $73,500 ($117,750 in the case of a joint return). Married individuals must file a joint return to be eligible for the exclusion. The ranges of income at which the exclusion is phased out are adjusted annually for changes in the cost of living.

This limited exclusion was intended to encourage savings for education; however, the purchase of savings bonds has barely increased since its enactment.

Dividends—Tax at a Max

Qualified dividends, like net long-term capital gain (see Chapter 5) are taxed at a maximum rate of 15 percent rather than up to the general maximum rate of 35 percent for both regular tax and alternative minimum tax (see Chapter 1) purposes. If qualified dividends would have been taxed at either of the lowest individual tax brackets of 10 percent or 15 percent in the absence of this special rule, a maximum rate of 5 percent applies to the dividends.

Qualified dividends are those received from a domestic corporation. Dividends received from a foreign corporation will also qualify if the entity was incorporated in a United States possession, is publicly traded on an exchange in the United States, or is privately owned but incorporated in a country which exchanges tax information with the United States. However, dividends on stock owned for less than 60 days in the 120-day period beginning 60 days before the ex-dividend date will not qualify. Neither will dividends from a corporation which was tax-exempt in the preceding year.

Question: I receive patronage dividends from a cooperative in which I participate. I also receive dividends from a credit union. Are these subject to the maximum tax on dividends?

Answer: No, a dividend for purpose of the maximum tax is defined as a distribution by a corporation with respect to its stock to the extent of current or accumulated earnings and profits. Consequently, both of these distributions which are commonly called "dividends" are not qualified dividends. For a similar reason, distributions on preferred stock also apparently cannot constitute qualified dividends. The character of money market dividends will usually depend on the nature of the earnings by the money market fund.

Caution

If you want a dividend to be counted as investment income for the purpose of applying the rule limiting the deduction of investment interest to the amount of investment income (see Chapter 4), you may not apply the maximum tax rate to qualified dividends. Because unused investment interest carries forward indefinitely, it makes sense to exclude qualified dividends from investment income in many instances to utilize the special rate on dividends.

Controversy

Constructive dividends include amounts paid by a C corporation (see Chapter 10) to a shareholder-employee as compensation but which are determined to be excessive. Because constructive dividends appear to constitute qualified dividends, a shareholder benefits if the IRS reclassifies salary or bonus as a constructive dividend while the corporation suffers from the loss of a tax deduction.

Caution

The maximum tax on dividends will not apply after 2008 unless extended. For 2007 the 5 percent rate for lower income individuals drops to zero.

Social Security—Netting the Benefit

Except for the lump sum death benefit that is never subject to tax, Social Security benefits are taxable pursuant to a formula.

If your AGI, determined without Social Security benefits but increased by tax-exempt interest plus one-half of the Social Security benefits (*modified AGI*), exceeds a base amount, up to 85 percent of the benefits is taxable. The net effect to an individual in the highest marginal tax bracket of 35 percent is a loss of almost 30 percent of the gross Social Security check. To an individual in a more modest 28 percent bracket, the loss to taxes is still almost one-fourth of the check. All in all, about 9.6 million individuals pay taxes on their Social Security benefits.

If you are single and your modified AGI is more than $25,000 but no more than $34,000, the computation will be relatively easy. One-half of your benefits (or, if less, one-half of the modified AGI greater than the $25,000 base) will be taxed.

Illustration

John, a widower, is retired and receives Social Security benefits of $10,000. His other income consists of a pension ($18,000), bank interest ($2,000), and tax-exempt interest ($3,000).

$18,000	Pension
2,000	Bank Interest
3,000	Tax-Exempt Interest
5,000	One-Half Social Security benefits
$28,000	Modified AGI
(25,000)	Base Amount, Single
$3,000	Excess

John must include in his income an amount equal to one-half of the excess of modified AGI over the base or one-half of the Social Security benefits, whichever is less. In this case, John includes $1,500 of his Social Security benefits in income (one-half of $3,000 is less than one-half of $10,000).

Different thresholds apply if you are married. If your modified AGI as a couple filing jointly is more than $32,000 but no more than $44,000, the computation also will be relatively easy. One-half of your benefits (or, if less, one-half of the modified AGI greater than the $32,000 base) will be taxed.

If you are single and your modified AGI is more than $34,000, or if you are married and your modified AGI is more than $44,000, the computation will be much more complex and, depending on the extent that your modified AGI exceeds this higher base, can result in a full 85 percent of benefits being taxed.

Illustration

Mildred and Pete file jointly. Together they receive a total of $8,000 in Social Security benefits. Their other income consists of Pete's military pension ($35,000), dividends ($4,500), and tax-exempt interest ($6,500).

$35,000	Pension
4,500	Dividends
6,500	Tax-Exempt Interest
4,000	One-Half Social Security Benefits
$50,000	Modified AGI
(44,000)	Base Amount, Married Filing Jointly
$6,000	Excess

Mildred and Pete must include in their income an amount equal to 85 percent of their Social Security benefits or, if less, the sum of (1) 85 percent of the excess of modified AGI greater than the base amount of $44,000; plus (2) one-half of the Social Security benefits (or, if less, $6,000). In this case, Mildred and Pete include $6,800 of their Social Security benefits in income (85 percent of $8,000 is less than the sum of 85 percent of $6,000 plus $4,000).

The following tables illustrate the taxable portion of $10,000 in Social Security benefits at various levels of modified AGI:

Single Individual with $10,000 of Social Security Benefits

TAXABLE AND TAX-FREE INCOME	MODIFIED AGI	TAXABLE SOCIAL SECURITY
$20,000	$25,000	$0
21,000	26,000	500
22,000	27,000	1,000
23,000	28,000	1,500
24,000	29,000	2,000
25,000	30,000	2,500
26,000	31,000	3,000
27,000	32,000	3,500
28,000	33,000	4,000
29,000	34,000	4,500

TAXABLE AND TAX-FREE INCOME	MODIFIED AGI	TAXABLE SOCIAL SECURITY
30,000	35,000	5,350
31,000	36,000	6,200
32,000	37,000	7,050
33,000	38,000	7,900
33,706	38,706	8,500

Married Individuals Filing Jointly with $10,000 of Social Security Benefits

TAXABLE AND TAX-FREE INCOME	MODIFIED AGI	TAXABLE SOCIAL SECURITY
$27,000	$32,000	$0
28,000	33,000	500
29,000	34,000	1,000
30,000	35,000	1,500
31,000	36,000	2,000
32,000	37,000	2,500
33,000	38,000	3,000
34,000	39,000	3,500
35,000	40,000	4,000
36,000	41,000	4,500
37,000	42,000	5,000
38,000	43,000	5,000
39,000	44,000	5,000
40,000	45,000	5,850
41,000	46,000	6,700
42,000	47,000	7,550
43,000	48,000	8,400
43,118	48,118	8,500

Thresholds for single individuals also apply to married individuals who live apart for the entire year and file separately. Married individuals who live together for at least part of the year and file separately usually are taxed on 85 percent of benefits.

Question: In 2004 I will receive a lump sum payment of Social Security monthly benefits covering periods back to 2002. The lump sum payment, when combined with my other income, will cause this check to be taxable. If I had received monthly payments all along, my income under the formula each year would have been less than $25,000. This does not seem fair.

Answer: It is not fair. Consequently, you may elect to compute the portion of the lump sum payment that would have been taxed in each year, if any, using the applicable threshold for each year and add these amounts together. The sum of the excess amounts is taxed in the year that you received the lump sum payment.

Year-End Reminder

When Social Security recipients make investments, they must keep in mind the potential that income generated by the investments will cause the otherwise nontaxable Social Security benefits to be taxable. This is particularly true when acquiring investments that throw off tax-exempt income. Even though the income generated by these investments is itself exempt from federal tax, this income may be sufficient to cause the Social Security recipient to be taxed on a portion of Social Security benefits. If your AGI, as modified previously, is approaching the applicable base amount, try to minimize your income for the remainder of the year. Buy CDs that mature next year or consider the use of installment reporting to defer recognition of the gain on sales of assets. Also, if you are comfortable in taking this step, give income-producing assets to your children. However, as discussed in Chapter 12, avoid gifts of highly appreciated assets and, in most cases, limit any gift each year to $11,000 per recipient ($22,000 if you are married) or as increased for cost of living.

Health Coverage—Insurance and Reimbursements

Employers may offer health insurance coverage in a select manner to employees as long as there is a *rational basis* for any discrimination. Subject to that subjective standard, an employer's payment of the cost of health (including dental) insurance coverage for employees, their spouses, and their dependents is not taxable. Payments made by the insurance carrier to employees or for their benefit (for example, to physicians providing medical care for the family) are also not taxable, except to the extent that you benefited from a deduction for the medical expenses in a prior year and received the reimbursement in a subsequent year.

If the carrier makes payments for the permanent loss of a part of your body or permanent disfigurement, such payments are not included in income unless the amount of the payment is computed by reference to the period of absence from work. For example, assume that an employer-financed insurance policy pays an employee $125 per week up to 52 weeks for absence from work as the result of the loss of an arm. The $125 weekly payment would be taxable because it is computed by reference to the employee's absence from work. However, if the payments from the health insurance plan were determined by the nature of the injury, rather than on the basis of service, the benefit payments would be excluded from income.

Tougher nondiscrimination rules apply to self-insured medical reimbursement plans. An employer's payment of medical and dental expenses of employees and their families pursuant to a written nondiscriminatory plan is not taxable to any employee. However, if the self-insured medical reimbursement plan fails to comply with the statutory nondiscrimination requirements mandating coverage generally for full-time workers over age 25 with three years of service, highly compensated employees, as defined under the law, will be taxed on the discriminatory portion of the medical reimbursements.

A medical reimbursement plan may be set up quite broadly to cover any medical expense that would be deductible by the employee as an itemized deduction were it not for the AGI floor (discussed in Chapter 3) or may be set up narrowly to cover only certain types of unreimbursed expenses including possibly only the deductible amount that the employee has to pay before the insurance carrier's coverage commences.

Through 2003 contributions by an employer averaging no more than 50 employees during the two preceding years to Archer medical savings accounts of employees with high deductible health insurance coverage are excludable from income. The maximum contribution is 65 percent of the individual deductible or 75 percent of the family deductible. Employer contributions may not discriminate among employees with extended health insurance coverage. However, unless extended, no Archer MSAs could be created after December 31, 2003. See Chapter 3 for a discussion of MSAs.

Tax Planning

Pursuant to a September 22, 2003 Revenue Ruling, nonprescription drugs such as pain relievers, allergy medicines, and cold medicines (but not vitamins and toiletries) are qualifying expenses under a medical reimbursement plan and a cafeteria plan (see the discussion later in this chapter) although they would not be deductible if paid individually.

Tax Planning

In the case of a small corporation in which the only employees are owners, group health insurance and a medical reimbursement plan are excellent fringe benefits, and no concern exists with the nondiscrimination rules. Few individuals, even among those who itemize deductions, are able to enjoy the benefit of itemizing medical and dental expenses due to the 7.5 percent of AGI floor. A health insurance or medical reimbursement plan permits the payment of these expenses with before-tax dollars. For example, a single individual with $85,000 of AGI in a 28 percent marginal tax bracket will save $1,260 in taxes under a medical reimbursement plan if he or she has $4,500 in medical expenses not covered by insurance.

The pretax payment of 100 percent of the cost of participation in a group health plan or in a medical reimbursement plan is not available to shareholders with more than a 2 percent interest in an S corporation. Sole proprietors and partners, who cannot be employees of their own unincorporated businesses, but not S corporation shareholders with more than 2 percent, can achieve pretax payment of all health costs in the event that their spouses can be placed on the payroll as bona fide employees. (See Chapter 10 for a discussion of various types of business entities.)

Business owners with medical reimbursement plans who must cover nonfamily members should consider a ceiling on benefits to protect against the possibility of catastrophic costs. Pursuant to a 2002 Revenue Ruling, if a plan has a ceiling, unused reimbursement amounts may carry over to a succeeding year.

Caution

See Chapter 3 concerning the special deduction of a portion of health insurance costs available to sole proprietors, general partners, and more than 2 percent S corporation shareholders. See Chapter 4, "Deductions—For Itemizers Only," concerning the cost of long-term care coverage as health insurance. Unless provided by a cafeteria plan (see the discussion later in this chapter), such employer-paid insurance will be tax-free (except for the same limitations for sole proprietors, partners, and shareholders of more than a 2 percent interest in an S corporation). However, tax-free benefits will be limited to the greater of $230 per day in 2004, adjusted for changes in the cost of living or actual expenses. Future tax legislation may end the ban on long-term care coverage through a cafeteria plan.

Question: My employer offers free family health coverage that extends to domestic partners of the same or opposite sex. My live-in girlfriend, who has a job but is not covered by health insurance, is afraid that she must pay taxes on this benefit. Is she right?

Answer: No, according to the IRS in a 1997 letter ruling, but you must pay taxes on the value of the coverage according to that ruling and another in 2001, because it is provided by your employer, and your girlfriend is not family (neither spouse nor dependent).

Question: Five years ago I organized a corporation. I now have six employees, four of whom work full-time (two salary and two hourly), and two of whom are part-time hourly and work only about four hours a day. Can the corporation pay for the four full-time employees' health insurance without paying for the two individuals who work only part-time?

Answer: It is clear that you have a "rational basis" for the distinction under which you would be providing health insurance for only the full-time workers. You should be able to provide this fringe benefit for all of them on a tax-free basis. Avoid coverage of only salaried or owner employees.

Excluding Disability Benefits

Payments by an employer for employee disability insurance coverage are nontaxable to the employee. However, if the premium cost is excluded from the employee's income, subsequent disability benefits would be taxable to the employee. In contrast, disability insurance paid by the employee (or paid by the employer as additional compensation to the employee and reported as income by the employee) will allow payments made by the carrier, in the event of disability, to be nontaxable.

In a closely owned corporation, or in a larger business when the employer offers disability insurance coverage to the employee, the initial reaction is to attempt to provide disability insurance on a tax-free basis. However, most disability insurance policies limit benefits to about two-thirds of an employee's usual income. A disabled employee, who receives two-thirds of his or her usual pay and is taxed on the benefit, may incur a cash shortage. A nontaxable disability benefit of two-thirds of usual compensation, however, may be comparable in after-tax dollars to the predisability situation.

Question: My employer pays my disability insurance premium. I have no reason to believe that I am ever going to draw benefits under the policy. Suppose that I exclude the premium cost from income now. In the unlikely event that I become disabled, I will have my employer report that year's premium cost on my W-2.

Answer: Good luck with the IRS. Under scrutiny, your idea would undoubtedly be considered a "sham," and your disability income determined to be taxable.

Excluding Worker's Compensation Benefits

If workers are injured on the job, they may be eligible to receive worker's compensation benefits. These benefits, to the extent that they are paid under a state or federal worker's compensation statute or under an equivalent law, are not taxable. No exclusion is available if payments are for non-work-connected disabilities or if the amount of payments is based on age or service.

Although a worker's compensation award is excludable from income, the Tax Court determined several years ago that interest on a back award is taxable. However, see "Damage Awards and Settlements" later in this chapter, which provides authority for a pro-taxpayer result if a state's worker's compensation law makes such interest part of the compensation itself.

Question: My husband was a county firefighter for 25 years. Six months ago he had a heart attack and was given a disability pension. The county determined that the heart attack was probably work related, inasmuch as it occurred two days after he had fought a major fire for 36 hours straight. Under worker's compensation, he was awarded disability pay of 50 percent of his compensation at the time that he had the heart attack plus an additional 1 percent for each year of service. Do we have to pay taxes on the payments?

Answer: If it was determined for other purposes that a disability was work connected, it should be accepted by the IRS. The base portion of the pension equal to 50 percent of pay will be nontaxable. The IRS would consider the balance as taxable income linked to years of service. However, the Tax Court probably would find the balance tax-free as well if the service add-on was a distinction between work-related injuries and others.

Question: I became disabled from work-related injuries after only five years on the police force. Now, 20 years later, I am at the age when I could have retired if I had been able to stay on the job, and, as a result, my disability pay is being reduced to the level of retirement pay. Will the payments still be tax-free?

Answer: The Ninth Circuit Court of Appeals reversed the Tax Court under similar facts in a 1999 decision and determined that the continuing payments related to the earlier injuries are tax-free in that the taxpayer was not employed long enough for retirement pay.

Question: My husband suffered an on-the-job injury and cannot work. Neither can I, because I need to stay home to take care of him. The state is paying me about $25,000 per year to tend to my husband. Is this tax-free worker's compensation?

Answer: No, according to a 2000 Tax Court decision, at least when payments to you are under a statute for assistance to a disabled beneficiary and not under the worker's compensation statute.

Acquiring Life Insurance Cheaply

Employers commonly offer an employee group life insurance coverage, usually with the amount of the insurance coverage being determined by the employee's salary. To the extent that the insurance coverage provided is term insurance and the amount of the coverage does not exceed $50,000, this benefit is nontaxable to the employee. If the amount of the insurance coverage exceeds $50,000, the employee is taxed on the deemed cost of this excess insurance. Following is the table for the current PS-58 cost of excess insurance coverage:

AGE	MONTHLY COST PER $1,000
Less than 25	5 cents
25–29	6 cents
30–34	8 cents
35–39	9 cents
40–44	10 cents
45–49	15 cents
50–54	23 cents
55–59	43 cents
60–64	66 cents
65–69	$1.27
More than 69	$2.06

Even though this excess insurance coverage is taxable to the employee, the employee will often still derive a benefit in that the tax cost of the excess insurance coverage should be less than the actual premium paid by the employer or what the employee would have to pay for the excess coverage if purchased individually.

Illustration

Sally's employer offers her group term life insurance coverage in an amount equal to twice her salary. Sally earns $60,000 a year. She is 37 years old and in a 25 percent tax bracket.

$120,000	Total Insurance Coverage
(50,000)	Exempt Insurance Coverage
$70,000	Taxable Insurance Coverage
$0.09	Monthly Cost per $1,000
$1.08	Annual Cost per $1,000
$75.60	Taxable Amount ($1.08 × 70)
$18.90	Added Federal Taxes ($75.60 × .25)

If the employer provides group term life insurance protection on a discriminatory basis, key employees, as defined under the law, are charged with income based upon the value of the discriminatory excess coverage. Sole proprietors, partners, and greater than 2 percent S corporation shareholders may not enjoy coverage with pretax dollars in any event.

Employer-paid group term life insurance providing a benefit on the death of a spouse or dependent of no more than $2,000 has historically been exempt from tax as a *de minimis* fringe benefit. Treasury Regulations that have been indefinitely delayed, if implemented, would require employees to include the cost of all spouse or dependent coverage in income.

Other employer-paid insurance premiums will be includable in the employee's income if the beneficiary of the insurance proceeds is the employee's personal beneficiary rather than the employer. Where the employer is the beneficiary (for example, in a key person policy), the employee is not taxed on the insurance coverage because he or she receives no policy benefit.

Life insurance proceeds received by the insured's beneficiary are generally tax-exempt even when the employer has paid the cost of the insurance protection.

Caution

Split-dollar life insurance is a means of providing additional insurance greater than group coverage to select employees. Under a typical split-dollar policy, the employer owns and pays for the policy and is the policy beneficiary to the extent of the premiums it paid; the employee's personal beneficiary receives

continues

Caution (cont.)

the difference. The employee has typically included in his or her income each year the one-year term cost of the insurance protection (determined under the PS-58 table issued by the IRS or, if lower, the rate charged by the insurer) plus policy dividends made to the employee less the amount the employee may have contributed to the premium.

However, on September 17, 2003, the IRS issued Final Regulations that would tax the employee on prospective policy acquisitions or material modifications based on the true "economic benefit", (typically the cost of current term life insurance protection plus the amount of the policy cash value to which the employee first has access during the year) of an employer-owned policy. The Regulations would require the employee to repay the employer with interest for premiums paid by the employer in the case of an employee-owned policy.

Tax Planning

Except in a business context, policy owners may receive tax-free accelerated death benefits from both insurance carriers and certain third parties. The law benefits both terminally ill (expected to die within 24 months) and chronically ill (substantial loss of physical or mental functions) individuals. Tax-free benefits to chronically ill individuals are limited to the greater of $230 per day in 2004, adjusted for changes in the cost of living, or the actual expenses when considered in conjunction with benefits paid out under long-term care insurance policies (see Chapter 4). Expenses do not include amounts paid to related individuals who are not health care professionals.

Employer-Provided Dependent Care Plans—A Benefit for You and Your Employer

A very valuable fringe benefit that an increasing number of employers are offering to their employees is the opportunity to participate in a dependent care plan. Through such a plan, an employer can provide the employee with the ability to exclude from income the value of the dependent care services up to the lesser of $5,000 per year ($2,500 in the case of a married couple filing a separate return), the employee's earned income, or the spouse's deemed earned income. (See the discussion of the dependent care credit in Chapter 3 as to a spouse's deemed earned income.)

Under a dependent care assistance program, the employer can pay the child care costs for the employees on a tax-free basis. To qualify, the dependent care assistance must be offered to both rank and file as well as to owners and other highly paid employees. No more than 25 percent of the amounts paid under the dependent care plan can be provided for more-than-5-percent owners, the employer, or their spouses or dependents, and the rank and file must receive benefits that are at least 55 percent of those paid to owners, officers, and certain other highly compensated workers.

(A related benefit for employees is an exclusion for employer-paid adoption expenses pursuant to a nondiscriminatory plan under which no more than 5 percent of the amounts paid can be provided to more-than-5-percent owners or their family members. The exclusion generally parallels the tax credit for employee-paid adoption expenses as discussed in Chapter 3.)

Question: I am a single parent earning $40,000 a year, and I am due to receive a $5,000 raise. My only child, Cathy, lives with me. I have to pay a babysitter $5,000 per year to care for Cathy while I go to work. If I expect $35,000 of taxable income for the year, how can I benefit from a dependent care plan?

Answer: If you do not participate in a dependent care plan, you will owe $3,150 in federal taxes on taxable income of $35,000, computed by using the head of household rates and taking into account a $600 dependent care credit and a $1,000 child tax credit (discussed in Chapter 3). If you participate in a dependent care plan, you will owe $3,000 in federal taxes on taxable income of $30,000, computed by using the head of household rates and claiming the child tax credit. By participating in the plan, you have $37,000 left ($40,000 − $3,000 taxes) of your $40,000 salary as opposed to $36,850 left of your $45,000 salary ($45,000 − $5,000 child care costs − $3,150 taxes). You save $150, but more significantly, you and your employer save another $383 each, because the $5,000 child care reimbursement is not subject to Social Security taxes.

"Cafeteria" Plans—A Full Menu

In a cafeteria plan, an employer provides employees with a menu of various nontaxable fringe benefits, such as health insurance, medical reimbursement, life insurance, and dependent care coverage. Each employee then can choose the benefits that best suit his or her particular needs. Such a plan provides employees with a great deal of flexibility. For example, an employee may not want to participate in any health insurance coverage offered by an employer if the employee is covered by the spouse's employer-provided insurance program. The employee then may choose the dependent care fringe benefit and the life insurance coverage instead of health insurance coverage with the cafeteria plan dollars. If the plan so provides, the employee can choose to receive unspent plan dollars in cash or have the unspent dollars contributed to a 401(k) profit-sharing plan.

Employees who select reimbursement under a cafeteria plan for uninsured medical expenses should be careful to limit this choice so that there is no unused portion at year-end. You may not make a new selection simply because you have not incurred uninsured medical expenses in excess of the amount of medical reimbursement coverage that you have elected. You will forfeit the unused portion, which could otherwise have been used by another benefit under the plan.

A cafeteria plan must be nondiscriminatory to qualify for favorable tax treatment, and key employees, as defined, may not received more than 25 percent of benefits.

Question: My employer has just instituted a cafeteria plan that allows me to choose coverage in a major medical plan, dental plan, group term life insurance plan, or a dependent care assistance plan. How often can I change my selection of benefits from the cafeteria plan menu?

Answer: Under Final Regulations issued in 2001, except in limited instances, generally involving the inclusion of a new plan benefit or a change in family circumstances such as your marriage or divorce, the death or change in employment state of your spouse, or the birth or death of a dependent, your selection of benefits under the cafeteria plan must be irrevocable for each plan year.

Tax-Free Meals and Lodging

When an employer provides an employee with free food and lodging, the employee usually pays a tax on the value of the benefit. However, employees are not taxed on certain employer-provided meals and housing.

To qualify for the tax-free treatment, the meal or lodging must be provided to the employee by the employer to further a business purpose of the employer (compensating the employee does not qualify), and it must be furnished on the employer's business premises. An additional condition qualifies the value of lodging (but not meals) for the exclusion—the employee must accept the lodging to properly fulfill job responsibilities.

Here are some typical situations in which the employee would not be taxed on the value of employer-provided meals or housing:

- Lunch served to a waiter or waitress who works the lunch shift
- Room and board provided to a live-in babysitter
- Meals and lodging provided by an employer at a remote job site where no other facilities other than those provided by the employer exist

If the value of a meal is taxable because one or more of the preceding conditions is not satisfied, the amount that is taxed is the cost of the meal to the employer, even though it may have cost the employee much more to have gone to a restaurant to eat.

The nontaxability of meals and lodging applies only to situations in which the meals or lodging are provided in-kind and not to cash allowances. If the employer provides supper money to employees who work late, the supper money will not be exempt from tax under the meals and lodging rule, although it may be exempt from tax as a *de minimis* fringe benefit.

The meals and lodging rule applies regardless of whether the employer is a closely held corporation and the employee is a stockholder in that corporation, so long as the statutory requirements are met. However, the IRS will not allow the value of meals or lodging furnished by an S corporation to a more-than-2-percent shareholder, by a partnership to a partner, or by a sole proprietorship to its owner to qualify for the exclusion.

Tax Planning

Suppose that you and an investor own and operate a motel in a resort area. You have converted three motel rooms into your home. You have to be at the motel 24 hours a day. If you run the business as a partnership, the value of the three rooms will be taxed to you. However, if you incorporate the business and work as an employee, the value of your home is not taxed.

However, the placing of real property in a corporation can cause double taxation in the event of sale—first at the corporate level and then again when remaining proceeds are distributed to the shareholders. Consequently, real property should be placed in a corporation only after extensive consideration of both the advantages and disadvantages.

The Company Car and Other Employer-Provided Transportation Benefits

Often an employer will provide an employee with an automobile as part of the employment package. More often than not, the vehicle provided will be used both for business purposes and for personal purposes. Any personal use of the company car, including commuting use, is taxable to the employee, but use of the vehicle for business purposes is not taxable. The value of personal use of the car is determined by the employer under various guidelines provided by the IRS, including annual lease value multiplied by the percentage of personal use or, for some cars costing less than $15,200 when placed in service during 2003, a standard mileage rate of 30 1/2 cents per mile (increasing to 32 cents for 2004). Both the dollar maximum for use of the standard mileage rate and the rate itself are indexed based on the automobile component of the Consumer Price Index. Under either method, if an employer provides gas and oil for the vehicle, the employee usually will report an additional 5.5 cents per personal mile as income.

The employer can choose to include 100 percent of the lease value of a car in the employee's income. The employee then deducts the business use portion as a miscellaneous itemized deduction subject to the 2 percent floor.

Even when the employee must include 100 percent of the lease value in income, he or she will be better off taking the company car than receiving reimbursement for business use of a personal car. The employee has to buy a car with after-tax dollars and must earn $30,769 to buy a $20,000 car if he or she is in the 35 percent bracket. If the employer buys the car and allows the employee to use it for personal as well as business purposes, the employee's income is increased by only $5,600 per year and the tax liability by $1,960. This $1,960 in extra taxes will be reduced as a result of the costs associated with the business use of the car if the employee itemizes deductions and if the costs coupled with other miscellaneous itemized deductions exceed 2 percent of AGI.

If an employer requires employees to commute to and from the workplace in the company car and has a written policy banning other personal use of the automobile, the employer has the option (usually favorable to the employee) of valuing the personal commuting use at $3 per round-trip commute. This method of valuing personal use is not available if the employee is an officer, director, or a 1-percent-or-more shareholder. Stock owned by your spouse, children, parents, and grandparents is considered to be owned by you for purposes of determining stock ownership in this case.

Careful substantiation records must be maintained when an employee uses a company car in order to establish business versus personal use. This is a high audit area.

Tax Planning

Employees who drive to work can enjoy employer-paid parking privileges or cash reimbursements on a tax-free basis up to $195 per month indexed for inflation in 2003 and succeeding years. This exclusion from income is not available to sole proprietors, partners, and greater-than-2-percent shareholders in an S corporation. (See Chapter 10 for a discussion of alternative types of business entities.)

Employee parking benefits are valued based on the regular commercial rate at the same or similar location. The IRS has acknowledged the lack of value in suburban and rural lots where free parking is offered; thus, the law is directed at employees who work in urban areas where parking is costly.

Employees who would otherwise walk or use public transportation to commute to or from their job site can receive an employer-paid taxi ride to or from work and need include only $1.50 per one-way trip in income as the deemed value of the fringe benefit. This special valuation rule is only available if the taxi

Tax Planning (cont.)

ride is furnished because of unsafe conditions, such as a high-crime area, and if the employer has a written policy to that effect. Only employees paid on an hourly basis are eligible for this special tax break. Other employees who receive a taxi ride home from their employer must include the actual value of the taxi service in income.

Public transit passes, fare cards, or tokens provided by employers to employees for their use in commuting as well as van pooling (six or more workers plus driver) costs paid by employer are not taxable to the extent of a benefit of up to $100 per month in 2003 (indexed for inflation in succeeding years). This exclusion, too, is not available to sole proprietors, partners, and greater-than-2-percent S corporation shareholders.

Stock or Property for Service—An Important Election

Particularly in the case of startup companies, many employers provide their employees with the opportunity to acquire stock (or other equity interest) in the company at a discount or for no consideration. If no restrictions exist on the ability to sell or otherwise transfer the stock or if there is a minimal chance that the stock will have to be forfeited, then the difference between the value of the stock and any amount that is paid for stock is taxable upon receipt of the stock. However, if the employer places restrictions on the transferability of the stock and imposes restrictions on the employee's ability to retain the stock in certain circumstances (for example, if the employee would be required to forfeit the stock upon termination of employment), the employee has no income tax consequences until such time as the stock becomes fully transferable or there is no longer a substantial risk of having to forfeit the stock.

Stock will be considered freely transferable when the employee can sell, assign, or pledge the stock without having the transferee subject to any conditions as an owner of the stock.

The IRS considers the following to be substantial risks of forfeiture:

- The stock is subject to a requirement that it be returned if the employer's earnings do not increase above a specified level.
- The stock must be returned to the employer if the employee terminates employment.

However, the following are not considered to be substantial risks of forfeiture:

- Return of the stock is required if the employee is terminated for cause.
- The employer is required to pay the employee the fair market value for the stock upon its return.

The existence of these conditions upon receipt of the stock would not prevent the employee from having to include the value of the stock less any amount paid for it in income in the year of receipt.

When such stock first becomes transferable or is not subject to a substantial risk of forfeiture, the value of the stock at that time less any amount paid for the stock is considered additional compensation. However, the employee has the option to include the value of this restricted stock in income in the year that it is received rather than in a later year when the stock becomes transferable or the substantial risk of forfeiture is eliminated. This Section 83(b) election permits the employee to be taxed prior to any rise in value of the stock, thereby reducing the compensatory element of the presumably appreciating property and ensuring that future appreciation will not be taxed until disposition of the property and that it will be taxed at capital gain rates.

The Section 83(b) election must be made within 30 days from the date that the employer transfers the property to the employee. The election is made by filing a written statement with the IRS Service Center where the employee expects to file his or her individual income tax return. A copy of that statement is attached to the tax return for the year in which the property is received. The Section 83(b) election must contain certain prescribed information.

After the Section 83(b) election is made, it is usually irrevocable. Consequently, even if the value of the stock declined rather than appreciated in value, the employee who has made the Section 83(b) election cannot change his or her mind.

The Section 83(b) election must be made even when no compensation element exists in the transfer (that is, when the property is purchased by an employee at its fair market value), or else the rise in value will be taxed as ordinary income when the property becomes transferable or a substantial risk of forfeiture no longer exists. For example, an employee who receives restricted shares of a second class of stock with no rights in existing equity and sharing only in future growth probably should make a Section 83(b) election and avoid any immediate tax or any tax, in fact, prior to disposition of the shares.

A partnership interest granted for services is taxed similarly. Several years ago the IRS announced that it was relenting from a prior position and agreeing that such partnership interests sharing only in future income (as opposed to interests in existing capital) generally are not taxed upon grant. Exceptions include interests in publicly traded partnerships (see Chapter 7), interests sold within two years of receipt, and interests in partnerships with a predictable income stream.

Although the IRS is silent on the issue, receipt of a corporate interest sharing only in future income should also be tax-free, whether a formal equity interest in a second class of stock (C corporations only) or a *phantom* interest under a contract giving the employee a percentage of future net income and gain.

The transfer of almost any property by an employer to an employee for services rendered is treated in the same manner as stock. If an employer gives an employee a house in exchange for services, the value of the house is taxable to the employee if the employee can transfer title to the house or if his or her rights to fully enjoy the property are not conditioned upon performance of future services or other substantial restriction. However, see the exception in Chapter 11 for members of the clergy.

Question: As part of my employment package, my employer, Mainco, Inc., will sell me 10 shares of Mainco stock for $10 per share. Mainco stock is currently worth $100 per share. If I terminate my employment within the next two years, I am obligated to sell the stock back to Mainco for $10 per share. In addition, I am prohibited from transferring the Mainco stock to any other person for two years. As I understand it, these conditions will be stamped on the face of the stock certificate. Mainco is doing very well, and every indication shows that in two years the stock will double in value. What are the tax consequences to me, if any, if I buy the 10 shares?

Answer: Because the Mainco stock is nontransferable and subject to a substantial risk of forfeiture, you have no tax consequences when you buy the stock. However, on the second anniversary, you will be taxed on the difference between the stock's value at that time and your $10 per share cost. If your estimate of value is correct, you would have to include $1,900 in income ($200 per share value − $10 per share cost × 10 shares). Alternatively, you should consider making the Section 83(b) election. By making the election, you would be taxed on your receipt of the Mainco stock. The amount on which you would be taxed is the difference between today's value of the stock and your cost, $900 ($100 per share value − $10 per share cost × 10 shares).

Tax Planning

Although the general rule is that property provided to employees for free or at a discount is taxable, some such fringe benefits can be provided on a tax-free basis. Employees who receive employer services costing the business little or nothing are not taxed on the value received. For example, as a no additional cost service, airline employees may be given the opportunity to travel for free or at a discount. Employee discounts on the purchase of merchandise are tax-free if the discount does not exceed the gross profit percentage or, in the case of services paid by the employer, 20 percent of the price of the service to customers. Employers must offer these fringe benefits on a nondiscriminatory basis.

continues

Tax Planning (cont.)

De minimis **fringe benefits—those of little value to justify the record keeping—are not taxed to employees. Examples include occasional personal use of business telephones, copiers, and postage meters. A 1994 IRS letter ruling distinguishes a *de minimis* fringe benefit from one of value. The IRS determined in its ruling that employer-paid tax return preparation is not a *de minimis* benefit, but use of the employer's computer equipment for electronic filing is a *de minimis* benefit. A 1999 IRS letter ruling concluded that company-paid financial counseling to family members of terminally ill and deceased employees is of value and taxable to the employee or family member, respectively. By statute, employer-provided nondiscriminatory retirement planning services are tax-free, including income tax planning, but not legal or brokerage services.**

Stock Options—A Premier Fringe Benefit

The ability to acquire stock in an employer corporation—an option to buy stock—remains one of the premier fringe benefits available to employees. The two general categories of stock options are nonqualified stock options and incentive stock options (ISOs). The tax consequences of the two types of options are significantly different.

The grant of a nonqualified stock option will not be taxable to the recipient unless the option can be valued. This is normally not the case unless the option is traded on an established market. Thus, the mere grant of a nonqualified stock option generally will have no tax consequences to the employee. However, when the employee exercises the option to buy the stock, the difference between the value of the stock at that time and the amount paid for the stock (the bargain element) is additional compensation. Any future appreciation in the stock received upon the exercise of the nonqualified stock option would not be recognized as income until the stock is sold. At that time, the appreciation would be considered a capital gain rather than ordinary income.

If the stock that is acquired upon the exercise of a nonqualified option is restricted, as previously discussed, then the taxation of the bargain element of the transaction is delayed until the stock becomes transferable or is not subject to a substantial risk of forfeiture. The Section 83(b) election, however, is available as a hedge against future appreciation of the stock.

If an employer establishes an ISO plan in accordance with the Internal Revenue Code, no tax consequences exist to the employee upon the grant of an ISO. Nor is there any regular income tax as a result of the exercise of the ISO, even if the value of the stock at the time of the exercise exceeds the option price. Upon exercise of an ISO, however, the spread between the value of the stock at the time of the exercise and the purchase price is a tax preference item and may result in the imposition of the AMT. With this exception, tax liability is delayed until disposition of the stock when it is taxed at capital gain rates.

To qualify as an ISO

- An option must be issued pursuant to a plan approved by the shareholders within 12 months of Board of Directors' approval.
- The option must be granted within 10 years from the earlier of directors' or shareholders' approval.
- The option must be exercisable within only 10 years from the date of grant.
- The price for which the option can be exercised must at least equal the value of the stock on the date the option is granted.
- No more than $100,000 worth of stock (valued at the time the option is granted) may become exercisable for the first time in any one year.
- The option must be nontransferable during the employee's lifetime.
- The employee to whom the option is granted cannot own more than 10 percent of the stock of the company unless the option is no less than 110 percent of the stock's value on the date of grant, and the life of the option is limited to five years.

The $100,000 limitation still permits your employer to grant you ISOs to purchase $1 million worth of stock (as valued at the time of the grant) so long as the terms of the option provide that only $100,000 worth of the stock can be purchased in 2004; a second $100,000 in 2005; and so forth. However, these rights to acquire stock are cumulative such that if in 2004 you decide to exercise your option with respect to only $20,000 worth of the stock, in 2005 you would be able to buy not only the $100,000 worth of stock that first became exercisable in 2005, but also the $80,000 worth of stock that you chose not to purchase in 2004.

If you sell the stock received upon the exercise of the ISO, any gain realized will be a long-term capital gain, as long as you hold onto the stock for two years from the time the option was granted to you and one year from the time you exercised the option. If the stock is disposed of prematurely, except in the case of options exercised after your death, the gain will instead be taxed as ordinary income.

Question: I have heard a lot about stock options as part of a compensation package. Should I insist that my employer comply with the ISO rules, or is it okay if my employer issues me an option to buy stock that does not comply with the ISO rules?

Answer: From your point of view, the ISOs certainly present an advantage. You will have no tax consequences on the receipt of the option or on its exercise;

however, on the exercise of the option, the spread between the value of the stock and the exercise price is a tax preference item that may expose you to the AMT (discussed in Chapter 1).

The disadvantage for you in being given an option to buy your company's stock under an ISO plan is that the option price may be higher than the price for which your employer is willing to sell you the stock under a nonqualified plan. The employer must make the option price under the ISO plan equal to or greater than the value of the stock on the date the option is granted; whereas the nonqualified option price need not be related to the stock's value.

Your employer may insist on the nonqualified option as opposed to the ISO. The ISO has more restrictions than does the nonqualified option, and your employer gets no tax deduction when an ISO is exercised but does get a deduction when a nonqualified option is exercised.

If your employer will not structure the option as an ISO, you might negotiate for your employer to pay you additional compensation equal to the extra tax that you are going to pay in the year that you exercise the option.

Year-End Reminder

Employees with stock options exercisable over a period of multiple years should not let December pass without considering the tax consequence of exercise versus nonexercise. Do not forget to consider the AMT.

Caution

Because tax liability is determined on exercise of stock options, regular tax in the case of a nonqualified option or AMT in the case of an ISO, the optionee bears risk of a cash shortfall if the value of the stock declines quickly after exercise of the option.

Individuals exercising nonqualified options may wish to sell a portion of their shares; however, individuals exercising ISOs and facing AMT must wait one year to dispose of shares lest the rise in value from date of grant to exercise be reclassified as ordinary income.

Nonqualified Deferred Compensation Arrangements

For any number of reasons, you may want to defer the receipt of your salary until a subsequent year. For example, you may want to defer income to a year in which you believe you will be in a lower tax bracket, or you may want to provide for financial security following retirement. To effectively defer the tax consequences of the compensation income to the time when you actually receive the salary, a binding agreement must exist between you and your employer entered into prior to the time that the compensation was earned—that is, before you render the services to which the compensation relates.

Unfortunately, you cannot turn your back on your employer's paycheck and avoid including it in income. If the paycheck is available on the last day of the year, even if you do not pick up the check until the following year, that salary check is included in your income in the earlier year.

A nonqualified deferred compensation arrangement is simply an employer's unfunded promise to pay the employee at a later date. For example, on December 31, 2003, you and your employee may enter into an agreement whereby $10,000 of your 2004 salary (plus perhaps a factor reflecting the time value of money) will be paid to you upon your termination of employment rather than in 2004.

Question: I can afford to defer a portion of my salary ($5,000) until I retire. The company that I work for has agreed to pay me my $5,000 plus a time value factor upon retirement. However, the company is fairly small, and I am concerned that, if I enter into a deferred compensation agreement, the company will not be around when I retire or will have spent "my" money for general operations. Can I do anything to protect what I am owed, yet not have to pay tax on it currently?

Answer: Your concerns are well justified. It does you no good whatsoever to defer compensation and then lose it completely. However, if your employer sets the funds aside or otherwise secures its obligation to you, you are exposing yourself to current income tax, even though you do not actually receive the money until retirement.

If you want to defer income, take two precautions. First, negotiate a trust arrangement (often known as a "Rabbi Trust"), whereby your employer will place the amount of deferred compensation in a special trust fund. The trust then will pay over the accumulated funds to you when you retire. The income generated by the trust will be taxed to your employer, and the trust fund will be within reach of the general creditors of the company. However, at least you know that the company has set the funds aside to cover its future obligation to you. Second, obtain personal guarantees from the owner and the owner's spouse. These unsecured personal guarantees should not accelerate taxation of your deferred compensation.

Year-End Reminder

Examine your income level as year-end approaches and determine whether it is advisable to defer future compensation. Note, however, that the IRS will closely scrutinize deferred compensation agreements and will disregard any agreement that does not impose substantial limits on your right to receive the salary. One factor the IRS will consider in its examination of the limits on your right to receive the deferred amount is the length of the deferral period. Where the deferral period is for just a few weeks, say from mid-December to mid-January, the IRS likely will rule that you must pay taxes on the deferred salary in the year you would have received the salary if there had been no agreement.

Tax Planning

Although income tax liability is delayed on nonqualified deferred compensation, Social Security and Medicare taxes are generally computed on the value of deferred compensation when earned. Payroll tax liability consequently may be lowered when compensation in that year (both paid and deferred) exceeds the Social Security base.

Caution

The employer gets no tax deduction for deferred compensation until the year that the employee must report income. Because a tax deduction is irrelevant to a governmental or tax-exempt employer, the maximum deferral to an employee in such cases is severely limited—generally to the 401 (k) limit (see Chapter 9, "Retirement Plans") unless the employee is willing to accept a "substantial risk of forfeiture" beyond the given risks associated with the deferral. Nonetheless, the affected employee may place net after-tax dollars in the Rabbi Trust for deferral of tax on the income. Because taxes have been paid on the principal, it is returned tax-free from the Rabbi Trust at retirement.

Losing Your Job—A Taxing Time

Unemployment compensation is fully taxable. Consequently, if you are receiving unemployment benefits, make sure that your withholdings from your job or your estimated tax payments are adequate to cover your obligation to prepay your current year's income tax liability, including the tax on the unemployment benefits.

Question: The division of the company that I work for was closed down. I received six months' severance pay and job placement assistance. I assume my severance pay is taxable. What about the job placement services?

Answer: Your assumption is correct; the severance pay is taxable. The value of the job placement assistance, however, is excludable from your income so long as you did not have the option of taking the job placement counseling in lieu of additional severance pay. The mere ability to choose between the counseling and the money would force you to include the value of the job placement counseling in your income.

Employer-Paid Educational Benefits

When an employer pays for an employee's education, the employee usually pays a tax on the value of the benefit. However, employees are not taxed on employer-provided educational assistance (tuition, fees, books, and supplies) to a maximum of $5,250 per year pursuant to an educational benefit plan even when the courses are primarily for the employee's benefit. Payment must be pursuant to a nondiscriminatory plan under which no more than 5 percent of the amounts paid can be provided for more than 5-percent owners of the employer or their family members. (See Chapters 3 and 4 concerning tax credits and deductions for employee-paid educational expenses.)

Tax Planning

Employer-provided educational assistance for the primary benefit of the employer is excludable without limit from an employee's income even if the courses are not pursuant to an educational benefit plan.

Family-Paid Educational Benefits

Section 529 plans and Coverdell Education Savings Accounts offer excellent tax-favored opportunities to fund future education costs.

Since 1997 states have been authorized to create, and all but five have created, Section 529 tax-exempt programs under which individuals prepay tuition at today's cost or participate in a choice of pooled savings trusts to pay future educational expenses including room and board. Since 2002 private educational institutions have also been permitted to create prepaid tuition programs.

The purchaser, usually a parent or grandparent, is considered to be making a gift to the beneficiary (see Chapter 12), which may be spread over the current and four succeeding years. The beneficiary, usually a child or grandchild, pays no tax on distributions from the plan to pay qualified educational expenses (effective 2004 for distributions from programs of private institutions). Contributions may be returned to the transferor, rolled over between plans (once in a 12-month period), or rolled over to other family members, but earnings that are returned to the transferor are subject to a 10 percent penalty.

The second family-paid educational benefit was added to the law in 1998. Individuals may contribute to nondeductible Coverdell Education Savings Accounts (formerly known as Education IRAs) of up to $2,000 per beneficiary under age 18 at the date of the contribution. A "special needs" beneficiary may receive contributions after age 18. The ability to make contributions is phased out at modified gross income between $190,000 and $220,000 for married couples filing jointly and between $95,000 and $110,000 for others.

Contributions to a Coverdell Education Savings Account may be made for the preceding year until April 15 of the following year.

Earnings from a Coverdell Education Savings Account are excludable from income unless distributions in a year exceed qualified elementary, secondary, undergraduate, graduate, or post-high school vocational education expenses (including room and board for at least a half-time student), in which case a *pro rata* portion of the contributions is recovered tax-free, and the balance is taxable. Thus, even though the contribution is not deductible, the value of a Coverdell Education Savings Account is in the tax-free growth over the years.

Any taxable portion of a distribution from a Coverdell Education Savings Account, meaning the portion not used to pay qualifying expenses, is subject to a 10-percent penalty unless the withdrawal is on account of death or disability, to the extent of a scholarship received by the account holder, or if the sole reason for taxability is waiver of the exclusion in favor of an educational credit. Except in the case of a special needs beneficiary, a Coverdell Education Savings Account must be distributed before the account holder is age 30; thus the penalty is likely to apply unless education is completed by that time.

No exclusion is available for a distribution from a prepaid tuition program or a Coverdell Education Savings Account to the extent that either of two educational credits, the HOPE scholarship credit or the lifetime learning credit, are used to offset the same for expenses of the same individual. Both credits are discussed in Chapter 3.

Question: What can my daughter do to avoid a penalty on her Education Savings Account? She is 28 years old and may not go back to school. In the meanwhile, what can be done to increase the yield on the account? It is earning 5 percent in the bank.

Answer: Before your daughter turns 30, she can transfer her account balance without penalty to a younger family member (and without gift tax considerations to a same generation beneficiary) by direct transfer or rollover with possession for up to 60 days. Prior to any such transfer, she may change investments in a similar manner by direct transfer or rollover.

Tax Planning

If a potential beneficiary's parents are barred from a Coverdell Education Savings Account contribution by high modified AGI, the $2,000 per beneficiary contribution alternatively may originate from grandparents with lower income or from the child's own money.

Damage Awards and Settlements

Amounts received as a result of litigation or settlement of litigation arising out of physical injury are exempt from tax if the payments are compensatory in nature, even if the payments represent back pay. The tax-free nature is unchanged even if payments are made to a decedent's estate or family, such as for lack of consortium. (However, as discussed in Chapter 4 on "Maximizing Medical Expenses," any recovery allocable to medical expenses reduces the available tax deduction.) With narrow exceptions, such as restitutions to Holocaust-era survivors, other damages including punitive damages and damages not arising out of physical injury are taxable as of August 21, 1996.

Payments under structured settlements, which are received throughout a number of years, although constituting in part the equivalent of interest, are also entirely tax-free when the underlying damages are tax-free. If the recipient of the settlement were to take a lump sum payment instead, interest received on the invested proceeds would be subject to tax. Of course, recipients of structured settlements must investigate the financial solvency of the insurance carriers or others who are legally liable for the deferred payments.

Prejudgment interest, arising when state law provides for interest from the date of contract breach or injury until judgment, and postjudgment interest on damages received in litigation are both taxable.

Question: I was the victim of a sexual assault by my employer. What started out as touching and suggestive remarks turned violent, and I was awarded a large amount by the jury. What part of the award is taxable?

Answer: If any portion of the award was punitive damages, that portion is taxable. According to the IRS in a 2000 letter ruling, the compensatory damages would be apportioned. The amount attributable to the period before the bodily harm is taxable, and the amount attributable and subsequent to the bodily harm is tax-free.

Tax Planning

If you receive a judgment in your favor and are entitled to prejudgment and/or postjudgment interest of a type nondeductible to the other party (see Chapter 4), everyone may come out ahead by entering into a consent judgment for a higher principal amount without the interest. However, the IRS might challenge such an arrangement. Similarly, in a situation involving physical injury when compensatory damages are tax-free and punitive damages are taxable, a settlement should allocate substantially to the compensatory damages. However, several courts of appeal have determined that the IRS is not bound to a settlement allocation of the parties and may seek to redetermine the taxable portion.

Filing Pointer

Here is how a corporate owner received tax-free compensation for injury on the job as the result of a Tax Court case several years ago. The corporate owner sued the corporation for medical expenses plus additional damages resulting from the injury, and the corporation made a quick cash settlement. The corporation deducted the amount of the settlement as a business expense, and the owner excluded the payment as settlement for physical injuries. The result was the conversion of otherwise taxable compensation into a tax-free payment.

Controversy

Suppose that you receive a taxable settlement or damage award and a percentage is paid to your attorney. May you report as income only the portion you receive, or must you report your gross settlement as income and deduct the attorney's fee as a miscellaneous itemized deduction (see Chapter 4)? If you must declare the full amount as income, your ability to offset the income with attorney's fees faces two limitations. First, as set forth in Chapter 4, the first 2 percent of miscellaneous itemized deductions are lost. Second, as set forth in Chapter 1, miscellaneous itemized deductions, such as professional fees, may not be used in the computation of AMT.

The Fifth, Sixth, and Eleventh Circuit Courts of Appeal as well as a Vermont Federal District Court permit the recipient of the settlement or award to report only the net amount as income. The First, Third, Fourth, Seventh, Tenth, and Federal Circuit Courts of Appeal as well as a Connecticut Federal District Court and the Tax Court agree with the IRS's position that the receipient must report the gross proceeds even if much of the benefit of the deduction will be lost. The Ninth Circuit Court of Appeals permits reporting of the net settlement in states where an attorney lien applies to the proceeds. The U.S. Supreme Court has declined three opportunities to resolve the issue, in each case letting stand a decision in favor of the IRS. Upon recommendation of the IRS Taxpayer Advocate, Congress is considering the Civil Rights Tax Relief Act which would adopt the taxpayer position as law.

Filing Pointer

Even if the entire settlement or award is subject to income taxes, only the portion actually paid to an employee or former employee for loss of pay subjects the worker and the employer to payroll taxes.

Question: My tax preparer made a mistake in preparing my return for last year. He reimbursed me $750 for a penalty and $250 in interest. Do I have to pay taxes on the $1,000 in which case he didn't really make me whole?

Answer: No, reimbursement for a filing error is not subject to tax even if the preparer were to pay the tax itself. However, reimbursement for erroneous tax advice is taxable. For example, if your attorney meant to negotiate a tax-free property settlement for you but the payments you received constituted taxable alimony income (see Chapter 8), he would need to "gross-up" the damages to fully pay your injury.

Gambling and Lottery Winnings

Taxable income includes any winnings from gambling or lottery drawings. If you itemize your deductions, losses can be deducted as miscellaneous itemized deductions to the extent of winnings (the gross amount of that is reported as "other income"). The apparent IRS position, untested in the courts, is that other gambling expenses of a nonprofessional are treated as gambling losses, but only if the gambling activity is one of skill, such as horse racing, and not if it is one of chance, such as the lottery.

If you are a professional gambler involved in gambling activities on a regular basis, your gambling losses are still deductible only to the extent of your gambling winnings (which include complimentary enticements by a casino, according to a 1996 Tax Court decision involving a gambler who lost more than $1.6 million in excess of $2.5 million in "comps" during a three-year period). However, income and expenses are reported on a Schedule C and, if the winnings exceed the losses, the profit is subject to self-employment tax.

Tax Planning

It makes sense to hold on to losing lottery tickets, losing horse track tickets, and the like so that, should you later get lucky, your losses can offset your winnings. The IRS looks with suspicion at losing tickets to see whether they were picked up off the ground or perhaps even borrowed. In 1996 a New Hampshire man and his accountant were indicted for *renting* 200,000 losing tickets to reduce the tax impact of a $2.7 million lottery payoff.

Question: I won a multiyear lottery payoff several years ago. I have been approached with an opportunity to collect in full right now—by selling the rights to future payments at discount. What would be the tax treatment if I go forward with the deal?

Answer: Days apart in 2002, an Oregon Federal District Court and the Tax Court each determined that the sale of rights to future payments is an *assignment of income* and, accordingly, constitutes ordinary income and not capital gain (see Chapter 5) to the seller.

Prizes—Wheel of Misfortune

With the principal exception that employees can exclude certain length-of-service and safety awards from their income, amounts received as prizes and awards will be fully taxable to the recipient.

Question: I appeared on a television quiz show and won a new car and a trip to Antarctica. I was given a Form 1099 that placed a value on the car at $4,000 more than my local dealer says would have been the price they would have charged me for the car. I had no interest in going to Antarctica, and I sold this trip to a crazy friend of mine for one-third of the retail value. How do I report all of this on my tax return? And, how do I handle my $1,800 of travel expenses to appear on the show?

Answer: The IRS takes the position that the value of the prizes must be measured by the fair market value at the time that you won them. However, the Tax Court has been liberal in determining what constitutes the value of a prize. As regards the car, it would be advisable to obtain an affidavit from your dealer and to hold onto it for use in the likely event that you are audited. Report the value of the car for the amount that you could have reasonably acquired it. In the case of the trip, as long as you made a reasonable effort to sell this prize, report the resale price. You may want to include a statement with your tax return explaining the difference between the amounts shown on the Form 1099 and the amounts reported on your tax return.

The Tax Court in 1995 determined that prizes from a television quiz show are not gambling winnings and, consequently, the expenses incurred in winning the prizes are not gambling losses fully deductible as miscellaneous itemized deductions to the extent of winnings. The expenses should be deductible as miscellaneous itemized deductions for expenses incurred in the production of income. However, as such, they would be subject both to the two-percent floor on most miscellaneous itemized deductions (see Chapter 4) and the overall phaseout levels of itemized deductions (see Chapter 1).

Loans and Gifts—Taxable Errors and Tax-Free Home Runs

Money or property received as a loan is not includable in the recipient's income. However, a loan taken without any intention of repayment may be considered as income in the year in which it is borrowed. Thus, under scrutiny by the IRS, a shareholder in a closely owned corporation who takes loans instead of compensation from the corporation may be charged with personal income in the year of the borrowing unless a promissory note and/or repayment pattern exists. An unauthorized loan is treated like a theft and will constitute income in the year of the borrowing despite an intention of repaying the loan.

Money or property received as a gift is not includable in the recipient's income. However, it is often difficult to distinguish between a gift and a transfer of money or property in exchange for services or other valuable consideration. (See the discussions of clergy and tip-earning employees in Chapter 11.) Accordingly, gifts of nominal value are often ignored. In a 2000 Revenue Procedure, the IRS stated that bank customers may ignore small handouts received from financial institutions, up to a $10 value for deposits of less than $5,000 and up to a $20 value for larger deposits.

A scholarship grant, usually excludable from income by a degree candidate to the extent of tuition, books, supplies, and equipment, is not a gift to the extent that the recipient must perform services, such as teaching or research, as a *quid pro quo*. Grants for room, board, and travel are taxable in any event. Thus, students receiving lump sum scholarship grants should keep records of qualifying expenses to minimize or eliminate the taxable portion of a grant.

Pursuant to a 1994 decision of the Tax Court, an individual, who is not required to perform services, is not in a trade or business and is not subject to self-employment tax (see Chapter 10), even though he or she derives taxable income as a nondegree candidate or as a degree candidate receiving free room, board, or travel.

Question: I received two scholarship grants for tuition from my college. One was on condition that I teach during the current term. The other was on condition that I engage in public service or nonprofit work after graduation for a period of at least five years. Do I have to pay taxes on the scholarships?

Answer: The IRS determined in a 1995 letter ruling that there is no *quid pro quo* regarding the second scholarship. In other words, the source of the grant is receiving no benefit from your future services. In contrast, the first scholarship is taxable in that the college was enjoying the benefit of your teaching.

Question: I have been living with a man for the past six months in an exclusive condominium that he bought me. My companion is a very generous man and has given me furs, jewelry, and two automobiles over the period of time that we have been together. Are the condominium, furs, jewelry, and automobiles taxable to me?

Answer: The tax treatment of property and money made in this context turns on the intention of the donor. If these items were given to you by your companion out of a "disinterested generosity" on his part rather than in exchange for any consideration from you, then none of these items, irrespective of their values, would be taxable to you. In contrast, the courts have ruled that individuals are taxable on the value of similar gifts received from their companions when the IRS successfully argued that the property was received in exchange for sexual services. However, in a case several years ago, an appeals court reversed the criminal conviction of twin sisters sentenced to jail for failing to report more than $1 million given to them by an elderly Milwaukee man.

Question: I work for a corporation that has a plan of "leave sharing" under which employees can donate their paid vacation time to other employees who need extra time off to take care of family emergencies but who have no remaining leave. If I donate my leave to the plan in order to help a friend with a sick child, will I be taxed on this transfer of unpaid vacation time?

Answer: According to the IRS, the employee who uses another employee's paid vacation time in a leave-sharing program will be taxed on the vacation pay received from the vacation bank. The employee who surrenders the paid vacation time to the leave-sharing program will not be taxed.

Question: I went out on strike and received union welfare benefits as gifts. I never worked for the union. All of us received $100 per workday, no questions asked. The union asked us only to walk a picket line two days a week. I also received another $200 per week in unemployment. Are these considered tax-free gifts or welfare benefits?

Answer: No, by law, unemployment benefits are taxable. Although public welfare benefits are tax-free, your union benefits will be taxable pursuant to a 1995 decision of the Tax Court. They are not welfare because everyone got them irrespective of need, and they are not gifts because there is no disinterested generosity on the part of the union.

Question: I am thinking of becoming a foster parent. The state will give me $600 per month for each child whom I assist. Are these payments taxable?

Answer: No; payments from a state or licensed nonprofit agency for foster care are usually tax-free. Exceptions include payments from an agency for a child who has reached age 19, unless he or she is handicapped. The statutory requirement that the foster child live in your home was interpreted by the Tax Court in 1998 to require that you reside in the property on at least a part-time basis. Unreimbursed costs of foster care under a state or nonprofit agency program qualify as a charitable deduction (see Chapter 4).

Question: I have a rare type of blood, and I am paid each time that I make a donation. The IRS is trying to tell me that this money is taxable. Is the IRS right?

Answer: The IRS does not consider the giving of blood to be a donation for tax purposes. Donors throughout the country are being taxed on the money they earn for donating their blood. Regular donors are also being subjected to the 15.3 percent self-employment tax.

Question: One of my friends caught one of Barry Bonds' final home runs of the 2001 season. He held onto the ball and rushed out of the stadium. It has been authenticated and appraised at $150,000. My friend has decided to sell the ball. Because he has held onto his trophy ball for more than a year, will he get long-term capital gain treatment on the sale?

Answer: The IRS appears to take the position that your friend had ordinary income in 2001. Articles of value that come into an individual's hands are almost always taxable unless received by gift or inheritance. Strike one. The 2001 value would then have created a tax basis (see Chapter 5) for measuring gain or loss. Income could apparently have been avoided, only if your friend had promptly returned the ball to the batter. And, according to IRS, this timely "disclaimer" would also have avoided a taxable gift of the ball upon its return, a result which would occur if he returned the trophy today. Strike two.

Easy to Forgive—Not with the IRS

The general rule is that taxable income includes the amount by which your liabilities have decreased as a result of a creditor's forgiveness of your obligation to that creditor. The additional income is the result of an increase in your net worth by the freeing of your assets that would otherwise have been required to be used to pay the debt. Thus, if you settle a personal or business obligation for less than the amount owed, the difference is generally taxable to you.

Limited exceptions to the debt cancellation rule do exist. When a disputed debt is compromised, the portion that is written off is not considered income. If a debt is forgiven in a gift context (for example, parents forgiving a loan that they made to their child), no debt forgiveness income would exist. In addition, if a debtor is insolvent, has filed for bankruptcy, or in the case of discharge of certain real estate debt, the forgiveness of debt does not result in income. However, such a debtor is required to reduce favorable tax attributes, such as net operating loss carryovers, credit carryovers, and capital loss carryovers, and may be required to reduce the tax basis of remaining assets.

Caution

Even without formal forgiveness of a debt, the IRS may take the position that relief from the indebtedness constitutes taxable income upon expiration of the statute of limitations on collection—in other words, at the time when you can raise a valid defense under state law that the creditor took too long to collect on the debt.

Question: When I put a short-term mortgage on my house several years ago, I was able to obtain a 4 3/4 percent fixed-rate mortgage. Because of rising rates, the bank contacted me and has offered to consider my mortgage paid off if I pay all but $3,000 of the outstanding principal. It would otherwise be paid off in a few years. Does it sound like a good deal?

Answer: Your bank is trying to clean out its loan portfolio by ridding itself of low-interest loans so that additional funds will be available to the bank to lend at a higher rate of return. Although it still would appear to make sense to accept the bank's offer, the $3,000 savings will be taxable to you as debt forgiveness income, which could mean about $1,000 in additional taxes if you are in a 33 or 35 percent tax bracket.

Controversy

A forgiven student loan may or may not constitute taxable income depending on the program under which the loan is discharged. The lack of clarity is causing litigation and may force modification of the law.

Question: I guaranteed a debt of my wholly owned corporation, which went bankrupt with no assets for creditors. I settled my guarantee for 15 cents on the dollar. Do I have debt cancellation income?

Answer: Not according to the Tax Court in a 1996 decision. The Court reasoned that forgiveness of debt income can arise only on an increase in net worth, which happens on an obligor's, but not a guarantor's, debt cancellation.

CHAPTER 3

Deductions and Credits—For Itemizers and Nonitemizers

Deductible Health Insurance

Although employees may enjoy employer-provided health insurance and medical reimbursements on a tax-free basis, self-employed individuals generally must claim their medical expenses as itemized deductions (see Chapter 4, "Deductions—For Itemizers Only")—where most often they are lost due to the 7.5 percent of AGI floor.

However, certain sole proprietors, general partners, and more-than-2-percent shareholders of S corporations, who generally are unable to enjoy the tax benefit of deducting costs of participation in a group health plan or medical reimbursement plan on a tax-free basis, as discussed in Chapter 2, "Taxable and Tax-Free Income and Benefits," are able to deduct their health insurance coverage and that of their families regardless of the 7.5 percent floor applicable to itemized medical deductions. This special deduction, limited to earned income from the business (wages in the case of an S corporation shareholder) is available even to those who do not itemize if they are self-employed and more-than-2-percent S corporation shareholders, who are not eligible to participate in another health plan by virtue of their employment or their spouse's employment. This test is applied on a monthly basis.

Caution

Congress has periodically considered legislation that, if enacted, would create a deduction for low- and moderate-income individuals and couples who purchase long-term care coverage as health insurance.

Deductible Archer Medical Savings Accounts

Without itemizing, an individual who participates in a health insurance plan of an employer that averaged no more than 50 employees during the two preceding years or who is self-employed may benefit from a deductible Archer Medical Savings Account (MSA) (or may receive excludable employer contributions as discussed in Chapter 2) if his or her health insurance coverage in 2004 has a deductible of between $1,700 and $2,600 (between $1,700 and $2,500 in 2003) with a maximum $3,450 ($3,350 in 2003) out-of-pocket limit for individual coverage or between $3,450 and $5,150 ($3,350 and $5,050 in 2003) with a maximum $6,300 ($6,150 in 2003) out-of-pocket limit for family coverage.

Under this experimental program, the maximum deductible amount is 65 percent of the individual deductible or 75 percent of the family deductible. Contributions can be made until April 15 for the preceding year; this date is not changed by placing a tax return on extension. Excess contributions are subject to a 6 percent penalty.

Distributions from an MSA are includable in income only if not used for medical expenses, in which case they are also subject to a 15 percent penalty unless paid out following age 65, death, or disability. An MSA may only retain its character following the death of the account holder if it passes to a surviving spouse. Otherwise, the beneficiary is taxed on the value at the time of the account holder's death.

Caution

Unless extended by legislative action, no new MSAs can be set up after December 31, 2003. Use of the MSA has not been substantial—about 100,000 taxpayers since the law was enacted in 1996. Nevertheless, Congress is considering legislation to extend MSAs in some form. HR 2596, the Health Savings and Affordability Act of 2003, if enacted, would replace MSAs with Health Savings Accounts (HSAs) and Health Savings Security Accounts (HSSAs) combining new sets of rules. HR.2596 was approved by the House on June 26, 2003.

Deductible Moving Expenses

Certain moving expenses are deductible to qualifying individuals regardless of whether they itemize. However, the deductibility of moving expenses is limited and, accordingly, the deduction is claimed by fewer than one million individuals each year, a small percentage of those who have actually relocated. To qualify for the deduction, your new place of employment must be at least 50 miles farther from your old residence than your former job was from your old residence. If you moved in order to start work at your very first job, then the job site must be at least 50 miles from your former residence. During the 12 months immediately following the move, you must be employed on a full-time basis for at least 39 weeks; alternatively, during the two-year period after the move, you must be a full-time employee or self-employed on a full-time basis for at least 78 weeks, half of which must have occurred during the first 12-month period.

You may claim the moving expenses even if you are not able to satisfy the 39-week/78-week requirement if your failure to do so was a result of death or disability, if your employment was involuntarily terminated (other than for willful misconduct), or if your employer transferred you to another job location.

Moving expenses that qualify for the deduction are limited to the cost of moving your household goods and furnishings and the cost of moving your family. If you drive, you can either claim your actual expenses of operating the car (gas and oil) or claim an amount equal to 14 cents for each mile traveled (12 cents in 2003) plus parking fees and tolls while en route to the new residence.

If your new or continuing employer pays your qualifying moving expenses, this payment will not constitute additional income unless you claimed a deduction in a prior year.

See the special rule in Chapter 11, "Special Groups of Taxpayers," for members of the military.

Question: I moved across the country in November. How can I file my tax return not knowing if I meet the time requirements for deducting moving expenses?

Answer: You are entitled to claim the moving expense deduction, even though the time test is not satisfied by the date your tax return is filed for the year in which the moving expenses were incurred. However, if after filing the return and claiming the deduction for the moving expenses, you fail to satisfy the time test (other than for reason of death, disability, involuntary termination, or transfer), then you must include the deducted amount as other income in the year you failed to satisfy the time test.

Deductible Education Expenses

A deduction of up to $4,000 ($3,000 for 2003) is available for "qualified education expenses" for post-high school academic or vocational courses. The deduction is for amounts paid during the year for tuition and fees of the taxpayer or a dependent student; expenses paid for books or room and board do not qualify.

The $4,000 deduction is available without itemizing to married couples filing jointly with modified AGI no greater than $130,000 and to single individuals with modified AGI no greater than $65,000. A deduction of $2,000 is available for married couples with modified AGI in excess of $130,000—but not in excess of $160,000—and for single individuals with modified AGI in excess of $65,000—but not in excess of $80,000.

Married individuals filing separately are not eligible for the deduction, nor can the deduction be taken by individuals claimed as a dependent by a parent or other taxpayer.

The deduction may not be claimed in the same year as the HOPE or lifetime learning credits discussed later in this chapter. No deduction is available for amounts taken into account in determining excludable portions of Coverdell Education Savings Accounts, education savings bonds, or qualified tuition programs, all of which are discussed in Chapter 2.

In addition to this partial deduction for tuition and fees, a partial deduction not requiring itemizing is available for interest paid on loans exclusively for educational expenses (tuition, fees, room and board) for the undergraduate, graduate, or vocational study of a taxpayer or a dependent at the time of the loan who was at least a half-time student.

The maximum deduction of $2,500 is phased out at modified adjusted income between $100,000 and $130,000 for married couples filing jointly and between $50,000 and $65,000 for single individuals, in each case indexed for cost of living beginning in 2004. This deduction, too, may not be claimed by a married individual filing separately or by an individual claimed as a dependent on a return of another.

Caution

The deduction for qualified education expenses is not phased out. Rather, if your modified AGI is $1 over the $65,000/$130,000 limit, or $1 over the $80,000/$160,000 limit, that dollar of income has cost you a $2,000 deduction worth $560 in a 28 percent tax bracket.

Year-End Reminder

A year-end payment of tuition and fees for courses starting in January will get you a tax deduction for the year ending in the previous December. However, no deduction is available for courses not commencing within three months of the start of the following year.

Caution

Congress has periodically considered legislation which, if enacted, would expand the qualified education expense deduction, scheduled to expire after 2005, to primary and secondary school expenses. The deduction for interest is not scheduled to expire.

Caution

Do not refinance by borrowing from a relative to pay off existing student loans. Payments to the relative are nondeductible.

Caution

Interest on a student loan does not typically qualify as a business expense as a doctor found out in a 1998 Tax Court decision. The Court determined that the interest expense did not relate to an existing business.

The Child Credit

Your children may give you credit—a tax credit claimed on about 31 million returns but inadvertently omitted on about 600,000 eligible returns. You receive a $1,000 reduction in your tax bill for each dependency exemption (see Chapter 1, "Introduction to Personal Tax Planning") for a child, grandchild, stepchild, or foster child under age 17 at year-end.

The child credit is phased out in $50 increments for each $1,000 or fraction of modified AGI in excess of $110,000 (one-half of that amount on a separate return) for married couples and $75,000 for single individuals.

Caution

The child must be a U.S. citizen or resident to be eligible for this credit. Additionally, the dependent must have a Social Security number to be eligible.

Tax Planning

A dependency allowance is more valuable in 2004 than it has ever been for individuals who can use the child credit. The exemption for a dependent of $3,050 before indexing in 2004 is worth $763 to a taxpayer in a 25-percent bracket. Tack on the child credit, and the dependency allowance is worth $1,763—right off your bottom line. Care should be given to avoid inadvertent loss of the ability to claim a dependent by failure to meet all of the conditions. Individuals going through a divorce should see Chapter 8, "Marriage and Divorce," for a discussion of how to keep the dependency allowance away from your ex-spouse.

Year-End Reminder

The child credit is refundable (meaning that you can get it paid to you beyond the amount of your tax liability) only in two circumstances. First, it is refundable to the extent of 10 percent of earned income (wages, tips, and self-employment income) in excess of $10,500 indexed for cost of living in 2004 and succeeding years. The 10 percent figure increases to 15 percent in 2005 and succeeding years.

Second, it is refundable to an individual with three or more eligible dependents to the extent that the individual's Social Security contribution, including one-half of the self-employment tax, exceeds the earned income credit (discussed later in this chapter).

In many cases, you should take income to the extent possible before year-end in order not to waste the credit.

Caution

The maximum child credit will be reduced to $700 for 2005–2008 and $800 for 2009 in the absence of new legislation. Congress is considering legislation which may extend the $1,000 maximum credit, if enacted. H.R. 1308, the All American Tax Relief Act of 2003 continuing this provision, was approved by the House on June 12, 2003. The Senate version, passed one week earlier, omits this provision. It contains a provision, not in the House bill, that, if enacted, would establish a uniform definition of "child," affecting the ability of some individuals to claim the child credit. Both versions would increase refundability of the credit and the income levels of the phaseout.

Filing Pointer

Many individuals received advance payment of $400 per qualifying child of their 2003 credit upon enactment of the Jobs and Growth Reconciliation Act of 2003 and, accordingly, will be limited to an additional credit of $600 per child on their 2003 return. Individuals receiving this advance payment need not repay the check even if they don't qualify for the credit when they complete 2003 returns.

Adoption Expense Credit

A nonrefundable tax credit claimed on about 50,000 returns applies to the first $10,390 of unreimbursed qualified adoption expenses per child ($10,160 in 2003), shared in the case of two unmarried individuals who are adopting. The full credit is available, irrespective of actual expenses in the case of a citizen or resident child determined by a state as a "special needs" child due to background, age, or disability. The adoption expense credit is phased out in 2004 at modified adjusted income levels of between $155,860 and $195,860 (between $152,930 and $192,390 in 2003). Unused credits carry forward for five years.

The definition of qualified adoption expenses is broad but excludes adoptions of stepchildren, surrogate parenting, and illegal adoptions. Expenses of unsuccessful adoptions of a citizen or resident child qualify.

Caution

The adoption expense credit usually is claimed in the year in which the expense was paid. However, the credit is claimed in the year after an expense was paid if the adoption is not completed by year-end.

Dependent Care Credit

If you incur expenses to care for your child so that you or, if married, you and your spouse can go to work, you may be eligible for a dependent care credit equal to at least 20 percent of your expenses (up to $3,000 of expenses for one child or $6,000 of expenses for more than one child).

To be eligible for the credit

- You must provide more than one-half of the cost of maintaining your household, which is also the principal residence of the child.
- The child must be your dependent (except in the case of divorced parents when only the custodial parent can claim the credit).

- The child must be under 13 years old or must be physically or mentally unable to care for himself or herself.
- You must file a joint return, if you file as married.

In addition to being able to claim a credit for the cost of caring for your child, the credit is available with respect to expenses incurred for the care of your spouse, any other dependent who is under 13 years old, or any dependents (including individuals who would be dependents but who earned more than the income limitation, which is $3,050 in 2003 and indexed in succeeding years for cost of living) who are physically or mentally unable to care for themselves.

The amount of the credit is 35 percent of the lesser of your earned income (or, if married, your spouse's earned income if that is less) or the expenditures incurred for the dependent's care (up to $3,000 of expenses, $6,000 if there is more than one dependent). The credit percentage is reduced, but not below 20 percent, by 1 percent for each $2,000 (or fraction thereof) by which AGI exceeds $15,000. Earned income means income from working, such as salary, tips, and self-employment income.

For the purpose of determining the deemed earned income of a spouse, who is a full-time student or is not capable of self-care, the spouse is considered to be employed and to have $200 of earned income ($400 if there are two or more dependents for whom expenses are incurred) for each month that he or she is a full-time student or is not capable of self-care. Without this special rule, no credit would typically be available when one of the spouses was a student or had a disability, because the spouse often would have no earned income.

The kinds of expenses that qualify for the credit include babysitting costs, day-care fees, and payments to a housekeeper (so long as the housekeeper's duties include care of the child or other individual) as well as nursery and kindergarten tuition. Tuition for first and higher grades does not count, although the expenses of before- or after-school care should qualify. Fees for overnight camps do not count.

To be eligible for the credit, your tax return must include the name, address, and taxpayer identification number of the person or organization providing the dependent care services, unless you can establish that you made diligent efforts to obtain the information and were unable to do so. See Chapter 11 concerning withholding requirements on certain household workers. Additionally, if you fail to provide the Social Security number of the person cared for, the IRS may disallow the credit by summary procedure—without a statutory notice of deficiency (discussed in Chapter 13, "Dealing with the Internal Revenue Service").

Question: My mother-in-law cares for our two infants while we go to work. We pay her $150 a week. Do we qualify for the dependent care credit?

Answer: Yes, you get the credit so long as you cannot claim your mother-in-law as a dependent. No credit is available for payments made to a dependent or for payments to your child who is under 19 years of age. If your mother-in-law comes to your house to care for the children, you are required to pay Social Security and unemployment taxes based on her salary as well as to withhold and pay over Social Security taxes from her wages. If you take your children to your mother-in-law's home, you will not have these payroll responsibilities, but she will still be subject to income and self-employment tax on the earnings.

Question: My husband and I both work full-time outside of the home, and we pay more than $11,000 annually for child care for our two children. I participate in my employer's dependent care assistance program, and as a result, I am reimbursed for $5,000 of these expenses. Are we still eligible to claim the dependent care credit with respect to the $6,000 of unreimbursed child care expenses?

Answer: Unfortunately, you will be able to claim the dependent care credit only by applying the applicable percentage to $1,000. The dollar limitations on the dependent care expenses ($3,000 for one dependent and $6,000 for two or more dependents) are reduced dollar for dollar for each reimbursement dollar that you receive from your employer's dependent care assistance program. Consequently, your maximum $6,000 ceiling is reduced to $1,000 as a result of the $5,000 reimbursement from your employer.

Caution

Congress is considering legislation that, if enacted, would establish a uniform definition of "child," affecting the ability of some individuals to claim the dependent care credit. H.R. 1308, the All American Tax Relief Act of 2003, containing this provision, was approved by the Senate on June 5, 2003. The House version, passed one week later, omits the provision.

Earned Income Credit

The earned income credit, traditionally of benefit to low-income workers with one or more children at home, now also benefits certain low-income workers not supporting a child at home. This credit is particularly valuable to the roughly 19 million eligible taxpayers because it is refundable. This means that, if your tax liability is less than the amount of the credit, the excess credit is refunded to you.

Certain low-income workers caring for a qualifying child (who may even be a grandchild, sibling, or foster child) at home are entitled to a tax credit in 2003 of 34 percent (40 percent if the worker has two or more children living at home for more than one-half of the year) of the first $7,490 of earned income ($10,510 for a worker with two or more children living at home). The credit amount is reduced when the AGI (or, if greater, earned income) exceeds $13,730 and no credit is available when AGI (or, if greater, earned income) exceeds $29,666 ($33,692 for a worker with two more children living at home). Earned income (wages, tips, and self-employment) is limited to income that is taxed and, thus, is determined after elective deferrals such as to cafeteria plans (see Chapter 2) and retirement plans (see Chapter 9, "Retirement Plans").

To be eligible for the earned income credit, if you have one or more qualifying children at home, you must

- File a joint return if you are married.
- Have less than the applicable annual thresholds of AGI and earned income.
- Not have taxable and tax-exempt interest, dividends, net rents and royalties, net capital gain, and other net passive income (see Chapter 2) of more than $2,600 prior to the increase for cost of living in 2004.
- Not be a qualifying child of another individual.
- Not be an illegal alien.
- Have a child who is under 19 years old, is a student under age 24, or is permanently disabled live with you more than one-half of the year.

Individuals at least 25 years old, but less than 65 years old, who satisfy the first three criteria, do not have an eligible child living with them, and cannot be claimed as a dependent on another's tax return qualify for the earned income credit on a reduced basis. These individuals are entitled to the credit at the rate of 7.65 percent of the first $4,990 of earned income. The credit for these individuals will begin to phase out when AGI (or, if greater, earned income) exceeds $6,240, and no credit is available when AGI (or, if greater, earned income) exceeds $11,230.

The dollar amounts on which the earned income credit is based will change in 2004 and succeeding years to reflect increases in the cost of living. Additionally, the phaseout level will be increased for married couples filing jointly by $2,000 for 2005–2007 and $3,000 for succeeding years.

Filing Pointer

You may receive an advance payment of the credit from your employer by filing a Form W-5 with your employer. A portion of the credit will be paid to you with each paycheck. Many individuals who are entitled to the earned income credit are unaware that they can receive advance payment during the year instead of waiting until they file their tax return. Notify your employer if you are eligible.

Caution

The IRS may disallow the credit by summary procedure—without a statutory notice of deficiency (discussed in Chapter 13, "Dealing with the Internal Revenue Service")—if you fail to provide the qualifying child's Social Security number. This harsh procedure results from years of abuse of the earned income credit by taxpayers and their income tax preparers. An individual who claims the earned income credit erroneously or due to reckless or intentional disregard of the rules is barred from claiming the credit for two years (10 years in the event of fraud). Additionally, the individual must be "recertified" by the IRS in order to claim the credit again.

Caution

Congress is considering legislation that, if enacted, would establish a uniform definition of "child," affecting the ability of some individuals to claim the earned income credit. H.R. 1308, the All American Tax Relief Act of 2003, containing this provision, was approved by the Senate on June 5, 2003. The House version, passed one week later, omits the provision.

HOPE Scholarship and Lifetime Learning Credits

Two education tax credits help ease the cost of higher education. First, the HOPE scholarship credit is designed to cover 100 percent of the first $1,000 and 50 percent of the next $1,000 of qualified out-of-pocket first- and second-year tuition and fees (not books or room and board) of a student attending school on at least a half-time basis in a program leading to an undergraduate degree or post-high school vocational certificate. This credit is computed on a per-student basis and each $1,000 threshold is indexed in 2004 and succeeding years for cost of living.

Second, the lifetime learning credit covers 20 percent of the first $10,000 of qualified out-of-pocket tuition and fees in a program leading to any degree or vocational certificate. This credit is computed on a per-taxpayer basis. For expenses of a particular student, this credit may not be claimed in any year in which the HOPE scholarship credit is claimed.

Both the HOPE scholarship and lifetime learning credits may be claimed by a parent of a dependent student or by a student who is not the dependent of another individual but not by both. A parent wanting to claim the credit must be careful to ensure that he or she, and not the child, is entitled to the dependency allowance (see Chapter 1), or, in the case of divorced parents, not the other parent.

A parent claiming the credit is entitled to tack on any expenses paid by the dependent child prior to computing the credit. A student claiming the credit is entitled to include any expenses paid by a parent or other family member.

Prior to indexing for cost of living in 2004, both the HOPE scholarship credit and the lifetime learning credit are phased out at modified AGI between $83,000 and $103,000 for married couples and between $41,000 and $51,000 for single individuals. The credits are not available to married individuals filing separately.

The HOPE scholarship credit, but not the lifetime learning credit, is denied to a parent or child if the student has been convicted of a felony involving distribution or possession of drugs. HOPE parents do not learn anything new from the IRS!

Year-End Reminder

A year-end payment of tuition and fees for courses starting in January will get you a tax credit for the year ending in the previous December. However, no credit is available as a prepayment for courses not commencing within three months of the start of the following year.

Filing Pointer

The HOPE scholarship credit may be claimed, whether by the parent or by the child, only for a particular student in two calendar years and may not be claimed for any year in which the student has third-year status as of January 1. If the first two years of higher education will be spread over three or more calendar years, the HOPE scholarship credit should be claimed in the two years of greatest benefit.

Credit for the Elderly

Individuals who are 65 or older may be entitled to a credit for the elderly equal to 15 percent of a base amount. The base amount is $5,000 for single individuals and for married individuals where only one spouse is 65 or older. The base amount is $7,500 for married individuals where both spouses are 65 or older. Married individuals who file separate returns do not qualify for the credit, unless the couple did not live together for the entire year. If such a married person has attained age 65, the base amount is $3,750.

Before calculating the credit, the base amount is reduced by nontaxable Social Security, veterans, Railroad Retirement, and disability pensions. The base amount is further reduced by one-half of the AGI in excess of $7,500 ($10,000 for married individuals who file jointly and $5,000 for married individuals who file separately).

Illustration

Harry and Mabel are married. They are both 70 years old. During the year they have received $4,000 in Social Security benefits, $8,500 in taxable dividends and interest—a $3,000 capital gain—and $5,000 in municipal bond interest.

$ 7,500	Base Amount
(4,000)	Nontaxable Social Security Benefits
(750)	One-Half Excess AGI ($11,500) Greater Than $10,000
$ 2,750	Credit Base
$ 413	Credit (15% × $2,750 Credit Base)

This credit is calculated in conjunction with the credit for disabled individuals discussed in Chapter 11.

Credit for Elective Retirement Plan Contributions

A credit for elective contributions to an employer-sponsored retirement plan or IRA first became available in 2002. The maximum credit is $1,000—50 percent of the first $2,000 of elective contributions. However, this maximum is available only to married couples filing jointly with AGI up to $30,000, heads of household with AGI up to $22,500, and other individuals with AGI up to $15,000. A lesser credit of 20 percent is available to individuals with AGI up to $32,500, $24,375, or $16,250, respectively, depending on filing status. A 10-percent credit may be claimed on AGI up to $50,000, $37,500, or $25,000, respectively.

This new credit is not available to an individual under 18 at year-end, to a full-time student of any age, or to anyone claimed as a dependent on the tax return of another.

See Chapter 9, "Retirement Plans," for a discussion of IRAs, 401(k), 403 (b), SEP, and SIMPLE plans that are the most common types of plans to which elective contributions can be made.

In calculating the available credit, the amount of elective contributions deemed made is reduced by taxable distributions from any of these plans, IRAs, or any other qualified retirement plans (see Chapter 9) during the year of the distribution, two prior years, or the succeeding year up to the extended due date of the return.

Tax Planning

An individual in a 15-percent tax bracket eligible for the maximum $1,000 tax credit goes out of pocket only $700 on a $2,000 contribution. The credit plus the deduction, which would be worth a savings of $300, together reduce taxes by $1,300.

Caution

The credit for elective retirement plan contributions, unless extended, will expire after 2006.

Credit for Health Insurance Costs

A credit for 65 percent of short-term health insurance costs is available for workers displaced by production shifted overseas and for workers age 55 or older who are receiving pension payments from the Pension Benefit Guarantee Corporation. Individuals who have other health insurance coverage or who may be claimed on another person's tax return are ineligible. Eligibility is determined on a monthly basis.

Caution

This new credit, first effective in December 2002, is extremely technical and quite narrow in scope. Call the Health Coverage Tax Credit hotline at 1-866-628-4282 to check your eligibility.

CHAPTER 4

Deductions—For Itemizers Only

Reporting Deductions Properly on Co-owned Property

Just as sources of income are the subject of sophisticated IRS matching programs (see Chapter 2, "Taxable and Tax-Free Income and Benefits"), certain deductions are also subject to the IRS matching programs. For example, mortgage interest paid to financial institutions is required to be reported to the IRS by those institutions. If there is a discrepancy between the taxpayer's reporting of the interest expense and that shown on the IRS records, an IRS inquiry will likely result.

When real property is owned by two or more persons, the deductions associated with the property must be reported in accordance with the type of co-ownership involved. Where a husband and wife own the property as co-owners and they file a joint return, it makes no difference whose deduction it is. However, when the co-owners are other than husband and wife, tracking the deductions becomes critical.

Under most states' laws, two types of co-ownerships exist for unmarried individuals—joint ownership with rights of survivorship and a tenancy in common. Each type of co-ownership has particular attributes under applicable state law. Generally, however, joint ownership with rights of survivorship means that the surviving owners will own the property upon the death of a co-owner. In a tenancy in common, each co-owner has a separate and distinct interest that passes pursuant to the deceased owner's will.

For tax purposes, each co-owner is entitled to deduct expenses associated with the real property only to the extent of his or her interest in the property as determined under state law. Ownership may be legal or equitable in nature, according to the Tax Court in a 1997 decision. In that case, family members of the taxpayer purchased a house and obtained a mortgage in their names because the taxpayer had bad credit. The taxpayer lived in the home, maintained the property, and paid the mortgage. The Court determined that the taxpayer, as equitable owner, could deduct the mortgage interest. The Tax Court reiterated its position two years later in a similar case.

Question: My brother and I own a condominium as tenants in common. From the time my brother was laid off from his job a year ago, he has been unable to contribute his share of the mortgage and taxes, and I have covered for him. Am I entitled to claim a deduction for the interest and taxes?

Answer: The answer depends on the law of the state in which the property is located. Very often, state law will dictate that you would be entitled to claim only one-half of the deductions (and report only one-half of the income) associated with the property because you were under no legal obligation to pay the expenses, or you were entitled to be reimbursed by your brother for his share of the expenses. Other states' laws would hold that you are jointly liable for the expenses. If state law makes you jointly liable for the expense or if your payment of the expense was required to protect your beneficial interest in the building, you may claim 100 percent of the expenses generated by the property.

Deductible versus Nondeductible Interest Expense

Interest expense of an individual must be classified into the following categories:

- Qualified residence interest
- Investment interest
- Passive activity interest
- Business interest
- Student loan interest
- Personal interest

Interest expense is allocated among the various categories based on the use to which the proceeds are put. Where the debt proceeds are commingled in a single account with unborrowed money, a complicated set of rules controls how to determine the use to which the proceeds were put.

Of the five classifications of interest, only qualified residence interest and investment interest are deductible as itemized deductions. They are discussed later in this chapter.

Business interest, meaning interest incurred in carrying on a trade or business in which you materially participate, is fully deductible without any limitations. In the case of a sole proprietorship, this interest is typically deducted on Schedule C (Schedule F for a farmer); in the case of a partnership of an S corporation (see Chapter 10, "Business Tax Planning") in which you materially participate, any interest that you pay is typically deducted as an adjustment to the income or loss flow through on Schedule E.

Passive activity interest, meaning interest incurred in a passive activity, is coupled with other expenses in passive activities and is compared with passive income. If the result is a loss, it is unusable except as a carryforward to future years. Rental of real estate, except on a short-term basis, is a passive activity, and interest expense associated with rental properties is deducted with other rental expenses on Schedule E. (However, see Chapter 6, "Real Estate—The Most Tax-Favored Investment," concerning the deductibility by certain taxpayers of up to $25,000 in rental losses and the special treatment for certain individuals in a real property trade or business.) In the case of a partnership or S corporation in which you do not materially participate, any interest that you pay is typically deducted also on Schedule E as an adjustment to the income or loss flowthrough.

Student loan interest—that is, interest on original or refinanced debt for educational purposes—may be wholly or partially deductible as an adjustment to income on page 1 of your tax return, whether or not you itemize. This is discussed in Chapter 3, "Deductions and Credits—For Itemizers and Nonitemizers."

Personal interest, meaning interest falling outside of the other five categories, is nondeductible. Personal interest includes credit card interest, interest incurred to purchase an automobile used solely for personal purposes, and interest paid to the IRS or to a state taxing authority.

Interest is deductible in any event only by an individual who is liable for the underlying debt. If you pay the interest on another person's obligation, no interest deduction is available. Where two or more individuals are jointly liable for a debt, each of the obligors is entitled to a deduction for the interest that he or she actually pays, subject to the statutory limitations, even if the obligor pays more than a proportionate share of the debt.

Meticulous record keeping throughout the year will be very important in order to maximize your deduction for interest expenditures. Properly classifying each of the expenditures and maintaining the appropriate records to trace the use of the loan proceeds will be crucial to the interest deduction.

Tax Planning

To avoid getting into the recordkeeping and complications of the allocation rules, consider establishing separate bank accounts in which to deposit loan proceeds earmarked for different purposes. For example, you might deposit loan proceeds to be used for investments in one account and deposit proceeds intended for personal purposes in another.

Caution

Interest may be classified as student loan interest only if the underlying loan was exclusively for educational purposes. Do not borrow for a dual use if one of the purposes is education and if the interest will not otherwise be deductible as qualified residence interest.

Qualified Residence Interest

Qualified residence interest on a principal residence or on a combination of a principal home and a designated second home is fully deductible subject to the overall reduction in most itemized deductions by high-income individuals (see Chapter 1, "Introduction to Personal Tax Planning"). In order to constitute qualified residence interest of the taxpayer, the debt must be secured by a qualified residence, and the debt cannot exceed certain dollar limitations. Qualified residence interest is claimed by almost one-fourth of individual filers.

The definition of a qualified residence is quite liberal, so you can deduct interest on financing to purchase not only typical single family homes, but also condominiums, cooperatives, mobile homes, boats, recreational vehicles, and time-share units. Temporary Regulations indicate that so long as the facility has basic living accommodations—such as a sleeping space, toilet, and cooking facilities—the boat, recreational vehicle, or similar "home" will fall within the definition of a qualified residence. The definition of purchase is also liberal, so as to include an acquisition from a spouse in a marital termination situation (see Chapter 8).

An individual can have two qualified residences, one principal residence and one secondary residence. Generally, determining an individual's principal residence will not be a problem except when that person spends considerable time in a number of homes throughout the year. The determination of what is a principal residence will depend on all the facts and circumstances, including where the individual votes, files a state income tax return, registers a vehicle, and spends more time.

In addition to an individual's principal residence, mortgage interest on a second residence may also be qualified residence interest. The second residence may be a home used by an individual for personal purposes such as a weekend retreat. When the second residence is not rented out to any other party, the mortgage interest on this home will constitute qualified residence interest. However, if the second residence is rented out to others, in order to be considered a qualified residence, the individual must use the property for more than 14 days or 10 percent of the time that the home is rented out, whichever is greater. Alternatively, the second residence may be a home used free of rent by another family member.

The law divides interest on a qualified residence into two different classifications—acquisition debt and home equity debt. If the debt involved is acquisition debt (debt incurred to purchase, construct, or substantially improve a qualified residence), the interest on such debt is fully deductible (subject to the overall reduction in most itemized deductions by high-income individuals) so long as the acquisition debt on a residence does not exceed the home's value and the total acquisition debt does not exceed $1 million ($500,000 in the case of a married individual filing separately).

Any mortgage debt incurred on or before October 13, 1987, and secured by the residence prior to that date, regardless of the dollar amount of the debt, will be considered acquisition debt but will reduce the $1 million/$500,000 ceiling for other acquisition debt.

Any debt incurred after October 13, 1987, to refinance a debt incurred prior to October 14, 1987, will also be considered acquisition debt, but only to the extent of the 1987 outstanding balance on the old debt. Thus, if you purchased your home in 1985 with an $800,000 mortgage, refinanced it in March 1987, and raised the indebtedness to $1.1 million, the debt is all acquisition debt, even though it exceeds $1 million. If this loan is refinanced again after October 13, 1987, the amount of the acquisition debt will be limited to the balance remaining on the refinanced debt.

Home equity debt is any other debt secured by a qualified residence that does not exceed the home's value. Total home equity debt may not exceed $100,000 ($50,000 in the case of a married individual filing separately). If the home equity loan exceeds the limits, then the deductibility of the interest allocable to this excess debt will depend upon the use of the proceeds, whether for personal expenditures, such as to pay off credit cards, for investment purposes, such as to increase a stock portfolio, or for a business or passive activity.

Tax Planning

Consider equity lines of credit or second mortgages to pay personal expenses so that the interest may be deductible. But do not overextend yourself and risk losing your home to the bank in a foreclosure proceeding.

Caution

Do not offer a single premium life insurance or annuity contract as additional collateral for a home loan generating qualified residence interest. As discussed in Chapter 6, interest paid to acquire or to maintain such a policy or contract is never deductible and, according to a 1995 IRS ruling, overrides the general rules on deducting home mortgage interest.

Filing Pointer

Check your year-end statements received from lending institutions to determine whether the lending institution has properly reflected the appropriate amount of interest payments you have made throughout the year. These interest statements usually will not include a payment you made on December 31, although they probably will include a payment you made on December 31 of the year before that. (See the discussion in Chapter 13 on audits for guidance regarding how to deal with this situation.) Also, check your settlement sheet if you purchased or refinanced any real estate during the year in order to pick up any interest paid from the date of the loan through the close of the month. The mortgage statement from the financial institution may not reflect any amounts shown on the settlement sheet.

Year-End Reminder

Even though you cannot claim a deduction for interest that you pay before it is due, do not forget that most home mortgages are paid one month in arrears; that is, your January payment is really the monthly payment for December. Thus, if you make your January payment by December 31, you will be entitled to claim a deduction in the earlier year for the interest portion of the payment (subject to the limitations on qualified residence interest and overall itemized deductions discussed previously). This January payment would not really be a prepayment of interest.

Controversy

Should the interest cost on the temporary rental of a principal residence be considered as qualified residence interest or as passive activity interest? If you continue to deduct the interest as qualified residence interest, you may benefit

Controversy (cont.)

by decreasing a passive activity loss that may be unusable. If you deduct the interest as passive activity interest on a rental schedule, however, you create a lower AGI, which, in turn, maximizes your ability to fund IRA contributions (see Chapter 9, "Retirement Plans") and to deduct medical expenses, casualty and theft losses, and miscellaneous itemized deductions as well as itemized deductions, and personal exemptions (see Chapter 1).

Due to the lack of clarity in the law, some individuals renting out their principal residence temporarily are seeking to achieve a double benefit by treating the interest cost as qualifying residence interest and also by deducting this expense on the rental schedule. The legislative history of these complex laws offers some support for this "best of both worlds" position.

Question: I need to take out a bridge loan to buy a new house while my present house is on the market. Is the interest on the bridge loan deductible?

Answer: Interest on the bridge loan may be deductible as qualified residence interest but only if it meets all criteria, including securing the loan by your principal residence or by a designated second home.

However, if you own a third piece of property, which you want to maintain as your designated second home for the purpose of the qualified residence interest deduction, all or a portion of the interest on the bridge loan may not be deductible. For example, assume that the bridge loan is secured by your old home, which is not sold prior to the time that you purchase the new home. After you vacate the old home, it will no longer qualify as your principal residence. If the third piece of property is maintained as the designated second home for the purpose of the qualified residence interest rules, your old residence loses its character as a qualified residence, and the interest on that bridge loan no longer meets the requirements for qualified residence interest.

Question: My home was destroyed in a fire. My insurance carrier is slow in paying, so I am continuing to make mortgage payments. Is my interest expense deductible on my nonexistent house?

Answer: According to an IRS Information Release, as a disaster victim, you may continue to deduct interest payments as qualified residence interest so long as you intend to rebuild and reoccupy the home within a reasonable time.

Question: My wife and I bought our home 30 years ago for $30,000. It is now worth about $250,000. No mortgage is on the property at this time. However, we would like to take out a mortgage for $175,000. Will the interest on this loan be deductible?

Answer: The interest on $100,000 of your $175,000 mortgage will be qualified residence interest, regardless of the use to which you put the proceeds. Your ability to deduct the interest on the remaining $75,000 will depend on the use to which the money is put. For example, if the excess proceeds are used to meet personal obligations, such as tuition or medical bills, no portion of the interest attributable to the excess proceeds will be deductible. If you use the excess proceeds to buy an interest in a partnership or an S corporation that is a passive activity, your interest on the excess loan will be passive activity interest. If you materially participate in the partnership or S corporation, that interest will be business interest. If you use the excess proceeds to buy an interest in a C corporation, however, your interest will be investment interest regardless of the nature and extent of your participation in the business.

Because your deduction of qualified residence interest is limited, you might consider selling your current home and purchasing a new one. No tax would likely be paid on the appreciation (see Chapter 6), and you can buy the new home with a small down payment and finance the rest of it. In this circumstance, the entire interest on the mortgage on the new home up to the $1 million/$500,000 ceiling will be qualified residence interest.

Question: My wife and I purchased a residential lot in the mountains many years ago. We own it free and clear. Now that my wife and I will be retiring, we plan to build a home on this lot and move away from the hustle and bustle of city life. We anticipate construction to begin in March 2003, and we should be able to move in the following year. Is the interest that we will be paying on the construction loan deductible? What about the permanent financing? Both loans will be secured by the lot and improvements.

Answer: You can treat the residence under construction as your secondary residence and, thus, the interest on the construction loan will be qualified residence interest so long as you have not elected to treat the interest on any other home (other than your current principal residence) as qualified residence interest and so long as the total acquisition debt on your current residence when added to the construction loan principal does not exceed the statutory limits. Homes under construction may be qualified residences for the purpose of the qualified residence interest deduction for only two years from the date that construction starts. The IRS has announced that forthcoming regulations will provide that your permanent financing (if incurred within 90 days of completion) will still be deemed to be acquisition debt to the extent of the construction costs incurred within the two-year period prior to the permanent financing.

Question: Every year I always seem to pay an alternative minimum tax due to some investments I have made. What is the effect of the qualified residence interest rules on me if I have to pay AMT again?

Answer: For AMT purposes, the rules governing home mortgage interest deductions are more restrictive. Only the interest on the acquisition debt is deductible in computing AMT income. No housing interest deduction is allowed for interest on home equity loans, unless the proceeds are used to rehabilitate the existing home. Interest on any debt incurred before July 1, 1982, which is secured by your principal residence (or second home), is deductible for AMT purposes, regardless of the use of the proceeds. (See Chapter 1 for a discussion of the AMT.)

Investment Interest

Investment interest is any interest incurred to purchase property held for investment, such as raw land or property that produces interest, dividends, or annuities. A typical example of investment interest is the interest charged on a margin account by your broker. Investment interest does not include interest expense associated with the acquisition or maintenance of rental real estate or with the acquisition or conduct of any other passive activity.

Investment interest is deductible as an itemized deduction but only to the extent of net investment income. It is not subject to the reduction discussed in Chapter 1 for high-income individuals. Net investment income is the excess of portfolio (investment) income, such as interest, over investment expenses, such as investment seminar fees. Unlike personal interest, any investment interest for which no deduction can be claimed in the current year is carried forward and deducted in a succeeding year if there is sufficient positive net investment income.

Income from dividends and gain on disposition of an income-producing investment asset would give rise to additional investment income. However, for the purpose of computing allowable investment interest, neither will be considered as investment income to an individual who claims a reduced tax rate for dividends (see Chapter 2) or capital gain (see Chapter 5, "Gains and Losses").

An individual in a high tax bracket who discovers that his or her investment interest expense is limited due to insufficient investment income should recompute investment interest to consider dividends and investment gains, while recomputing overall tax liability with dividends and investment gains taxed at ordinary income rates. Keep in mind that, although the recomputation may save immediate taxes, it still may not be the better approach due to loss of the investment interest carryforward.

Filing Pointer

Make sure that you reduce interest income if you bought any bonds between interest payment dates. Show the reduction for the accrued interest, which you paid at the time of purchase, on Schedule B as a reduction of the gross interest figure that will be reported by the borrower on IRS Form 1099. Do not show the accrued interest as an investment interest expense on Schedule A.

Filing Pointer

Suppose that you are the sole shareholder of your C corporation, and the company needs money for operations. If you borrow the funds and lend them to the corporation or contribute them as additional capital, the interest you pay the bank will not be business interest but will be investment interest subject to deduction limitations. Have the corporation borrow the money directly and let it deduct the interest in full. In contrast, interest paid by an S-corporation shareholder or by a partner on borrowed funds loaned or contributed to the entity is usually characterized as business interest when that owner materially participates in the business, and as passive activity interest when the owner does not. For an S corporation, this approach will also give the shareholder an added tax basis to absorb losses. A change in status from a C corporation to an S corporation or vice versa should change the nature of the interest on funds loaned or contributed to the business, according to a 1997 letter ruling of the IRS.

Deducting Points

Points are charges made by financial institutions when loans are made and usually are expressed as a percentage of a loan amount. For example, two points on a $100,000 loan would be $2,000. When the points are paid for the use of money, they will receive the same tax treatment as interest payments. Thus, points paid on a loan to purchase a principal residence will be fully deductible (subject to the overall reduction in most itemized deductions by high-income individuals) in the year paid so long as all mortgage debt on qualified residences does not exceed $1 million ($500,000 for married individuals filing separately).

Points paid on a loan to purchase a second qualified residence are claimed ratably over the term of the loan so long as all mortgage acquisition debt does not exceed the $1 million/$500,000 ceiling. The portion not written off previously may be deducted in full if the loan is paid off early.

A 1994 Revenue Procedure sets forth the IRS position as to when points are fully deductible in connection with the acquisition of a principal residence. The points must be incurred in connection with the indebtedness and not in connection with lender services. If amounts are designated as points in lieu of normal settlement charges, these loan charges will not be deductible. The points must conform to an established business practice in the geographic area. The IRS will not allow an immediate deduction for excessive points caused by electing to *buy down* the interest rate of the loan.

An amount must be paid or applied at closing from the buyer's own funds in excess of the dollar amount of the points. In other words, the buyer may not borrow the amount of the points.

However, if your seller, upon acquisition of a principal residence, is willing to pick up some of your up-front costs, you do not have to pay your own points and have the seller pay nondeductible costs associated with the closing. The 1994 Revenue Procedure allows a buyer to deduct points paid by a seller if all other requirements for the deduction are satisfied. The buyer is treated as having paid the points and reduces the purchase price by the amount of the points.

Year-End Reminder

Closing on your principal residence by December 31 allows you to accelerate any deduction for the points that you may pay at closing.

Filing Pointer

According to the IRS in a 1999 letter ruling, points that are deductible may instead be amortized over the life of the loan (and the unamortized portion may be written off on prepayment). If you do not itemize in the year that you acquire your principal residence or if you get little or no tax benefit from the full deduction of points in that year, you should amortize your points and claim a ratable portion in succeeding years.

Caution

On a refinance, besides issues related to points, be careful of earmarking portions of the new borrowing to pay off interest on the old loan with the same lender. In a 1996 decision, the Tax Court ruled that such interest was not immediately deductible.

Controversy

Points paid when a mortgage is refinanced present additional issues. Because the points are a cost of obtaining the loan, the benefit of which extends over the entire period of the loan, it is the IRS's position, which was upheld by the Tax Court, that such points are not currently deductible unless the refinancing proceeds are used to improve a principal residence (but not a second qualified residence). If the loan proceeds are not used to improve a principal residence, the IRS's view is that the points are additional interest that may be claimed ratably over the term of the loan as qualified residence interest if the mortgage debt on all qualified residences is within the $100,000/$50,000 limit on home equity debt.

However, the Eighth Circuit Court of Appeals ruled in 1990 that the IRS and the Tax Court incorrectly barred the deduction on points paid in connection with a refinancing. The facts of the case were that the taxpayers had purchased a principal residence with a secured loan calling for a balloon payment after three years. Eighteen months later, the taxpayers obtained a home improvement loan and secured that second loan with their principal residence. Less than three years after the taxpayers purchased their principal residence, they obtained a permanent 30-year mortgage and paid off the two prior loans. The taxpayers incurred points in acquiring the permanent mortgage, and the Eighth Circuit ruled that these points could be claimed in the year paid rather than ratably over the life of the loan. The Court of Appeals ruled that the 30-year permanent mortgage was clearly contemplated at the time the residence was purchased and, as such, was sufficiently integrated in the overall transaction to acquire the home that the points could be said to be "in connection with" the purchase of their principal residence.

The IRS is required to follow the decision of the Eighth Circuit only for those taxpayers who live within that Court's jurisdiction (Arkansas, Iowa, Minnesota, Missouri, Nebraska, North Dakota, and South Dakota). Pursuant to a 1991 announcement, the IRS will maintain its contrary position for residents of other states.

Caution

In a land contract sale, legal title remains with the seller until full payment and the buyer assumes the responsibilities of ownership. The buyer may make a single mortgage payment to the seller (who pays existing mortgages with the funds) or may pay existing mortgages and an additional payment to the seller. If the buyer subsequently puts his or her own financing in place and takes legal title, this step is a refinance according to Treasury Regulations.

Filing Pointer

Points paid on other loans for business, investment, or passive activity purposes are also deducted ratably over the term of the loan subject to the respective limitations applicable to investment interest or passive activity interest. Deduct the unamortized portion of the points if the loan is paid off early.

Maximizing Medical Expenses—Some Weighty Issues

Another itemized deduction not subject to the overall reduction for most itemized deductions by high-income individuals (see Chapter 1) exists for unreimbursed medical expenses of a taxpayer, his or her spouse, dependents, and individuals who would be dependents but who exceed the income limitation. However, the deduction is available only to the extent that the total unreimbursed medical expenses for the family exceed 7.5 percent of AGI. Consequently, only about 4.5 percent of individual taxpayers claim medical expenses as itemized deductions. However, if you have high medical expenses that exceed or approach this 7.5 percent figure, do not overlook any unreimbursed medical expenses. All amounts paid to physicians and other medical personnel to diagnose, treat, or prevent illness will fall within the category of deductible medical expenses.

The types of medical expenses that qualify for a deduction include payments for acupuncturists, alchohol or drug treatment, ambulance services, bandages, birth control pills, capital improvements (discussed later in this chapter), chiropractors, crutches, dental charges, diagnostic devices, hearing aids, health insurance, *in vitro* fertilization costs (including all costs associated with egg or sperm donation including the donor's fee and legal expenses), laboratory fees, medical supplies, medical travel (discussed later in this chapter), nursing services, ophthalmologists, optometrists, osteopaths, prescriptions, prescription eyeglasses and contact lenses, psychiatrists, psychologists, wheelchairs, and X-rays.

Nonprescription drugs, in contrast to nonprescription medical supplies, are not deductible.

Certain amounts paid for long-term care insurance qualify as potentially deductible health insurance. The maximum payment to be considered in 2003 and 2004 respectively as health insurance is $250/$260 if the insured is under age 41, $470/$490 if age 41 to 50, $940/$980 if age 51 to 60, $2,510/$2,600 if age 61 to 70, or $3,130/$3,250 if over age 70 and is indexed in 2004 and succeeding years for the cost of living. Benefits received are tax-free up to the greater of $230 per day ($220 in 2003) indexed for cost of living or actual unreimbursed costs. The maximum exclusion is coupled with the exclusion for accelerated death benefits discussed in Chapter 2. See Chapter 3 concerning the ability of certain sole proprietors, general partners, and more than 2-percent shareholders of S corporations to deduct health insurance coverage regardless of whether they itemize.

Expenses for cosmetic surgery are not deductible medical expenses unless resulting from a congenital defect, an accident, or a disfiguring disease. Cosmetic surgery is defined as a procedure that "does not meaningfully promote the proper function of the body or prevent or treat illness or disease." In a 1996 letter ruling and again in a 2003 Revenue Ruling, the IRS determined that lasik surgery to correct eyesight, an increasingly popular procedure, is not cosmetic in nature. However, in the 2003 Ruling, the IRS determined teeth whitening to be cosmetic in nature.

You can deduct medical expenses paid on behalf of your child (or any other dependent), but these payments will be subject to a floor of 7.5 percent of your income. If it looks like you will not have medical expenses that exceed that floor or if the benefit from those deductions is modest, have the child pay the expenses personally. If the child has enough itemized deductions, the child may get to use the deductions when you would not. The 7.5 percent of your child's income is probably much less than 7.5 percent of yours. Be careful, however, to make sure that this move will not cost you your ability to claim the child as a dependent. Following divorce, either parent may deduct medical expenses of their child (subject to the 7.5 percent of AGI floor) to the extent paid by that parent, regardless of which parent is entitled to claim the child as a dependent.

Tax Planning

If your medical expenses always seem to be just under the 7.5 percent of AGI floor, consider attempting to claim the deduction in alternate years by timing your payments. For example, it may make sense to pay the orthodontist or other health care professional in a lump sum rather than to pay the bill over time.

Year-End Reminder

If you are close to the 7.5 percent floor for the year, try to accelerate planned medical and dental expenses. Remember, after you get over the 7.5 percent floor, your ability to deduct further medical expenses is worth anywhere from 10 cents to 35 cents on the dollar.

Question: What about a deduction for marijuana? I use it legally in my state to alleviate severe chronic pain. I even have a prescription.

Answer: The IRS said "no" in a 1997 Revenue Ruling. It remains an illegal controlled substance under federal law.

Question: I had an abortion last year. Can I deduct the portion not paid by insurance?

Answer: The IRS has ruled that the unreimbursed costs of a legal abortion are deductible. Of course, total unreimbursed medical expenses must exceed 7.5 percent of your AGI to save you any taxes.

Question: Can I deduct the cost of a stop-smoking program? What about the cost of nicotine patches and gum?

Answer: In 1979 the IRS issued a letter ruling denying a deduction for stop-smoking programs not entered into to cure a specific ailment. After maintaining this position for 20 years, the IRS in 1999 did an about-face and ruled that the costs of smoking cessation programs and prescription drugs to alleviate nicotine withdrawal can be deducted as a medical expense (of course, subject to the 7.5 percent floor). Nonprescription nicotine patches and gum remain nondeductible.

Question: I am in good health, but I have a stressful job, and my doctor told me to lose weight. So, I bought a roomful of exercise equipment and work out an hour a day. I have lost 15 pounds; I feel great; and my doctor says that I have never tested better. Can I deduct the equipment? What about the other costs of losing weight such as a health club if I were to join.

Answer: You cannot claim a medical expense deduction because the weight loss and exercise in your case is not for prescribed alleviation of a particular disease.

While the IRS takes the position that the cost of maintaining good health is an "inherently personal" expense, in a 2002 Revenue Ruling it retreated from its longtime position and conceded that obesity is a disease. Although you won't qualify for any deduction, individuals diagnosed as obese (or being treated for another specific ailment such as high blood pressure) can deduct treatment costs such as weight loss programs. However, special foods will not qualify if they are a substitute rather than a supplement for normal nutritional needs. If a physician prescribes exercise as part of a treatment program for obesity or other ailment, the cost of the exercise equipment will be deductible pursuant to a 2003 information letter.

Concerning health club fees, the IRS issued a letter ruling in 2002 indicating that costs of a health club could be deductible if directed by a physician because of obesity or other specific ailment. However, less than a year later, the IRS retreated in the 2003 edition of Publication 502, denying a deduction for these fees in all cases.

Question: Can I deduct the cost of my weekly massage?

Answer: Not ordinarily prescribed for a specific ailment, massages will generally not be deductible as indicated in a 1995 decision of the Tax Court.

Question: My son has been diagnosed with attention deficit hyperactivity disorder (ADHD). Are the treatment costs deductible as a medical expense?

Answer: According to a 1998 letter ruling, the costs of diagnosis, cure, and treatment of ADHD qualify as a medical expense subject to the 7.5 percent floor. (See the discussion on special education costs later in this chapter.)

Controversy

To the extent that resolution of a damage claim allocates to past medical expenses, they are considered to have been reimbursed. Even if the settlement or judgment is silent, the IRS will presume that medical expenses have been reimbursed "off the top"; the courts back this position. In the case of an allocation to future medical expenses, they will be treated as reimbursed and therefore nondeductible. However, what if future medical expenses are incurred but the resolution is silent? The IRS believes that it can impute a portion of the award to future medical expenses based on trial testimony, for example; the Ninth Circuit Court of Appeals has disagreed.

Out-of-the-Ordinary Medical Expenses—Special Schools, Travel, and Homes

The cost of schools may be a medical expense if the institution is for the mentally or physically disabled, and the resources of the institution for alleviating the disability are the principal reason for attendance there. The curriculum at the school must be directed primarily at the treatment of the disability but may also include regular educational programs. Consequently, schools that train the blind or emotionally disturbed, for example, will fall within this special classification, and the cost of attendance will be deductible as a medical expense subject to the 7.5 percent of AGI floor. However, only 50 percent of any cost of attending the school that is attributable to meals is deductible.

If the school does not direct its curriculum at the treatment of the disability but supplements its regular educational programs with special programs targeted for the disabled students, only the added cost of attendance at these programs will be deductible subject to the floor.

Also qualifying as a medical expense is the cost of travel to and from the physician. An individual is entitled to claim transportation expenses to and from a medical facility, at the rate of 14 cents a mile if by automobile (12 cents in 2003). According to the IRS in a 2000 Revenue Ruling, this includes transportation costs for a parent and dependent child attending a medical conference for patients with a particular affliction. If an out-of-town trip is for medical treatment, 50 percent of the cost of your meals and 100 percent of the lodging expenses will also be considered a medical expense.

Whether costs associated with travel to a more favorable climate can be deducted as a medical expense is doubtful as a result of a 1990 decision by the Tax Court in favor of the IRS. In that case, a woman followed medical advice that she should seek a warmer climate during the winter in order to alleviate heart and lung ailments. While her husband remained in Michigan, she spent the winter in Florida. Although the Court conceded that the wife "did not enjoy any significant elements of personal pleasure, recreation, or vacation" due to her poor health, it took a narrow view and denied a deduction for the costs associated with the travel.

The issue of whether the cost of capital improvements to an individual's home qualifies as a medical expense has given rise to many factual clashes with the IRS. The general rule is that these expenditures do not qualify for a deduction. However, a deduction can be claimed for the total cost of a medically prescribed capital improvement to the extent that the cost exceeds any increase in the property's value.

For example, if a heart patient requires the use of an in-home elevator, the cost of that elevator is a deductible medical expense to the extent that the value of the home is not increased by the addition of the elevator. A swimming pool is a capital improvement to a residence, but its cost may also qualify in part as a medical expense deduction under this rule where exercise in the pool is prescribed by a physician for treatment of a medical condition.

Illustration

Ken has a chronic back problem, and his physician instructed him to swim 30 to 60 minutes a day. Ken installed a swimming pool at a total cost of $35,000. Before the pool was installed, Ken had his house appraised at $250,000. After the pool was put in, the appraiser said the house was worth $270,000. Ken has a medical expense of $15,000, the amount by which the cost of the pool ($35,000) exceeded the increase in value to Ken's home ($20,000). To the extent that this $15,000 medical expense and Ken's other medical expenses paid during the year exceed 7.5 percent of Ken's AGI, he will have a medical expense deduction.

Filing Pointer

If your physician has prescribed the addition of an elevator or similar capital improvement to your home or regular exercise in a swimming pool, it would be well worth your time and effort to have the home appraised both with and without the new addition in order to qualify any excess cost as a medical expense deduction.

Filing Pointer

What if the capital expenditures made to your home for medical purposes are incurred over more than one year? Because of the 7.5 percent of AGI floor, you stand to end up with a lesser deduction, unless the expenses can be concentrated in a single year. However, a Minnesota federal district court in 2000 determined that the increase in a home's value cannot be established until the improvements are complete, at which time costs in excess of the rise in value are deductible in a single year subject to the AGI floor for that year.

Claiming Charitable Contributions

Subject to the overall reduction in most itemized deductions by high-income individuals discussed in Chapter 1, you may claim deductions for your donations to certain charitable organizations. In order to qualify, the recipient of your donation must be organized and operated exclusively for religious, charitable, scientific, literary, educational, or certain other narrow allowable purposes. Contributions to other organizations that receive tax-exempt status do not qualify for the deduction unless they maintain separate funds for allowable purposes to which you contribute.

If you are in doubt as to whether a gift to an exempt organization will qualify for a deduction, request a copy of the organization's IRS tax-exemption letter, which will indicate clearly whether contributions will qualify for a deduction. Alternatively, the IRS publishes a list of organizations to which contributions are necessarily deductible (*Publication 78*).

If you donate property to a charitable organization, the amount of the charitable contribution is generally equal to the property's fair-market value. If the property that you are contributing would have generated short-term capital gain (see Chapter 5), or ordinary income if you had sold it, however, the amount of the contribution is equal to the property's cost or other tax basis. For example, if you purchase stock for $1,000 and three months later (when it is worth $5,000) you give it to your local church, the measure of your contribution will be $1,000. If, however, you wait until you have owned the stock for more than one year, the charitable contribution amount will be the property's value at that time. Another rule similarly limits the measure of your contribution to the property's basis if the charitable organization is expected to sell the donated property and only retain the proceeds or if the donated property is otherwise unrelated to the recipient's tax-exempt purpose, such as an old car (not an antique) given to a museum.

Although you are not entitled to a charitable contribution deduction for the value of your time that you donate to a charitable organization, you may claim a contribution for unreimbursed expenses made in connection with the contribution of services. For example, volunteers can deduct the cost of their uniforms and travel expenses (including actual gas and oil expenses or at the standard mileage rate of 14 cents per mile, plus tolls and parking). Foster parents (see Chapter 2) can deduct their unreimbursed costs.

The general rule is that the charitable contribution deduction computed prior to the overall reduction by high-income individuals cannot exceed 50 percent of your AGI; however, the deduction for contributions of appreciated property cannot exceed 30 percent of your AGI. Contributions that cannot be deducted because of the 50/30 percent limits can be carried forward for up to five years.

No deduction for any contribution of $250 or more may be claimed unless the charity has previously provided you with written substantiation that reports the amount of the contribution, the value of any goods or services received in exchange for the contribution, and (in the case of a noncash contribution) a description of the donated property. A check is not sufficient to satisfy this record-keeping requirement.

A formal appraisal of contributed property is not required unless the property is worth more than $5,000. However, an appraisal may be warranted for the donation of any significantly valued property in order to validate the claimed market value. Subject also to the overall reduction in most itemized deductions by high-income individuals, the cost of the appraisal can be claimed as a miscellaneous itemized deduction if your total miscellaneous itemized deductions exceed 2 percent of your AGI.

If you overstate the value of your charitable contribution by more than 200 percent and the overvaluation results in an additional tax liability of more than $5,000, you may owe a special penalty. The penalty is significant—20 percent of the underpaid tax attributable to the overvaluation of the charitable gift.

Year-End Reminder

Furniture, equipment, linens, recordings, books, and cookware, as well as clothing, can be subjects of year-end donations. Always get a receipt from the charity to verify the contribution. When an appraisal is not required, have the charity indicate the value of the donated property. Your estimate of value, even when permitted, can be challenged. Former President Clinton took criticism for valuing used underwear at $1 to $2 per pair on several of his tax returns from the 1980s that were released to the public. Ironically, the underwear today would fetch a substantial price!

Year-End Reminder

You can claim a charitable contribution for amounts charged to your credit card in the year that the charge is made even if you do not pay the credit card charge until the following year. A credit card may be the best way of making charitable contributions late in the year; according to the IRS, if you send a check that is lost by the charity, your contribution is considered made in the succeeding year if replaced after December 31.

Filing Pointer

Does your credit card company give a percentage of your purchases to a charity? In a 1996 letter ruling, the IRS said that you get to claim the charitable contribution at least where you can choose among several charities or a personal rebate.

Filing Pointer

Rather than donate investment property that has declined in value, sell the property first and then donate the proceeds. The loss that you realize on the sale is deductible (subject to the limitation on deductions for capital losses discussed in Chapter 5), and the gift of the sale proceeds qualifies as a charitable contribution. Assume that you bought stock five years ago for $4,000. Today, it is worth $1,000. If you sell it for $1,000, you will have a capital loss of $3,000. If you donate the $1,000 proceeds to a charitable organization, you will have a $1,000 charitable contribution deduction as well.

Question: I just bought a new car and want to get rid of my old car. I heard that the local vocational school needs old cars for the students to work on. Can I get a tax break if I give the car to the school?

Answer: Yes, you can claim the car's value as a charitable contribution if you give it to the vocational school. Take the car to your mechanic or to a couple of used-car dealers and ask them to give you a written statement of the car's value. Then get a written receipt that describes the vehicle from the school.

Caution

The donation of used cars to charities has become a big business (733,000 returns in 2000 claimed a vehicle donation), and the IRS has noticed. First, the IRS will disallow a deduction where the charity does not directly benefit from the donation—such as when its name is used in a solicitation in exchange for a fixed fee. It is currently considering how to handle donations where the charity gets only a small percentage of the contribution while the marketer gets the lion's share. Second, the IRS will scrutinize the actual value of the donated vehicle. Many advertisements are claiming that a donor may claim the bluebook value of the vehicle even if it is a beat-up clunker that needs to be towed away. In a 2002 Revenue Ruling, the IRS indicated that a car must be in at least average condition to claim bluebook value.

Question: Our 18-year-old son spent a year working as a missionary for our church. We put $200 each month into his checking account to support the activities and to pay for his rent, food, and transportation while serving in the mission. Can we claim a charitable deduction for our support of the mission?

Answer: The U.S. Supreme Court ruled in 1990 that a parent supporting a child's mission by paying living expenses may not deduct these costs. However, certain of the costs may be deductible by your child in the unlikely event that the dependent makes enough to itemize. Even if you had paid the $200 each month directly to the church, the IRS might have denied you the deduction. In a 1994 letter ruling, the IRS disallowed a deduction for a charitable contribution parents made to a church when their child was engaged in a divinity program even though there was no formal commitment by the church to use the funds for the child's benefit.

Question: Each year my husband and I have a high school exchange student stay in our home. We spend about $100 a month during the child's stay with us for food, books, etc. Can we claim a tax deduction for these expenditures?

Answer: Yes, you may be able to claim a charitable contribution for these expenses, up to $50 for each month that the child is a member of the household and a full-time student. However, to qualify for the deduction, the exchange student must be living with you under a written agreement between you and the sponsoring organization. The organization must be a charitable organization. No deduction can be claimed if you are fully or partially reimbursed by the sponsoring organization for your costs. In order to claim the $50 per month charitable contribution, the exchange student cannot be claimed as your dependent.

Caution

Congress is considering legislation that, if enacted, would allow nonitemizers to deduct a limited amount of charitable contributions. S 476, the CARE Act of 2003, containing such a provision, was approved by the Senate on April 9, 2003. HR7, the Charitable Giving Act, with a similar provision was approved by the House on September 17, 2003.

Deducting State Income Taxes

Subject to the overall reduction in most itemized deductions by high-income individuals (see Chapter 1), state income taxes are deductible against federal tax liability in the year when they are actually paid or applied. Consequently, individuals who itemize should not deduct withholding, estimated taxes, and other payments of state taxes in the year for which they are to be credited by the state. Deduct these taxes in the year that your employer withholds, or you write the check.

Year-End Reminder

If you expect to owe taxes when you file your state return, pay the difference before December 31. That way, you will not have to wait a year to deduct your state tax payment. For example, if you will owe $3,000 in state taxes and you are in a 35-percent bracket, you will reduce your federal taxes by $1,050, and the cost will be just a few months' interest on the $3,000 that would otherwise be due on April 15.

Property Tax Deductions

Subject to the overall reduction in most itemized deductions by high-income individuals (see Chapter 1), itemizers may claim a deduction for state and local personal and real property taxes that are paid during the year. To qualify for this deduction, the personal property tax must be imposed on a periodic basis on the value of the property; the real property tax must be similarly imposed; and the tax must be levied for the general public welfare. Taxes assessed for a local benefit are deductible as a tax only to the extent that the charge is allocable to interest and maintenance costs. For example, no deduction can be claimed for taxes imposed to provide a local improvement, such as a sidewalk if no breakdown shows interest and maintenance charges. These nondeductible fees are added to the basis of the property to reduce future gain.

When you own property together with another person, each of you is entitled to claim whatever portion you pay of the real property taxes assessed against the property, even if you pay more than your proportionate share.

If you own a condominium, you are treated as owning your particular unit outright. In contrast, if you have an interest in a cooperative, you do not own the property outright but rather own stock in a corporation that owns the real property. As the shareholder in a cooperative corporation, you are entitled to occupy a particular apartment unit. Regardless of whether you own the residence in a condominium form of ownership or in a cooperative form of ownership, for tax purposes you are treated in the same manner as the owner of any other real property. Condominium owners are assessed real property tax directly, and cooperative apartment owners make monthly payments to the corporation for their proportionate share of the real estate taxes. The taxes may be claimed by both condominium owners and cooperative owners.

Question: I bought my new house in August 2003. My year-end statement from the lender shows no payment of taxes, although I am required to pay $225 per month toward property taxes. Can I deduct the $1,125 that I paid in 2003 for these taxes?

Answer: If you finance the acquisition of real property through a financial institution, the lender may require you to pay your property taxes directly to the institution as part of your monthly mortgage payment. You may claim these property taxes included in your payment only when the financial institution pays the taxing authority.

Year-End Reminder

If your property taxes are not escrowed, pay the bill for current taxes prior to year-end in order to accelerate the deduction.

Caution

Look for increased IRS scrutiny of property tax deductions. Local assessments of user fees for such services as sewer, water, and trash are often included in property tax bills. Nearly half of the largest jurisdictions do not separately state these nondeductible user fees. The General Accounting Office believes that taxpayers are improperly deducting almost $2 billion each year in property taxes.

Deducting the Cost of Your Education

The cost of your tuition, books, supplies, and the like not available for an exclusion (see Chapter 2), a credit (see Chapter 3), or a deduction irrespective of itemizing (see Chapter 3) will be deductible when you itemize your deductions if the educational course is required by your employer or by law so that you can keep your job or if the course maintains or improves your skills at your existing job. No deduction can be claimed if the educational course is required to meet the minimum requirements to qualify you for a new job. For example, continuing professional education courses attended by accountants, doctors, and lawyers are deductible, but the costs of an accountant attending law school are treated as nondeductible, because a law school degree qualifies an individual for a new trade or business.

Educational expenses are deductible as miscellaneous itemized deductions but only to the extent that, together with any other miscellaneous itemized deductions, they exceed 2 percent of AGI. They are further subject to the overall reduction in most itemized deductions by high-income individuals (see Chapter 1).

Year-End Reminder

If you will be taking a deductible course in the term beginning in January and your miscellaneous itemized deductions will exceed 2 percent of your AGI, pay for it in December.

Question: I am currently a third-grade teacher at the local public school. I would like to move out of elementary school teaching and begin to teach at the high school level. I was a math major in college, and our school system needs math teachers desperately. However, before I can teach in high school, I need to take a couple of courses in secondary school education, although these courses are not required by the school system for high school teachers. Can I deduct the cost of these courses?

Answer: You will be able to claim a tax deduction for these courses, subject to the AGI limitations. Although going from elementary to secondary school teaching may appear to be a new business, IRS Regulations specifically provide that a move by an elementary school teacher to the secondary school system does not constitute a new trade or business.

Other Miscellaneous Itemized Deductions

In addition to educational expenses, you may claim a deduction for certain other miscellaneous expenses that you incur during the year, but only to the extent that the aggregate of the educational and miscellaneous expenses exceeds 2 percent of your AGI and subject again to the overall reduction in most itemized deductions by high-income individuals (see Chapter 1). Examples of these miscellaneous itemized deductions are legal fees to the extent related to taxable income, investment fees, safe deposit box fees, tax return preparation fees, tax consulting fees, uniforms, professional subscriptions, the cost of looking for a new job, union dues and other professional organization membership fees, and other unreimbursed employee business expenses.

The IRS does not like employees to claim business expenses, and consequently these itemized deductions are heavily scrutinized (see Chapter 13). The IRS especially seeks tax returns on which the 2 percent floor is avoided by claiming employment-related expenses on a Schedule C as expenses offsetting small amounts of self-employment income. One tact of the IRS, especially when the employee owns the business, is to claim that the expenses belonged to the business and should have been reimbursed rather than deducted. However, the Tax Court in a 1996 decision determined that, especially when the employee owns the business, it is the employee who sets the conditions for reimbursement and, as such, he or she can deduct those reasonable expenses that are not reimbursed.

Employee business expenses must be reasonable in nature, or they will be disallowed. For example, in a 1997 decision the Tax Court agreed with the IRS that a mathematics professor who served as advisor to a comic book club could not deduct the cost of 16,000 comics that he purchased over a three-year period.

However, in a 2000 decision, the Tax Court permitted a high school English teacher to deduct more than $13,000 in travel expenses over two succeeding summers. The travel was in the form of organized courses, and the Court found that the primary purpose was to improve job skills. The Greek mythology curriculum helped in literature classes, and the Southeast Asia course helped the teacher relate to her primarily Asian students.

Only a few types of miscellaneous itemized deductions are not subject to the 2 percent floor including, most importantly, gambling losses of a nonprofessional (see Chapter 2) and certain employee business expenses of a worker with a disability (see Chapter 11, "Special Group of Taxpayers"). Itemized gambling losses are also not subject to the overall reduction by high-income individuals.

Filing Pointer

Allocate tax preparation and consulting expenses, when appropriate, to the Schedule C or (in the case of rental real property) to the Schedule E in lieu of claiming the entire cost on Schedule A as a miscellaneous itemized deduction subject to the 2-percent limitation. The IRS sanctioned a division of costs in a 1992 ruling. The Tax Court in 1994 even allowed an individual to claim his entire $55 tax preparation fee on a Schedule C when the business schedule constituted most of the line items on the return. The Tax Court did not explain its decision; instead, it criticized the IRS for litigating only $15 in taxes. If the case is broadly read, no allocation is required when return preparation charges relate primarily to a single schedule. Even with this interpretation, individuals who itemize are probably looking at allocating charges.

Year-End Reminder

If you are close to the 2-percent floor for your miscellaneous expenses (or just over it), be on the lookout to accelerate other expenses from early 2003 into 2002. That way, you will be sure to get a deduction for them.

Filing Pointer

Because of the 2-percent floor on the deduction for employee business expenses and the heavy IRS scrutiny, you should take the opportunity to negotiate with your employer so that the employee business expenses are reimbursed by your employer.

Question: I am a financial officer and earn $50,000 per year. Each semester I teach a financial accounting course at the local community college and am paid $3,000. This past semester my work schedule prevented me from teaching a couple of the classes, so I got a substitute and paid her $800 to teach those classes for me. Can I claim this $800 as a deduction on my tax return, and if so, where? If you need to know, my AGI for the year, including the salary I receive for teaching, will be about $60,000.

Answer: Unfortunately, it is unlikely that you will be able to claim a deduction for the $800 you paid your substitute teacher, even though it was a direct cost of producing the $3,000 of teaching income. The $800 you paid the substitute teacher would qualify as a miscellaneous itemized deduction, but miscellaneous itemized deductions may be used only to the extent that the aggregate exceeds 2 percent of your AGI (in your case, 2% × $60,000 = $1,200). Consequently, no deduction is available to you for the $800 unless you have more than $400 of other expenses that qualify as miscellaneous itemized deductions. Before you face this situation again, see whether you can negotiate with the school so that it will pay your substitute teacher directly and reduce your salary payment by the substitute's fee.

Question: My husband and I just purchased a computer system that will be set up in our family room. To what extent, if any, can we deduct the $3,000 cost of the system? I will be using the computer in my catering business, which I operate as a sole proprietor, and my husband will be using it to complete projects for his employer, a government contractor. Of course, we will also keep track of our investments on the computer, and the children will be using the system for school projects.

Answer: You must determine how much time the computer is being used for each of the different functions that you have identified, including business use, investment use, and personal use. If you use the computer more than half of the time in your business, you will be able to either write off the percentage of the cost attributable to your use (see Chapter 10 for a discussion of expensing the cost of tangible personal property used in business), or you may elect to depreciate the percentage allocable to your use on an accelerated basis over five years. If the computer is used 50 percent or less in your business, you may depreciate the allocable percentage only on an equal basis over the five-year life. The election to expense the allocable percentage of the cost in the year of purchase would not be available.

Your husband's use of the computer probably would not be considered business use. An employee's use of a home computer is considered business use only if it satisfies a stringent two-prong test that it be "for the convenience of the employer" and "a condition of employment." The IRS and the courts have been very reluctant to find that an employee's use of a home computer is for an employer's convenience.

To the extent that the computer is used for tracking your investments, you are entitled to a depreciation deduction over five years calculated on an equal basis each year. However, this depreciation is a miscellaneous itemized deduction and is deductible only to the extent that it and any other miscellaneous itemized deductions exceed 2 percent of your AGI and is further subject to the overall reduction in most itemized deductions by high-income individuals (see Chapter 1).

The personal use of the computer is not deductible.

Question: I charged my payment for federal taxes on a credit card and was assessed a fee by the credit card company. Can I deduct this fee?

Answer: According to the IRS in a 2001 Service Center Advice, the fee is a nondeductible personal expense.

Filing Pointer

Statutory employees, independent contractors treated under the law as employees for Social Security purposes only, are unaffected and may deduct business expenses on a Schedule C. Full-time life insurance salespersons (see Chapter 11, "Special Groups of Taxpayers") and certain other outside salespersons constitute the largest groups of statutory employees whose numbers also include food, beverage (except milk), and laundry drivers, as well as certain home workers. Eligible workers may want to seek reclassification as statutory employees to avoid the 2-percent floor.

Filing Pointer

Employees other than statutory employees, including apparently S-corporation owners who receive an IRS Form W-2 from their business, must deduct unreimbursed business expenses as miscellaneous itemized deductions subject to the dual limitation. Partners in an unincorporated business may deduct any unreimbursable expenses without limitation. Of course, automobile-related expenses are limited based on the percentage of business use, and only one-half of the costs of business meals and entertainment is deductible.

Claim partner business expenses on Schedule E as an adjustment to your share of the income reported by the partnership. The adjustment will reduce self-employment income for purposes of Social Security contributions.

Casualty and Theft Losses

If you suffer a loss of property as the result of a sudden, unexpected, or unusual event and that loss is uninsured, or if you are the victim of theft, you may be able to claim a loss measured by the lesser of the property's adjusted basis or fair-market value (or decline in value if the casualty is not total).

A casualty loss requires physical injury to the claimant's property. Accordingly, a California Federal District Court in 1999 denied a casualty loss to neighbors of O. J. Simpson. The neighboring couple had claimed that the proximity of their home to that of the acquitted murder suspect lowered their property value by $400,000. Another neighbor claiming a $750,000 loss fared no better in a 2000 Tax Court decision. Similarly, because the claimant's own property suffered no damage, a Utah Federal District Court in 2000 denied a casualty loss to the owner of vacation property that became inaccessible during nearby winter avalanches.

The IRS follows state law as to the definition of theft. Consequently, courts reach different results (generally pro-IRS) in cases involving alleged misrepresentations of stockbrokers and corporate management. (See Chapter 5 regarding securities losses other than by theft.) In other situations, the Tax Court ruled in 1990 that payments to a fortune teller under New York law gave rise to a tax deduction for theft loss. Both an Oklahoma federal district court and the Tax Court (applying New York law) determined in separate cases in 1994 that a woman who was swindled by her new companion could claim a theft loss.

However, unlike a casualty or theft of business or income-producing property, which is fully deductible beyond insurance recovery, such a loss of personal use property is only potentially deductible as an itemized deduction. In such cases, the loss in excess of $100 will be deductible to the extent (when aggregated with any other casualty or theft losses of personal use property less separate $100 deductibles) that it exceeds 10 percent of your AGI. Casualty and theft losses are not subject to the overall reduction in most itemized deductions by high-income individuals (see Chapter 1).

A casualty loss must be deducted in the year of loss to the extent of the portion for which there is no further reasonable prospect of recovery. Additional loss, or gain if recovery is greater than expected, may be claimed in a subsequent year upon receipt of insurance or other recovery. A theft loss is deductible in the same manner; however, a theft loss that is not immediately discovered may be claimed no earlier than the year of discovery of the loss.

Question: Over the course of the past month all of my ornamental pine trees that served as a buffer between my home and the neighbor's home died. My arborist has identified the problem—an attack by a swarm of pine beetles. Can I claim the cost of replacement as a deduction on my tax return?

Answer: There is no clear-cut answer for you. If you can establish that the attack was "sudden" and had not previously occurred on your property or in the area, you will have a good argument for claiming a casualty loss. The courts and even the IRS approve of a casualty loss deduction in cases such as yours so long as the loss of the trees was sudden and unexpected and the loss occurred over a relatively short period of time. In one case, however, the IRS ruled that a loss of trees as a result of an attack of pine beetles was not deductible when it took the insects nine months to destroy the trees. In your case, it appears as though your loss would be deductible because of the relatively short period of time involved.

Assuming the loss falls within the definition of a casualty loss for tax purposes, the measure of your loss is the lesser of your cost basis (see Chapter 5) in the trees or the decline in your property's value. The cost of replacing the trees is a factor that may provide evidence of the decline in value.

Question: I forgot to winterize my car, and the engine blew up. Can I claim a casualty loss?

Answer: Personal neglect does not give rise to a casualty loss. So spoke the Tax Court in a 1996 decision. A business taxpayer would not get a casualty loss either but would be able to deduct the repair bill if actual expenses are deducted rather than optional mileage (see Chapter 10).

Question: I backed my car into my boss's Cadillac this past January. I submitted the claim to my carrier, and it paid all except my $500 deductible, which I paid out-of-pocket. My wife started a new business this year, and I do not think we will have much income after applying her losses against my salary. Can I claim the $500 as a loss?

Answer: Even if the $400 loss after subtracting the $100 floor exceeds 10 percent of your AGI, you are not permitted to deduct losses to the property of others (even if you caused the loss).

Question: Over the past few years my car stereo has been stolen three or four times. As luck would have it, my car was broken into again last week, and the stereo system was taken. In the past, I have always submitted a claim to my insurance company, but I cannot afford to have my car insurance rates go up any more as a result of these continued claims against my policy. Because I will have fairly low income this year, should I claim the loss of the stereo system as a casualty loss on my tax return?

Answer: Unfortunately, you are not allowed to claim a theft loss deduction of personal use property if the loss is covered by insurance, and you fail to make the insurance claim. The law allows a deduction for uninsured losses only and not for losses in which no insurance claim is made.

Get an Immediate Refund for Disaster Losses

If you suffer a loss as a result of a disaster, you are given the option of deducting that loss in the year in which the disaster occurred or in the preceding tax year. A disaster loss is any loss (whether to personal property or to property used in a trade or business or held for investment purposes) attributable to a disaster occurring in an area that has been declared by the President of the United States to be a disaster area entitled to federal assistance. Areas affected by a terrorist attack may be declared as disaster areas. The IRS lists the designated disaster areas each year.

If you suffer a loss to personal use property as a result of a disaster, the loss is deductible only if it would otherwise qualify as a casualty loss—that is, the loss was the result of a sudden or unexpected event. For example, you may suffer damage to your landscape around your personal residence as a result of a drought, and you live in a county that the President has declared a disaster area. However, drought damage more often than not does not qualify for casualty loss treatment because the drought generally causes damage through a progressive deterioration rather than as a result of a sudden and identifiable event. Consequently, the damage to the landscaping around your residence would not be deductible as a casualty loss or under the disaster loss rules. If the damage had been to a rental property, for example, the disaster loss rules would apply, and a loss could be claimed either in the year in which it occurred or in the preceding year.

If you do suffer a disaster loss to personal use property and the disaster loss qualifies as a casualty loss (for example, hurricane damage to your home and the President has declared the area to be a disaster area), the loss is deductible in the current year or the preceding year but is subject to the same limitations as would have applied to a casualty loss. In other words, no loss is deductible except to the extent that it exceeds $100 and (with other casualties and thefts greater than the separate $100 floors) 10 percent of your AGI.

Illustration

Steve lives in a county that has been declared a disaster area because of flooding. Steve's house was flooded in the storms, and he suffered $5,000 of damage for which he carried no insurance. In 2003, the year of the loss, Steve's AGI is $40,000. In 2002, Steve's AGI was $25,000.

Steve would be entitled to a larger deduction if he amended his 2002 return and claimed the disaster loss deduction in that year, rather than in 2003.

	2003 Loss	2002 Loss
	$5,000	$5,000
	(100)	(100)
	$4,900	$4,900
10% AGI	(4,000)	(2,500)
Deduction	$900	$2,400

See Chapter 6 for a discussion of how to avoid gain after a disaster, if your insurance recovery exceeds your tax basis in an asset. See Chapter 1 for a discussion of net operating loss arising from a disaster.

The election to claim a disaster loss deduction in a year prior to its occurrence is made by filing the return (or an amended return if the prior year's return has already been filed) and attaching an election statement to the return. The original return (or the amended return) claiming the disaster loss in the year before its occurrence must generally be filed on or before April 15 of the year following the year in which the disaster actually occurred. For example, if a disaster loss was actually suffered in 2003, the election to claim the disaster loss on the 2002 return must generally be made by April 15, 2004.

Filing Pointer

The IRS has authority to extend certain filing, payment, and retirement plan funding deadlines for up to 120 days for individuals living, owning a business, or maintaining records within a disaster area. Penalties and interest will not apply. Such action also extends the time period in which the IRS can assess or collect. (See Chapter 9 for a discussion of retirement plan funding deadlines and Chapter 13 for a discussion of filing and payment deadlines.)

CHAPTER 5

Gains and Losses

Capital Assets and Section 1231—Special Treatment

Most assets owned by individuals are capital assets. Exceptions include ordinary income property, such as inventory and accounts receivable, as well as Section 1231 property discussed later in this chapter.

When you sell a capital asset at a profit, even if it is personal to you, such as jewelry, a collectible, or a season ticket to your favorite football team, you must report the recognized gain—although it is capital in nature unless the selling activity has become a trade or business.

The distinction between capital gain and ordinary income is important in that the capital gain realized by individuals on dispositions of qualifying assets held more than one year is taxed at lower rates than ordinary income (except dividends, which are taxed through 2008 at long-term capital gain rates), typically at 15 percent. (See Chapter 4, "Deductions—For Itemizers Only," concerning an option to waive the lower rates on capital gain and dividends to receive a larger investment interest deduction.)

Additionally, the distinction between ordinary income assets and capital assets is significant due to the fact that individuals are limited in deducting capital losses to the amount of capital gains plus $3,000 ($1,500 in the case of married individuals filing separately). Unused amounts carry forward to subsequent years until the loss is fully used.

Most depreciable property and land held long-term and used in a trade or business, including rental activity, is Section 1231 property. If an individual's gains from Section 1231 sales exceed the losses from such sales, all of the gains and all of the losses will be treated as long-term capital gains and losses. In contrast, if Section 1231 losses exceed Section 1231 gains, all of the gains and losses will be ordinary in nature. Section 1231 net gain, however, will be ordinary and not capital to the extent of any net Section 1231 losses deducted in the five preceding years.

Section 1231 is overridden by the depreciation recapture rules. Under these rules, all gain is ordinary on the disposition of personal property to the extent of depreciation previously claimed. As discussed later in this chapter, for individuals the gain, which is attributable to depreciation previously claimed on real property held long-term, usually is subject to a 25 percent maximum rate. However, under a complex provision, all or a portion of the gain attributable to depreciation previously claimed on real property placed in service before 1987 may be taxed at ordinary income rates.

Question: During the past year, I have, in two separate transactions, sold equipment and real estate used in my business. All of the property was acquired in 1988. The transactions resulted in the following gains and losses:

$25,000 gain from the sale of equipment used in business

$50,000 loss from the sale of unimproved land used in business

How should I treat these gains and losses on my tax return?

Answer: Assuming no depreciation recapture, these transactions will be lumped together to compute your net Section 1231 gain or loss for the year. Your Section 1231 losses ($50,000) exceed your Section 1231 gains ($25,000). Therefore, the gain will be treated as ordinary income, and the loss will be treated as an ordinary loss. If your 1231 gains had totaled more than $50,000, all of the gains would have been treated as long-term capital gain, and the loss would have been treated as a long-term capital loss.

Caution

Look for stepped-up audit activity by the IRS of Internet sales transactions in an attempt to find unreported gain. The IRS has announced that businesses will be allowed to swap ads on web sites in a tax-free manner; however, this is a limited decision that does not affect sales transactions on the Internet.

The Many Capital Gain Rates

Capital gain on assets held for more than one year usually enjoys long-term treatment at a maximum tax rate of 15 percent. If the gain would have been taxed at either of the lowest individual tax brackets of 10 or 15 percent if it were ordinary income, the long-term capital gain rate is instead 5 percent. These same rates also apply in computing an individual's AMT (see Chapter 1, "Introduction to Personal Tax Planning").

Certain assets are not eligible for the maximum 15 percent/5 percent rate on long-term capital gain. Collectibles such as art, jewelry, stamps, and coins are taxed at a maximum rate of 28 percent on long-term capital gain. Small business stock (see Chapter 7, "Other Tax-Favored Investments"), which is eligible for a 50 percent exclusion if held more than five years, also remains taxed at a maximum rate of 28 percent on long-term capital gain; the exclusion effectively creates a maximum tax rate of 14 percent. As discussed, gain attributable to prior depreciation on real property is taxed at a maximum 25 percent rate or, in some instances, at ordinary income rates.

Caution

For payments received before May 6, 2003, the usual long-term capital gain rate was 20 percent (10 percent for individuals in the lowest two tax brackets). Thus, installment payments received after May 5, 2003 on prior sales enjoy the lower rates. For payments received in 2008, the current 5 percent rate is reduced to 0 percent. However, for payments received thereafter, the 20/10 percent rates applicable before May 6, 2003 are scheduled to be restored.

The 18 percent (8 percent for individuals in the lowest two tax brackets) capital gain rate scheduled to apply beginning in 2006 for qualifying assets held more than five years has been abolished even before taking effect.

Caution

Sale treatment without an actual sale is required when an estate transfers appreciated property to satisfy a monetary bequest. In 2010 the same rule will continue to apply but only to the extent the property has increased in value from the date of death, even though the estate may have a carryover basis (see the discussion on carryover basis for estates and heirs later in this chapter).

Effective in 2010, transfers of appreciated property to a nonresident alien will be treated as sales.

Controversy

Must mutual fund investors hold their shares for more than one year to receive long-term capital gain on their portion of a fund's long-term gain? The answer appears to be in the affirmative; however, the IRS is preparing guidance.

Netting Capital Losses with Capital Gains

Capital losses offset capital gains through a complex netting process. First, net your short-term capital gains and losses and net your long-term capital gains and losses. If each netting yields a gain, you have both net long-term and short-term capital gain. If each netting yields a loss, you have both net long-term and short-term capital loss. If one netting yields a gain and the other yields a loss, net these two numbers, and you will derive a net long-term capital gain, a net long-term capital loss, a net short-term capital gain, or a net short-term capital loss.

What if your one-step or two-step netting of losses against gains leaves you with some remaining long-term capital loss and you started with 15 percent, 25 percent, and 28 percent long-term capital gain? Losses offsetting long-term capital gain first offset gain of the same type (28, 25, or 15 percent) and then offset the highest-taxed remaining gain.

Question: During 2003 (all after May 5), I had the following capital gains and losses:

- $10,000 gain on the sale of a coin collection acquired in the 1980s
- $40,000 gain on the sale of a building acquired in 1987 of which $35,000 is attributable to prior depreciation
- $2,000 gain on the sale of stock acquired in 1996
- $20,000 loss on short-term commodities trading

How should I treat these gains and losses on my tax return?

Answer: After netting you have $32,000 of net long-term capital gain, $7,000 of which will be taxed at a maximum rate of 15 percent and $25,000 of which will be taxed at a 25 percent maximum. With no other short-term transactions, the short-term loss first offset 28-percent long-term capital gain and then reduced your 25-percent long-term capital gain. The $7,000 of 15-percent long-term capital gain that remained was derived from the stock sale and from the building sale to the extent of gain in excess of the original purchase price.

Computing Gain or Loss Correctly

To calculate gain or loss on the sale of any asset, whether it is a capital asset, Section 1231 asset, or otherwise, you need to know

- Selling price
- Expenses of sale
- Adjusted basis

Your selling price in a transaction is the amount of cash and the fair market value of other property received, including the amount of mortgages on which your liability is discharged. For example, if the property is sold subject to an existing mortgage or if the buyer assumes an existing mortgage, the selling price includes the principal balance of that mortgage. You must reduce your selling price by expenses of sale. This determines the amount realized on the sale.

Your adjusted basis in the property being sold will depend on how you acquired the property. Usually, your basis will be the amount you paid for it plus all capital expenditures you made with respect to the property. In the real estate area, capital expenditures would include improvements to the property, surveying costs, and legal fees paid at the time the property was purchased.

It is crucial that all records related to the purchase price of real property (plus improvements), stocks, and other assets be retained indefinitely. In the event of an audit, you are required to prove your tax basis for assets you sold. On his 1992 tax return, former President Clinton reported a $1,000 gain on sale of an interest in an unsuccessful land development corporation. A spokesperson indicated that, even though the President had lost thousands of dollars on the investment, he was unable to establish basis.

Records related to the purchase price of other assets must also be retained indefinitely to prove basis. For example, in computing basis in a mutual fund, reinvested dividends constitute part of your basis. You have paid taxes each year on the dividends, but you must be able to show your reinvestment to avoid a second tax on the same profit.

If you acquired the property by gift, your basis will be the same as your donor's basis (in other words, the basis of the person who gave the property to you), increased by any gift tax paid and increased further by any capital expenditures you made with respect to the property. If you inherited the property, your basis will be its fair market value at the time of the death, increased by your subsequent capital expenditures. Unless you were the estate's personal representative, you are not bound to use the value shown on the decedent's estate tax return, according to a 1999 IRS letter ruling.

In any of these situations, if you were entitled to claim depreciation with respect to the property, your basis is reduced by the depreciation allowed or allowable (the amount that you could have deducted but did not) to determine your adjusted basis. To the extent that the amount realized exceeds your adjusted basis, you have a realized gain. To the extent that the amount realized is less than your adjusted basis, you have a realized loss, which may or may not be deductible.

All realized gain is recognized unless deferred under a specific provision of the law. All recognized gain is taxed unless excluded under a specific provision of the law. (See other deferral strategies later in this chapter and in Chapter 6, "Real Estate—The Most Tax-Favored Investment.")

Except for casualty and theft losses (discussed in Chapter 4), individuals are entitled to recognize only losses incurred in their business or investment transactions.

If property is held for business purposes, any loss is deductible in full in the year of sale as an ordinary loss. If property is held for investment purposes, any loss is deductible in the year of sale to the extent of capital gains and a $3,000 limitation ($1,500 in the case of a married individual filing a separate return) on offsetting ordinary income with capital losses; unused amounts are carried forward to subsequent years until the loss is completely used.

Caution

Congress has periodically considered legislation which, if enacted, would increase the amount of capital loss which could be used annually as an offset to ordinary income.

Question: I listed some land costing $200,000 for sale with a broker for $450,000. After 18 months on the market, I sold the property on July 25, 2003 for $430,000. I paid the broker a commission and incurred advertising and legal fees related to the sale of the property totaling $25,000. What will this mean to me in taxes?

Answer: The amount realized on this sale is $405,000, and the gain realized is $205,000.

$430,000	Selling Price
(25,000)	Commissions and Fees
$405,000	Amount Realized
(200,000)	Adjusted Basis
$205,000	Gain Realized

All of the gain on the sale will be taxed as a capital gain unless you defer gain through a tax-free exchange (discussed in Chapter 6). The $205,000 in capital gain will mean an additional tax of $30,750 at 15 percent.

Question: My late wife and I bought a second home at the beach in 1978 at a price of $110,000 plus $5,000 in closing costs. In 1979 we added a screened porch at a cost of $6,000. My wife died in 1991, and this property in Delaware was valued at $200,000 on the federal estate tax return that I had to file. I now have a contract to sell the house at $255,000, and my selling costs will be $14,000. What is my gain on the sale?

Answer: One-half of the property received a step-up in its basis in 1991 upon the death of your wife. The other half did not. Consequently, it is easiest to compute your basis by looking at the house as two separate halves.

On the half of the property that you have always owned, your cost was $55,000 plus closing costs of $2,500 and improvements of $3,000, giving you a basis of $60,500 on this portion. On the half interest that you acquired through inheritance from your wife, your basis is the $100,000 value of the fractional interest at the time of death. Improvements prior to this date are disregarded, inasmuch as they are reflected in the fair market value.

Consequently, your adjusted basis in the property as a whole is $160,500. Your amount realized will be $241,000, reflecting the selling price of $255,000 less $14,000 in commissions and fees. Your gain is $80,500.

Filing Pointer

In the case of joint interests created before 1977, the step-up in basis would not necessarily be on one-half of the property. Under pre-1977 law, husband-wife jointly held property with right of survivorship (that is, assets passing automatically to the surviving spouse by operation of law, outside of the will) was included in the estate of the deceased spouse to the extent that the decedent contributed to the acquisition of the property. When the decedent was the only working spouse during the course of the marriage, the entire property in such cases may be entitled to a step-up in basis. If a federal estate tax return were filed, both the date-of-death value and the degree of contribution from the spouse who died could be determined from the return. If no return had to be filed, this information would have to be obtained from local probate records, other documentation, or recollection.

Filing Pointer

Under a quirk in the law, surviving spouses domiciled in community property states get to step up their tax basis for inherited community property (except real estate and its contents in noncommunity property states) to the full fair market value on the date of death. The same 100 percent step-up in basis is available to all surviving spouses as to real estate in community property states. See Chapter 1 for a list of the nine community property states.

Caution

One of the great tax shelters remaining today is that capital gain on the rise in value of assets is, in essence, forgiven at death. As a trade-off for the scheduled abolition of the estate tax in 2010 (see Chapter 12, "Estate Planning Strategies"), the Economic Growth and Tax Relief Reconciliation Act of 2001 provides for the carryover basis for property inherited after 2009, just as in the case of gifts. However, an estate would be able to select $1.3 million of property to receive a step-up in basis plus an additional $3 million when there is a surviving spouse beneficiary. Nonresident aliens would receive only a $60,000 exception.

How To Determine the Best Year for Recognizing Gain or Loss

Nontax considerations often control the timing of sales of assets. For example, sales of securities are often made solely for investment purposes in order to diversify your portfolio or to liquidate a stock when you believe it has reached its zenith. However, tax considerations, whenever possible, should be part of your sales analysis.

Here are some of the factors that you should keep in mind before making any dispositions that will involve significant taxable gains or losses:

- *Your marginal tax bracket in the current year vis-à-vis your marginal tax bracket next year.* Will the contemplated transaction add sufficient income or loss to your federal taxable income to raise or lower your marginal tax bracket?
- *Sales earlier in the year.* Prior sales generating capital losses allow subsequent sales of appreciated property in the same year with no additional taxable income. Prior sales of appreciated property can be offset by year-end sales of capital assets in a loss position.
- *Likelihood of additional congressional activity affecting tax rates.* Although the chance of congressional activity affecting tax rates is often difficult to assess in a timely manner, it should not be overlooked.

Year-End Reminder

As year-end approaches and sales of stock, real estate, or other investments are contemplated either in the current year or in the next year, an overall assessment of comparative tax brackets and the nature of already existing transactions should be made to determine the impact of additional taxable transactions on your overall tax liability.

Deferring Gain through Conditional Sales

Gain or loss is recognized in the year in which the transaction is completed for tax purposes. Usually, a sale will be closed when the title has been transferred from the seller to the buyer or when all of the benefits of ownership are transferred to the buyer. A sale will not be closed, and the gain or loss will not be recognized when the sale is subject to conditions that have not been fulfilled. These conditional sales are handled through escrow arrangements, with the escrow agent being instructed to dismantle the sale should the conditions not be fulfilled by returning the consideration to the buyer and the subject property to the seller.

A conditional sale will not be closed for tax purposes until the condition has been fulfilled, only if the condition is precedent. A *condition precedent* is a condition allowing either of the parties to turn its back on the transaction. For example, parties to a real estate contract can transfer the deed and purchase money to an escrow agent with the condition that the sale not be completed until the title is examined and determined to be marketable. For tax purposes, no completed transaction and no gain or loss will be recognized until the condition precedent—the examination of and finding of a marketable title—has been completed. If the condition involved is a condition subsequent to the sale, however, the transaction will be closed, and gain or loss will be recognized in the earlier year.

Year-End Reminder

Use of a condition precedent, especially for sales near year-end, can delay taxation of a transaction until the close of the escrow in the succeeding year.

Question: I have been trying to sell my house, and I have a prospective buyer. However, I have heard rumors that the swim and tennis club located in the neighborhood may be closing, and the property sold to a developer. The swim and tennis club is a big attraction for the buyer, and he would not be interested in the house if the club were not there. I understand that the current membership of the club will be voting in early January on the issue of whether to sell the club property to the developer.

I am happy with the price that I have been offered, but I would like to enter into a deal with the club and sell the property with that of the club's should the membership vote to sell to the developer. What can the buyer and I do to protect our interests under these circumstances?

Answer: One suggestion is that your contract to sell the house to the buyer be conditioned on the club's membership voting against selling the club property to the developer. If the condition is satisfied, you will sell the house for the price and under the terms of the contract to which you and your buyer have agreed. If the membership votes to sell the property to the developer, you are relieved of the obligation to sell the property to your buyer and can join the club and sell the property to the developer if that is your desire.

For tax purposes, if you enter into such a contract, the sale of the property will not be closed, if at all, until next year, when the membership takes its vote on this issue. Should they decide in favor of selling the property to the developer, you do not go through with the contract to sell the property. If the membership votes against selling the club property to the developer, however, your sale will be closed for tax purposes next January rather than in the year you entered into the contract.

Deferring Gain through Installment Sales

Whenever an individual sells property (other than such items as inventory or marketable securities) and receives all or a portion of the payment after the year of sale, in the absence of an election to the contrary, that person will report the realized gain as payments are received from the buyer—on the installment basis. However, if the individual realizes any depreciation recapture income on the sale, all of the recapture income must be reported as ordinary income in the year of sale.

Recapture income is all gain from the sale of depreciated personal property up to the seller's original cost. The recapture rules on real property do not apply to post-1986 acquisitions. However, complex rules applicable to certain pre-1987 real property purchases can convert a portion of the gain up to the seller's original cost from capital gain to ordinary income reportable in the year of the sale.

Any gain not subject to recapture is reported as payments are received from the buyer on an installment basis. Pursuant to IRS Regulations, when other gain is attributable to depreciation previously claimed on real property and held long-term, such that the 25 percent rate applies in part on the capital gain, the 25 percent gain is frontloaded. Only when all of the 25 percent gain has been taxed in installments is the 15 percent gain taxed.

If any property other than farm property is sold on the installment basis and the selling price is more than $150,000, a special rule may apply. Under a complex provision, the seller will be required to pay interest to the IRS on the deferred tax if the seller's total outstanding obligations from sales during the year exceed $5 million.

Caution

When you hold an installment note, be careful of tax traps! Should an installment obligation be used to secure a loan made to the taxpayer, the loan amount is considered to have been a payment on the installment note, accelerating gain recognition to the taxpayer. Another trap for the unwary is the *balloon* date—when the installment obligation becomes due. If the due date is extended before the date of the balloon, the taxpayer continues to report the payments as they are received. However, the Ninth Circuit Court of Appeals in a 1998 decision agreed with the Tax Court that the extension of an obligation after the due date leaves the taxpayer in *constructive receipt* of the proceeds and subject to immediate tax on the deferred payments.

Question: I own a tract of land that I bought a couple of years ago for \$300,000. I have just signed a contract to sell the tract for \$500,000, with \$100,000 payable at closing. The buyer is giving me his promissory note for \$400,000 to cover the remainder of the purchase price. The promissory note will be paid off in eight years in equal amounts of \$50,000, and the buyer will be paying me the market rate of interest. How can I report this gain?

Answer: You can report the gain realized on this transaction on the installment method. Your gain on the property is \$200,000, and a portion of this \$200,000 gain will be taxable to you in the year of sale as well as in the eight years during which you receive payments on your buyer's promissory note in accordance with the following ratio:

$$\frac{\text{profit}}{\text{contract price}} \times \text{payment} = \text{reportable gain}$$

$$\text{Year of Sale: } \frac{\$200{,}000}{\$500{,}000} \times \$100{,}000 = \$40{,}000$$

$$\text{Subsequent Years: } \frac{\$200{,}000}{\$500{,}000} \times \$50{,}000 = \$20{,}000$$

Question: How do the installment sales rules work if my buyer assumes the mortgage on the property? I own an apartment building that is worth \$500,000. My buyer will be assuming the existing mortgage of \$200,000 and will be giving me \$100,000 in cash at closing. The remaining \$200,000 will be paid in equal annual installments over the next five years. In addition, the buyer will be paying me the going rate of interest. My basis in the apartment building is \$300,000.

Answer: If the buyer assumes a mortgage on the property or takes the property subject to a mortgage, the calculation of the amount of gain that you must report each year is different. The contract price, the denominator of your profit ratio, is reduced by the amount of the mortgage to which the property is subject or the amount of the mortgage assumed by the buyer, except to the extent that such liabilities exceed your basis in the property.

In the year of sale, you will be required to recognize a gain of \$66,667 (\$200,000/\$300,000 × \$100,000) and in each of the next five years, you will be required to report \$26,667 of gain on the sale (\$200,000/\$300,000 × \$40,000 note payments).

Now assume that your basis in the property was only \$150,000. Your gain of \$350,000 (\$500,000 − \$150,000) can be reported on the installment method, but the calculation changes because the mortgage assumed by the buyer exceeds your basis in the property by \$50,000. The \$50,000 excess amount will be included in the denominator of your profit ratio and will be considered a payment in the year of sale.

$$\text{Year of Sale:} \frac{\$350,000}{\$350,000} \times \$150,000 = \$150,000$$

$$\text{Subsequent Years:} \frac{\$350,000}{\$350,000} \times \$40,000 = \$40,000$$

As you can see, whenever the buyer assumes a mortgage in excess of the seller's basis, the full amount of each payment on the promissory note as well as the full amount of the down payment and the excess of the mortgage over the basis will be taxable income.

Question: My brother wants to buy my apartment building. Can I report the gain on the installment method?

Answer: Yes, but special rules will apply if your brother sells the apartment building within two years of the date he purchased it from you and before he had made all of the payments on your installment obligation. If this occurs, an acceleration of the reporting of your gain will occur. This acceleration rule is designed to prevent tax avoidance by having the related party pay the initial owner of the property on an installment basis while the related party buyer turns around and sells the property at little or no gain in a conventional sale, receiving the full market value of the property immediately.

For the purpose of this related-party rule, spouses, children, grandchildren, parents, siblings, and certain corporations and partnerships are considered related. The related-party sale rule applies only for two years after the initial installment sale. After two years have passed, the related party buyer can dispose of the property without accelerating gain recognition on the initial transaction. Furthermore, the related-party sale rule will not apply upon a disposition by the related party buyer if the IRS can be convinced that neither the first installment sale nor the second sale was entered into for a tax-avoidance purpose.

Tax Planning

In-laws do not come within the definition of a related party. Thus, if there is a *bona fide* sale to an in-law, for example, to a son-in-law, installment reporting is still available. However, if the true buyer of property was in fact the related party (in our example, the daughter), the IRS will view the transaction as a sale between the related parties and disregard the terms of the contract listing the in-law as the purchaser.

Minimizing Taxable Gain on Sales of Securities

Gain on the sale of marketable securities is reported in the year of the sale even if payment for the stock is not received until the following year. Under rules governing the New York Stock Exchange, payment is received on the settlement date, which is usually five full business days after the date of the sale. Despite this difference in the sale date and the settlement date, the seller must report the gain in the year of the sale, rather than in the year of the settlement. For example, if the individual sells stock on December 29, 2003, payment will not be received until 2004. However, because installment reporting is not available for marketable securities, the gain from this transaction will be reported in 2003, even though no payment is received until 2004.

Although installment reporting is not available for stock sales, you can postpone paying taxes on the sale of securities from one year to the next by using a technique known as a *short sale*. In a short sale, you enter into a contract to sell stock that you do not currently own. (You may also sell short even if you own the stock by "selling short against the box.") To go through with the sale, you borrow shares from your broker to deliver to your buyer. At a later date, the short sale will be closed by your delivery of stock to your broker of the same company that you just sold.

For tax purposes, if you close the short sale by January 30 and you continue to own identical stock for at least 60 days after you close the transaction, the gain is reported that year upon repayment of the borrowed stock and not in the prior year when you sold the borrowed stock. For example, in December you enter into a contract to sell 100 shares of XYZ stock. To complete this transaction, you borrow 100 shares of XYZ stock for delivery to your buyer. By January 30, you close this short sale by delivering another 100 shares of XYZ stock (shares that you either own or that you purchase on the market) to the lender, usually your broker. For tax purposes, the transaction is closed in January, and the gain is reported in that year and not in the preceding year if you continue to own at least 100 shares of XYZ stock for at least 60 days after closing.

However, using short sales merely for tax purposes without considering the economic volatility of the stock market is one-sided and could lead to a disaster if the stock market takes off and you have locked in your profit at a lower level.

Filing Pointer

When an individual has acquired stock holdings over a period of time and does not dispose of all holdings at the same time, that person must specifically identify which shares of stock are being sold in the transaction in order to properly compute gain. If the individual is unable to identify the lot from which the sold shares are derived, IRS Regulations require that person to treat the shares being sold as coming from the oldest lot first. The seller can adequately identify the securities to be sold by delivering a certificate or by specifically identifying the securities to the broker who holds the certificate. This allows disposition of the higher basis shares, thereby reducing gain.

Year-End Reminder

Suppose that you have a substantial profit on a stock and you want to shift your taxable gain into next year. You can guarantee your present profit by buying a put (an option to sell) on your stock at its current price, good for a long-enough period to carry you into the next year. If the stock keeps climbing, do not exercise the put. Instead, sell the stock at a higher price.

Year-End Reminder

Mutual fund trading poses special tax issues; the timing of purchases and sales of shares is important. Many funds distribute capital gains to shareholders in December, and a shareholder of record must report the entire gain even if the individual just acquired the shares. Make purchases of mutual fund shares after the record date.

Question: I told my broker last year to sell 400 shares of stock, but he sold 4,000 shares. By the time I discovered his error and bought 3,600 shares back, the stock had climbed $4 per share. Following arbitration early this year, the brokerage firm split the difference with me and gave me $7,200 (one-half of what the error cost me) and dropped the commission charges. However, my accountant says that I have to report a gain on the sale of all 4,000 shares. Is this really a correction of my broker's error?

Answer: Not according to the Tax Court in a 1996 decision. According to the Court, a rescission requires that you be restored to your exact original position, usually through mutual consent or court order, in the same tax year. You met none of the conditions. Rather, through arbitration you were awarded damages in the following year (see Chapter 2, "Taxable and Tax-Free Income and Benefits"). Under the Court's reasoning, it is virtually impossible for an error by a brokerage firm to be rescinded because you cannot typically get back the exact shares.

Maximizing Tax Loss on Sales of Securities

If you sold any stocks or bonds at a loss or if you own any stocks or bonds that become totally worthless during the year, you are entitled to claim a capital loss deduction. As with other capital losses, these losses will offset any capital gains recognized during the year and will offset up to $3,000 of ordinary income. Any unused capital loss can be carried forward.

However, a special rule applies with respect to the disposition of certain small business stock, known as Section 1244 stock. Although gains from Section 1244 stock are taxed as capital gains, losses are deductible as ordinary losses. The maximum ordinary loss from Section 1244 stock in a single tax year is $50,000 ($100,000 on a joint return), but no more than your basis in stock. The stock must be issued by a domestic corporation for money or other property (not services), and the total of capital stock and paid-in surplus must not be in excess of $1 million. For the five tax years ending before the loss, more than 50 percent of the corporation's gross receipts must have come from the active conduct of a trade or business. No formal corporate action is now required for a shareholder to benefit under this special rule, but if the stock was issued before November 7, 1978, the corporation had to formally adopt a written plan for the issuance of such stock.

Section 1244 treatment is not available if you receive your stock from another shareholder rather than from the corporation itself. In certain situations, it is possible to structure a stock issuance in either manner. Original issuance of the stock by the corporation will ensure desirable ordinary loss treatment, provided all criteria have been met.

Tax Planning

When funding a new corporation, it is often desirable to lend needed funds rather than to commit to an equity contribution. However, the loss on a worthless loan will be ordinary in nature only if the obligation can be characterized as a business bad debt. As discussed later in this chapter, such a characterization is difficult to show. The result is that favorable tax treatment, if you do not get your money back, may be lost by structuring the corporate funding as debt.

Financing a corporation with debt carries multiple hazards. A proper debt-equity ratio must be maintained, or the IRS can recharacterize debt on the books as disguised equity. Additionally, if you transfer property with a value in excess of its tax basis to a corporation, you will pay taxes on the rise in value if you take back any debt from the corporation.

Caution

A *wash sale* of stock occurs when, within a 60-day period, beginning 30 days before the sale of securities, the seller replaces the sold stocks with substantially identical stocks or securities. If the wash sale results in a loss, the loss cannot be recognized. The wash sale rules are designed to prevent an individual from disposing of the stock to create a tax loss but preserving a position in the market by a quick replacement of the sold shares. To avoid the application of the wash sale rules without changing your basic investment position, either wait the required 31-day period or replace the securities sold with securities in the same or a related industry.

Controversy

What if the seller does not replace a sold stock with identical securities acquired individually during the 60-day period but uses an Individual Retirement Account (IRA) (see Chapter 9) to accomplish the replacement? The IRS is considering this issue but has not announced its position.

Question: I have been dabbling in the stock market this year and have had four transactions dealing with some XYZ stock. Here are the four transactions. Please explain to me what impact the tax rules are going to have on these transactions:

- June 1—bought 100 shares at $10 per share
- August 1—sold 20 shares at $8 per share
- August 27—bought 40 shares at $7 per share
- October 1—sold 50 shares at $9 per share

Answer: Your sale of the 20 shares of XYZ stock on August 1 resulted in a loss of $2 per share. However, because you acquired 40 shares of XYZ stock (at $7 per share) within 30 days of that loss sale, you will not be able to deduct the $2 per share loss that you realized on the August 1 sale. Your basis in 20 of the 40 shares that you bought on August 27 will be their cost basis, $7 per share, but the remaining 20 shares will have a basis equal to $9 per share (the $10 basis of the 20 shares sold on August 1 less the $1 difference between the August 1 sale price and the August 27 purchase price).

The sale on October 1 is not subject to any wash sale rule, assuming that no other XYZ transactions took place before November 1. If you identified that the 50 shares of stock that were sold on October 1 came from your June 1 lot, then you will recognize a loss of $1 per share ($9 less $10 cost basis). If you identified that 40 of the shares that were sold on October 1 came from your August 27 purchase, then 20 of the 50 shares will have been sold at a gain ($9 less $7 cost basis), 20 at no gain or loss ($9 less $9 cost basis), and 10 at a $1 loss ($9 less $10 cost basis). If you failed to identify from which lot the 50 shares that were sold on October 1 came, then you will be deemed to have sold 50 of the shares that you bought on June 1 under the first-in, first-out rule discussed previously.

Filing Pointer

In contrast with the usual three-year statute of limitations discussed in Chapter 13, a claim for refund attributable to a worthless security can be submitted up to seven years after the original due date of the return for the year that the security became worthless.

Year-End Reminder

In the absence of an identifiable event, such as a bankruptcy, to show worthlessness of a security, you may be able to sell the equity or debt instrument to a third party for a small amount prior to year-end and claim the loss.

Controversy

What is the proper tax treatment for the activities of day traders? Although the IRS has issued no formal guidance, day traders would appear to properly report trading gains and losses as capital in nature, expenses as ordinary in nature, and no self-employment tax applicable to any net gains. Traders who make a *mark-to-market* election for the succeeding year report trading gains and losses as ordinary in nature but would appear to handle expenses and the self-employment tax in the same manner as those not making the election.

Convert Your Personal Losses to Deductible Losses

Individuals are entitled to claim a tax loss on the sale of an asset only if the property was used in business or was investment property. As a result, if you sell your personal residence at a loss, the loss will not be deductible. Similarly, when you sell your 1980 Chevrolet for less than what you paid for it, the loss is not deductible unless the car was used in a business.

If you convert property that had been used in strictly personal activities to use in a trade or business, or for use in an investment activity, the property loses its personal character and assumes the business or investment character. For example, if you move out of your personal residence and rent it, you have converted it so that the loss suffered on its sale will be deductible to the extent that it is attributable to the decline in value after you rented it.

Caution

The IRS will scrutinize the rental of inherited property to a family member. If the lease is for less than fair rental value, it will consider the property to be personal (nondeductible loss) instead of rental (Section 1231 loss) upon a subsequent sale not generating a gain.

Tax Planning

If the housing market in your area is depressed and you anticipate that the sale of your personal residence will result in a loss, consider renting the property prior to the sale to clearly establish that the home is no longer your personal residence. When the house is sold at a loss, the decrease in value since its conversion to rental property will be a Section 1231 ordinary loss; whereas, if you had sold it without converting it from personal use, the loss would not be deductible.

Controversy

The courts are split as to the level of rental activity required to treat the rental property as a trade or business, thus giving rise to Section 1231 treatment. In the most recent case of significance, the Tax Court in 1993 disallowed a Section 1231 loss claimed by an individual who was transferred by an employer to another state and who leased his home to the original builder for a low rental. The builder maintained the property and showed it to prospective buyers. The Tax Court held that the lease was a caretaking arrangement lacking a primary rental or investment purpose.

Controversy

Although the Tax Court has ruled on multiple occasions that the sale at a loss of inherited property not converted to personal purposes or to rental property gives rise to a capital loss measured by the difference between the date of death value and the amount realized, the IRS continues to challenge the deductibility of such losses.

Writing Off Your Uncollectible Loans as Losses

When you have lent someone money and you are unable to collect the debt because it is worthless, you are entitled to claim a bad debt deduction on your personal tax return. If the loan was made in a nonbusiness context—any debt other than one created or acquired in the course of a business which gives rise to an ordinary loss—you are entitled to claim a short-term capital loss in the year that the debt becomes worthless. The short-term capital loss will offset capital gain income recognized in the same tax year and will offset ordinary income to the extent of $3,000. Any capital loss that is not deductible as a result of these limitations can be carried forward to subsequent years.

Like a security, an uncollectible loan can be claimed as a deduction only in the year in which it is totally worthless. So long as there is some expectation that the debt will be repaid, it is not totally worthless and, therefore, is nondeductible unless the debt paper is sold at a loss.

Loans to family members that become worthless during the year will also qualify for the bad debt deduction, even though the debtor is a member of your family. However, you must be able to establish that the loan to the family member was in fact a loan and not a gift. The IRS will strictly scrutinize any transaction between related parties to determine whether the advance of money was a loan or a gift. In order to establish that the advance was a loan, you should document the advance with a promissory note that establishes an interest rate and a fixed time for repayment. The more businesslike the transaction, the more likely it is that, should the debt become worthless because of the debtor's insolvency or other inability to repay, you will be entitled to a bad debt deduction. For example, a dad who loaned his daughter $37,000 to open a skating rink was permitted to claim a bad debt when business dried up and went bust. The Tax Court in its 1995 decision cited a long history of family loans and repayments.

Question: Several years ago I set up a corporation for the purpose of maintaining a kennel for dogs and cats. A number of veterinarians promised that they would make me referrals, so I put $5,000 of my own money into the corporation and guaranteed a corporate obligation to the bank of $50,000. The veterinarians promised me that I could make a lot more money than what I had been making as an animal trainer. The business has gone under, and I had to sell everything that I owned in order to pay off the bank as well as the IRS for payroll taxes and the state for payroll and sales taxes. Can I write this off?

Answer: As to the loan, you are entitled to claim a bad debt deduction on payments made as a result of your guarantee. The issue is whether the loss is a nonbusiness bad debt, in which case it will be a capital loss, which you will have to use at $3,000 per year over a number of years in the absence of capital gain from the sale of your assets, or a business bad debt, in which case it will be an ordinary loss that is usable in full this year.

The test used to make the distinction centers on whether the loan (or, in this case, the guarantee of the loan) was connected with a business of yours as opposed to a business of a corporation owned by you. This subtle distinction is very important. The IRS and the courts take the position that a shareholder's loan to a corporation, even one that is 100 percent owned by the shareholder, is a nonbusiness bad debt when the motivation is to make or protect an investment. However, it appears as though your dominant motive was to give yourself a better income. The courts view a loan that is for the purpose of earning a higher income as being business motivated—meaning in your case the business of being an employee of the kennel. Claim the business bad debt.

As to the unpaid taxes to the IRS that you paid personally, you cannot deduct this penalty, which is imposed when a corporation defaults. (See "The Trust Fund Recovery Penalty—Personal Liability for Payroll Taxes" in Chapter 10, "Business Tax Planning.") However, the Ninth Circuit Court of Appeals ruled in 1995 that one who personally pays a tax obligation when state law makes the individual a co-obligor with the corporation for the liability, as opposed to a guarantor, can claim a nonbusiness bad debt upon payment.

If you personally must pay corporate state withholding or sales tax, check whether you were equally liable for payment from the beginning under state law. If so, you may be able to claim a deduction, although both the IRS and the Tax Court may take a different position outside of the Ninth Circuit (California, Oregon, Washington, Idaho, Montana, Alaska, and Hawaii).

The alternative, or your only choice if you will be required to pay federal withholding taxes or state withholding or sales taxes for which you are not automatically liable as a co-obligor, is to lend money to the corporation to make payment and then to claim a bad debt on the loan. However, if you lend money when it is clear that you will not be repaid, the IRS will challenge your claim of a bad debt.

Filing Pointer

Like a refund claim because of a worthless security, a refund claim on account of a worthless debt can be made up to seven years after the original due date of the return for the year that the debt became worthless.

Question: My former husband is thousands of dollars behind in child support. Can I claim a bad debt? He will never catch up.

Answer: Even if the obligation is totally worthless, you have no basis in the debt, which would allow a write-off according to a 1993 Revenue Ruling reiterating a prior Tax Court decision.

CHAPTER 6

Real Estate—The Most Tax-Favored Investment

Owning and Titling Real Estate for Tax Advantage

Ownership of real estate offers the most tax-favored investment. As discussed in Chapter 4, "Deductions—For Itemizers Only," in the case of real estate held for personal use, taxes, interest in most instances, and borrowing costs (points) paid to acquire a principal residence are deductible. As discussed later in this chapter, individuals may in most cases exclude gain recognition on disposition of a principal residence.

In the case of real estate held for investment purpose, numerous tax advantages exist as well, which are also discussed later in this chapter. Ownership of real estate offers exceptions to the passive activity rules discussed in Chapter 2, "Taxable and Tax-Free Income and Benefits," while often allowing deductible losses in excess of outgoing cash or generating incoming cash in excess of taxable income from the property. Further exceptions discussed in Chapter 11, "Special Groups of Taxpayers," apply for real estate professionals.

Individuals can own real property either in their own names or as sole shareholders of corporations that own the property. In most states, an individual can own real property as the sole member of a limited liability company (LLC) that owns the property. Real estate held for personal use should be held in your name. Whether real estate held for investment purpose should be owned individually, in corporate form, or in LLC form, however, will depend in part on tax considerations as well as nontax considerations such as limited liability.

From a tax point of view, any profit or loss generated by the investment property will be reported on the personal tax return if the individual owns the property in his or her own name. Any operating losses suffered by the individual may be subject to disallowance on account of inadequate basis (see Chapter 5, "Gains and Losses"), or at risk limitations (see Chapter 7, "Other Tax-Favored Investments"), or on account of not being an activity entered into for profit (see Chapter 10, "Business Tax Planning"). More often, operating losses will be subject to the passive activity rules that allow losses from such activities to be deducted only to the extent of the income generated from such activities. However, if the investment real estate is rented, up to $25,000 of the losses incurred by the individual from the rental activity may be deductible if that person actively participates in the rental activity. (See the discussion of rental activity losses later in this chapter.)

If the investment real estate is owned in a corporate name, the individual shareholder of the corporation will obtain no personal tax benefits from that ownership unless the corporation elects to be an S corporation. If such an election is made, the individual shareholder will be able to report the income or losses from the corporation's ownership of the real estate on his or her personal return. Losses incurred by the S corporation are deductible by the individual shareholder to the extent of tax basis, meaning investment in the company either in the form of an equity investment or in the form of loans to the corporation. The limitation on passive losses will still apply.

The passive loss limitation also applies to personal service C (regular) corporations such as incorporated medical, legal, and accounting practices. The passive loss limitation applies to other C corporations in modified form. Passive losses incurred by nonpersonal service C corporations can offset net active income—but not portfolio income.

If the investment real estate is owned by an LLC with one individual owner, as is permitted in all but a few states, the LLC is disregarded as an entity for tax purposes, which does not adversely affect the limited legal liability under state law. Any profit or loss is reported on the personal tax return as if the individual owns the property in name.

If two or more individuals invest in real estate, they can do so by owning the property in a corporate name, jointly (either with a right of survivorship or as tenants in common), or through a partnership or LLC (which usually is taxed as a partnership if it has two or more owners). If the investment real estate is merely rented out, a partnership in the tax sense need not exist. Each co-owner may report his or her respective share of the rental income or loss on a personal return. If services (such as attendant parking) are provided, however, a partnership does exist for tax purposes. If a partnership exists, each partner reports his or her share of the partnership income or loss on a personal return. Once again, the rules on passive losses will affect the ability of individual co-owners or partners to claim losses. (See Chapter 10 for a further discussion of alternative types of entities, in the context of an active trade or business.)

Tax Planning

Although you are not required to file a partnership return when multiple individuals share passive ownership of real property through a general partnership as opposed to a limited partnership or LLC, this approach is easier than reporting percentages of each income and expense item for each of the separate properties on the rental income schedule of your tax return. However, opting not to file a formal partnership return may allow greater flexibility in tax planning. For example, a partnership interest in real property cannot be swapped tax-free (see the subsequent discussion in this chapter on tax-free exchanges) for a similar partnership interest or for real property itself. In contrast, a fractional interest in real property through co-ownership can be swapped for a whole or fractional interest in other realty. In a 2002 Revenue Procedure, the IRS generally sanctioned swaps of fractional interests in real property held as tenants in common by no more than 35 co-owners (with husband and wife treated as one and heirs through a single co-owner treated as one).

Question: Two friends and I are planning to acquire rental properties. We hope to acquire several of them in order to minimize our exposure in the event that one stays vacant for a long period of time. We are looking for break-even cash flow during the year and for appreciation to make an above average rate of return on the cash down payment. How should we own the properties?

Answer: Use of a regular C corporation is clearly inadvisable. Because a regular corporation is taxed on its profit at the corporate level, it will be difficult to avoid double taxation—once at the corporate level on any operating profit or upon sale of a property and then again at the individual level upon distribution of the operating cash flow or sale proceeds to you and your co-owners. Additionally, a C corporation will not be able to take advantage of the provision that allows deductions for up to $25,000 of rental losses in excess of passive income. An S corporation is a possibility; however, unless a significant cash contribution exists by the three of you, you may not have enough tax basis to use the losses likely to arise as a result of depreciation.

In a partnership or co-ownership context not constituting a formal partnership, you will receive additional basis (unless you are a limited partner and the financing is recourse) from your share of liabilities. Consequently, partnership or co-ownership is probably best for you. If limiting personal liability is a concern, you can have the benefits of this favorable tax treatment and of maximum protection from creditors by using an LLC.

Caution

See the discussion in Chapter 10 on an important 1994 Tax Court case applying the *hobby loss* rules to real property ownership in two component parts—the first as to the property rental and the second as to the holding for potential appreciation.

Excluding Gain on the Sale of a Principal Residence

Most gain on home sales is free of tax as a result of a $250,000 exclusion available once every two years to an individual, regardless of age, who has owned and used the property as a principal residence for at least two of the previous five years. (See Chapter 11 concerning pending legislation which, if enacted, would give military personnel a suspension of the two-year period for up to five years.) The two years of ownership and occupancy need not occur at the exact same time. Married couples filing jointly get a $500,000 exclusion if both individuals lived in the house for two years even if only one owned the house for the required period. Alternatively, if a husband and wife each sell qualifying properties within two years of each other, even in the same year, they may each claim maximum $250,000 exclusions on their respective sales. Unmarried couples, or any two or more individuals sharing a home, may each claim maximum $250,000 exclusions on sales of their respective interests in the same home.

Under Temporary Regulations issued in 2002, even if the two-year ownership or occupancy period is not satisfied, or even if another principal residence has been sold within two years, a *pro rata* portion of the $250,000/$500,000 exclusion will apply (based on the portion of the two years that has been satisfied) if the change of residence is on account of casualty to the residence, loss of or changed employment, health, death, marital termination, multiple births from the same pregnancy, or other circumstances that may be designated by the IRS or determined to be applicable to the specific individual.

Short temporary absences for vacations, including seasonal absences (even when the house is rented out during the temporary absence), count as periods of occupancy according to the Final Regulations issued in 2002. If an individual actually occupies a home as a principal residence for at least one year, time in a nursing facility counts toward the second year of occupancy.

What qualifies as your residence for purposes of the exclusion? For this purpose a residence includes a condominium or a cooperative and even a houseboat or a mobile home, so long as it is equipped with cooking, sleeping, and sanitation facilities. However, a retirement home or life care facility, even though an individual may purchase the right to exclusive lifetime occupancy, cannot qualify in the absence of a legal interest in the underlying property.

When an individual has multiple homes, the question arises as to which is the principal residence. This is a facts and circumstances analysis applied on a calendar year basis requiring consideration of situs of employment, family, and community ties among others; however, the Final Regulations state that an individual's principal residence is ordinarily where he or she spends a majority of time during the year. The situs of an individual's domicile (what he or she considers as home) or tax home (location of principal place of business—see Chapter 10) will not always determine the result.

Special rules apply when an individual wishes to sell his or her entire ownership interest in fractional parts. Under the Final Regulations, only a single \$250,000/\$500,000 exclusion is available, which may be spread over multiple years. However, the exclusion must be used in full on sale of a remainder interest, which gives full title to the purchaser following the seller's death.

Tax Planning

Whether vast acreage around a home is eligible for the exclusion has been a source of controversy for many years. However, the Final Regulations not only clarify that a home includes contiguous land unless used inconsistent with residential character but also allow the single exclusion to apply to multiple land sales within two years before or after sale of the parcel containing the home.

Controversy

Does use of a property as a principal residence require physical occupancy? The IRS and the Courts have historically said "yes," except for temporary absences. However, the Court of Federal Claims in 1998 disagreed with all existing authorities and determined that "use" does not depend solely on physical occupancy but rather is determined based on all "facts and circumstances." Although this case was decided under pre-1997 law, current law also requires a time period of "use" to obtain the exclusion. The Final Regulations indicate that the IRS will continue to challenge an exclusion when physical occupancy does not exist for two out of the five years preceding sale (except when the nursing facility exception applies).

Tax Planning

Two tacking rules facilitate use of the exclusion. To avoid inequities to divorcing taxpayers, an individual's home occupancy includes periods in which the property was occupied by the spouse pursuant to a written agreement or court order. To benefit a surviving spouse who was not on the title, a widow or widower's home ownership or occupancy includes periods in which the property was owned or occupied by the deceased spouse. Effective 2010, when carryover basis is scheduled to commence (see Chapter 5), a third tracking rule will allow estates and heirs to claim the exclusion by adding the decedent's periods of ownership and occupancy to their own.

Question: My husband died in January of this year. We purchased our home in 1962 for $85,000. It is now worth $850,000. I want to sell the house this year and move into a small condominium. How much will I lose in taxes?

Answer: Unbelievably, nothing—if you can close on the sale by the end of December. One-half of your $765,000 in gain is "forgiven" by the 50 percent step-up in basis when your husband died (see Chapter 5). The balance qualifies for a $500,000 exclusion if a joint return is filed for the year of your husband's death, according to the Final Regulations. Next year, you can get only a $250,000 exclusion filing individually. Had your husband died late in the year, for example December, you would be without sufficient time to use the larger exclusion.

Caution

What if you have been claiming a depreciation deduction for your office-in-home (see Chapter 10) or on account of a rental of a portion of your home? First, all depreciation ever claimed will reduce the basis of property (see Chapter 5). Second, gain will be recognized to the extent of depreciation attributable to periods after May 6, 1997. However, under the Final Regulations, a disqualifying use of one or more rooms for more than three of the five years preceding the sale will not usually cause a loss of the exclusion on a portion of the principal residence. An exception applies if the portion of the home used for business or rental purposes is a separate structure. Affected individuals will lose the exclusion on the portion of gain attributable to the separate structure.

Filing Pointer

Use of the exclusion is optional. Under certain circumstances, it may be desirable not to claim the exclusion on an earlier sale in order to have the full $250,000/$500,000 exclusion available on a subsequent sale within two years. You may make or revoke an election to claim the exclusion during the three-year period beginning with the original due date of the return.

Make Full Use of the $25,000 Write-Off for Rental Real Estate

As discussed earlier in this chapter, except for certain individuals in a real property trade or business whose special treatment is discussed in Chapter 11, rental real estate is automatically considered a passive activity. Under the general rule, losses arising from such rental activity can offset only passive income and cannot be used to offset active income (salary and self-employment income, for example) or portfolio income (interest and dividends, for example).

However, the statute carves out an exception to this general rule, allowing individuals to offset up to $25,000 of active or portfolio income with losses generated by rental of real estate in which the taxpayer actively participates. The $25,000 ceiling is reduced to $12,500 in the case of a married individual filing a separate return who lives apart from the spouse for the entire year. For spouses who live together during any part of the year but who file separate returns, the $25,000/$12,500 rule does not apply.

For those taxpayers with higher levels of income, the $25,000/$12,500 amount is reduced one dollar for every two dollars that the taxpayer's modified AGI (AGI excluding passive losses, taxable Social Security, and IRA deductions) exceeds $100,000 ($50,000 in the case of a married individual filing a separate return). Thus, if the taxpayer's (other than a spouse filing a separate return) modified AGI is $150,000 or more, the rental activity loss will not be able to offset active or investment income. The $12,500 amount of a spouse who files a separate return and is eligible for the deduction is completely phased out if his or her modified AGI is at least $75,000.

To qualify under the $25,000/$12,500 rule, the individual must actively participate in the rental activity both in the year the loss arose and in the year the loss is allowed. To be considered an active participant with respect to the rental real estate, the individual must own at least a 10 percent interest in the property and, unless also a general partner, usually may not own the interest as a limited partner.

The active participation requirement may be satisfied without continuous and substantial involvement in the operations of the rental activity so long as the individual is involved in a significant way (such as making management decisions involving approval of tenants, terms of the rental contract, or capital expenditures). The individual should be able to engage a management company that undertakes supervision of the rental property, as long as the individual exercises independent judgment over the recommendations of the management company and makes all significant management decisions.

On multiple occasions, the Tax Court has upheld the IRS's position that the $25,000/$12,500 exception to the passive loss rule for rental real estate is not applicable to short-term rentals (seven days or less; 30 days or less if services are provided). An owner of property rented on a short-term basis must show material participation (see Chapter 2) to use losses. For example, in a 1998 decision, the Tax Court found that a resort property owner satisfied the "100-hour and more time than anyone else" test by his arranging of rentals, handling of calls, and arranging repairs despite the front desk's own handling of reservations, arrivals, departures, and cleaning services.

Question: What can I do if my income as a corporate executive is greater than $150,000 and I do not have the option to write off $25,000 in rental losses? I expect my AGI to be about $225,000 before losses. In 1987 I purchased an apartment building that produces $40,000 of gross income. The mortgage on the apartment house requires an interest payment of $15,000 per year. My depreciation is about $20,000 a year, and my other expenses on the property, such as insurance, management fees, and repairs, are about $15,000. I expect a loss of about $10,000. What are my options?

Answer: If you do not have any passive income, you will lose the ability to claim your $10,000 loss. Your best choice is to reduce or pay off the mortgage on the apartment building so as to reduce your interest expense. You might do this by securing a second mortgage on your principal residence and using the proceeds to pay down the apartment building's mortgage. The interest on the second mortgage on your principal residence will be deductible so long as the amount of the second mortgage does not exceed the lesser of the home's equity or $100,000 ($50,000 if you are married and file a separate return). This qualified residence interest will either be fully deductible, or a small portion may be lost, depending on the extent of your other itemized deductions, as you must reduce most itemized deductions by 3 percent of the amount by which your AGI exceeds the threshold ($139,500 in 2003, $69,750 if you are married filing sepa-

Year-End Reminder

Prior to year-end, make sure that you are structuring your rental activities in an appropriate manner in order to maximize the use of your $25,000 write-off. Ascertain that you can satisfy the active participation test by maintaining an appropriate rein on the management decisions. Watch the timing of year-end expenditures with respect to the property. When necessary and when possible, structure the timing of your income to keep your modified AGI less than $100,000.

Caution

A single individual with modified AGI in the $100,000 to $150,000 range and losses from rental properties can be in the highest marginal tax bracket of any taxpayer. A single individual falling within this range can lose 44 cents on each additional dollar of earnings when caught in the phaseout of the $25,000 deduction for rental real estate, the phaseout of itemized deductions, and the phaseout of personal exemptions. Add a dependent and, with the phaseout of the child credit, the effective tax bracket is about 63 percent. Married couples caught in the phaseout fare only slightly better.

rately), subject to a maximum loss of 80 percent of affected deductions. (See Chapter 1 for a further discussion of the phaseout of itemized deductions.)

Maximize Your Depreciation and Amortization Deductions

If real property is residential in nature, the adjusted basis of the building portion (as opposed to the land portion) is recovered ratably over 27 1/2 years. If the real estate is nonresidential real estate, meaning it is used for commercial purposes including rentals usually 30 days or less, the write-off is over a 39-year period. In either case, first-year depreciation does not give a full year write-off, inasmuch as a proration of a full year's depreciation is used depending on the month of acquisition. The IRS publishes tables for use in computing depreciation.

Do not forget to include acquisition costs in the basis of your real property. Most such costs, including construction period interest and taxes, transfer taxes, and recordation fees, are added to the basis of property and, to the extent that the property is depreciable (meaning the extent to which costs can be allocated to a building used in a trade or business or for investment purposes), will be recovered through depreciation deductions. The allocable portion of the purchase price and additions to the land, as opposed to the structure, is not depreciable.

Points, loan origination fees, and loan commitment fees are not added to the basis of property. Rather, they are amortized over the term of the loan.

After acquisition of real property, the owner will undoubtedly make any number of expenditures with respect to that property, some of which will be currently deductible and some of which must be added to the property's basis and then cost-recovered through depreciation. If the expense is a repair or maintenance cost, the owner receives an immediate benefit from the expenditure by being able to currently deduct the expense. If the expenditure is structural and materially enhances the value of the property or prolongs its life, however, it is considered a capital expenditure and must be capitalized and then cost-recovered over time, 27 1/2 years in the case of residential property or 39 years in the case of nonresidential property. Nonstructural capital expenditures as well as furnishings and appliances are written off over a shorter period, typically seven years (five years for most property used in residential rentals).

The following are examples of the various types of expenditures that might fall into the repair category or the capital expenditure category:

Repairs	Capital expenditures
Painting	Plumbing system installation
Maintenance on furnace	New furnace
New roof	Structurally changed roof

Year-End Reminder

Where a cash outlay will be a repair as opposed to a capital expenditure, a repair at year-end will offer a valuable deduction unless you will have unusable losses. In fact, all bills related to rental properties should be paid in December.

Caution

A group of repairs accomplished at the same time may be considered as a rehabilitation project—a capital expenditure—even if each cost incurred individually could have been deducted. Do your repairs as needed rather than saving them to do in a group.

Renting to Family Members at a Loss

You can provide housing to your family members at a reasonable cost and still get a tax break. If a property is rented at its fair rental value and the home is the family member's principal residence, you will be able to claim a rental loss deduction with respect to the property, subject to the usual limitations on deducting rental losses. For example, a couple can purchase a home, rent it to their daughter as her principal residence, charge her the full market rent on the property, and be eligible to claim a rental loss deduction with respect to that property. If a couple purchases a home and lets their daughter use the property rent-free or if the property does not constitute the daughter's principal residence, however, the daughter's use of the property will be attributed to the couple and no loss can be claimed.

Question: I own a piece of investment property near the location where my parents want to retire. When my current tenant's lease expires, can I rent the property to my parents and get the same tax breaks that I am getting now from my tenant?

Answer: Yes. So long as you charge your parents the same amount of rent that you would charge an unrelated party, the fact that your parents are your new tenants will not change your tax treatment of the rental losses that have been generated. However, you must limit your visits as well as the visits of other family members to your parents to no more than the greater of 14 days or 10 percent of the number of days that the property is rented at fair value, because those days would be treated as personal to you. (See "Renting, Using, and Writing Off Your Vacation Home," which follows.)

Question: My son and his wife have found their dream home but cannot afford the necessary down payment. I am able to lend them the money for the down payment, but I would like to get some tax breaks from this loan. Any suggestions?

Answer: Rather than lending the couple money, you and your son and his wife should consider a shared equity arrangement. In a shared equity arrangement, you and your son and his wife will each own a share of the dream home. So long as your son and his wife pay you for the fair rental value of your fractional share, you will be able to offset the income not only with the interest, taxes, and other expenses that you pay but also with the depreciation of your percentage interest in the property. The passive activity rules, including the $25,000/$12,500 rule, will be applicable to your ownership interest.

If your son and his wife itemize deductions, they can write off the taxes and interest, subject to the qualified residence interest rules.

Caution

Do not lease a portion of your home to your S corporation. By statute, you must report the income but cannot get an offsetting deduction for expenses other than the business portion of mortgage interest and taxes. Rather, have your S corporation (this prohibition is not applicable to C corporations) reimburse you personally for a *pro rata* share of cash expenditures. Except for the inability to claim depreciation, you achieve the same result. Alternatively, you may qualify for the office-in-home deduction regarding the portion of your home that you use for business as an employee of your S corporation. See Chapter 10 for a discussion of business entities, depreciation, and the office-in-home deduction.

Renting, Using, and Writing Off Your Vacation Home

Any residence that you own as an investment may fall within the definition of a *vacation home*. This is a generic term applied to property that an individual or members of the individual's family use personally, at least in part. In addition to the traditional home, the term vacation home includes condos, apartments, boats, and mobile homes equipped with living accommodations. If there is any personal use of the home by the individual or by family members, write-offs with respect to that property are limited.

Personal use by an individual includes not only his or her own use of the premises but also use by family members even if fair rent is charged, by any other individual if less than the fair rent is charged, by a co-owner, or by any person under an arrangement in which that person's investment property is made available for use. Consequently, if you rent your beach house to your grandchild's family for three weeks, that time will be considered your personal use of the beach house even if you charge your grandchild the same rate that you charge the general public. Similarly, if you let your next-door neighbor use the beach house and only charge one-half of the going rate, your neighbor's time at the beach house will be considered your personal use of the property.

Use of a property during a period substantially devoted to full-time repair and maintenance does not count as personal use of the property. Under a 1993 Tax Court decision, the period of repair and maintenance includes the time expended in making capital improvements.

If a vacation home is rented for 14 days or less during the year and there is any personal use, the individual gets to pocket the rental income. The individual does not have to report the income; however, that person is permitted to claim no expenses other than mortgage interest (if the property is treated as the second residence under the qualified residence interest rules) and property taxes.

If a vacation home is rented for more than 14 days and personal use does not exceed the greater of 14 days or 10 percent of the days that the property is rented at fair value, expenses must be prorated based on the number of rental days and the number of personal days. The rental income is compared to the expenses allocable to the rental days. Any loss offsets other passive income and, as discussed earlier in this chapter, can offset other types of income in the case of certain real estate professionals and individuals eligible to use the $25,000/$12,500 write-off. However, as discussed earlier in this chapter, few vacation home landlords qualify for a write-off under the $25,000/$12,500 rule because it does not apply to short-term rentals according to the IRS.

In such case, the personal portion of the property taxes may be claimed as an itemized deduction; however, the personal portion of the mortgage interest is not eligible for treatment as qualified residence interest.

If a vacation home is rented for more than 14 days and personal use exceeds the greater of 14 days or 10 percent of the fair rental days, expenses also must be prorated based on the number of rental days and the number of personal days. However, an individual is penalized in that no loss is permitted to be claimed in connection with the rental aspects of the property. Regarding the personal use aspects, property taxes may be claimed as an itemized deduction as may the mortgage interest if the property is treated as the second residence of the individual.

Caution

A home with multiple bedrooms, one of which is occupied by the homeowner and the others of which are rented to housemates, is treated as one home. The owner has made personal use of the home, and no rental loss is allowed. In contrast, if the home had separate cooking facilities, bathrooms, and entrances, such as in a duplex, the owner's occupation of one portion of the building would not taint the other portion, and the rental loss would be allowed subject to the $25,000/$12,500 rule.

Year-End Reminder

Care should be exercised if significant tax benefits would be lost by allowing personal use to exceed the greater of 14 days or 10 percent of the number of rental days. In some cases it may be possible to reduce the number of personal days.

Controversy

The Tax Court backs up the IRS's position that you may count only days of actual use as rental days and not days in which a unit is in a rental pool, even if the rental agent gives you a fixed or minimum annual fee. However, in a decision binding the IRS and the Tax Court only in Michigan, Ohio, Kentucky, and Tennessee, the Sixth Circuit Court of Appeals determined in 1996 that the total number of days that a unit is available in the rental pool counts as rental days, at least when fair rental value is received for the year.

Tax Planning

Individuals with homes in seasonably desirable locations, such as Louisville during Derby Week or New Orleans during Mardi Gras, should consider taking advantage of the tax-free windfall of legally putting cash in their pockets for up to 14 days of rent. Owners of beach homes or ski resort properties may fare best by renting their units for seven weekends and keeping the cash, especially in light of the IRS position that short-term rentals do not qualify for the $25,000/$12,500 exception to the passive loss rule for rental real estate. Congress has periodically considered legislation that, if enacted, would end the 14-day rule, requiring property owners to account for income and expenses of all rentals regardless of duration.

Controversy

The IRS takes the position that mortgage interest and property taxes are prorated between the rental activities and personal activities based on the number of days of each use. However, the courts have rejected the IRS approach, instead prorating just these two expenses based on the number of rental days and the number of other days in the year (reasoning that interest and property taxes accrue even when the property sits vacant). The effect is to increase the interest and property taxes allocable to the personal days and to decrease the interest and taxes chargeable to the rental days.

Question: I own a beach house and rented it 160 days during the year. My family and I used the house for 20 days; it is vacant the remainder of the year. I received $16,000 in rent. The mortgage interest was $5,000, I paid $3,000 in property taxes, and my insurance and repair costs totaled $4,000. My depreciation allowance for the year, based on the total cost of the structure itself (ignoring the land), would be $8,000. How is all of this handled on my tax return?

Answer: Because your personal use of the property (20 days) exceeds the 10 percent of the number of days that the house is rented, you will not be able to claim a tax loss on the property. First, however, determine whether the position of the courts or the IRS position gives you a better result. Using the favored allocation method of the courts, limit your deductions chargeable to the rental activity by applying a fraction (160/365 to interest and property taxes and 160/180 to other expenses) to the whole amounts of the expenses as shown:

	Rental Portion	Personal Portion
Mortgage Interest	$2,192	$2,808
Property Taxes	1,315	1,685
Insurance & Repairs	3,556	N/D
Depreciation	7,111	N/D
	$14,174	$4,493

Because the portion of the expenses attributable to the rental period is less than the $16,000 of rental income, all of the $14,174 in expenses will be deductible. The remaining property taxes and mortgage interest (if the interest is treated as qualified residence interest on a second home) will be used as itemized deductions.

Using the IRS method of allocating interest and taxes between rental portion and personal portion, interest and taxes charged to the rental days would be $4,444 and $2,667, respectively. Rental expenses would total $17,779; thus, $1,779 of expenses would be disallowed with the depreciation deduction for the year reduced by that amount.

Maximize Passive Income by Maximizing Your Rental Receipts

Individuals with passive losses from nonrental activities or passive losses from rental activities in excess of the amount deductible to them, if any, need to try to generate passive income. One way to do this is to maximize rental income, which is considered passive income against which passive losses can be offset. Review rental contracts to be certain that the rent being charged is the maximum that the market will bear.

If a property owner rents to his or her family-owned corporation, the owner should consider a rent increase within the limits of fair rent and a decrease in salary payments. This will save Social Security taxes if the decrease reduces the salary to less than the Social Security base of $87,900 ($87,000 in 2003) and will help to reduce passive losses. Before taking this step, however, consider the impact on reduced retirement benefits.

Question: I am leasing an office townhouse that I own personally to my professional corporation in which I conduct a psychiatric practice. The rental income pays the 8 percent mortgage and other expenses associated with the property; however, I always end up with losses on the property each year on my tax return due to depreciation. I have no other passive activities, and I expect my income to be greater than $150,000. What should I be doing to avoid unusable losses?

Answer: Determine whether you are charging your professional corporation a below-market rent. If you are charging too little, raise the rent to avoid unusable passive losses. If you cannot avoid passive losses by raising the rent to the highest possible fair rental amount, you may want to pay off a portion of the mortgage with available cash or borrow against your home. It makes little sense to have idle cash earning about 2 1/2 percent in a certificate of deposit and paying taxes on this income while you are carrying a mortgage of 5 percent and not enjoying the deduction for the full mortgage interest.

Caution

When the landlord and tenant are related parties (such as an individual taxpayer leasing real estate to a family-owned corporation), special care should be taken. Although you can increase rent (as long as it remains a fair amount) in order to wipe out losses, the courts have upheld IRS Regulations stating that positive net income arising from a leasing arrangement to an entity in which the taxpayer materially participates will not generate passive income capable of offsetting passive losses from other activities.

Filing Pointer

Can your sole proprietorship rent space from you personally? No, because your unincorporated business is your alter ego. However, the Eighth Circuit Court of Appeals in 1997 agreed with the Tax Court that a sole proprietorship can rent one-half of property owned jointly by the sole proprietor and his wife, allowing the couple to enjoy 50 percent of the advantages of rental property. Had the real estate been in the spouse's name alone, the Court would apparently have allowed the full tax benefit to the couple, even on a joint return.

Deferring Gain by Exchanging Properties

A taxpayer who owns investment or business real property can exchange it for like-kind investment or business real property. The gain realized on the exchange (the difference between the value of the property received and the adjusted basis in the property exchanged) will not be recognized. Use IRS Form 8824 to report the exchange. The taxpayer's basis in the exchanged property will carry over and become the basis of the newly acquired property. If the taxpayer, in addition to receiving investment or business real property, receives personal property, cash, or other consideration, collectively referred to as *boot*, the taxpayer's gain will be recognized to the extent of the value of the boot received. Deferred gain is taxed upon subsequent sale of the property received in the exchange.

A very simple tax-free exchange transaction involves two parties, each of whom owns a piece of real estate that the other party desires to acquire. The parties simply exchange the real estate and, if necessary, equalize the values by the addition of boot.

However, in everyday life it is quite unusual to find two parties who want to acquire each other's property. The more likely transaction involves three or more parties. Assume that Alex wants to dispose of Tara and wants to acquire Twin Oaks, which is owned by Betty. Charles wants to acquire Tara. To best effectuate a tax-free exchange, Alex will need Charles to purchase Twin Oaks from Betty and then swap Twin Oaks with Alex in exchange for Tara.

The law permits some delay in the exchange of properties so long as the property to be received in the exchange is identified within 45 days after the date on which the taxpayer transferred property. Additionally, the closing on the acquired property must take place within 180 days after the date of transfer or, if earlier, the due date of the return, including extensions, for the year of the transfer. This 45-day/180-day provision now permits taxpayers to contract for an exchange of properties without having a particular replacement property in mind and allows some flexibility with respect to the identification and closing on the new property. In order for the multiexchange situation to work, there must be contractual interdependence in the transactions.

Mortgages are a reality in today's real estate market. The existence of mortgaged property on either side of the exchange will have an impact on the tax-free nature of the exchange. If the other party to the exchange assumes a taxpayer's mortgage, this assumption is also considered boot, and the taxpayer's gain will be recognized to the extent of this and any other boot. However, if the taxpayer receives property subject to a mortgage in the exchange or pays some cash for the new property, either will reduce or eliminate the taxpayer's gain recognition. In other words, any mortgage that is assumed or cash that is paid out will be netted against any mortgage of which the taxpayer is relieved. Only to the extent that a taxpayer is relieved of a mortgage greater than that which he or she assumes plus the cash that he or she pays will gain be recognized.

If you exchange depreciable real estate for other real estate, you will not be able to avoid all gain recognition. The depreciation recapture rules (see Chapter 5) override the general nonrecognition of gain rules in these situations.

Question: I am interested in this tax-free exchange. I own a rental property in Houston worth $250,000. I have found a buyer who is willing to assume my existing $50,000 mortgage and pay me $200,000 for the property. I would like to buy another rental property in California. I have found a number of possibilities in the San Francisco area. What do I do next?

Answer: You should engage an attorney in Texas to draft the appropriate contract language to effectuate an exchange. You will have to determine which

California property or properties you want within 45 days after you close on the Texas property, and you must close on the California property within 180 days after the Texas closing. Unless you assume a mortgage on the California property of at least $50,000 or pay at least $50,000 in cash (or a combination of the two), you will be required to report your gain to the extent of the $50,000 mortgage assumed by your buyer. Suppose that the California property that you find is worth $300,000. You must necessarily assume a mortgage of $100,000 or pay cash of $100,000 (in addition to the $200,000 received from your buyer) or a combination of the two in order to equalize the equities of the two properties.

An independent escrow agent who is unrelated to you and has not served in a professional or agency role for you during the most recent two years would hold the $200,000 proceeds from the Texas property's closing and then use those funds pursuant to your written instruction to acquire the California property for you. Your access to the proceeds from the Texas property must be substantially limited to qualify for the tax-free exchange treatment. What will not work is for you to sell the Texas property in a conventional sales transaction and then take possession of and use the proceeds to reinvest in other property. The tax-free exchange treatment for investment or business property differs in this material respect from the deferral of gain rules on the sale of a principal residence.

Question: I want to purchase a piece of investment property. However, I need to sell one of my four existing real property investments. Can I do a like-kind exchange in reverse?

Answer: The IRS appeared to frown on reverse like-kind swaps until 2000 when it issued a Revenue Procedure sanctioning these exchanges. Title to your new piece of property must be held initially by an independent escrow agent under an arrangement put in writing within five business days after the title transfer. The property to be sold must be identified within 45 days after transfer and closed upon within 180 days of transfer.

Deferring Gain from Involuntary Conversions

The law permits taxpayers whose property (business, investment, or personal) has been taken by the government or involuntarily converted (seizure or destruction, for example) to defer gain by using the condemnation or insurance proceeds to reinvest in property similar or related in service or use to the property that was condemned or otherwise destroyed. If all of the condemnation or insurance proceeds are reinvested within the replacement period, no gain will be recognized.

The replacement period usually ends two years after the close of the tax year in which the condemnation or other conversion occurred. The replacement period is extended an additional year for business or investment real estate that has been condemned and an additional two years for a principal residence involuntarily converted as the result of a disaster. (See Chapter 4 for the tax treatment of disasters and other casualties causing tax losses.)

The similar or related in-service or use standard is a very strict test. A more lenient replacement test applies if the transaction involved is the condemnation of business or investment real estate. In these circumstances, the taxpayer can satisfy the law if mere like-kind property is the replacement. Under this latter test, unimproved realty would qualify as an appropriate replacement for improved real estate. An even more lenient rule applies for business or investment property converted as the result of a disaster loss. It may be replaced in a timely manner by any tangible business property.

Where the converted property is rental property, the replacement property's use is viewed at the landlord level; so long as the landlord is providing similar services, the test will be satisfied. For example, the IRS has ruled that a landlord or investor can qualify for the deferral of gain on the conversion of warehouse property by using the conversion proceeds to build a gas station that would then be leased to an oil company.

In lieu of acquiring replacement real estate, an individual who has received conversion proceeds can acquire at least an 80 percent interest in a corporation owning the appropriate replacement property. However, if the individual is seeking to replace the real estate with like-kind property instead of property that is similar or related in service or use, that person must acquire the property directly. The individual cannot acquire an 80 percent interest in the corporation that owns real estate in order to satisfy the like-kind test.

The reinvested proceeds of any involuntary conversion must be used to acquire the replacement property from an unrelated person if the gain realized exceeds $100,000 or if the taxpayer is a C corporation (see Chapter 10) or a partnership with one or more C corporations owning more than one-half of the partnership interests.

Filing Pointer

If a principal residence is condemned or otherwise involuntarily converted, the realized gain usually will not be recognized under the general $250,000/$500,000 exclusion applicable to sales of principal residences discussed earlier in this chapter. If the realized gain exceeds the amount of the available exclusion, gain recognition requires the reinvestment of the conversion proceeds less the excluded gain.

Question: I do not understand how I can have an income tax gain when my apartment building is destroyed by fire. Please explain.

Answer: It does seem unfair to tax you after such a catastrophe, but that is what will happen if you do not act. Here is the reason for the tax. Suppose that you receive $200,000 from the insurance company, but your basis in the building is $90,000. Because you received proceeds in excess of your basis, you have realized a gain. The gain of $110,000 can be deferred by timely purchasing (or reconstructing) a qualifying replacement property for at least $200,000. Note that, if your destroyed building were mortgaged and you received only your equity in cash from the insurance company, the mortgage amount plus the cash you receive is the amount that must be spent on the replacement property.

Low-Income Housing—A High-Income Shelter

Although investing in low-income housing projects presents substantial economic risks, many individuals are interested in this type of investment because it is one area still offering some real tax breaks. Before investing in such projects, however, consider not only the tax ramifications but also the economic risks of the investments and the fact that you may not be able to receive your cash contributions back as a result of an inability to dispose of the property at an appreciated value.

Taxpayers who construct or substantially rehabilitate low-income housing are permitted to claim the low-income housing credit. In the case of nonsubsidized housing, the credit is an amount equal to 70 percent (91 percent in high-cost areas) of the construction and rehabilitation costs. In the case of subsidized housing, the credit is an amount equal to 30 percent of the construction and rehabilitation costs.

This credit is claimed over a 10-year period, and the amount of the credit that can be claimed each year is determined by the IRS so that the present value of the 10 credit amounts will equal the applicable percent of the qualified costs. For low-income housing projects placed in service during 2003, the maximum credit available in each of the 10 years is approximately 7.9 percent for nonsubsidized housing and approximately 3.4 percent for subsidized housing. The actual percentage is tied to the month in which the project is opened.

To qualify for the credit, the acquisition or rehabilitation costs must involve low-income housing as determined under a complex definition.

After an individual makes an investment in a low-income housing project and a credit is made available, it can be used only to offset the tax generated by the passive income and to provide a credit equivalent of a $25,000 deduction. If you are in the 25-percent tax bracket and have no passive income, this credit equivalent rule would allow you to claim up to a $6,250 low-income housing credit (25 percent multiplied by $25,000). The credit increases to a maximum of $8,750 in a 35-percent tax bracket. In other words, investors in low-income housing projects are in essence subject to the $25,000 rental real estate rule previously described.

Two important differences exist, however, for low-income housing project investors. First, there is no requirement that you actively participate in the low-income housing project in order to be eligible for the credit. Consequently, investors who are limited partners will still qualify for the low-income housing project credit. Second, the credit is available for all individuals regardless of modified AGI.

For married individuals who live apart for the entire year and who file separately, the credit is an equivalent of the $12,500 deduction. Married individuals who file separately, but who do not live apart for the entire year, do not qualify for the credit equivalent of the $25,000/$12,500 deduction.

The amount of the credit, unlike the rehabilitation tax credit subsequently discussed, does not cause a reduction in the tax basis of the housing project. Consequently, the full cost of the building is eligible for depreciation. The building's basis will be depreciated on a straight-line basis (equal depreciation every 12 months) over 27 1/2 years.

If the project does not remain qualified as a low-income housing project for 15 years, the low-income housing credit is subject to recapture. A sale of the project or of an interest in the project will also trigger a recapture of the credit, unless the seller furnishes a bond to the IRS, and it is reasonably expected that the project will continue to meet the definition of a low-income housing project.

Tax Planning

An additional benefit is provided for investors in low-income housing projects. If the project is sold in a qualified sale, the investor can elect to defer recognition of the gain realized on the disposition if that person reinvests the sales proceeds in another low-income housing project in a timely manner. The reinvestment must occur within a two-year period beginning one year before the disposition.

To qualify for the deferral of gain on the sale of a low-income housing project, the project must be sold to the tenants of the project or to a cooperative or other tax-exempt organization established solely for the benefit of the tenants. In addition, the sale must be approved by the U.S. Department of Housing and Urban Development.

This rule provides for the deferral of gain recognition and not for its exclusion from income. This deferral is accomplished by requiring the taxpayer to reduce the basis in the new project by the amount of the gain that is deferred, so that when the new project is sold and no election is made to reinvest in another low-income housing project, the deferred gain is then taxed.

The Rehabilitation Tax Credit for Aged and Historic Buildings

Taxpayers who incur rehabilitation expenditures with respect to commercial buildings constructed before 1936 are eligible for a tax credit equal to 10 percent of the rehabilitation costs. For those taxpayers who invest in certified historic structures (both commercial and residential rental), the credit amount will be 20 percent of the rehabilitation expenditures.

To qualify for the credit with respect to certified historic structures, all expenditures must be certified by the U. S. Department of the Interior as being in character with the property in the area in which the property is located. With respect to rehabilitations on any property not a certified historic structure, a taxpayer must:

- Retain at least 50 percent of the existing external walls of the building as external walls.
- Retain at least 75 percent of the existing external walls as either internal or external walls.
- Retain at least 75 percent of the internal structure framework of the building.

To qualify for the credit, a taxpayer must, during a 24-month period, make rehabilitation expenditures at least equal to the adjusted basis in the building (or $5,000, if that is greater). For example, if your adjusted basis in a building is $80,000, to qualify for the rehabilitation credit you must spend at least $80,000 to renovate the building while complying with the wall retention rules described previously.

As with the low-income housing credit, the rehabilitation tax credit is subject to the rules on passive activities. Once again, Congress has provided a tax break for those investors who qualify for this credit. There is no requirement that the taxpayer actively participate in the management of the project. As a result, you can invest in the project as a limited partner and still qualify for the rehabilitation credit. The phaseout of the $25,000 equivalent does not begin until modified AGI exceeds $200,000, rather than at the general phase-out level of $100,000 applicable to rental losses. For a taxpayer with modified AGI between $200,000 and $250,000, the rehabilitation tax credit is phased out. A taxpayer with modified AGI in excess of $250,000 cannot use the rehabilitation tax credit.

Remember, the credit equivalent rule does not mean that you can offset $25,000 of tax. What it means is that you can offset your tax liability to the same extent that a $25,000 deduction would have reduced your tax liability. If you are in the 25-percent tax bracket, you will be able to claim a tax credit equal to $6,250. If you are in the 28-percent tax bracket, the credit equivalent will be $7,000. In a 33-percent bracket, the credit equivalent rises to $8,250. For married individuals who live apart for the entire year and who file separately, the credit is an equivalent of the $12,500 deduction, and the phaseout levels are one-half of the levels for other taxpayers. Married individuals who file separately but who do not live apart for the entire year do not qualify for the credit equivalent of the $25,000/$12,500 deduction.

Unlike the low-income housing credit, the taxpayer is required to reduce basis in the rehabilitated building by the full amount of the tax credit claimed. For example, if you purchase a building that qualifies as a certified historic structure for $100,000 and spend $150,000 to renovate the structure, the rehabilitation credit for which you would be eligible is $30,000 (20% × $150,000). For the purpose of depreciation, your basis in the building would be $220,000 (the $100,000 cost of the building plus $150,000 in rehabilitation expenditures less the $30,000 rehabilitation tax credit), written off over the applicable recovery period depending upon whether it is used for residential rental or commercial purposes.

Caution

If the building is sold within five years, a ratable portion of the rehabilitation tax credit is recaptured. There is no recapture of the credit after five years.

CHAPTER 7

Other Tax-Favored Investments

Is the Tax Shelter Dead or Breathing?

It has been almost two decades since the Tax Reform Act of 1986 took away much of the desire and most of the means to shelter income. Given the Act's maximum effective individual tax bracket of 28 percent as of 1988, investors chose to pay taxes and keep 72 cents on the dollar rather than risk the full dollar on speculative sheltering investments. Additionally, the passive activity rules discussed in Chapter 2, "Taxable and Tax-Free Income and Benefits," coupled with the existing basis rules and at-risk rules imposed obstacles.

The basis rules limit your ability to claim losses beyond your unreturned investment in a venture plus your share of the venture's liabilities if it is unincorporated. The at-risk rules further limit your ability to claim losses to the extent that your investment, regardless of basis, arises from nonrecourse financing (that is, financing for which you are not personally liable). Your loss is limited to what you have put on the line. However, in the real estate field your at-risk amount will include nonrecourse financing, so long as the financing was provided by a commercial lender. The passive activity rules generally limit your ability to shelter business and portfolio income with passive losses.

So what remains of tax shelters almost two decades after the Tax Reform Act of 1986?

The real estate lobby convinced Congress to retain some of the benefits of real estate investments and, as described in the preceding chapter, you will still be able to find a tax shelter by investing in a second home, rental real estate, low-income housing, or rehabilitation of older buildings or certified historic structures. Of course, your own primary residence is the best tax shelter.

Investing through an individual retirement account or employer-sponsored retirement plan, as discussed in Chapter 9, "Retirement Plans," is an excellent way of sheltering income while securing your future.

Notwithstanding the Tax Reform Act of 1986, passive activities can still be tax-favored investments, if leveraging is eliminated or reduced or if investments producing passive losses are coupled with those producing passive income. Additionally, oil and gas, insurance, and annuity investments continue to be tax-favored.

The Revenue Reconciliation Act of 1993, with its maximum marginal individual tax bracket of 39.6 percent, since reduced to 35 percent, rekindled the desire to shelter income. Despite its expressed purpose of deficit reduction, the 1993 Act created two new significant tax-favored investments: *small business stock* and *empowerment zones*. The Community Renewal Tax Relief Act of 2000 added tax-favored treatment for investments in *renewal communities*.

The Job Creation and Worker Assistance Act of 2002 provided numerous tax incentives to New York City employers within the targeted zone affected by the September 11, 2001 terrorist attacks.

Question: My investment in a video store is $5,000. The remainder of the capital for the business was made available to me by a financial institution. I have signed a commercial note, which my attorney tells me is a nonrecourse note in the amount of $20,000. I work every day in the store. Am I limited in the losses I can deduct?

Answer: Yes. You may claim deductions with respect to the video operations beyond the income generated by the venture only to the extent of $5,000. If you are personally liable on the bank loan, your initial at-risk amount would be $25,000.

Any net loss for which a deduction is denied under these at-risk rules may be deducted in a subsequent year during which the business venture produces income or additional contributions of capital are made by you.

Reduce Leveraged Investments

The old rule of thumb with respect to passive activities was "leverage the deal to the greatest extent possible." In other words, make your investment with as much borrowed money as possible. Two advantages exist to the leveraged passive activity. First, the investor could obtain significant write-offs with minimal cash output. Second, the interest paid on the borrowed funds was fully deductible by the investor so that the cost of the mortgage money was significantly reduced.

As a result of the adoption of the passive loss rules, the rule of thumb is to minimize leverage in a passive activity so that it at least breaks even from a tax point of view. When the activity produces tax write-offs, such as depreciation in the case of real estate or depletion in the case of natural resources, which do not require a cash expenditure, the activity may generate positive cash flow.

Illustration

The cost of a small apartment building is $200,000, of which $140,000 is allocable to the building. You put up $75,000 and finance the rest over 30 years at 10 percent. Projections for the property indicate that you can expect to receive $21,500 in income. Real estate taxes and insurance could run $4,000. Your annual mortgage payment will be slightly greater than $13,000. Here are the specifics for the first year:

$21,500	Rent	$21,500	Rent
(3,000)	Taxes	(3,000)	Taxes
(1,000)	Insurance	(1,000)	Insurance
(13,164)	Principal & Interest Payments	(12,469)	Interest Payments
		(4,879)	Depreciation
$ 4,336	Cash Flow	$ 152	Passive Income

This investment would produce an annual positive cash flow of which virtually all is sheltered for tax purposes.

Filing Pointer

If you presently have highly leveraged passive activities generating unusable passive losses, curtail the debt with any available cash. Not only do you reduce or eliminate passive losses, but in many cases you rid yourself of debt typically at a higher interest rate than the rate of earnings on your idle money.

Passive Income Generators (PIGs)

If you have existing passive activities generating unusable losses, rather than curtail existing debt, you can buy a PIG—a passive income generator. A PIG is designed to give you the passive income needed to offset existing passive losses. You may buy a PIG, often through an all-cash deal, or an existing investment may become a PIG.

If you invested in a tax shelter some years ago, you may find yourself holding what is often known as a burned-out shelter. A burned-out shelter is one that produced tax write-offs in its early years of operation, but these write-offs diminished over the years and the investment is now producing taxable income. If the shelter is not making cash distributions, the investors find themselves with increased taxable income resulting from their investment in the shelter but no cash distributions. This kind of taxable income is known as *phantom income*, because the investor has no cash to go along with the increase in income.

Certainly being in a position of an investor with phantom income is not good. However, the phantom income investment will likely be a PIG, allowing use of passive losses.

Your PIG will be fatter, however, if your gain on disposition of a passive activity is accompanied by receipt of cash. For example, if you have unusable passive losses, you can create a PIG by selling a rental property at a gain on an installment basis if sufficient principal can be collected each year. Rather than amortizing the obligation, consider having the purchaser curtail equal amounts of principal each year while paying interest on the unpaid balance. This creates more passive income and less portfolio income in the early years.

If you buy a PIG, do not work it more than 100 hours per year. Income otherwise passive in nature will be recharacterized as nonpassive under the significant participation activity regulations to prevent individuals from structuring activities in such a way as to generate passive income in order to shelter passive losses from other activities.

A significant participation activity is one in which an individual taxpayer is involved for more than 100 hours per year but in which the individual does not materially participate. (See Chapter 2 for a discussion of material participation.) If one engages in significant participation activities during the year and the gross income from these activities exceeds the deductions from these activities, IRS Regulations will treat the net income as income from a nonpassive activity. The result of this recharacterization is that an individual has less passive income against which to offset passive losses.

Question: A friend of mine told me that he has been able to use something called a "master limited partnership" as a tax shelter. What is a master limited partnership? How does it work?

Answer: A master limited partnership (MLP), also known as a publicly traded partnership, is an unincorporated entity offered on a public exchange or a secondary market that is generally designed to distribute significant tax-free return of capital and long-term capital gain along with ordinary income. Such interests are much more marketable (and potentially more liquid) than in the case of other partnerships. As a result, MLPs have been instituted in all sorts of businesses.

MLPs formed after December 17, 1987, are usually taxed as corporations. Thus, income and loss will not pass through to the partners. However, partnership treatment will apply if 90 percent or more of the MLP's gross income is from interest, dividends, real estate rents, gains from the sale of capital assets, income or gains from certain oil and gas activities, and gains from the sale of certain business assets. The MLP must have met this passive income requirement for each year after 1987.

Under special rules, a partner's share of net business income from an MLP treated as a partnership cannot be used to offset losses from other MLPs or other passive loss activities. A partner's share of loss from such an MLP is suspended and carried forward until the MLP generates net business income. The MLP loss may not be used against passive income from any other MLP or passive business interest. Suspended losses not offset by future net business income are deductible when the partner completely disposes of the MLP interest. (See Chapter 2 for a discussion of suspended losses from passive activities.) In any event, partners in an MLP taxed as a partnership may claim tax credits for rehabilitation expenses and low-income housing expenses in each case up to the $25,000/$12,500 deduction equivalent (discussed in Chapter 6, "Real Estate—The Most Tax-Favored Investment").

The Benefits of Oil and Gas Investments

If you are willing to assume some risk with respect to investments in the oil and gas industry, consider investing in a working interest in an oil and gas property but not as a limited partner or shareholder in a corporation. Working interests in oil and gas properties are excluded from the definition of a passive activity so long as the investor's liability in the working interest is not limited.

Although most investments in the oil and gas field were previously structured as limited partnerships, many deals now are being structured as general partnerships in which the investor becomes a general partner. Because no material participation requirement exists for such working interests, meaning the investor need not be involved in the management of the property, the losses generated by the partnership will flow through to the investor general partner and be deductible on the general partner's personal return subject only to the at-risk rules. However, as a general partner the investor would be individually liable for the partnership's debts, even if they exceed the amount of investment, so a significant degree of risk is assumed in this kind of deal.

Question: What sort of write-offs are available if I buy a working interest?

Answer: Investment in the oil and gas industry can provide an immediate write-off of intangible drilling costs, should the partnership elect to expense rather than capitalize these costs. If the partnership elects to capitalize the costs, they are recovered through depletion and depreciation. More than likely, however, the partnership will elect to expense the intangible drilling costs; then the partners can elect to either expense their proportionate shares of the intangible drilling costs personally or amortize them over a 10-year period of time. If a partner elects to expense the intangible drilling costs, to the extent that they would be considered excess intangible drilling costs, they are a tax preference item, and the alternative minimum tax may be triggered. Excess intangible drilling costs are those costs incurred in drilling productive wells, which exceed the amount of the deduction for the intangible drilling costs, had the taxpayer elected to amortize them over a 10-year period of time.

Depletion is the second incentive attracting investors to the oil and gas industry. The depletion deduction allows the investor who has purchased an interest in a producing well to shelter the cash distributions. This deduction is either computed on a cost basis or a percentage basis.

Cost depletion allows the investor to deduct each year a ratable portion of the individual's cost basis in the producing well, determined by the number of barrels of oil sold, until the basis is fully recovered. Percentage depletion allows annual write-offs usually of 15 percent of the gross income derived from the property and continues to be available to the taxpayer, even though the basis in the producing well has been recovered. However, to the extent that the taxpayer's percentage depletion deduction exceeds that person's basis in the well, the depletion allowance will be a tax preference item that may trigger application of the alternative minimum tax.

Insuring Your Future

Now more than ever, the key to your investments should be the economic return available to you and not the tax benefits derived from the investments since, in most cases outside of the real estate area, little or no tax benefits will be available. Life insurance is an investment that continues to receive favorable tax treatment, although it produces no write-offs or tax credits.

Investing in whole life insurance or universal life insurance allows you to obtain both life insurance protection and a savings vehicle. The savings vehicle in the life insurance contract, the cash surrender value, accumulates tax-free until the policy is surrendered. If the policy is never surrendered, but the insurance company pays the death benefits to the beneficiary, the payout usually will be free of income tax.

Question: Is my understanding of life insurance products correct? I can pay my premiums under the contract, have the policy accumulate in value tax-free, and get my money back tax-free.

Answer: Your understanding is basically correct; however, the definition of a life insurance contract has been more strictly written than was the case in the past. For life insurance contracts entered into after June 20, 1988, if the contract does not meet a strict definition, withdrawals from the contract's cash surrender value and loans against the policy will be taxable to you as income. Only if withdrawals and loans exceed the earnings under the contract would they be tax-free. All taxable amounts received under the contract prior to death would be subject to a 10-percent penalty unless received after you reached age 59 1/2, became disabled, or the distribution was one of a series of payments to be paid each year over your life expectancy.

A contract will not meet the new strict definition of a life insurance contract if, at any time during the policy's first seven years, the cumulative amount paid under the contract is greater than the net level premiums that would have been paid prior to that time if the contract had provided for paid-up future benefits at the end of seven years. This revised definition hurts those life insurance products designed and purchased primarily as investment vehicles rather than for life insurance protection.

Caution

Future tax legislation may bring about a change, even an end, to the general tax-free "inside build-up" of life insurance contracts. See Chapter 2 for information about the tax-free surrender by terminally ill individuals of all or portions of life insurance contracts without causing income tax liability.

Annuities as Investments

Commercial annuity contracts also enjoy tax-favored treatment. You purchase the annuity contract either in a lump sum or over a period of time. The contract will then provide you with a fixed annual payment beginning at a specified age (for example, beginning at age 65). As with life insurance contracts, the earnings generated by the annuity contract build up tax-free. Only when the annuitant begins receiving distributions from the contract will taxes be due.

Payment under an annuity contract will be subject to a 10 percent penalty on the taxable portion if made prior to age 59 1/2 unless the payment is on account of disability or is one of a series to be paid over the life expectancy of the recipient. If you borrow from the annuity contract, the loan amount will be considered a taxable cash withdrawal, to the extent of the interest buildup, and will be subject to the 10 percent penalty rule. If the loan exceeds the interest buildup, this excess is a tax-free recovery of your investment.

When you begin receiving the annuity, a portion of each payment will be tax-free to allow you to recover your investment in the contract. After your investment in the contract has been recovered, the entire annuity payment will be taxable as ordinary income.

A private annuity is simply an individual's promise to pay a fixed amount to another (the annuitant) for life in return for the annuitant's transfer of property or cash to the person paying the annuity. The tax rules governing the taxation of a private annuity are somewhat different from those governing a commercial annuity where there has been a transfer of property (as opposed to cash) to purchase the annuity. The annuitant will be deemed to have sold the property in exchange for the private annuity so that the annuity payment will consist of three elements: The recovery of basis in the property, the gain element, and the annuity element.

As with a commercial annuity, a portion of the private annuity payment will be tax-free until the basis in the transferred property has been recovered. The gain portion of the annuity is determined by subtracting the basis of the property from the present value of the annuity, using valuation tables. If the present value of the annuity is less than the value of the property, the excess will be considered a gift by the annuitant to the person paying the annuity, and compliance with the federal gift tax laws will be required.

Question: I am 69 years old, and I want to sell my business to my son. He has offered to pay me over 10 years. The sales proceeds and my Social Security will be my only retirement income. I am scared about how I will live when my son has finished paying for my business. Can I sell my business to him and receive an annuity instead of payments for a fixed time period?

Answer: Yes, you can sell your business and take back an annuity. However, depending on how many years you live, your son may pay for your business a couple of times over, or he could get a windfall.

Small Business Stock— Exclude Half of Your Gain But Get Minimal Shelter

Individuals investing in certain C corporations (see the discussion in Chapter 10 on "Organization Choices for Your Business") after August 10, 1993, and holding on to their Section 1202 small business stock for more than five years, will be able to exclude one-half of their gain from income. However, gain on sale of qualifying stock is taxed at no more than 14 percent, in that small business stock has a maximum 28-percent rate on the capital gain that is not excluded and not the general 15-percent rate (see Chapter 5, in "Gains and Losses").

As a result, until the scheduled reinstatement in 2009 of a general 20-percent rate on capital gain, the benefit of small business stock on your federal tax liability is small. However, the exclusion of one-half the gain will continue to have significant benefit on state income taxes in many jurisdictions.

Your excludable gain is limited to the greater of 10 times your basis in the stock or $10 million. A portion of your excluded gain is a tax preference item for alternative minimum tax purposes, 7 percent for gain after May 5, 2003 when the capital gain rates dropped. (See Chapter 1, "Introduction to Personal Tax Planning," for a discussion of the AMT.)

Your stock must be of original issue by the corporation, whether acquired for cash, property, or services. If acquired for services, the five-year holding period commences when you report income on receipt of the stock. (See Chapter

2 for a discussion of stock received for services.) The corporation must not be engaged in certain activities, including professional services, financial and brokerage services, consulting, or any other business in which the principal asset is the reputation or skill of one or more employees.

The issuing corporation must not have a basis of more than $50 million in its assets; neither real property nor portfolio securities may constitute more than 10 percent of assets. During the five-year period, the corporation must use at least 80 percent (by value) of its assets in the active conduct of a business.

Question: I am a general partner in a family partnership that has a number of investments, mostly in publicly traded stocks. Can the partnership invest in small business stock? If I make an additional investment personally, can I give it to my children during the five-year holding period?

Answer: Yes, partnerships and S corporations (see Chapter 10, "Business Tax Planning") can invest in a qualifying corporation. A partner or shareholder must hold his or her interest in the entity during the entire investment period in order to share in the exclusion of one-half of the gain. Recipients of a gift or inheritance of small business stock get to add the time the stock was held by transferors to their own holding period in order to determine whether the five-year requirement has been met.

Tax Planning

If you (or a partnership or S corporation in which you have an interest) sell small business stock that you owned for more than six months, you have a 60-day period in which to reinvest at least as much as the sales price in order to avoid gain recognition. If you acquire new small business stock for less than the sales price but for more than the basis of the stock (see Chapter 5), you will avoid recognition of a portion of the gain. Any gain not recognized is deferred until sale of the replacement stock. For stock owned more than six months but not more than one year, reinvestment offers the opportunity for any gain to receive favored long-term treatment on taxable disposition of the replacement stock, even if the five-year holding period for preferential treatment will not be satisfied. After the one-year holding period is satisfied, taking into account the period that the first stock was owned, any gain will be considered long-term.

Caution

The term *small business stock* is also used as another name for Section 1244 stock, discussed in Chapter 5. Section 1244 small business stock is eligible for ordinary loss treatment upon its worthlessness or sale at a loss. However, the criteria for small business stock under Section 1244 are significantly different than the criteria for exclusion of gain under Section 1202.

Investments in Empowerment Zones and Renewal Communities

Businesses that operate in certain areas of the country designated as "empowerment zones" or "renewal communities" qualify for certain tax breaks. The Secretaries of Housing and Urban Development and Agriculture are authorized to designate certain urban and rural areas of the country as empowerment zones or renewal communities. These designated areas meet certain statutorily prescribed criteria, including size, population, unemployment rate, and poverty level. State and local governments may assist in the development of empowerment zones and renewal communities by providing funding for businesses. The interest from bonds, the proceeds of which are invested in businesses located in empowerment zones and renewal communities, are exempt from federal income tax and may be exempt from state income tax.

The first $15,000 of wages paid to a resident of a designated empowerment zone who also works in the empowerment zone will qualify the employer for a 20-percent tax credit. In a designated renewal community, the credit is 15 percent on the first $10,000 of wages. The cost of buildings in a renewal community may be written off much faster than in other communities (see Chapter 10).

Additionally, a renewal community or empowerment zone business can write off up to $135,000 of the cost of tangible personal property purchased for use in the business prior to indexing the $100,000 base amount for cost of living in 2004. As discussed in Chapter 10, other businesses are limited to $100,000. Empowerment zone and renewal community businesses get an added $35,000 per year. The phaseout of the ability to expense this tangible personal property at $400,000 of qualifying purchases (prior to indexing in 2004) is computed by counting only one-half of the cost of such property used in the empowerment zone or renewal community.

All capital gain on the sale of renewal community business interests and assets is free of tax; whereas the exclusion of gain from the sale of small business stock, discussed earlier in this chapter, held for more than five years is 60 percent for empowerment zone businesses rather than the usual 50 percent.

Caution

The tax benefits for empowerment zones run out at the end of 2004 or 2009, depending on when the particular zone was designated; the tax beneffts for renewal communities expire at the end of 2009. The maximum writeoff for the cost of tangible personal property used in a renewal community or empowerment zone is scheduled to be reduced to $60,000 in 2006 with the phaseout commencing at $200,000 of qualifying purchases.

Filing Pointer

Did you ever want to live in the nation's capital? The Taxpayer Relief Act of 1997 created many tax benefits for the District of Columbia empowerment zone and provided a tax credit of $5,000 for first-time homebuyers who purchase a principal residence anywhere in the city. A first-time homebuyer is defined as an individual or a married couple who has not owned another principal residence in the District of Columbia during the year leading up to the date of contract or construction. The credit is phased out at modified AGI levels of between $110,000 and $130,000 for married couples and $70,000 and $90,000 for single individuals. Reduce your tax basis by the amount of the credit. Any unused credit carries forward indefinitely. However, the credit was scheduled to expire at the end of 2003.

CHAPTER 8

Marriage and Divorce

Your Wedding—Often a Taxing Experience

When two lower-income people marry, they usually discover that they will pay less taxes as husband and wife than they did as two individuals. When two middle-income people marry, they may not notice a difference in their tax bill. However, when two upper income people marry, they usually discover that they will pay more taxes as husband and wife than they did as two individuals. Some of these couples marry in December, causing them to be treated for tax purposes as married for the entire year. By waiting a few weeks until January, they might save enough in taxes to pay for their honeymoon.

Question: John and I are planning a holiday wedding. For the year coming to an end, we will each earn about $100,000 from wages and interest. We each have itemized deductions of about $15,000. Should we get married in December or wait a few weeks?

Answer: You will save about $1,194 by putting off the wedding until January, or you can schedule a New Year's Eve bash but recite your vows after midnight.

The computations that follow do not reflect the scheduled indexing of the middle brackets, the standard deduction, and the personal exemption for 2004.

They reflect the required reduction in most itemized deductions for married couples with modified adjusted gross income over $139,500 prior to 2004 indexing. (See Chapter 1, "Introduction to Personal Tax Planning," for a discussion of the phaseout of the ability to use most itemized deductions.)

	JOHN	MARY
Wages and Interest	$100,000	$100,000
Itemized/Standard Deduction	(15,000)	(15,000)
Exemptions	(3,050)	(3,050)
Taxable Income	$81,950	$81,950
Tax	$17,692	$17,692
Total Tax as Single Individuals	$35,384	

	JOHN AND MARY
Wages and Interest	$200,000
Itemized Deductions	(28,195)
Exemptions	(6,100)
Taxable Income	$165,705
Tax as a Married Couple	$36,578

Year-End Reminder

Couples planning to marry usually should wed before year-end if either has little or no income but are usually better off waiting until next year if both have a high income. The following table illustrates the *marriage tax penalty* for two high-income individuals and the equally significant disadvantage of being unmarried when at least one-half of a couple has little or no income. It is based on AGI and assumes no dependents, itemized deductions of 15 percent of AGI, and no other tax benefits limited as a result of income level. Computations do not reflect the scheduled indexing for inflation of the middle tax brackets, the standard deduction, and the personal exemption for 2004.

Year-End Reminder (cont.)

INDIVIDUAL 1 INCOME	TAX AS SINGLE	INDIVIDUAL 2 INCOME	TAX AS SINGLE	TAX AS MARRIED FILING JOINTLY	MARRIAGE PENALTY (−) OR BONUS (+)
$0	$0	$50,000	$6,673	$4,460	+ $2,213
$0	$0	$25,000	$2,230	$940	+ $1,290
$25,000	$2,230	$50,000	$6,673	$8,033	+ $870
$50,000	$6,673	$50,000	$6,673	$13,346	$0
$75,000	$11,985	$50,000	$6,673	$18,658	$0
$75,000	$11,985	$75,000	$11,985	$24,261	−$291
$100,000	$17,692	$75,000	$11,985	$30,421	−$744
$100,000	$17,692	$100,000	$17,692	$36,578	−$1,194

The Filing Status Trap upon Separation

If a marriage sours and children are involved, the custodial parent (this means the spouse with primary actual custody when there is legal joint custody) becomes eligible to file as head of household prior to divorce or legal separation under a decree of separate maintenance. However, the noncustodial parent is forced into using the highest tax brackets for individuals—those for married individuals filing separately. (See Chapter 1 for a detailed discussion of filing status alternatives.)

Question: My wife, Jane, and I separated in June 2003, and Jane has custody of our four-year-old daughter. What are the alternatives concerning our filing status for 2003?

Answer: Under a special rule, Jane will be considered as unmarried and eligible for head of household status because you were not a member of her household for the last six months of the year, provided the household is the principal residence of your daughter (regardless of whether Jane claims the dependency exemption or passes it to you). In contrast, unless you can persuade Jane to file a joint tax return, you will be forced to file as married filing separately until such time as your divorce is final or there is a legal decree of separate maintenance (a court decreed separation—not just a signed separation agreement between the parties).

You should negotiate with Jane to get her consent to a joint return. She may require that the tax liability be divided in such a way that she pays nothing more than what she would have paid filing as head of household. You should still come out ahead despite this guarantee; the premium that you would have to pay Jane probably will be made up by your retention of lower marginal tax brackets.

Caution

If you live in a community property state (see Chapter 1), you will normally need to divide community income equally on a separate return. However, if you and your spouse lived apart for the entire year and no community income was transferred between spouses, each should report what he or she made separately. See Chapter 1 for additional circumstances under which community property laws may be ignored.

Are You an "Innocent Spouse"?—Underpayments and Understatements

Because the IRS can collect from whichever individual it chooses on a joint return, as a divorcing individual with little or no separate tax liability, you should not sign a joint return if your spouse is insolvent, is fiscally irresponsible, or is unwilling to give you the return to mail with a certified check attached for any unpaid tax liability. You could pay the entire unpaid tax liability—a terrible price!

Even if you do not sign a joint return, you may have some legal exposure, especially if you were required to file a tax return and failed to do so. On a couple of occasions, most recently in a 1997 decision, the Tax Court determined that a former spouse "intended" to file a joint return and allowed the other spouse the benefit of the joint filing. To provide relief to the many affected spouses and former spouses, the "innocent spouse" rule was broadened in 1998. In the first three years afterward, new cases poured in to the IRS at the rate of almost 1,000 per week. The IRS granted innocent spouse relief in 27 percent of applications.

For liability shown on a joint return, an individual can obtain relief from the *underpayment* only if, "taking into account all the facts and circumstances, it is inequitable to hold a spouse liable for any portion of any unpaid tax." This situation is particularly intended to apply where the individual signed returns under duress or the other spouse diverted funds intended to pay taxes. However, pursuant to an August 11, 2003 Revenue Procedure, innocent spouse status for an underpayment is not available in the event of fraud or to the extent you received assets from your spouse for tax avoidance purpose. An applicant for relief should have a good tax compliance record for the years after those for which innocent spouse status is sought.

For liability not shown on a joint return but resulting from an *understate-*

ment of proper tax liability (see Chapter 13, "Dealing with the Internal Revenue Service"), an individual who is divorced, legally separated under a decree of separate maintenance (see the discussion later in this chapter), or has lived separate and apart from a spouse for more than one year due to estrangement can elect to be taxed only on the portion of the understatement, if any, attributable to him or her. The election may not be filed before your divorce or legal separation is final or before you have been otherwise separated for more than one year. You will not be let off the liability to the extent of an understatement of liability for which you had actual knowledge (unless you signed the return under duress) or to the extent that you received assets from your spouse for tax avoidance purposes. You will not be let off the liability at all if you and your spouse are conspiring in a fraudulent scheme.

An individual who is not divorced, legally separated under a decree of separate maintenance, or who has not lived separate and apart from a spouse for more than one year has a liberalized standard for innocent spouse relief in the case of an understatement of tax liability, but not nearly as favorable as one who is ending a marriage. Except when a return is signed under duress, such an individual must show not only that he or she had no actual knowledge of the understatement of tax but also that he or she had no reason to know of this shortfall. Additionally, the prospective innocent spouse must show that it would be inequitable to hold him or her liable.

An individual who is potentially liable for an understatement who does not meet either of the two formal standards for relief may still be removed of liability at the discretion of the IRS if it would be inequitable to hold that person liable.

If you must prove duress to get innocent spouse treatment, you must show a causal connection between the threats and your signing of the return. For example, in a 1994 case, the Tax Court was unsympathetic to an abused ex-wife's claim that her signature on two joint returns during their marriage was provided under duress. Despite testimony that she was verbally and physically abused, the former wife was found liable for more than $1 million in taxes arising out of a financial scam. The Court ruled that the taxpayer failed to prove that she was under duress at the precise time when the tax return was signed and that she would not have otherwise signed the return. In contrast, in a 2000 case, a Florida Bankruptcy Court found that an ex-wife signed two returns under duress in fear of what her husband, an attorney with masters degrees in both business and taxation, might do to either himself or her.

Use IRS Form 8857 to request innocent spouse treatment under any of the alternatives. You must file the form within two years of the commencement of collection activity by the IRS. Innocent spouse treatment cannot be applied to employment taxes on household workers (see the discussion of the "Nanny Tax" in Chapter 11, "Special Groups of Taxpayers") although they are reported and paid with the income tax return.

Caution

Watch for the earliest possible expiration of the two-year rule, particularly if you are awaiting divorce, legal separation, or one year of actual separation. The law does not give clear guidance as to the measurement date; future regulations should clarify. The legislative history indicates that the two years do not commence until the IRS attempts to reach assets or income of the potentially innocent spouse. For individuals who have faced IRS collection activity before July 22, 1998, the date of enactment of the law, the two years is measured from the earliest collection activity after enactment.

Caution

You cannot escape "knowledge" of an understatement of tax liability by turning a "blind eye" toward your spouse's actions. Additionally, you do not escape "knowledge" by failing to learn of the applicable tax law when you are aware of an item of income or expense.

Caution

Expect the IRS to talk to your spouse or former spouse to get a different view as to whether you are truly an innocent spouse. In a pair of 2000 decisions, the Tax Court determined that the "not so innocent" spouse has the right under the law to intervene in innocent spouse litigation. If you fear retaliation, you should write "Potential Domestic Abuse Case" at the top of Form 8857 and attach an explanatory statement to enjoy "additional safeguards."

Form **8857** (Rev. May 2002) Department of the Treasury Internal Revenue Service

Request for Innocent Spouse Relief

(And Separation of Liability and Equitable Relief)

▶ **Do not file with your tax return.** ▶ **See instructions.**

OMB No. 1545-1596

Do not file this form if:

- You did not file a joint return for the year(s) for which you are requesting relief. However, if you lived in a community property state, see instructions.
- All or part of your overpayment was (or is expected to be) applied against your spouse's past-due debt (such as child support). Instead, file **Form 8379,** Injured Spouse Claim and Allocation, to apply to have your share of the overpayment refunded to you.

TIP *To see if you may qualify for* ***Innocent Spouse Relief,*** *go to* ***www.irs.gov,*** *click on "Individuals," "Innocent Spouses," and "Explore if you are an Eligible Innocent Spouse"; or see* ***Pub. 971,*** *Innocent Spouse Relief.*

Part I See **Spousal Notification** in the instructions.

Your current name (see instructions) | Your social security number

Your current home address (number and street). If a P.O. box, see instructions. | Apt. no.

City, town or post office, state, and ZIP code. If a foreign address, see instructions. | Daytime phone number

If you have been a victim of domestic abuse and fear that filing a claim for innocent spouse relief will result in retaliation, check here . . . . ▶ ☐

Part II

1 Enter the year(s) for which you are requesting relief from liability of tax ▶ ______

2 Information about the person to whom you were married as of the end of the year(s) in line 1.

Name | Social security number

Current home address (number and street). If a P.O. box, see instructions. | Apt. no.

City, town or post office, state, and ZIP code. If a foreign address, see instructions. | Daytime phone number

3 Do you have an **Understatement of Tax** (that is, the IRS has determined there is a difference between the tax shown on your return and the tax that should have been shown)?
☐ **Yes.** Go to Part III. ☐ **No.** Go to Part V.

Part III

4 Are you divorced from the person listed on line 2 or has that person died?
☐ **Yes.** Go to line 7. ☐ **No.** Go to line 5.

5 Are you legally separated from the person listed on line 2?
☐ **Yes.** Go to line 7. ☐ **No.** Go to line 6.

6 Have you lived apart from the person listed on line 2 at all times during the 12-month period prior to filing this form?
☐ **Yes.** Go to line 7. ☐ **No.** Go to Part IV.

7 If line **4, 5,** or **6** is **Yes,** you may request **Separation of Liability** by **attaching a statement** (see instructions). Check here ▶ ☐ and go to Part IV.

Part IV

8 Is the understatement of tax due to the **Erroneous Items** of your spouse (see instructions)?
☐ **Yes.** You may request **Innocent Spouse Relief** by **attaching a statement** (see instructions). Go to Part V.
☐ **No.** You may request **Equitable Relief** for the understatement of tax. Check **Yes** in Part V.

Part V

9 Do you have an **Underpayment of Tax** (that is, tax that is properly shown on your return but not paid) or another tax liability that qualifies for **Equitable Relief** (see instructions)?
☐ **Yes.** You may request **Equitable Relief** by **attaching a statement** (see instructions).
☐ **No.** You cannot file this form unless line 3 is **Yes.**

Under penalties of perjury, I declare that I have examined this form and any accompanying schedules and statements, and to the best of my knowledge and belief, they are true, correct, and complete. Declaration of preparer (other than taxpayer) is based on all information of which preparer has any knowledge.

Sign Here Keep a copy for your records. ▶ Your signature | Date

Paid Preparer's Use Only Preparer's signature ▶ | Date | Check if self-employed ☐ | Preparer's SSN or PTIN

Firm's name (or yours if self-employed), address, and ZIP code ▶ | EIN | Phone no.

For Privacy Act and Paperwork Reduction Act Notice, see instructions. Form **8857** (Rev. 5-2002)

ISA STF FED9049F

Form 8857, Request for Innocent Spouse Relief

Filing Pointer

If you feel that you are an innocent spouse because your husband or wife agreed to indemnify you against tax liability on a joint return, but you did not meet the standard for being off the hook with the IRS, there may be added hope for recovery. In 1995 the U.S. Supreme Court declined to hear an appeal from a decision of the Fourth Circuit Court of Appeals holding that a spouse's indemnification to the other spouse is not dischargeable in bankruptcy.

Separation and the Dependency Allowance

A controversial issue over the years has involved the question of who gets to claim the children as dependents on a separate return. Given that personal exemptions may be used in full without phaseout by individuals in some cases with marginal tax brackets as high as 33 percent, an exemption in 2004 may be worth as much as $1,017 (even prior to that year's indexing for inflation)—irrespective of any state tax savings. Add the child credit of $1,000 or an educational tax credit if you are eligible (see Chapter 3, "Deductions and Credits—For Itemizers and Nonitemizers") and the right to claim a child as a dependent, from birth through college years, can be worth more than $30,000 in tax savings. For that reason, dependency allowances are usually an issue in negotiating a separation agreement.

Present law awards the exemptions automatically to the custodial parent (again, that parent who has actual physical custody of the child for the greater part of the year) unless the custodial parent releases the right to claim the benefit. This release can be claimed by having the custodial parent sign IRS Form 8332 on an annual basis, an indefinite basis, or for a specific number of years. The noncustodial parent attaches Form 8332 to his or her tax return.

However, in a 1997 decision, the Tax Court determined that the general rule giving the dependency allowance to the custodial parent in the absence of a waiver is not applicable in the year of separation when the separation occurs in the second half of the year and there is no divorce or court-decreed separation by year-end. Rather, the dependency allowance goes to the spouse providing majority support of the dependent. See the discussion on court-decreed separations later in this chapter.

Pre-1985 instruments are governed by prior law, allowing the exemption to the noncustodial parent when authorized in the instrument and where the noncustodial parent provides at least $600 per year in child support.

In a September 26, 2003 decision, the Tax Court determined that the same rules applicable to divorced and separated individuals also apply to never married individuals disputing a dependency allowance for their child.

Tax Planning

Noncustodial parents are well advised to have a specific provision placed in the separation agreement requiring the custodial parent to execute Form 8332 or, even better, get the Form signed with the separation agreement. The Tax Court ruled in 1995 and again in 2000 that a noncustodial parent cannot claim the exemption without an executed Form 8332, even if the custodial parent signed an agreement or is under court order to pass the exemption on to the noncustodial parent. Custodial parents are well advised to sign the IRS Form on an annual, rather than an indefinite, basis so that a noncustodial parent delinquent in child support does not get the dependency allowance.

Form **8332**
(Rev. December 2000)
Department of the Treasury
Internal Revenue Service

Release of Claim to Exemption for Child of Divorced or Separated Parents

▶ Attach to noncustodial parent's return **each year** exemption is claimed.
Caution: *Do not use this form if you were never married.*

OMB No. 1545-0915

Attachment Sequence No. **115**

Name of noncustodial parent claiming exemption

Noncustodial parent's social security number (SSN) ▶

Part I **Release of Claim to Exemption for Current Year**

I agree not to claim an exemption for ______________________
Name(s) of child (or children)

for the tax year 20 ______

______________________ Signature of custodial parent releasing claim to exemption
______________________ Custodial parent's SSN
______________________ Date

Note: If you choose not to claim an exemption for this child (or children) for future tax years, also complete Part II.

Part II **Release of Claim to Exemption for Future Years** (If completed, see **Noncustodial parent** below.)

I agree not to claim an exemption for ______________________
Name(s) of child (or children)

for the tax year(s) ______________________
(Specify. See instructions.)

______________________ Signature of custodial parent releasing claim to exemption
______________________ Custodial parent's SSN
______________________ Date

General Instructions

Purpose of form. If you are a **custodial parent** and you were ever married to the child's **noncustodial parent,** you may use this form to release your claim to your child's exemption. To do so, complete this form (or a similar statement containing the same information required by this form) and give it to the noncustodial parent who will claim the child's exemption. The noncustodial parent must attach this form or similar statement to his or her tax return **each year** the exemption is claimed.

You are the **custodial parent** if you had custody of the child for most of the year. You are the **noncustodial parent** if you had custody for a shorter period of time or did not have custody at all. For the definition of custody, see **Pub. 501,** Exemptions, Standard Deduction, and Filing Information.

Support test for children of divorced or separated parents. Generally, the custodial parent is treated as having provided over half of the child's support if:

- The child received over half of his or her total support for the year from one or both of the parents **and**
- The child was in the custody of one or both of the parents for more than half of the year.

Note: *Public assistance payments, such as Temporary Assistance for Needy Families (TANF), are not support provided by the parents.*

For this support test to apply, the parents must be one of the following:

- Divorced or legally separated under a decree of divorce or separate maintenance,
- Separated under a written separation agreement, or
- Living apart at all times during the last 6 months of the year.

Caution: *This support test does not apply to parents who never married each other.*

If the support test applies, and the other four dependency tests in your tax return instruction booklet are also met, the custodial parent can claim the child's exemption.

Exception. The custodial parent will not be treated as having provided over half of the child's support if **any** of the following apply.

- The custodial parent agrees not to claim the child's exemption by signing this form or similar statement.
- The child is treated as having received over half of his or her total support from a person under a multiple support agreement (**Form 2120,** Multiple Support Declaration).
- A pre-1985 divorce decree or written separation agreement states that the noncustodial parent can claim the child as a dependent. But the noncustodial parent must provide at least $600 for the child's support during the year. This rule does not apply if the decree or agreement was changed after 1984 to say that the noncustodial parent cannot claim the child as a dependent.

Additional information. For more details, see **Pub. 504,** Divorced or Separated Individuals.

Specific Instructions

Custodial parent. You may agree to release your claim to the child's exemption for the current tax year or for future years, or both.

- Complete Part I if you agree to release your claim to the child's exemption for the current tax year.
- Complete Part II if you agree to release your claim to the child's exemption for any or all future years. If you do, write the specific future year(s) or "all future years" in the space provided in Part II.

TIP To help ensure future support, you may not want to release your claim to the child's exemption for future years.

Noncustodial parent. Attach this form or similar statement to your tax return for **each year** you claim the child's exemption. You may claim the exemption **only** if the other four dependency tests in your tax return instruction booklet are met.

Note: *If the custodial parent released his or her claim to the child's exemption for any future year, you must attach a copy of this form or similar statement to your tax return for each future year that you claim the exemption.* ***Keep a copy for your records.***

Paperwork Reduction Act Notice. We ask for the information on this form to carry out the Internal Revenue laws of the United States. You are required to give us the information. We need it to ensure that you are complying with these laws and to allow us to figure and collect the right amount of tax.

You are not required to provide the information requested on a form that is subject to the Paperwork Reduction Act unless the form displays a valid OMB control number. Books or records relating to a form or its instructions must be retained as long as their contents may become material in the administration of any Internal Revenue law. Generally, tax returns and return information are confidential, as required by Internal Revenue Code section 6103.

The time needed to complete and file this form will vary depending on individual circumstances. The estimated average time is:

Recordkeeping . . . . 7 min.
Learning about the law or the form . . . . 5 min.
Preparing the form . . . . 7 min.
Copying, assembling, and sending the form to the IRS . . . . 14 min.

If you have comments concerning the accuracy of these time estimates or suggestions for making this form simpler, we would be happy to hear from you. You can write to the Tax Forms Committee, Western Area Distribution Center, Rancho Cordova, CA 95743-0001. **Do not** send the form to this address. Instead, see the Instructions for Form 1040 or Form 1040A.

ISA
STF FED6615F

Form **8332** (Rev. 12-2000)

Form 8332, Release of Claim to Exemption for Child of Divorced or Separated Parents

Caution

Who is the custodial parent and who is the noncustodial parent when the former spouses alternate weeks of physical custody? In a 2002 decision, the Tax Court denied both spouses the dependency exemption and the child credit since neither could prove the *greater* period of custody. The sparring parties would have fared better by agreeing to claim the benefits in alternate years.

Tax Planning

As discussed in Chapters 1 and 3, personal exemptions, the child credit, and educational credits are phased out and become unavailable for high-income individuals. If one parent may have AGI greater than the level when the benefits would be unavailable, it may be advisable to provide for transfer of the benefits to the parent who will be able to use them. This can be done within the separation agreement.

Controversy

Can a state court require a custodial parent to relinquish the right to claim a child as a dependent? Although federal law prevails over conflicting state law, a majority of state courts have deliberated the issue and consider the federal law to be silent, such that they can order the passing of one or more exemptions to the noncustodial parent.

Separation and Credit for Tax Prepayments

With the filing of a separate return for the first time following marital separation, along with the issue of who gets to claim the children as dependents, there may be a short-term larger issue of who gets credit for tax prepayments.

Prepayments take one of three forms:

1. Withholding at the source (usually on wages)
2. Application of a prior year's tax refund to estimated taxes
3. Other estimated tax payments

Withholding is credited to the spouse who earned the underlying income, equally in community property states (see Chapter 1) where the spouses each report 50 percent of the income. Although estimated taxes caused by the application of a prior year's separate tax refund or by payment with one name on the voucher are credited solely to that individual, it is unclear who receives the credit on the separate return for these tax prepayments when they arise by application of a prior year's joint tax refund or by payment with both names on the voucher.

Controversy

The IRS position is that, in the absence of an agreement between the spouses, estimated taxes (including application of a prior year refund to estimated taxes pursuant to a 2001 IRS Legal Memorandum) are credited based on their proportionate tax liabilities. However, recent court decisions have tended to look to the source of the funds; that is, whose prior year's income and payments caused the prior year's tax refund and whose money was paid in with the joint voucher. These questions raise additional issues as to the ownership of cash, and ownership issues are generally determined by state law.

Planning Your Divorce—More Tax Considerations

The timing of a divorce has tax considerations similar to the timing of a marriage.

Question: My wife, Paula, and I will soon be divorcing, but we can finalize the divorce after year-end. Paula has been a housewife and has had no income of her own while raising our two children. My income, exclusively from wages, is $80,000. Our itemized deductions, all belonging to me or paid by me, are $11,000. Should the divorce become final this year or next?

Answer: Look at the numbers, and you see a big difference by waiting until after year-end.

	AS MARRIED FILING JOINTLY	AS SINGLE
Wages	$80,000	$80,000
Itemized Deductions	(11,000)	(11,000)
Exemptions	(12,200)	(9,150)
Taxable Income	$56,800	$59,850
Tax after Credit of $1,000 per Child	$5,820	$9,772

These computations do not reflect the scheduled indexing of brackets, the standard deduction, and the personal exemptions for 2004. It is also assumed that the separation agreement gives the dependency allowances for the children to you.

More than $3,900 is saved by delaying the divorce until after December 31. In the succeeding year, your increased tax liability may be mitigated if you are required to make deductible alimony payments to Paula.

Year-End Reminder

When a marriage is terminating, the timing of the divorce or court-decreed separation needed to be unmarried for tax purposes is flexible in light of the local court calendar. If both spouses have significant income, it is usually best to be unmarried before year-end. However, when one spouse has little or no income, it is usually best (from a tax perspective) to delay divorce or court-decreed separation until after year-end.

Caution

A court-decreed separation has different meanings in different states. In any event, the mere signing of a separation agreement does not make a couple unmarried in and of itself.

Maximizing the Alimony Deduction

Alimony constitutes taxable income to the recipient and is deductible to the payer, regardless of whether the payer itemizes. Alimony means any payment in cash if

- The payment is received by or on behalf of a spouse under a divorce or separation instrument, which includes annulment if the support requirements under state law are similar for divorce and separation.
- The divorce or separation instrument does not designate the payment as an amount other than alimony (for example, property settlement or child support).
- In the case of an individual legally separated from a spouse under a decree of divorce or of separate maintenance, the spouses are not members of the same household at the time the payment is made.
- Liability to make future payments as alimony, or otherwise, stops by agreement or by law upon the death of the recipient spouse.

Cash payments of rent, mortgages, life insurance premiums on the payer's life where the recipient spouse is the owner of the policy, and other obligations of the payer spouse are examples of payments received on behalf of a spouse which qualify as alimony. In the case of mortgage payments, the payer spouse would deduct the entire amount of the mortgage as alimony if it otherwise qualifies, and the recipient spouse would report this amount as income. The recipient would then be able to deduct mortgage interest and property taxes paid on behalf of the recipient spouse to the extent otherwise permitted under the tax law. (See Chapter 4, "Deductions—For Itemizers Only," concerning limitations on qualified residence interest and Chapter 1 concerning the phaseout of most itemized deductions by high-income individuals.)

If the payer spouse continues to have an ownership interest in the property for which he or she makes payments in full, the law is more complicated. When a divorce is final and the ownership is typically 50-50 between the former spouses as tenants in common, the payer spouse treats one-half of the mortgage payments and one-half of other home-related expenses as deductible alimony and one-half of property taxes and one-half of mortgage interest (subject to qualified residence interest limitations) as itemized deductions. The recipient spouse treats one-half of the mortgage payments and one-half of the other home-related expenses as alimony income, offset in part by one-half of property taxes and one-half of mortgage interest (also subject to qualified residence interest limitations).

However, prior to the final divorce, most couples in noncommunity property states (see Chapter 1) hold real property as tenants by the entireties or as joint tenants with right of survivorship. The IRS and the courts agree in such cases that one-half of mortgage payments allocable to principal are deductible alimony to the payer and, accordingly, alimony income to the recipient. They agree that the entire property taxes are an itemized deduction to the payer and are not alimony income to the recipient. With the exception of mortgage interest, where the IRS and the Tax Court differ, they agree that other home-related expenses are neither deductible alimony expense to the payer nor alimony income to the recipient.

Controversy

The IRS and the Tax Court disagree as to the handling of mortgage payments allocable to interest in the case of tenants by the entireties property or joint tenants with right of survivorship property. The Tax Court accords the same treatment for mortgage interest as it does for property taxes, allowing the interest as an itemized deduction subject to the qualified residence interest limitation. In contrast, the IRS treats one-half of the mortgage interest in that manner and treats the other one-half as deductible alimony to the payer and alimony income to the recipient. Until resolution of the issue, affected taxpayers may want to use whichever approach is more favorable.

Tax Planning

When a joint return cannot or will not be filed following separation, the after-tax costs of spousal support to the payer will be increased in the absence of a written instrument compelling payment. The payer of marital support should strive to obtain a written agreement or court order in order to get the deduction. Otherwise, support payments will be treated as voluntary and nondeductible.

Year-End Reminder

In general, make your current alimony payment by December 31 to get the tax deduction in the year coming to an end. However, prepayment of more than one month in advance may be challenged by the IRS as nondeductible.

Caution

The IRS is matching the alimony payer's deduction to the income reported by the recipient using the recipient's Social Security number as reported by the payer. Along with improper deductions and unreported income, the IRS can expect to find inconsistencies when a check was mailed in late December and properly deducted by the payer but was received in early January and properly deferred by the recipient.

Question: My former wife and I were divorced in August 2003. During 2003 I paid my attorney $9,000 to negotiate the terms of our separation and property settlement agreement, which included child custody provisions and the terms of spousal and child support obligations. Can I deduct this amount on my 2003 income tax return? I also paid my wife's attorney fees of $12,000. Can I deduct these payments?

Answer: Unfortunately, legal expenses paid in connection with divorce proceedings usually are classified as personal nondeductible expenses. However, the legal expenses that can be allocated to tax advice, to the protection of business income, or to securing alimony can be claimed as a miscellaneous itemized deduction to the extent the total exceeds 2 percent of your AGI (see Chapter 4). Ask your attorney to break down the $9,000 fee to show how much of the fee is properly allocable to tax planning advice (for example, alimony versus child support, dependency exemption) and how much is properly attributable to protection of business income.

Note that the legal fees are not deductible merely because income-producing property or even business property may have to be transferred to a former spouse under the terms of a property settlement agreement. Amounts paid to your former wife's attorney are in any event nondeductible unless you remain eligible to file a joint return with her and elect to do so.

Avoid Rapid Declines in Annual Alimony Payments

In the third calendar year of alimony payments, the payer spouse must pick up income under a complicated recapture provision for excess payments from year two to the extent that the amount of alimony payments paid during the second year of alimony exceeds the amount paid during the third year by $15,000. Additionally, there is recapture in year three when the amount of payments during the first year exceeds the average of the payments in the second year (after that year's recapture) and the third year by more than $15,000.

This recapture rule is not applicable to court-ordered support during the pendency of litigation for divorce or separate maintenance. The rule is also not applicable if either spouse dies before the close of the third year of alimony or if the recipient spouse remarries before the close of that third year, when the alimony payments cease by reason of the death or remarriage. Similarly, this rule is not applicable when payments are contingent upon a percent of compensation or business income. Additionally, this rule may be rebutted by either a taxpayer or the IRS by showing that the reduction in alimony was determined independently of any events related to the children.

Illustration

Bob pays Susan $1,500 per month in alimony for each of the 12 months of 2004 and 2005. Alimony ceases with the December 2005 payment under the terms of the agreement. There is $3,000 in excess payments for the second year, because the $18,000 paid in 2005 exceeds by $3,000 the amount paid in 2006 ($0) plus the $15,000 base. No excess payments exist for 2004, the first year. The $18,000 paid in 2004 does not exceed by $15,000 the average of $15,000 and $0, the former being the 2005 payments less the $3,000 excess for that year and the latter being the 2006 payments.

Consequently, Bob will report $3,000 in income from the recomputation, and Susan will get a deduction of $3,000 from the recomputation, with the taxable event occurring in 2006 in each case.

Tax Planning

To avoid the recapture rule, alimony payments should not drop by more than $15,000 between the second year of payments and the third year of payments. Additionally, although the drop in alimony from the first year of payments to the third year of payments can exceed $15,000, payments for the first year should not be more than $15,000 larger than the average of the payments for the second and third years.

Question: I have agreed to pay rehabilitative alimony to my wife for three years to enable her to complete her education. We have agreed on $3,000 per month as alimony for each month of calendar year 2004, $2,250 per month during calendar year 2005, and $1,500 per month during calendar year 2006. Will all of the payments be fully deductible to me as alimony without any recomputation required in 2006?

Answer: Yes, no excess payments exist for 2005, because the difference in payments between 2005 and 2006 is only $9,000. Also, no excess payments exist for 2004, because the $36,000 to be paid during that year exceeds the average payments for 2005 and 2006 by only $13,500.

Convert Cash Payments Intended As Property Settlements into Alimony

The purpose behind the excess front loading rule requiring recapture of certain purported alimony payments was to discourage characterizing property settlements as alimony. However, it is still possible to set up payments arising from property settlements as deductible alimony to the payer, provided the payments are made over three calendar years (in as little as 14 months) and do not reduce from year to year in a manner giving rise to liability on the excess payments. The payments would have to cease upon death of the spouse receiving alimony.

Question: I have agreed to pay my wife $500 per month as alimony for five years. Additionally, I am going to remain in our house, but my wife wants $12,000 for her equity in the property. I cannot afford to pay her the payments in a lump sum. Is there any way that I can deduct these additional payments?

Answer: If the payments on account of the house are made part of the alimony package in which, for example, you would pay her $700 per month as alimony or perhaps a bit more to take into account an interest factor on the equity, you would be permitted to deduct these additional payments provided that they are labeled as alimony or spousal support and otherwise meet all of the criteria for deductibility. Your wife, however, would be taxed on the payments.

If she is in a much lower marginal tax bracket than you, this approach could be particularly valuable.

Filing Pointer

Just because a state court considers payment under a separation agreement as constituting a property settlement does not necessarily mean that the payment is not alimony for tax purposes. In 1989 the Tax Court ruled that monthly payments labeled as combined alimony and property settlement were deductible alimony to the payer despite a prior state court's determination that the payments represented a property settlement under state law. Similarly, the Court held in 1994 that it could determine based on all facts and circumstances whether monthly payments labeled as alimony and enforced by a state court were really a property settlement.

Convert Cash Payments Intended as Child Support to Alimony

Until two decades ago, a spouse making a combined payment for the support of the other spouse and children could get a deduction for the entire amount by using such wording as "for the support of my wife and children." Unless an amount was specifically allocated to child support, nondeductible to the payer and tax-free to the recipient, the payments had to be treated as alimony, even when they declined as a result of a child reaching adulthood, for example. This was known as the "Lester Rule," named after a famous 1961 U.S. Supreme Court case.

The ability to "Lesterize" payments is diminished today; however, opportunities are still available. When the intention is that both alimony and child support be paid, amounts considered by the parties to be child support can be labeled as alimony provided the reduction does not occur on the happening of a contingency related to the child, such as the child's attaining a certain age, marrying, dying, or leaving school.

Temporary Regulations provide that a reduction within six months before or after the date when a child attains the age of 18, 21, or the local age of majority is presumed to be clearly associated with a contingency relating to the child unless the reduction is a complete termination of payments that have been made in at least six calendar years. Additionally, the presumption applies when payments are to be reduced on two or more occasions within one year before or after different children of the payer spouse attain a certain age between 18 and 24. These presumptions are tricky; computations are based on years, months, and days.

Illustration

John's older child was born on January 1, 1987, and his younger child was born on October 12, 1989. He and his wife have agreed on a combination of alimony and child support, which will be reduced on two occasions. Assuming a legal age of 18 or 21, the first presumption will jeopardize an alimony deduction if the initial decline in alimony occurs between July 1, 2004 and July 1, 2005, between April 12, 2007 and July 1, 2008, or between April 12, 2010, and April 12, 2011. Even if the initial decline in alimony occurs during either window, July 2, 2005, to April 11, 2007, or July 2, 2008 to April 11, 2010, the second presumption could also cause loss of the deduction if the second reduction occurs before April 12, 2010.

Why? If a reduction in support occurs when the older child is between 18 1/2 and 20 1/2, no further reduction may occur when the younger child is within this age range. Two reductions would exist within one year before or after different children attained a certain age between 18 and 24. Here, that age would be 19 1/2; one reduction would have occurred within one year before that age 18 1/2, and the other would have occurred within one year after that age 20 1/2.

If a second reduction of alimony is desired before April 12, 2010, the first reduction must occur before July 1, 2004, when the older child reaches age 17 1/2. Then a window is created for the second reduction. Assuming a first reduction in support on June 30, 2004, the second reduction may occur after April 12, 2009, and before April 12, 2010, (when the younger child is between age 19 1/2 and 20 1/2) without running awry of either presumption, which could convert deductible alimony to nondeductible child support.

Question: My wife and I have one 13-year-old son. The age of majority in my state is 18. I want to maximize my tax deduction over the four years that I have agreed to pay alimony to my wife and the three years for which I am obligated to pay child support. How can I maximize my tax benefit?

Answer: Do little or no allocation specifically to child support. Make the preponderance of payments for the benefit of your wife and have these payments terminate on a specific calendar date, which is not within six months of your son's 18th birthday or within six months of his 21st birthday.

Caution

Despite the favorable tax considerations of an allocation to alimony, be careful. In many states, alimony may be made nonmodifiable under the terms of a separation agreement. However, the general rule is that child support cannot be made nonmodifiable. Consequently, too low an allocation to child support could have your spouse asking a court for an increase in payments.

Ensuring the Tax-Free Nature of Property Settlements

One of the most widely heralded changes in the tax law in recent years was legislation making the transfer of appreciated property between spouses generally tax-free upon the termination of their marriage. Prior to the law change, when appreciated property was transferred to a spouse in consideration for a reduced alimony payment or for no alimony payment, not only did the transferor spouse give up the property or an interest in the property, but that spouse also could be taxed on the appreciation.

Now interspousal property transfers are not taxed (except for certain ordinary income assets, as discussed in the next section) if they occur during the course of a marriage or thereafter, but only if the transfer occurs within one year after divorce or can otherwise be shown to be "related to cessation of the marriage." Where interest on a delayed transfer of property is not stated, none will be imputed under the rules set forth in Chapter 10, "Business Tax Planning." However, stated interest is taxed to the recipient.

Under Temporary Regulations, a transfer of property is related to the cessation of the marriage if it occurs not more than six years after the date on which the marriage ceases and is pursuant to a written instrument. Transfers that occur more than one year after divorce and that are not made pursuant to a written instrument or transfers that occur more than six years after divorce are presumed not to be related to the cessation of the marriage; however, even this presumption may be rebutted based on the facts and circumstances.

Transfers to nonresident alien spouses and transfers of installment obligations or property with liabilities in excess of the tax basis in the underlying property into trust are exceptions to the general nontaxability rule.

Caution

The importance of proper wording of a separation agreement to place any tax burden where intended cannot be overstated. Poor wording can cost dollars, even hundreds of thousands of dollars. Even a court judgment can be both ambiguous and costly as a New Jersey woman found out in a 1994 decision of the Third Circuit Court of Appeals, which reversed a Tax Court decision in her favor.

A state court had previously awarded the woman a "one-third interest in the business operation of the sole proprietorship . . ." This "non-management interest" was to be "solely held for the purposes of receiving the plaintiff's one-third interest at the time the property may be sold . . ." The state court did not make it clear whether it created an "ownership interest" in the wife (making her share of the cash proceeds taxable to her) or a "payment of money contingent as to time and amount" (leaving the entire cash proceeds taxable to the husband). The federal appeals court found that the wife, in fact, received an ownership interest and had to pay her own taxes.

continues

Caution (cont.)

The Tax Court, faced with a similar issue in a case decided in 2002, determined that the former wife of a dentist receiving a portion of proceeds paid to her former husband from the sale of his practice had not received an ownership interest in the note and, accordingly, received tax-free payments of principal. The interest amount that she received from her former husband was taxed to her. (Note that he had to report what was, in essence, the same interest income on payment from his purchaser, but can he offset that interest income with interest expense?)

Controversy

The IRS holds that interest paid directly to a spouse is necessarily personal in nature and nondeductible unless qualified residence interest (see Chapter 4). However, the Tax Court disagrees, and twice since 1997 has permitted interest on debt between spouses to be characterized based on the nature of the interspousal transfer giving rise to the interest payment. Consequently, for example, you should be able to successfully argue (in Tax Court, at least) that the interest is other than nondeductible personal interest when paid on a marital monetary award attributable to dividing business, investment, or passive activity assets (see Chapter 2, "Taxable and Tax-Free Income and Benefits").

Question: My husband and I will be getting a divorce within the next few months, and we are in the process of negotiating a property settlement. As part of that settlement, my husband wants his share of the equity from the marital home, but I want to continue living in the house. If I take out a loan to buy his share of the house, can I deduct the interest on my tax return?

Answer: The IRS has announced that, under forthcoming regulations, debt incurred to acquire your husband's interest in the house will be considered acquisition debt (see Chapter 4). However, the interest may be deductible as qualified residence interest only if the house remains your principal residence (or is your second residence), the total acquisition debt does not exceed the lesser of the home's value or $1 million, and, finally, the loan that you take out to buy your husband's interest is secured by the home.

Suppose that your house is currently worth $100,000, and the mortgage incurred to buy the property has been paid down to $40,000. This would mean that you would need $30,000 to buy your husband's equity in the property. This $30,000 loan, together with the $40,000 existing mortgage, would both consti-

Controversy

Sometimes the IRS gets "whipsawed" and loses tax cases both against the wife and the husband on the same facts and legal issue. It happened in 1994 when the Tax Court decided that a husband could not be taxed on a corporate buyout of his wife's shares in a hamburger franchise, owned 50 percent by each, when the separation agreement stated that the parties "shall cause the corporation to pay wife . . . for wife's stock in the corporation." The Ninth Circuit Court of Appeals had determined two years previously that the wife could not be taxed either.

Thus, under a property settlement, when a payment for the benefit of one spouse is made by a corporation to be retained by the other spouse, is the transaction a taxable redemption to the first spouse or is it constructively a taxable redemption to the second spouse followed by a tax-free transfer to the first spouse? In two separate 2000 decisions, one by the Eleventh Circuit Court of Appeals and the other by the Tax Court, payments by the corporation were determined to be tax-free to the spouse who was terminating her interest in the corporation.

To prevent future whipsaw, the IRS issued Final Regulations on January 12, 2003 that generally cause the spouse terminating an interest in the corporation upon the marital termination to enjoy tax-free treatment. The spouse using the corporation to accomplish a property settlement faces taxation on the stock redemption. However, the spouses by clear written instrument can shift tax on the redemption to the spouse terminating an interest.

tute acquisition debt, and the interest on both of these debts would be qualified residence interest. (See Chapter 6, "Real Estate—The Most Tax-Favored Investment," concerning each spouse's ability to exclude $250,000 of gain if the principal residence is sold rather than transferred to one spouse.)

Question: My former husband and I purchased some land in 1979 for $25,000. When we divorced in 1986, it was worth $75,000, and he transferred the property to me under the terms of our separation agreement. I have a contract to sell the land for $100,000. Will I pay taxes on a gain of $25,000, $75,000, or $25,000 plus an additional amount representing my share of the appreciation while we were married?

Answer: You will pay taxes on a gain of $75,000, because your tax basis in the property is $25,000, reflecting a carryover of the original basis (see Chapter 5, "Gains and Losses") in the property that you had with your former spouse. Because the transfer of his interest in the property to you in 1986 was not taxable to him, you are not entitled to adjust your basis upward. If the transfer of the house to you had occurred before July 19, 1984, and the transfer was in consideration for a reduction or elimination in alimony, you probably could have added one-half of the appreciation during the marriage to your original $25,000 basis (unless the transfer occurred in 1984 before July 19, and you agreed that the transfer would be nontaxable).

Question: My ex-wife and I have agreed to divide the proceeds on the sale of a rental property 75 percent to her and 25 percent to me, even though we own the property equally. Could the IRS tax me on 50 percent?

Answer: Your fears are well founded. In a 1997 decision, the Tax Court determined that gain on property sales between divorcing spouses must be divided based on the percentage of ownership. If you had not gotten scared, you might have walked away with nothing.

Filing Pointer

Change the percentages of legal ownership by deed prior to the sale to shift the tax burden to parallel the distribution of proceeds. However, if the spouse who receives the greater proceeds is in a lower tax bracket than the other spouse, the IRS could view any transfer of title at or shortly before closing as a sham. However, if the spouse receiving the larger share keeps the extra amount, a challenge by the IRS probably would be unsuccessful.

Question: I live in a "marital property" state in which property acquired during the marriage is considered marital until divorce, even if it is titled in your spouse's sole name. My estranged husband is selling a piece of real estate that was just in his name, even though we bought it together two years after we were married. We will definitely not file a joint return. Is there any chance that I might be stuck for some of the taxes?

Answer: Not according to the Tax Court in a 2001 decision. A marital interest is not an ownership interest but is rather an intangible right. This differs from a community property state (see Chapter 1) in which actual ownership of community property is 50-50.

Cutting the Retirement Pie (and Other Ordinary Income Sweets)

Although the transfer of property between spouses is usually tax-free, this rule does not apply to ordinary income assets. With several significant exceptions, the transfer of such assets is considered an impermissible *assignment of income.*

Courts have the statutory authority to divide a retirement plan account balance or an accrued benefit between the employee and the spouse upon a marital termination. The trustee of a qualified retirement plan (see Chapter 9, "Retirement Plans") must comply with a proper Qualified Domestic Relations Order (QDRO). Each spouse becomes taxable on amounts that he or she ultimately receives from the retirement plan. A QDRO requires more than a separation agreement between the spouses. It must be submitted to the local court in order to obtain a judgment, decree, or order.

The QDRO must set forth the following:

- The name and last known mailing address of the participant and alternate payee
- The amount or percentage of benefits to be paid to the alternate payee or the manner in which a computation of the amount or percentage is to be determined
- The number of payments or period to which the order applies
- A designation of each plan to which the order applies

Special rules apply to civilian and military government pensions requiring strict compliance in order to shift taxation from the employee spouse to the other spouse.

A QDRO is not needed to divide an IRA. A written agreement to transfer all or a portion of an IRA from one spouse to another upon separation or divorce suffices to direct the trustee to comply and shifts future taxation of the transferred balance to the recipient spouse.

According to a 1994 Tax Court case, if a QDRO is legally deficient, the tax liability caused upon payment to the nonemployee spouse remains with the employee spouse. Similarly, IRA transfers must meet the requirements of the law in order to shift taxation to the recipient spouse. One of these requirements is that the IRA transfer must be pursuant to a marital termination—separation or divorce. According to an IRS letter ruling, any other IRA transfer causes tax liability to the original owner. Must a QDRO be pursuant to separation or divorce? There is no specific authority; however, the IRS could be expected to take such a position.

In a 2002 Revenue Ruling, the IRS reversed its longtime position and indicated that nonqualified deferred compensation including stock options can be transferred between spouses upon a marital termination without income realization by the transferor spouse; the transferee spouse under the Ruling reports the income at such time as if he or she had earned the compensation. (See Chapter 2, for a discussion of nonqualified deferred compensation and stock options.)

Caution

Pursuant to a Notice issued at the same time as the Revenue Ruling, the IRS is seeking comment on its proposed position that the liability for Social Security taxes would remain with the spouse who earned the nonqualified deferred compensation or option.

Caution

The interspousal transfer of Incentive Stock Options, tax-favored to the employee as discussed in Chapter 2, will convert them into less favorable nonqualified stock options.

Question: My husband and I are divorcing, and we have entered into a separation agreement. For so long as my husband has been employed, he has been a participant in his employer's retirement plan and has accrued benefits of approximately $200,000. As part of the property settlement, my husband has agreed that I am entitled to one-half of his retirement benefits. What are my options when I receive the $100,000?

Answer: A QDRO will have to be signed by a judge from your local court awarding you the $100,000 from your husband's retirement plan. After the order is signed, it will be submitted to the administrator of your husband's retirement plan for compliance. The timing and form of payment to you will be governed by the terms of your husband's plan. If you receive the $100,000 in a lump sum, you will be eligible for favorable income tax treatment in lieu of ordinary income if your husband met the requirements for special treatment. In any event, you will not have to pay the usual 10 percent penalty for premature withdrawal, even if you have not reached the age of 59 1/2. If you have the $100,000 transferred directly into an IRA or your own eligible retirement plan, you will not be subject to income tax liability until you withdraw the funds. (See Chapter 9 for a full discussion of Retirement Plans.)

CHAPTER 9

Retirement Plans

Planning for Your Retirement

Planning for your retirement makes sense not only from a tax point of view but also from a financial and economic point of view. Social Security benefits probably will not be sufficient to meet your living expenses after retirement, so planning is needed to augment any government-provided retirement benefits. Retirement plans come in many types: Those typically funded by employers (profit-sharing plans, money purchase plans, defined benefit plans, and SEPs), those that we fund ourselves (IRAs), and those that are funded both by our employers and ourselves (401(k) plans and Simple plans). To assist lower income employees in planning for their retirement, a tax credit, discussed in Chapter 3, "Deductions and Credits—For Itemizers and Nonitemizers," exists for the years 2002–2006 under which the government is subsidizing a portion of employee elective contributions.

Caution

Employers are cutting back company contributions or even eliminating plans in order to control costs. To encourage the creation and maintenance of retirement plans for employees, small employers may be exempt for five years from *user fees*

continues

Caution (cont.)

charged on submitting plans to the IRS for approval. They also may receive a tax credit for 50 percent of the first $1,000 in administrative and plan education expenses for each of the first three years of the plan. A small employer has 100 or fewer employees who received at least $5,000 in compensation in the preceding year. To be eligible for the waiver of user fees and for the tax credit, the employer must have had no predecessor plan in the current or three preceding tax years and must have at least one participant not considered "highly compensated" under the law.

Additionally, to stimulate retirement savings, Congress is considering various proposals to simplify the retirement plan laws and to increase allowable contributions.

Traditional IRAs

Individual retirement accounts (IRAs) are government-sanctioned savings vehicles for workers and recipients of alimony. Although an IRA is typically a personal account, it may also be a subaccount of a participating employer plan. The traditional IRA has been supplemented by the Roth IRA discussed later in this chapter.

Contributions to a traditional IRA may be made until the year an individual reaches age 70 1/2, and the earnings generated by the contributions accumulate tax-free. When withdrawals are made from the traditional IRA, the owner pays tax not only on the amount of the contributions but also on the earnings that have been accumulating.

The *maximum* annual IRA contribution and deduction is $3,000, subject to rules discussed below limiting IRA deductions for workers who are active participants or whose spouses are active participants in employer-sponsored retirement plans. If you earned less than $3,000, you can contribute all of it, but no more, to an IRA and claim a full deduction for your contribution. Consequently, if you earned $1,500, your IRA contribution can be no more than $1,500. What you made includes the earned income as reported on your W-2s and self-employment, as well as any alimony payments that you received. Unearned income such as interest, dividends, and rents does not count for this purpose.

A special rule exists for nonworking spouses or individuals who made no more than $3,000. Under these circumstances, your total contribution as a couple can be increased to the lesser of what the two of you made or $6,000, although no more than $3,000 can be put in either spouse's account.

Individuals who have reached age 50 by year-end can contribute an additional $500 annually to their IRA contributions if supported by sufficient earned income plus alimony.

Although the general rule permits deductible IRA contributions up to the dollar maximum, not all individuals are eligible for the tax deduction. If either you or your spouse is an active participant in an employer-sponsored retirement plan, your ability to make a deductible contribution to your IRA may be reduced or eliminated.

However, if you and your spouse file a joint return and your modified AGI (essentially AGI before the IRA deduction) is no more than $65,000 in 2004, both of you are entitled to continue to make full deductible contributions to your own IRAs, even if one or both of you is an active participant in an employer-sponsored retirement plan.

If you and your spouse's modified AGI on your 2004 joint return is between $65,000 and $75,000, each of you will be looked at separately, and either or both of you will phase out your ability to make deductible IRA contributions depending on your individual status as an active participant in an employer-sponsored retirement plan. For example, if you and your spouse have a modified AGI of $70,000, and you are an active plan participant but your spouse is not, you may make a $1,500 deductible IRA contribution while your spouse may make a $3,000 deductible contribution.

If you and your spouse's modified AGI is between $75,000 and $150,000, the ability of each of you to make a deductible IRA contribution depends on your own lack of active plan participation. If your and your spouse's modified AGI is between $150,000 and $160,000, the ability of a spouse who is not an active plan participant to make a deductible IRA contribution phases out if the other spouse is an active plan participant. At $160,000 of modified AGI, neither of you can make a deductible IRA contribution if either of you is an active plan participant.

If you file a separate return while married, you can make a deductible IRA contribution so long as neither you nor your spouse is an active participant in an employer-sponsored retirement plan. For the individual who files a separate return but who is or whose spouse is an active participant in an employer-sponsored retirement plan, no deductible contribution to an IRA can be made if his or her modified AGI is $10,000 or more. If the separate modified AGI is less than $10,000, a *pro rata* deductible contribution can be made not to exceed earned income plus alimony.

If you are married and file a separate return but you and your spouse have lived apart for the entire year, you will not be considered as married for the purpose of the IRA contribution. Thus, your spouse's status as an active participant in an employer-sponsored retirement plan will have no impact on your ability to make a deductible IRA contribution for yourself. If you are not an active participant in an employer-sponsored retirement plan, you are eligible to make a deductible IRA contribution. If you participate in an employer-sponsored retirement plan, you are eligible to make a deductible IRA contribution subject to the modified AGI limitation as though you were single.

If you are single and an active participant in your employer's retirement plan, you can still make a deductible contribution to your own IRA in 2004 so long as your modified AGI does not exceed $45,000. If your modified AGI is between $45,000 and $55,000, the deductible contribution to the IRA will be phased out. If your modified AGI is $55,000 or more and you are an active participant in an employer-sponsored plan, no deductible IRA contribution can be made.

Where any phaseout formula may have reduced your deductible IRA contribution to less than $200 (but more than $0), the law permits a minimum deductible contribution of $200.

Caution

The contribution limit will rise from the current $3,000 to $4,000 in 2005 and to $5,000 in 2008 and thereafter will be indexed for cost of living in $500 increments. The maximum added contribution for individuals who have reached age 50 will rise from the current $500 to $1,000 in 2006.

For 2003 the ability to make a deductible IRA contribution was phased out between $60,000 and $70,000 of AGI for a married individual filing jointly when that individual was an active participant in an employer-sponsored retirement plan. The phaseout was between $40,000 and $50,000 for single individuals actively participating in a plan. The phaseout levels for married couples filing jointly and for single individuals are rising annually. By 2007 the level of phaseout for married couples will be $80,000 to $100,000; by 2005 the level of phaseout for single individuals will be $50,000 to $60,000. Other phaseout limits are not scheduled to change.

Question: I contributed to my IRA believing that I was not an active participant in my employer's retirement plan. I now find that I will be considered an active participant in the plan. Because my AGI will exceed the amounts that would allow me even a partial IRA deduction, what are my options?

Answer: Unless you treat the contribution that you made to the IRA as a nondeductible contribution or as a Roth IRA (see the discussion later in this chapter), you will be liable for a 6 percent penalty for each year that the excess contribution remains in the IRA. To avoid the 6-percent penalty, you should withdraw the contribution and the earnings that it has generated before the due date of your tax return, including extensions. The withdrawn contribution is not taxable to you, but the earnings on the contribution are taxable in the year that you made the excess contribution, not in the year that the earnings were withdrawn. There also will be a 10-percent penalty on the amount of the earnings that are withdrawn. The 6-percent penalty will continue to apply each year that you do not correct the excess contribution.

Question: Who is an active participant in an employer-sponsored retirement plan for purposes of the IRA rules? I retired from the federal government two years ago following the death of my husband, and I receive my monthly government pension. I have decided to take a job for a small company without a retirement plan. Will I be able to make a deductible IRA contribution this year? I expect to have an AGI of about $65,000.

Answer: Anyone who participates in a profit-sharing plan, money purchase pension plan, defined benefit plan, government or church retirement plan, tax-sheltered annuity, simplified employee pension plan (SEP), or Simple plan in which contributions or forfeitures are added to an account maintained in that person's name or who has benefits that accrue on his or her behalf is an active participant in an employer-sponsored plan. Form W-2 indicates whether or not an employee is an active participant for any part of the year.

Even though you receive a government pension, you will be eligible for a deductible IRA contribution. Receipt of retirement benefits is not considered active participation in an employer-sponsored plan.

Caution

Participants in a profit-sharing plan might find that no contributions are made on their behalf in a lean year for the employer. However, if an employee receives a few dollars of forfeitures from the accounts of departing participants, that individual would be considered an active participant in an employer-sponsored retirement plan, and the result could be disqualification of the employee and possibly the employee's spouse from deductible IRA contributions, depending upon income levels. An employee repeatedly faced with this situation and wanting to deduct an IRA contribution may want to consider opting out of the employer's plan, if permitted.

Filing Pointer

If you or your spouse cannot make a deductible contribution to an IRA because of your modified AGI level, you can still make a nondeductible contribution to an IRA of up to $3,000 and have the earnings on the account accumulate tax-free. As a result, even though you receive no current tax benefit for your retirement savings, the earnings on the account are accumulating on a tax-deferred basis, thus allowing for a greater accumulation of capital. By filing IRS Form 8606 with your return, you designate the amount of your nondeductible IRA contribution. However, a nondeductible Roth IRA contribution would be preferable to a nondeductible traditional IRA for individuals who are eligible.

Year-End Reminder

You may open an IRA and make a contribution for the previous year until April 15 of the succeeding year. If you are eligible for a deductible IRA, this is one of the very few steps that you can take after year-end to reduce your taxes from the previous year. Note that filing an extension on your tax return does not extend the April 15 deadline for making IRA contributions.

Tax Planning

If your tax return information is completed early, you can file your tax return showing a deductible contribution, obtain your refund (hopefully by April 15), and then make the contribution.

Roth IRAs

The Roth IRA is a nondeductible IRA under which qualified withdrawals of contributions and earnings are tax-free and penalty-free (see "Avoiding Penalties on Retirement Plan Distributions" later in this chapter) after the fourth calendar year following the initial contribution. Qualified withdrawals are those on account of death or disability, after age 59 1/2, or (to a limited extent as discussed later in this chapter) to purchase a "first home."

Even nonqualified withdrawals from Roth IRAs enjoy some degree of favorable tax treatment. Unlike partial distributions from a traditional IRA, in which basis (see Chapter 5, "Gains and Losses") is recovered tax-free on a *pro rata* basis over the period of the anticipated income stream, distributions from a Roth IRA are first allocated to tax-free recovery of your own contributions.

Unlike a traditional IRA, a contribution to a Roth IRA can be made after age 70 1/2, and withdrawals need not commence at that age. Regardless of participation in an employer-sponsored retirement plan, the ability to make Roth IRA contributions is phased out at modified AGI levels between $150,000 and $160,000 for married couples filing jointly, between $95,000 and $110,000 for single individuals, and between $0 and $15,000 for married individuals filing separately.

Tax Planning

The decision as to whether to make an IRA contribution will vary with an individual's particular circumstances. However, most individuals whose personal preretirement needs will be met should make IRA contributions. Over a period of many years, the greatest tax savings is not in the initial deduction for the IRA contribution but in the tax-free compounding of earnings.

For this reason, a Roth IRA in most cases is more valuable than a traditional deductible IRA. (The $3,000 IRA contribution limitation is a combined one for traditional IRAs and Roth IRAs.) The value of a $3,000 deduction today ($750 to an individual in the 25-percent bracket) from a traditional IRA will pale against the value of the exclusion in the future after the $3,000 has grown tax-free for many years in a Roth IRA. See "Unhappy with Your Yield?—Direct Transfers and Rollovers" later in this chapter for a discussion about how to convert a traditional IRA into a Roth IRA.

Tax Planning

You are never too young to start an IRA. A youngster who starts early with paper route savings or with compensation paid by a parent for household work will enjoy the benefit of decades of compound growth. At 10-percent growth, just four years of $3,000 contributions beginning at age 12 will make your child a millionare by age 70.

Maximizing Elective Deferrals under a 401(k) or Simple Plan

A 401(k) plan is an employer-sponsored retirement plan that gives employees the option of deferring a portion of compensation by directing it to be contributed to the plan. These plans have increased in popularity as employers have sought to have employees share the cost of their retirement security.

An employee who participates in a 401(k) plan (or a 403(b) or 457 plan of certain government and nonprofit organizations) can elect a tax-free deferral far in excess of the IRA limitation. The largest elective deferral possible under the law in 2004 is 100 percent of compensation before taking the subtraction of the deferred amount into account up to a maximum of $13,000 plus an additional $3,000 if the employee has reached age 50 by year-end. The elective deferral maximum is the total amount that can be deferred for all plans.

Employers can contribute additional amounts to the 401(k) plan that are not subject to the employee's election up to an amount that, when combined with the employee's elective deferral amount, does not exceed the ceilings applicable to profit-sharing plans (discussed later). In fact, many 401(k) plans provide for the employer to match a percentage or dollar amount of employee elective deferrals up to a maximum. This incentive is particularly important in a small- or medium-size business, because the maximum elective deferrals of highly compensated workers are tied to the average elective deferrals of the rank and file unless the employer contributes at least 3 percent of compensation for all plan participants irrespective of whether they make elective deferrals.

A Simple plan is another employer-sponsored retirement plan that gives employees the option of elective deferrals. An employee who participates in a Simple plan can make an elective deferral of 100 percent of compensation before taking the subtraction of the deferral amount into account—up to a maximum of $9,000 in 2004 plus $1,500 if the employee has reached age 50 by year-end. Employers are required to make certain levels of contribution to a Simple plan.

As in the case of an IRA, the earnings on employer, employee 401(k), and Simple contributions accumulate tax-free until withdrawal. The employee's right to contributions that he or she chose to put into the plan and the earnings on those contributions are fully vested, as are most employer matching contributions and the related earnings, except in certain 401(k) plans. Also, as in the case of an IRA, no Social Security or Medicare taxes are saved.

See Chapter 11, "Special Groups of Taxpayers," for information on a special "catch-up" rule on elective deferrals by members of the military.

Year-End Reminder

Employees who can contribute to a 401(k) or Simple plan should consider maximizing their contributions before year-end. An employee in a 25-percent tax bracket electing a deferral of $13,000 to a 401(k) plan will save $3,250 in taxes; an employee in a 35-percent bracket will save $4,550.

Caution

For 2003 the maximum 401(k) elective deferral was $12,000, and a $2,000 additional deferral was permitted by an individual 50 years old or more. The maximum Simple plan elective deferral was $8,000, and a $1,000 additional deferral was permitted by those over age 50. The maximum 401(k) elective deferral rises by $1,000 each year after 2004 until it reaches $15,000 in 2006; thereafter, it will be indexed for cost of living in $500 increments. The 401(k) over-50 addition rises by $1,000 each year after 2004 until it reaches $5,000 in 2006; thereafter, it will be indexed in $500 increments. The maximum Simple plan elective deferral rises to $10,000 in 2005; thereafter, it will be indexed in $500 increments. The Simple plan over-50 addition rises by $500 each year after 2004 until it reaches $2,500 in 2006; thereafter, it will be indexed in $500 increments.

Tax Planning

Looking ahead to 2006, elective deferrals to a 401(k) plan will be possible in after-tax dollars, in which case qualified distributions will be totally free of tax. These 401(k) plans will be known as Roth 401(k) plans and will generally follow the Roth IRA rules on qualified distributions as discussed earlier in this chapter. Although you may be passing up a hefty deduction, as in the case of a Roth IRA, a Roth 401(k) in most cases will be more valuable than a traditional 401(k). A similar arrangement will exist for 403(b) plans created by public school systems and certain tax-exempt organizations.

In Business for Yourself?—Funding Larger Contributions

If you are in business for yourself, you have the opportunity to defer larger amounts and let the contributions and earnings grow tax-free through one or more qualified retirement plans or SEPs. However, you must treat employees in a nondiscriminatory manner, which usually means making a contribution on behalf of each of them in the same percentage of compensation as you make for yourself. You may exclude part-time employees and those under the age of 21. Qualified retirement plans may exclude workers with less than one or two years of service, depending on the type of plan and how quickly benefits become nonforfeitable and vest; SEPs may exclude workers with less than three years of service.

Qualified retirement plans come in two varieties—defined contribution plans and defined benefit plans. Defined contribution plans come in two primary types—money purchase pension plans and profit-sharing plans.

In a defined contribution plan, whether it is a money purchase pension plan or a profit-sharing plan, a separate retirement account is maintained in the name of each participating employee, and employer contributions to the plan are allocated to each account. Each employee's account then is increased by a proportionate share of investment earnings, and any losses suffered by the plan will be proportionately allocated to the employee's account. If an employee is terminated, he or she may forfeit all or a portion of the account depending upon the vesting schedule selected by the employer. Any amounts forfeited by the employee are usually allocated to the accounts of the remaining employees. The total *annual addition* (employer contributions, employee contributions, and forfeitures) allocated to an employee's account each year cannot exceed 100 percent of the employee's compensation or, if less, $41,000 ($40,000 in 2003) indexed in 2005 and succeeding years in $1,000 increments for increases in the cost of living. Earnings are not part of the annual addition.

Employers contribute a fixed percentage of employee compensation to a money purchase plan each year regardless of employer profitability. In contrast, contributions by the employer to a profit-sharing plan may be set up to be completely discretionary. Contributions need not be made each year, and the amount of the contribution may vary annually. For this reason, profit-sharing plans are very attractive for companies that are first starting out and have not yet established a history of profits or for companies that incur peaks and valleys in their profits, while, in contrast, money purchase pension plans have fallen into disfavor. The employer may claim a tax deduction with respect to a defined contribution plan only to the extent that total contributions do not exceed 25 percent of the compensation paid to the eligible employees as a whole. A 401(k) plan, previously discussed, is a type of profit-sharing plan. A Simple plan, also previously discussed, may be similarly set up, or it may be set up as a group of IRAs. Employee elective deferrals into a 401(k) plan or Simple 401(k) plan are not counted against the 25 percent limitation.

The amount of an employer's contribution to a defined benefit plan depends on the retirement benefit established in the plan. An actuary must determine the employer's contribution each year depending on assumptions made with respect to the salary progression and the ages of the participating employees as well as the investment return of the plan. Contributions to defined benefit plans must be made in periodic installments, or an interest charge is imposed.

A defined benefit plan can provide for an annual retirement benefit in a straight-life annuity at age 62 of no greater than $165,000 ($160,000 in 2003) indexed in 2005 and succeeding years in $5,000 increments for increases in the cost of living (or, if less, the amount of the employee's average compensation during that individual's highest-paid three consecutive years). Therefore, a defined benefit plan must limit the annual retirement benefit of employees to this amount, and employer contributions to the plan must be based on projecting this maximum annual benefit.

A SEP is a hybrid between a qualified retirement plan and an IRA. Like qualified plans, SEPs have nondiscrimination rules, although they differ from those of qualified plans. SEPs have an annual contribution limit per participant and a deduction limit in the aggregate of 25 percent of compensation (determined exclusive of the contribution itself) to a maximum deduction of $41,000 ($40,000 in 2003) indexed in $1,000 increments in 2005 and succeeding years for cost of living.

Tax Planning

If you are an employer looking into establishing a retirement plan or if you are the only worker and are seeking to maximize the benefit for yourself and you make more than $164,000, a discretionary profit-sharing plan will allow you to make the maximum $41,000 contribution to a defined contribution plan. However, if you are near retirement and want to maximize your tax deduction and future benefit, consider establishing a defined benefit plan instead. Such a plan probably would provide you with the largest current contribution (and also the largest current tax deduction) available. Actuarially determined contributions to a defined benefit plan on behalf of a high-income individual nearing retirement age can be far in excess of $41,000.

Tax Planning

If you have other workers in your business, the selection of features for your particular type of retirement plan will be important. Although discrimination against employees is supposedly not permitted, owners may minimize the cost of covering others through such means as delayed vesting schedules, integration with Social Security, and, in the case of profit-sharing plans, age-weighted and comparability formulas.

Year-End Reminder

Although contributions to a qualified retirement plan need not be made until after year-end to be deductible, the plan itself must be in place before the end of the employer's tax year.

The employer's retirement plan will be in existence if a written plan is executed before the end of the year and has been formally adopted by the employer before year-end. So long as the contribution is made to an established retirement plan before the due date of the employer's income tax return, including extensions, a deduction can be claimed. For example, if a calendar-year corporation has established a retirement plan before December 31, 2003, the corporation need not make its contribution for 2003 before March 15, 2004, the due date of the corporation's tax return for 2003. The contribution deadline can be extended for an additional six months if the corporation files a request to extend the due date of its corporate return in a timely manner.

A SEP may be started by an employer for its employees and funded for the prior year until the extended due date of the tax return—as late as October 15 of the succeeding year.

Question: What is a Keogh plan?

Answer: A Keogh plan is a qualified retirement plan (whether a profit-sharing plan, money purchase plan, or defined benefit plan) established by a sole proprietor for the benefit of the proprietor and the employees or by an entity taxed as a partnership (see Chapter 10, "Business Tax Planning") for the benefit of the partners and the employees. The same rules generally govern the operation of a Keogh plan as govern the operation of a qualified retirement plan established by a corporate employer.

However, the deduction for contributions on behalf of a sole proprietor or partner to a defined contribution plan is effectively limited to 20 percent of self-employment income (instead of 25 percent) determined after deducting one-half of the self-employment tax. The reason for this difference is to avoid a windfall to owners of unincorporated businesses who apply the percentage limitations to business profit before plan contributions, as compared to the owners of incorporated businesses who apply the percentage limitations to their salaries while retaining sufficient funds in the corporation for plan contributions. The result is parity between owners of unincorporated and incorporated businesses. The computations are quite complex, however, and are even worse for a defined benefit plan which follows the same principles.

Question: I am going to earn $410,000 in 2004. I have two support employees who make $40,000 each. If I am to receive a profit-sharing plan contribution of the $41,000 maximum, do I need to put in 10 percent for each employee?

Answer: You may need to put in 20 percent for them. Even if you made $4.1 million, you are treated as if you made $205,000, which is the maximum covered compensation for 2004, indexed in 2005 and succeeding years in $5,000 increments for increases in the cost of living. The maximum for 2003 was $200,000. If your employees are younger than you and you do not want to lock yourself into mandatory contributions to a defined benefit plan, consider an age-weighted profit-sharing plan that favors older workers. Integrating the plan with Social Security will also cut your costs.

Invest Your Retirement Plan Savings Wisely

Your retirement plan money can be invested in anything prudent; however, an IRA, SEP, or self-directed qualified plan cannot be invested in antiques, precious metals, art, or other collectibles (except certain coins).

In the event of a poor retirement plan investment, no tax loss can be claimed on the investor's personal return. Consequently, you should act conservatively with plan investments and reserve any speculative investments for nonretirement plan money.

Tax Planning

Although not prohibited as a retirement plan investment, you should never invest plan money in tax-exempt bonds because the interest earned from tax-exempt bonds is already tax-free. If retirement plan money is used to buy tax-exempt bonds, the interest in the plan account will be taxed when you take the money out of the account, even though it was all generated by tax-exempt bonds. In other words, if you invest your plan money in tax-exempt bonds, you will be converting tax-exempt income into taxable income as well as receiving the lesser yield usually associated with tax-exempt securities. Real estate syndications are not attractive investments either, inasmuch as tax-deferred retirement plans do not need the sheltering benefits associated with real estate.

Unhappy with Your Yield?—Direct Transfers and Rollovers

If you are unhappy with the yield of your retirement plan and you are the trustee (permitted only with certain types of plans) or you have a plan in which you direct the investments, you can change investments without changing plans. In other cases, you may seek to change the trustee without changing plans. In certain plans sponsored by financial institutions, however, you may need to change the plan itself.

Alternatively, you may receive notice that you are to receive a distribution from a qualified retirement plan in which you have participated.

In many cases, you can avoid paying taxes by a direct trustee-to-trustee transfer of funds between plans or by rollover in which you can negotiate and hold funds for up to 60 days (120 days as discussed later in this chapter for acquisition delays of "first-time" home buyers) before reinvestment.

Any portion of a distribution from a qualified retirement plan not attributable to the tax-free return of employee after-tax contributions can be transferred tax-free to a traditional IRA or another qualified retirement plan unless the distribution is a periodic (one of a series of substantially equal payments either tied to life expectancies or over a specified period of at least 10 years) or minimum (discussed later) distribution. A distribution from a qualified retirement plan may also be transferred to a 403(b) or 457 plan for certain public school, tax-exempt organization, or state government employees.

Any portion of a distribution from a qualified retirement plan attributable to employee after-tax contributions and otherwise eligible for transfer can be moved only to an IRA or (by direct transfer only) to a defined contribution qualified retirement plan.

However, any amount transferred out of a qualified retirement plan cannot ultimately qualify for the special tax treatment that is available for lump sum distributions from such plans (discussed later in this chapter). However, if otherwise eligible for special treatment and not commingled with other IRA money, an amount may be transferred from a qualified plan into a *conduit* IRA and back into a qualified retirement plan in order to qualify for the special treatment.

The transfer rules on traditional IRAs are similar to those of qualified retirement plans. In a traditional IRA, you may direct an IRA-to-IRA transfer at any time; however, an IRA-to-IRA rollover of the same funds is permitted only once every 365 days. After-tax contributions otherwise eligible for transfer can be moved only to another IRA. A SEP usually is treated as an IRA for purpose of transfers.

Simple plans have their own rules, limiting transfers in the first two years to just transfers into other Simple plans.

Roth IRAs also have their own rules, too. They may be transferred only into other Roth IRAs. Like traditional IRAs, a direct Roth IRA to Roth IRA transfer is permitted at any time; however, a rollover between Roth IRAs is permitted only once every 365 days.

Tax Planning

Traditional IRAs, SEPs, and certain Simple plans may be transferred into Roth IRAs without penalty by reporting the rollover amount less the amount attributable to any nondeductible contributions as income. Such transfers are not available to married individuals filing separately and to others with modified AGI in

Tax Planning (cont.)

excess of $100,000, which is computed without taking the taxable amount of the transfer into account.

Despite the requirement of current tax payment, the transfer of amounts in traditional IRA accounts into Roth IRAs will make sense for many individuals. Prime candidates for moving into Roth IRAs from existing traditional IRAs are those individuals with small balances or those with larger balances that have many anticipated years of in-plan growth. Individuals with net operating losses (see Chapter 1, "Introduction to Personal Tax Planning") may even be able to absorb the income without the payment of any taxes. On a transfer from a traditional IRA into a Roth IRA, pay the tax liability from current income or savings in order to transfer the gross distribution into the Roth IRA for maximum future tax-free growth.

If you act early in a year to convert a traditional IRA into a Roth IRA and the portfolio subsequently declines in value, you may avoid the tax by reconverting to a traditional IRA no later than the extended due date of the tax return. IRS regulations permit subsequent conversions into a Roth IRA beginning in the calendar year following the reconversion to a traditional IRA—provided at least 30 days has passed.

Tax Planning

If a Roth IRA makes sense for you, and your retirement funds are in a qualified retirement plan under which you can control distributions, especially one to which no new contributions will be made, consider a transfer of funds into a traditional IRA and a second transfer to a Roth IRA.

Caution

What happens if you convert your traditional IRA into a Roth IRA, showing modified AGI of $100,000 or less on your tax return and a subsequent audit by the IRS increases your income above the threshold? According to a 2001 Service Center Advise, you face a penalty of 6 percent per year on the excess contribution until withdrawn and a penalty of 10 percent on the withdrawal unless you are at least 59 1/2 years old (see the next heading, "Avoiding Penalties on Retirement Plan Distributions"). However, inasmuch as you would be beyond the time period in which you can automatically reconvert to a traditional IRA, you must apply to the IRS for relief and show you acted "reasonably and in good faith."

Caution

Income tax withholding is required at a rate of 20 percent on any distribution of $200 or more from a qualified plan that is eligible to be transferred tax-free and is not the subject of trustee-to-trustee direct transfer. Recipients of distributions from qualified plans not intending to use distributed funds should arrange direct transfers of their balances rather than rollovers. Distributions from IRAs and SEPs are not subject to withholding.

Tax Planning

If you are waiting for a tax refund or other funds needed in order to make an IRA contribution for the current filing year, an alternative, although it is a bit risky, is to take a distribution from your existing IRA. Use the funds to make the needed current contribution. In 1990 the IRS issued a letter ruling not binding on other individuals that would allow a tax-free rollover within the 60 days back to the same account from which the funds were withdrawn.

Tax Planning

The IRS may extend the 60-day rollover period if failure to waive the deadline would be "against equity or good conscience," such as in the event of casualty, disability, postal, or bank error. Approval is automatic under a January 27, 2003 Revenue Procedure in the case of bank error corrected within one year from the start of the 60-day period. Other requests for relief require application to the IRS with payment of a user fee. The IRS will consider all facts and circumstances including the use of the amount distributed and the time elapsed since the distribution.

Avoiding Penalties on Retirement Plan Distributions

A taxable distribution from a qualified retirement plan, which is not directly transferred or rolled over, is subject to a 10-percent penalty unless the distribution is made:

- On or after the date the participant reaches the age of 59 1/2
- After the death of the participant (in which case special distribution rules apply to the beneficiary)
- On account of the participant's disability

- As part of a series of substantially equal periodic payments made over a period of time equal to the participant's life expectancy or the joint life expectancy of the participant and the beneficiary
- To cover medical expenses when the payment does not exceed the amount allowable as a medical expense deduction
- On account of an IRS levy
- As a transfer to the nonparticipant spouse or former spouse pursuant to a Qualified Domestic Relations Order (QDRO) (discussed in Chapter 8, "Marriage and Divorce")
- Upon termination of employment in or after the calendar year in which the participant reaches age 55.

A taxable distribution from an IRA (including a SEP), which is not directly transferred or rolled over, is subject to a 10-percent penalty unless the distribution is made:

- On account of any of the first six items listed previously
- As a transfer to a spouse or former spouse upon a marital termination
- To the extent of family health insurance premiums after 12 consecutive weeks of receiving unemployment compensation (or after 12 consecutive weeks without self-employment) and until 60 days of re-employment (or self-employment) provided that the withdrawal is made in the same or succeeding year of eligibility for the withdrawal
- To the extent of tuition, fees, and room and board paid during the year for undergraduate, graduate, or post-secondary vocational study of the taxpayer or spouse, child, or grandchild
- To a maximum of $10,000 less similar lifetime withdrawals to purchase a principal residence within 120 days for the taxpayer, spouse, child, grandchild, or ancestor of the individual or spouse. Eligibility requires that neither the recipient of the funds nor the recipient's spouse have owned a principal residence within the two years leading up to the date of contract or construction. In the case of a delay in acquisition of a principal residence, funds may be restored to the IRA within 120 days of withdrawal.

A taxable distribution from a Simple plan that is not directly transferred or rolled over will also be subject to a 10-percent penalty unless the distribution is made on account of one of the exemptions. However, the penalty is usually 25 percent in the first two years of plan participation.

Not only are you penalized for a premature distribution, but you also are penalized for a late distribution unless from a Roth IRA. You may be fortunate enough not to need your savings from your retirement plan, either because you are continuing to work or because you have other sources of income. In that case, you want the retirement plan savings to accumulate tax-free as long as possible. You are required to receive your entire benefit maintained in the plan no later than the April 1 following the year in which you attain age 70 1/2, or you must take a minimum distribution by that same April 1 date and have subsequent annual minimum distributions paid to you no later than each December 31, commencing in the same calendar year, over your life expectancy or that of you and your beneficiary. If you continue to work, unless you are a greater-than-5-percent owner, minimum distributions from a qualified plan, but not a traditional IRA, can be delayed until April 1 of the year following your retirement.

Failure to begin distributions by the required distribution date will subject the retirement savings to a 50 percent penalty tax computed on the difference between the minimum amount you were required to take out and the amount that was actually distributed to you.

Year-End Reminder

You should not wait until the early months of the year following the year when you reach age 70 1/2 to commence distributions if two distributions in the same calendar year would move you into a higher marginal tax bracket. Rather, take your initial distribution by December 31 of the year in which you reach age 70 1/2.

Caution

You should avoid a premature retirement plan distribution if at all possible, even if the purpose is a valid one. The net proceeds to you may be quite small after taxes and penalty.

Illustration

Bob needs $15,000 to make a down payment on a vacation home. He has faithfully made contributions to an IRA, all of which were deducted by him. The IRA has a total balance of $15,000. Bob withdraws $15,000 from the account to use for his down payment. If Bob is less than 59 1/2 years old at the time of the distribution, not only must he include the $15,000 in income, but he also must pay a $1,500 penalty on the premature withdrawal. So after taxes, Bob, who is in the 28-percent bracket, nets only $9,300 from the withdrawal before any state income taxes ($15,000 less $4,200 in federal taxes and less the $1,500 penalty). Bob should consider borrowing the $15,000 down payment from family or other lenders. If Bob borrows $15,000 at 7 percent for five years, his monthly payment will be less than $300, and the interest can be claimed as an itemized deduction if the loan is secured by the home.

Tax Planning

When you must commence distributions, it usually makes sense to take only minimum distributions when you have no need for the extra funds. By taking only the minimum distribution required by law, you are spreading the income over a number of years as well as allowing amounts remaining in the plan to grow due to the continuing tax-free nature of the earnings. IRS regulations coupled with new mortality tables reflecting increased longevity have significantly reduced the amount of the required minimum distribution. When you commence minimum distributions at age 70 1/2, you will be treated as having a designated beneficiary who is 10 years younger than you even if you have not named a beneficiary or if the beneficiary is more or less than 10 years younger than you. The effect is that at age 70 1/2 you will be required to distribute less than 4 percent of your account balance. Even if you earn as little as 6 percent on your money, you will be age 83 before your account balance goes down. Only if your designated beneficiary is your spouse, who is more than 10 years younger than you, are you permitted to disregard the uniform table and compute the required minimum distribution using the actual joint life expectancy.

Caution

In part as a result of the significant decline in stock values between 2000 and 2002, Congress is considering legislation to modify the general requirement that distributions commence at age 70 1/2, perhaps changing the age to 75.

Tax Options on Distributions from Retirement Plans

When you can receive money that has been accumulated for your benefit in a qualified retirement plan depends on the terms of the plan itself. Usually, the plan will provide that the benefits will be payable at normal retirement age or upon death. Some plans will provide that the benefits can be paid upon termination of employment even if that occurs before retirement. You control the payment date from an IRA.

The full amount of any distribution to you from a retirement plan which is not properly rolled over or directly transferred to another eligible plan will be taxable unless you have made nondeductible contributions to the plan, in which case you will recover your contributions tax-free. If you are receiving payments over time, a portion of each payment from the retirement plan will be deemed to be a nontaxable recovery of your after-tax contribution to the retirement plan.

For most individuals, the taxable portion of a retirement plan distribution is taxed as ordinary income. However, special rules apply to individuals who reached age 50 before January 1, 1986. They may use 10-year averaging for a lump-sum distribution based generally on 1986 tax rates for single individuals if they are a plan participant for at least five years preceding the year of distribution. You basically compute the tax as though the payment were received over a 10-year period, even though the full tax is paid in the year you receive the distribution. Additionally, those individuals who were participants in a plan prior to 1974 can treat a portion of the distribution as capital gain computed at the 1986 maximum rate of 20 percent.

A SEP is considered an IRA for the purpose of distribution rules. Thus, a SEP distribution is not eligible for averaging or capital gain.

Tax Planning

If you have the opportunity to receive a distribution eligible for favored averaging or for capital gain, and you do not have immediate need of the funds, you must make a determination as to whether you will be better off taxwise and economically by paying taxes in the year of the distribution at favored rates and then reinvesting the remaining amounts or by transferring the distribution and taking portions as ordinary income only when needed or required by law. A determination must be made on the facts of each case; however, the latter approach is usually preferable particularly when the distributee has a number of years before distributions must commence under the law.

Question: Can I borrow money from my retirement plan? What are the rules?

Answer: Subject to the terms of the qualified retirement plan, the law allows you to borrow a limited amount against your account. Unless the borrowing is to acquire a principal residence, full repayment must be within five years. In any event, installment payments must be made on at least a quarterly basis. You can borrow up to the lesser of (1) $50,000 or (2) the greater of $10,000 or one-half of your vested benefit.

The $50,000 amount is reduced by the excess of your highest outstanding loan balance during the one-year period prior to a subsequent loan over the loan balance on the date of the subsequent loan. For example, assume the following facts:

Vested Account Balance	$200,000
November 1, 2003, Loan Balance	$30,000
November 1, 2004, Loan Balance	$20,000
Maximum Additional Loan on November 1, 2004	$20,000

On November 1, 2003, the participant borrowed $30,000 from his qualified retirement plan. On November 1, 2004, when his outstanding loan balance was $20,000, he sought to borrow an additional amount from the plan. The most that he could borrow on November 1, 2004 was an additional $20,000 because the normal $50,000 cap was reduced by $10,000, representing the excess of $30,000, the highest outstanding balance, over the $20,000 outstanding balance on the date of the new loan. Any distribution over these legal limits will be considered a taxable distribution from the plan and includable in income.

Caution

Interest paid by key individuals, including most owners and officers, on loans from retirement plans is not deductible regardless of the use to which the loan proceeds are put or whether the loan is secured by a qualified residence. Furthermore, no interest deduction is allowed to any employee if the loan's repayment is secured by the employee's account balance representing elective deferrals in a 401(k) plan or a 403(b) plan. In any event, a SEP or IRA cannot lend money to the account holder except indirectly through a 60-day rollover once every 365 days.

CHAPTER 10

Business Tax Planning

Organization Choices for Your Business

When you decide to start a business, whether it will be your full-time occupation or a part-time venture to make extra dollars, your next decision should be to decide the legal form in which the business will operate. Should operations be conducted as a sole proprietorship, a partnership, or a corporation? No single right answer exists for everyone. Rather, various tax and nontax factors must be considered, and each individual situation must be evaluated on its particular facts. Also, after the initial legal form of the business organization has been established, the facts and circumstances may change so as to warrant modifying the structure of the business to another legal form.

Business can be conducted under three basic structures—corporation, partnership, or sole proprietorship. Corporations, for federal income tax purposes, can operate as regular taxable C corporations or, if eligible, can elect to be treated as S corporations, which usually are not subject to federal income taxes at the corporate level. About 56 percent of corporations have made S elections. Partnerships can be organized as either general partnerships or as limited partnerships. As discussed in Chapter 6, "Real Estate—The Most Tax-Favored Investment," partnerships also include multi-member limited liability companies (LLCs), which usually allow all co-owners the benefit of limited liability

Form **2553** (Rev. December 2002) Department of the Treasury Internal Revenue Service

Election by a Small Business Corporation

(Under section 1362 of the Internal Revenue Code)

▶ **See Parts II and III on back and the separate instructions.**

▶ **The corporation may either send or fax this form to the IRS. See page 2 of the instructions.**

OMB No. 1545-0146

Notes: 1. ***Do not file Form 1120S,*** *U.S. Income Tax Return for an S Corporation, for any tax year before the year the election takes effect.*

2. *This election to be an S corporation can be accepted only if all the tests are met under* ***Who May Elect*** *on page 1 of the instructions; all shareholders have signed the consent statement; and the exact name and address of the corporation and other required form information are provided.*

3. *If the corporation was in existence before the effective date of this election, see* ***Taxes an S Corporation May Owe*** *on page 1 of the instructions.*

Part I Election Information

Please Type or Print	Name of corporation (see instructions)	A Employer identification number
	Number, street, and room or suite no. (If a P.O. box, see instructions.)	B Date incorporated
	City or town, state, and ZIP code	C State of incorporation

D Check the applicable box(es) if the corporation, after applying for the EIN shown in **A** above, changed its name ☐ or address ☐

E Election is to be effective for tax year beginning (month, day, year) . . . . . ▶

F Name and title of officer or legal representative who the IRS may call for more information

G Telephone number of officer or legal representative

H If this election takes effect for the first tax year the corporation exists, enter month, day, and year of the **earliest** of the following: (1) date the corporation first had shareholders, (2) date the corporation first had assets, or (3) date the corporation began doing business . . . . . ▶

I Selected tax year: Annual return will be filed for tax year ending (month and day) ▶ ____________

If the tax year ends on any date other than December 31, except for a 52-53-week tax year ending with reference to the month of December, you **must** complete Part II on the back. If the date you enter is the ending date of a 52-53-week tax year, write "52-53-week year" to the right of the date.

J Name and address of each shareholder; shareholder's spouse having a community property interest in the corporation's stock; and each tenant in common, joint tenant, and tenant by the entirety. (A husband and wife (and their estates) are counted as one shareholder in determining the number of shareholders without regard to the manner in which the stock is owned.)	K Shareholder's Consent Statement. Under penalties of perjury, we declare that we consent to the election of the above-named corporation to be an S corporation under section 1362(a) and that we have examined this consent statement, including accompanying schedules and statements, and to the best of our knowledge and belief, it is true, correct, and complete. We understand our consent is binding and may not be withdrawn after the corporation has made a valid election. (Shareholders sign and date below.)		L Stock owned		M Social security number or employer identification number (see instructions)	N Shareholder's tax year ends (month and day)
	Signature	Date	Number of shares	Dates acquired		

Under penalties of perjury, I declare that I have examined this election, including accompanying schedules and statements, and to the best of my knowledge and belief, it is true, correct, and complete.

Signature of officer ▶ **Title ▶** **Date ▶**

For Paperwork Reduction Act Notice, see page 4 of the instructions. Form **2553** (Rev. 12-2002)

ISA
STF FED4589F.1

Form 2553 Election by a Small Business Corporation (page 1)

from creditors, and limited liability partnerships (LLPs), which are recognized in most states and typically allow all co-owners the benefit of limited liability in certain circumstances. Sole proprietorships include one-member LLCs conducting a business; they have gained recognition in every state since being sanctioned by the IRS in 1997. One-member LLCs file a Schedule C like any other sole proprietorship.

Nontax considerations, such as limiting personal liability, are of equal importance as tax considerations in determining the appropriate form of business operation. In terms of income tax considerations, however, the sole proprietor includes the net profit or loss generated by the business on his or her personal return; any profit is subject to the normal applicable personal income tax rates. Similarly, an individual partner (whether general, limited, or an LLC/LLP member) is taxed at the personal tax rates on that partner's share of the partnership business operations.

A C corporation is a taxable entity and pays federal taxes on its taxable income at the following marginal rates:

IF TAXABLE INCOME IS	MARGINAL TAX RATE IS
Up to $50,000	15%
$50,001–$75,000	25%
$75,001–$100,000	34%
$100,001–$335,000	39%
$335,001–$10,000,000	34%
$10,000,001–$15,000,000	35%
$15,000,001–$18,333,333	38%
More than $18,333,333	35%

This creates an effective tax rate of 34 percent for most corporations with taxable incomes greater than $335,000 and one of 35 percent for the most profitable corporations. However, personal service corporations, providing medical, legal, accounting, and similar services, are taxed at a flat rate of 35 percent from the first dollar of taxable income.

The corporate structure offers the owner-employee the opportunity to enjoy tax savings from participation in certain fringe benefit programs, which is not available when the business is operated in unincorporated form. If the business operates as a C corporation (but not as an S corporation), the shareholder-employees, subject to nondiscrimination rules when there are other employees, can have the cost of group term life insurance as well as unreimbursed medical expenses paid for on a tax-deductible basis. (Health insurance on shareholder-employees can also be paid for and deducted by a C corporation and not by an S corporation, but as discussed in Chapter 2, "Taxable and Tax-Free Income and Benefits," an S corporation shareholder-employee can usually get the same benefit in full but on his or her individual return.)

Although C corporation status may save taxes in the short run, the effect of double taxation, initially at the entity level and ultimately at the individual level, will normally cause C corporations to pay more tax in the long run. However, with qualified dividends taxed at a maximum rate of 15 percent through 2008, the effect of double taxation is at least temporarily alleviated.

C corporations retaining too much in profits risk an additional *accumulated earnings tax*, and C corporations paying out too much in compensation to shareholder-employees risk that the IRS will deny a deduction for the excess as unreasonably high compensation in relation to the value of services performed. Additionally, larger nonpersonal service C corporations averaging more than $5 million in sales, unlike other business entities, must use accrual basis accounting even if inventories are not material in the production of income. For most businesses, accrual accounting is costly as income is taxed when earned—not when it is collected and enjoyed.

An S corporation shareholder is taxed at the personal tax rates on his or her share of the S corporation business operations. Although an S corporation shareholder is taxed similar to a partner in a partnership, restrictions on qualifications and use of losses make operating as an S corporation more hazardous from a tax perspective than operating as a partnership.

The salary paid to a shareholder-employee of a C or S corporation is treated like all other compensation and is subject to all payroll taxes, including unemployment and Social Security taxes. The Social Security costs of operating in incorporated form are the same as in unincorporated form. The employee's share of the Social Security tax in 2004 is 7.65 percent on the first $87,900 of salary ($87,000 in 2003). The corporation pays an additional 7.65 percent for a combined total on the shareholder-employee salary of 15.3 percent, which is the self-employment tax rate on the unincorporated owner. The Medicare portion of 1.45 percent to the employee and an additional 1.45 percent to the employer (the combined rate of 2.9 percent being the same for the unincorporated owner) applies to all wages and self-employment income.

Caution

Although operating as a sole proprietorship or general partnership requires no formal filings, the requirements of state law must be satisfied to obtain legal status as a limited partnership, LLC, LLP, or corporation. Additionally, a corporation must file Form 2553 with the IRS within 2 1/2 months from the start of the year for which it seeks S corporation treatment. The IRS in its discretion may accept late-filed S elections inadvertently forgotten.

Tax Planning

As a general rule, if you incorporate, S corporation status is most attractive to start-up corporations if the losses to the shareholders will be active rather than passive (see Chapter 2) and to personal service or profitable nonpersonal service corporations when income will be taxed personally in a lower or comparable bracket to corporate rates of 34 or 35 percent. In contrast, C corporation status is most attractive to nonpersonal service corporations able to take advantage of the 15-percent and 25-percent corporate marginal rate brackets, especially when attractive fringe benefits exist. C corporation status is required to obtain a 50 percent exclusion on stock gains in certain small business corporations. See Chapter 7, "Other Tax-Favored Investments," for a discussion of small business stock.

Tax Planning

S corporation shareholder-employees can keep Social Security contributions low by setting modest salaries below the Social Security base. Although they will pay Social Security taxes on such compensation, they will not pay any Social Security tax on remaining amounts distributed by the corporation as dividends or on earnings that are retained. This loophole, and the fact that a few jurisdictions do not yet recognize one-person LLCs, are the primary reason why new businesses may want to operate as S corporations as opposed to LLCs, which are otherwise more flexible in operation.

Unreasonably low compensation in relation to the value of services performed by an S corporation owner may be challenged. The IRS has commenced an audit program of the compensation paid to S corporation shareholder-employees. An audit nabbed an Idaho law firm, which in 1994 lost its case in federal district court. The firm, which operated as an S corporation, never paid salary to its owner-employees, and the IRS successfully reclassified amounts distributed to the shareholders from dividends to compensation. Expect more audits in the future. In a 2002 report, the Treasury Inspector General for Tax Administration cited unreasonably low compensation to S corporation shareholder-employees as a continuing problem and made recommendations for finding scofflaws.

Congress has periodically considered legislation that would restrict or eliminate the ability of S corporation owner-employees to avoid Social Security taxes through this loophole. Certain proposals have been directed at all businesses, although others have targeted only service-related businesses including health, law, engineering, architecture, accounting, actuarial services, performing arts, consulting, athletics, and most financial services as well as any other business that the IRS determines to require little capital to produce income.

Controversy

If the IRS denies a deduction for "unreasonable" compensation paid to a C corporation shareholder-employee, the employee is still taxed on the income but as a dividend rather than wages. Is the newly-classified dividend eligible for the 15 percent maximum rate through 2008 (see Chapter 2), allowing the shareholder to receive an unexpected benefit individually? The law is unclear.

Tax Planning

All small businesses averaging less than $1 million in sales and not keeping books on an accrual basis may use the more favorable cash basis of accounting pursuant to a 2000 IRS Revenue Procedure. At $1 million in average sales, noncustom manufacturers, wholesalers, and retailers must use accrual accounting pursuant to a 2002 Revenue Procedure. All other C corporations, except personal service businesses, must use accrual accounting at $5 million in average sales. All other S corporations, except those in which inventories are not material in the production of income, must use accrual accounting at $10 million in average sales. Contractors carrying over jobs from year-to-year have special rules.

Selection of the Business' Fiscal Year

A business operated as a sole proprietorship will use the calendar year to report its business activity. C corporations, other than personal service corporations, can select any fiscal year. These corporations should consider selecting a fiscal year based upon the business' natural business year. Closing the corporation's books and records for tax purposes in the middle of the business' busiest time may be an administrative headache and may cause the highest possible taxable income due to high inventory levels.

Partnerships, S corporations, and personal service corporations are usually required to use a calendar year to report their business activities. Alternatively, if the entity can establish that a fiscal year coincides with the entity's natural business year, the entity can request IRS permission to use that fiscal year for its business reporting. Except for certain businesses that are seasonal in nature, a natural business year will be difficult to show.

If a partnership or S corporation wants to adopt a fiscal year that does not coincide with its natural business year, it may do so by selecting a fiscal year of September 30, October 31, or November 30. However, if an S corporation or partnership selects a September, October, or November year-end, it must make a tax payment to the IRS roughly equal to the value of the tax deferral available to the partners or shareholders of the partnership or S corporation.

Personal service corporations unable to show a natural business year may also elect a September, October, or November year-end. A personal service corporation that opts for a September, October, or November year-end will lose deductions for payments to the shareholder-employees if the corporation fails to pay proportionate shares of their salaries during the entire fiscal year.

Tax Planning

Selecting a year-end of January 31 for a nonpersonal service C corporation can provide some tax savings. The corporation can pay a bonus to the shareholder-employee early in the calendar year. The bonus payment is deductible by the corporation, but the individual does not pay taxes (other than through withholdings) on the bonus until April 15 of the following year.

Tax Planning

Personal tax planning is facilitated when eligible corporations select fiscal years other than December 31. For example, if a shareholder-employee finds himself or herself in the 28-percent tax bracket but realizes that a normal December salary payment would cause creeping into the 33-percent bracket, that individual can enter into an agreement with the corporation in November to defer receipt of December's salary until January. This effectively avoids having December's salary taxed at the 33 percent rate and has no impact on the corporation's taxable income, because the January payment is in the same fiscal year as a December salary payment would have been.

However, the IRS closely scrutinizes agreements between corporations and shareholder-employees to defer compensation. To be an effective deferral, the agreement between the employer and the employee must be entered into before the time that the compensation is earned, and the corporation's obligation must be unsecured. See the further discussion of deferred compensation arrangements in Chapter 2.

Allocating Price on an Asset Purchase

In many instances a business commences by purchasing assets from a seller, as opposed to purchasing an interest in a business entity itself or starting from scratch. The allocation among assets will be extremely important to the buyer in an asset purchase.

Form **8594** (Rev. October 2002) Department of the Treasury Internal Revenue Service

Asset Acquisition Statement Under Section 1060

▶ Attach to your income tax return. ▶ See separate instructions.

OMB No. 1545-1021

Attachment Sequence No. 61

Name as shown on return	Identifying number as shown on return

Check the box that identifies you:

☐ Purchaser ☐ Seller

Part I General Information

1 Name of other party to the transaction	Other party's identifying number
Address (number, street, and room or suite no.)	
City or town, state, and ZIP code	
2 Date of sale	3 Total sales price (consideration)

Part II Assets Transferred — All filers of an original statement must complete.

4 Assets	Aggregate fair market value (actual amount for Class I)	Allocation of sales price
Class I	$	$
Class II	$	$
Class III	$	$
Class IV	$	$
Class V	$	$
Class VI and VII	$	$
Total	$	$

5 Did the purchaser and seller provide for an allocation of the sales price in the sales contract or in another written document signed by both parties? . . . . . ☐ Yes ☐ No

If "Yes," are the aggregate fair market values (FMV) listed for each of asset Classes I, II, III, IV, V, VI, and VII the amounts agreed upon in your sales contract or in a separate written document? . . . . . ☐ Yes ☐ No

6 In the purchase of the group of assets (or stock), did the purchaser also purchase a license or a covenant not to compete, or enter into a lease agreement, employment contract, management contract, or similar arrangement with the seller (or managers, directors, owners, or employees of the seller)? . . . . . ☐ Yes ☐ No

If "Yes," attach a schedule that specifies **(a)** the type of agreement and **(b)** the maximum amount of consideration (not including interest) paid or to be paid under the agreement. See instructions.

For Paperwork Reduction Act Notice, see separate instructions. Form **8594** (Rev. 10-2002)

ISA
STF FED6841F.1

Form 8594, Asset Acquisition Statement under Section 1060 (page 1)

For an allocation to inventory, the buyer will write-off the cost upon the disposition of the merchandise. Capital assets such as furniture, fixtures, equipment, and vehicles will be written off over prescribed periods of time as discussed later in this chapter. When a below-market lease is acquired, an allocation to the leasehold rights is written off over the remaining period of the lease. Most intangibles, including goodwill, covenants, and lists of customers, clients, and patients, are written off over 15 years.

In many cases the seller or one or more officers of the seller will provide significant or not-so-significant consultation services. When part of the consideration for the deal is the consulting payments, these amounts will be deductible to the business, provided that they reflect the value of the services.

Purchasers generally seek allocations to those assets, such as furniture, fixtures, and equipment, as well as consulting agreements, which provide a quick write-off period. Individual or S corporation sellers seek allocations to those assets that will result in capital gain. These assets include capital items such as furniture, fixtures, and equipment but only to the extent that the allocation is more than the seller's original purchase price. Allocations to goodwill, leasehold interests, and lists also offer capital gain treatment to a seller. C corporation sellers seek allocations that avoid a double layer of taxation, such as to individual consulting agreements or covenants.

IRS Form 8594 must be attached to the tax return of both the buyer and seller when mass assets of a business are sold and a goodwill or going concern value applies. The form will allow the IRS to overturn allocations that clearly lack substance.

Tax Planning

The allocation among assets is important to both buyer and seller. Their interests are adverse, except both a buyer and an individual S corporation seller may benefit from an allocation to leasehold rights or to capital assets beyond the seller's original purchase price. However, most transactions cannot offer any economic substance to support a significant allocation in either manner. Both a buyer and a C corporation seller may benefit from an allocation to a consulting agreement. Of course, the arrangement must have substance, or the IRS can challenge the allocation.

Sellers at or near retirement age, however, should be aware of an allocation to consulting services. Such payments constitute earned income and affect the right to draw Social Security benefits until age 65 when the income limitation is no longer applicable. Additionally, Social Security or self-employment tax, depending on whether the structure is under an employment or independent contractor agreement, must be paid on the income.

Caution

Many states impose a sales tax to the extent that a purchase price is allocated to furniture, equipment, and similar property. Additionally, certain jurisdictions seek to apply their sales tax to seemingly intangible assets, such as customer lists, to the extent that they are transferred on such tangible media as paper or computer disks. Given that lists have the same tax treatment to both buyer and seller as goodwill, no benefit exists in such an allocation.

Capitalize on Your Depreciation Deduction

You can recover the cost of assets used in a trade or business over a period of time, usually five or seven years, depending upon the particular type of property and the year in which you first acquired the asset.

Tangible personal property acquired by a taxpayer for use in a trade or business (as opposed to an investment such as nontransient lodging) can be expensed to a maximum of $102,000 in 2004 ($100,000 in 2003) with this annual maximum indexed for cost of living in 2005. This benefit, which must be elected by the due date of the tax return including extensions, eliminates the need for many small businesses to maintain depreciation schedules and accelerates the tax benefit associated with capital expenditures. The expensing of tangible personal property to these maximums is phased out in any year for a taxpayer placing in service tangible personal property costing more than $405,000 in 2004 ($400,000 in 2003) indexed for cost of living in 2005. Expensing, in any event, cannot be used to cause or increase a business loss. Married individuals filing separately are treated as one taxpayer for the purpose of expensing. See Chapter 7 for special expensing rules for businesses within empowerment zones and renewal communities.

For new tangible personal property acquired after May 5, 2003 but before January 1, 2005, an additional first year write-off of 50 percent of the purchase price, computed after expensing up to $100,000 indexed in costs if eligible, may be taken before calculating normal depreciation and irrespective of annual acquisitions or taxable source.

Although automobiles usually qualify for write-offs over five years, it takes many more years to fully depreciate expensive automobiles. The maximum normal write-off for an automobile used 100 percent in a taxpayer's business and placed in service 2003 is only $10,910 in the aggregate over the first three years and is only $1,775 in each subsequent year. The actual annual write-offs are adjusted upward or downward for changes in the automobile component of the Consumer Price Index. The expensing rule for tangible personal property acquired during the year cannot be used to increase the first-year write-off. However, for new automobiles acquired after May 5, 2003 but before January 1, 2005, an additional first-year write-off of $7,650 usually applies.

The maximum annual write-offs assume 100-percent business use. If an automobile is used primarily—but not exclusively for business—the actual annual write-offs must be determined by multiplying these maximums by the actual percentage of business use. Special rules apply to automobiles in which business use does not exceed 50 percent.

Tax Planning

Consider buying one of 20 sport utility vehicles or vans weighing more than 6,000 pounds for your business; they are exempt from the luxury car rules. As a result, you may be able to write off the entire cost of the vehicle in the year of purchase. Congress is considering legislation to close this "loophole" by limiting first year expensing to $25,000 for such vehicles. The provision was combined in S. 1637, the Jumpstart Our Business Strength Act, which was approved by the Senate Finance Committee on October 1, 2003.

Year-End Reminder

Buy needed tangible personal property by December 31 if you are eligible for the expensing of capital assets and you have not reached your limit. The dollar-for-dollar write-off will give an immediate reduction of taxable income.

Filing Pointer

Although the expensing of tangible personal property may not cause or increase a business loss, the test is applied by considering all taxable income from the active conduct of any trade or business. IRS Regulations indicate that compensation earned as an employee is considered taxable income from a business. Consequently, most employees with W-2 income and small-side businesses will be able to expense qualifying capital purchases up to the maximum.

Caution

Where more than 40 percent of the basis of newly acquired personal property, exclusive of expensed items, is acquired in the fourth quarter of the year, the normal depreciation deduction for personal property may be reduced under a formula that looks at the quarter in which each asset was acquired. If a taxpayer is not careful and this rule applies, the depreciation deduction for fourth-quarter purchases will be one-fourth of the deduction that otherwise would have applied.

Caution

All capital expenditures are subject to the depreciation rules irrespective of cost. In a 2001 case, the Tax Court backed up the IRS position that a business could not automatically expense purchases of less than $500 and ignore the limitations.

Caution

For tangible personal property acquired in 2003 before May 6, the additional first-year write-off was 30 percent. For new automobiles, the usual additional first-year write-off for cars was $4,600. In 2005 the additional first-year write-off will expire. In 2006 the maximum annual expensing is scheduled to be reduced to $25,000 with a phaseout for taxpayers placing more than $200,000 of such property in service.

Making the Imputed Interest Rules Work for You

When a property sale occurs and at least one payment for the property is deferred (for more than six months in some cases and for more than one year in others), an adequate rate of interest must be charged or the IRS will impute interest on payments due more than six months after the sale. Depending on the subject matter of the sale and the parties involved in the transaction, the required rate of interest will vary.

The interest that must be charged is usually the lesser of 9 percent, or a rate set monthly by the IRS tied to U.S. government securities rates. The 9 percent alternative is unavailable on 2003 sales in excess of $4,280,800 (prior to indexing in 2003 and succeeding years). Many exceptions exist. For example, on the sale of land between certain related parties for $500,000 or less, an interest rate of at least 6 percent, compounded semiannually, must be charged. Interest is not imputed in transfers related to a marital termination.

The imputed interest rules also apply to loans in excess of $10,000.

If the stated interest rate on a sale is less than that required by law, a portion of each note payment will be recharacterized as interest, deductible by the payer and taxable as interest income to the recipient. Because a portion of the amount paid by the purchaser will be recharacterized as interest, the purchaser must reduce the basis of the purchased assets by the amount that has been recharacterized as interest.

If the stated interest rate on a loan is less than that required by law, the foregone interest is deemed to have been transferred from the lender to the borrower and then *paid* by the borrower to the lender as interest. The constructive transfer from the lender to the borrower will be characterized as a gift if the context of the transaction is other than a business setting.

If the loan is made in a business setting, such as a loan to an employee or to a shareholder, the amount of the foregone interest is taxable as additional compensation (subject to Social Security taxes) if the loan is made to an employee with no equity interest or as a dividend if the loan is made to a shareholder. The constructive payment from the borrower to the lender is taxable as interest income to the lender and perhaps deductible as an interest expense for the borrower. See Chapter 4, "Deductions—For Itemizers Only," for the rules governing the deduction for interest expense by an individual.

Tax Planning

Although the IRS sets a minimum interest rate, it does not set a maximum rate on sales or loans. Two parties must use a rate that is *reasonable* or face a tax restructuring if scrutinized by the IRS, but purchasers in a sales transaction may particularly seek faster write-offs through a lower sales price with a higher interest rate.

Tax Planning

Because the imputed interest rule is not applicable to loans up to $10,000, you can use your corporation as a bank and borrow up to $10,000 without interest. The $10,000 will be recognized as a true loan only if certain steps are taken. As with all loans, document the books of the corporation and have evidence of a promissory note, which calls for loan repayment. Of course, the loan should be paid down on some regular basis.

Paying Your Children

One method of family tax planning that is often overlooked is the ability of a business owner to pay children for services that are performed for the business. So long as the children are actually performing services for the business, they can be paid a salary that will provide the business with a current tax deduction. Although the salary will be taxable to the children, this earned income will be taxed at the children's own tax rate (perhaps as low as 10 percent) and will not be subject to the "Kiddie" tax (see Chapter 1, "Introduction to Personal Tax Planning"). And, as discussed in Chapter 9, "Retirement Plans," the child can open an IRA and enjoy years of tax-free compound growth.

An additional saving can result from the exemption from Social Security taxes for children under age 18 on the payroll of their sole proprietor parent. Nevertheless, the self-employment income of the parent is reduced by the payment to a child. When the parent is below the Social Security base ($87,900 in 2004), payments justifiably made to a child of a sole proprietor as a *bona fide* employee result in substantial self-employment tax savings coupled with the income tax savings.

Caution

For wages paid to a child to be deductible, they must be both "ordinary and necessary" to your business and "reasonable" for the work that was actually done.

Illustration

This example of the savings that can be achieved by having your child on the payroll uses 2003 tax rates before indexing for 2004. Assume that you have your own sole proprietorship and that your 13-year-old child works for you every day after school and on weekends, cleaning up and doing general filing. Assume further that you would have to pay $10,000 to any other person to perform the same job that your child is doing. Your business shows a profit of $40,000 before considering your child's salary and any deduction relating to self-employment tax. You are in the 28-percent federal tax bracket, and the salary that you pay your child is his or her only income.

	CHILD EMPLOYED	CHILD NOT EMPLOYED
Business Net Profit (before child's salary and self-employment tax deduction)	$40,000	$40,000
Child's Salary	($10,000)	$0
Business Net Profit	$30,000	$40,000
Federal Income Tax on Net Profit	$7,806	$10,409
Self-Employment Tax	$4,239	$5,652
Parent's Federal Taxes on Net Profit	$12,045	$16,061
Child's Federal Income Tax	$525	$0
Family's Combined Federal Taxes on Net Profit	$12,570	$16,061

By choosing to pay your child, your family's total federal tax liability is reduced by almost $3,500. The self-employment tax and the federal income tax were computed after the adjustments relating to the deduction for one-half of the self-employment tax, as discussed in Chapter 1.

Caution

Make sure that you consider the impact of the child's salary on your ability to continue to claim the child as a dependent. Loss of the exemption for the child in 2004 prior to that year's indexing would mean the loss of a $3,050 deduction, which translates to $854 more in federal taxes for a taxpayer in the 28-percent bracket (28 percent × $3,050) plus an additional $1,000 from the loss of the child credit if the dependent is under age 17. Loss of the exemption also means loss of any available education credit if the child is in college or vocational school. See Chapter 3, "Deductions and Credits—For Itemizers and Nonitemizers," for a discussion of these credits.

Paying Your Other Workers—Independent Contractor versus Employee

Whether to classify a worker as an independent contractor or as an employee is an important decision for any business owner. If the worker is properly classified as an independent contractor, the service recipient has no obligation to pay Social Security taxes or unemployment taxes on the worker's compensation or to withhold income taxes or the employee's share of Social Security taxes. The worker is solely responsible for paying his or her own tax obligation, including self-employment tax. Additionally, the worker does not qualify for fringe benefits.

What allows a worker to be classified as an independent contractor, reducing the costs of business operations? An independent contractor is a worker who is free to complete a designated task by whatever means he or she feels appropriate and is under the control of the service recipient only as to the end result. An employee, however, is subject to the direction and control of the service recipient both as to the end result and as to the means used to achieve that result. Twenty questions have been developed to ascertain whether an employer-employee relationship exists. Among the most important factors indicating employee status are the following:

- The work relationship is continuing, as opposed to intermittent.
- The worker is performing services solely or primarily for one service recipient.
- Training is being offered to the worker by the service recipient.

In recent years the IRS has increased its activity in the independent contractor/employee classification area despite a lack of clarity in the tax law. No industry is immune. The General Accounting Office believes that independent contractors, who comprise only 15 percent of individual taxpayers, account for 40 percent of unreported income and owe 75 percent of delinquent taxes.

Because of the lack of clear guidelines governing proper classification of workers, Congress provided some relief. Under Section 530 of the Revenue Act of 1978, if the business has consistently treated a worker as an independent contractor, has filed all tax returns (including the information return to the worker reporting the amount of remuneration) consistent with independent contractor status, and has a reasonable basis for such treatment, the IRS is barred from assessing payroll taxes against the business. For purposes of this Section 530 relief, a judicial precedent, an IRS ruling, a prior audit of the taxpayer, or a practice by a significant segment of the industry will be sufficient to establish that the business owner had a reasonable basis for treating the worker as an independent contractor. A post-1996 audit may be relied upon only if worker classification was an issue in the audit. Pursuant to 1996 tax legislation, 25 percent of an industry constitutes a significant segment in all cases, but a smaller percentage may suffice on a case-by-case basis. Section 530 relief is not available for certain technical personnel such as engineers, computer programmers, and system analysts.

Caution

Failure to properly classify workers as employees not only means substantial exposure to the business for the unpaid taxes but also may create personal liability for unpaid withholding tax. See "The Trust Fund Recovery Penalty—Personal Liability for Payroll Taxes" later in this chapter. The improper classification of workers as independent contractors also jeopardizes qualification of the retirement plans of the business because the workers were not covered.

Tax Planning

Businesses wanting to continue to treat workers as independent contractors should have written agreements with their help providing, among other things, that they may work for other businesses as well. IRS Form 1099 should be used to report compensation to independent contractors in excess of $600 in any year and to report all amounts paid to attorneys.

The Trust Fund Recovery Penalty—Personal Liability for Payroll Taxes

Although the business owner in a sole proprietorship (which includes a single owner LLC according to the IRS in a 2003 Chief Counsel Advice) is responsible and all general partners in a partnership are jointly and individually responsible for the payment of payroll taxes, responsibility in a corporation, multi-member LLC, or LLP requires assessment of the Trust Fund Recovery Penalty, formerly called the 100-percent penalty. This penalty, when imposed, is a personal assessment for income and Social Security taxes withheld in trust from the wages of employees (or not withheld due to the alleged misclassification of workers as independent contractors). When it appears that payroll taxes cannot be paid by the business entity at any time in the foreseeable future, the IRS seeks to determine the identities of the responsible persons and to collect the trust portions of the payroll tax liability from them.

There has been much litigation, and the courts and IRS appeals offices remain crowded with Trust Fund Recovery Penalty cases. For an individual to be held responsible for the Trust Fund Recovery Penalty, that person must have been one of the persons responsible for the collection and payment of payroll taxes. Additionally, the individual's failure to pay over taxes must have been "willful."

In any business entity, there will be at least one person, and perhaps many, who have the responsibility for paying over taxes. The IRS usually interviews stockholders, directors, officers, and authorized signators of a corporation (or their LLC/LLP equivalents) to determine whether they are responsible persons. Many factors are considered in determining who is responsible; however, the issue usually comes down to whether the individual had or shared responsibility for financial decisions.

The most frequent cases involve:

- A management team blaming outside investors and outside investors pointing fingers at the management team
- Bookkeepers with signature authority over the bank account but who deferred to others in making the financial decisions
- Family members of clearly responsible business owners (often spouses with ownership interests or who hold offices in name only)

The results in each case will depend upon the particular facts. Successful defenses to the imposition of the Trust Fund Recovery Penalty usually involve the absence of willfulness as shown by one or more of the following:

- Lack of knowledge of the delinquent payroll taxes
- Lack of funds to pay the taxes after learning of the delinquency
- Lack of ability to make payment after learning of the delinquency due to no signature authority or lack of an actual ability to cause others to make or order payment

Those individuals determined to be liable are jointly and individually responsible for the payment of the Trust Fund Recovery Penalty. If the penalty is collected from one person, it is not collected from any others. As a result, many of these matters are not resolved quickly in the hope that payment will be made by someone else.

A person held liable for the Trust Fund Recovery Penalty is liable only to the IRS for the federal income tax withholding and Social Security withholding collected from employees (or not collected due to the alleged misclassification of workers as independent contractors). No personal liability exists for the employer matching Social Security or for unemployment taxes. Interest begins to run on the Trust Fund Recovery Penalty after a personal assessment occurs, usually only after an unsuccessful appeals conference.

After payment by a person found to be liable, other individuals may remain liable for other tax periods for which the prior payer was not responsible. The business, if it is still in existence, also remains liable for remaining unpaid trust portions, matching Social Security, unemployment taxes, and for penalties and interest. An individual making payment has the right to bring suit under federal law for *pro rata* reimbursement by other individuals found liable for the penalty. Upon written request, the IRS must inform a responsible individual of the extent of collection activity against and the amount of payment by other responsible individuals.

See Chapter 13, "Dealing with the Internal Revenue Service," for a discussion of the procedures for contesting a proposed Trust Fund Recovery Penalty.

Caution

You should avoid being involved in any capacity with a business that does not fulfill its responsibilities concerning employee withholding. Recent court decisions have strongly backed up the IRS in most Trust Fund Recovery Penalty assessments. That you were only following orders is not in itself a defense. In one 1994 case, a federal district court found a corporate officer liable although he "essentially acted as a cabin boy on a sinking ship." That you should be met with sympathy is not in itself sufficient to cause a favorable decision. In a 1996 case, the Ninth Circuit Court of Appeals backed up a Hawaii Federal District Court decision finding a quadriplegic personally liable for the Trust Fund Recovery Penalty scant months following his crippling injury. However, in a 1999 case, the Third Circuit Court of Appeals reversed a New Jersey Federal District Court decision holding corporate officers liable for unpaid payroll taxes arising when federal agencies would not pay outstanding bills or award new contracts to the corporation without the payment of bribes.

Controversy

To be considered a responsible person, must you have actually *exercised* authority in financial matters, or does it suffice that you have *exercisable* authority? Going against the weight of authority, the First Circuit Court of Appeals in 2000 determined that the standard is exercised authority. The IRS has announced its disagreement with the decision. Even outside of the New England states composing the First Circuit, individuals with exercisable authority are not without a defense. They may still show that their conduct was not willful—best shown by the absence of knowledge of the tax delinquency.

Tax Planning

Voluntary payments can be allocated to the trust portion of the employment tax liability, thereby reducing the subsequent personal liability of persons who are individually liable. Designations should be made both on the check and on accompanying correspondence that payment is to be applied against the withholdings from employee wages and not employer matching Social Security. Payments under an installment agreement with the IRS (see Chapter 13) are not considered as voluntary payments. Neither are payments made while in bankruptcy, although the court may direct application of payments to the trust portion first.

Caution

Be careful not to let a corporate charter lapse. In such a case, the IRS may be able to hold all directors and/or officers responsible for the entire corporate debt for employment and unemployment taxes if state law renders them personally liable for corporate debt upon lapse of charter.

Combining Your Business and Personal Travel

The cost of travel away from home for business purposes is usually a deductible expense. The expense of your hotel room during the business trip is fully deductible so long as your trip requires you to be away from home overnight. However, only 50 percent of the cost of your meals is deductible on the theory that the meal contains an element of personal living expense, regardless of the meal's relationship to your business activities.

If you combine a business trip with a vacation, you may be able to write off part of the cost of the trip as a business expense. If the trip is taken primarily for business purposes, the cost of traveling to and from the destination is fully deductible (with the exception of special rules that apply to trips outside the United States). The costs of your meals and lodging while on the trip are deductible (subject to the percentage rule for the costs of the meals) to the extent that they are allocable to business activities.

All of the circumstances surrounding a combined business/pleasure trip may be examined in the event of an audit to determine whether the primary purpose was business or personal. Obviously, the amount of time spent on business activities in relationship to the personal activity time will be an important factor.

Special rules cover combined business and personal trips that you take outside the United States for more than seven days. Under these circumstances, if you spend 25 percent or more of your time on personal activities, only the cost of the travel allocable to the business portion of the trip will be deductible, even if the trip was primarily business-oriented.

If you do not have substantial control over arranging the itinerary for the trip abroad or if you can establish that a personal vacation was not a major consideration in deciding to take the trip, no allocation will be required, and your entire travel costs will still be deductible as a business expense. If the trip abroad is primarily personal in nature, none of the travel expenses will be deductible, although the expenses incurred at the destination that are allocable solely to business activities will be deductible.

Besides airfare, meals, and lodging, other types of expenses are often overlooked when tallying up out-of-pocket costs away from home on business. Do not forget tips for the skycaps and porters, taxicabs or other transportation costs from the airport to the hotel and between the hotel and the various business sites, tips to the hotel maid, and tips for valet service.

If you own income-producing property, such as rental property, you can deduct the costs of reasonable travel to look after the property. For example, if you own a beachfront condominium in Florida, you probably can deduct the costs of travel to and from Florida in the middle of fall to get the property ready for the season and then again at the end of the rental season to close up the property. However, not all investment-related travel is deductible. You cannot deduct the costs of attending investment seminars or similar conventions. Similarly, the costs of traveling to a shareholders' meeting are usually not deductible.

Filing Pointer

Even though you are unable to deduct your spouse's travel costs unless he or she is a bona fide employee of the business, you will nonetheless get some break with the cost of your lodging. Only to the extent that your hotel room costs more than hotel accommodations at a single rate is a portion of the deduction denied. If no difference exists between the cost of the hotel room whether you are alone or with your spouse, the hotel room is fully deductible even though the spouse's travel costs will not be deductible.

Filing Pointer

Even though a corporation may not fully deduct certain expenses, such as spousal travel and 50 percent of meals, the disallowed amounts are not income to an employee if a business reason exists for the expense, thereby avoiding a *double-hit* (no business deduction yet income to the employee).

Question: I live in Chicago, and I will have to travel to San Francisco on business. I have scheduled meetings with business associates in San Francisco for each day, Monday through Friday. I hope to finish up on Friday afternoon and then spend the weekend in the wine country before my return flight to Chicago. Can I write off the cost of this trip?

Answer: The entire cost of the flight to and from San Francisco will be deductible as a business expense, because it is clear that the primary purpose of this trip will be business. The cost of your hotel room in San Francisco for Sunday night through Thursday night will also be fully deductible. The applicable percentage of the costs of your meals in San Francisco will also be deductible as a business expense.

Although the costs of the meals and lodging incurred during your trip into the wine country will not be deductible inasmuch as they are personal in nature, an exception may apply if you fly home on the Sunday following your meetings. In a 1992 letter ruling not binding on other taxpayers, the IRS indicated that the cost of lodging and the deductible cost of meals may be written off on a day without business activity if a net saving in travel cost results by staying over a Saturday night. For example, if your airfare is $300 instead of $1,200 by staying in California through Saturday night, the extra cost of meals (to the extent of the allowable percentage) and lodging are deductible if they do not exceed $900.

Getting Meat Out of Your Business Meals and Entertainment

The deduction for business meals, including the cost of meals incurred while traveling away from home and on business, and business entertainment expenses usually is limited to 50 percent of the total costs incurred. Exceptions do exist. For example, the 50 percent limitation on meals is not applicable to meals offered to the general public such as prior to a marketing presentation.

To be able to deduct the applicable portion of the cost of a business meal, you must be able to establish that more than a general expectation of deriving a business benefit exists and that business discussions actually occurred directly before, during, or after the meal. No deduction for a meal expense usually is allowable unless you or one of your employees is present at the meal.

Similar rules govern the deductibility of entertainment expenses. You must have more than a general expectation of deriving a benefit related to your business. Consequently, unless the entertainment is in a business setting, significant business discussions must occur before or after the event. For example, you can deduct the applicable portion of the cost of taking your biggest customer to a play on Broadway so long as you can establish that bona fide business discussions took place either before or after the play. However, according to a 1994 Tax Court decision, you cannot deduct the cost of taking your clients on Canadian and Alaskan fishing trips when business is discussed casually but when the primary purpose is keeping client goodwill.

No deduction can be claimed for costs associated with an entertainment facility that you own or rent, such as a yacht or tennis court; however, taxes and allowable interest remain deductible on the entertainment facility. Where the facility is used for entertainment purposes, the costs of the actual entertainment, such as food and beverages, are deductible subject to both the percentage rule and the ability to prove the validity of the entertainment expense.

The 50 percent limitation on entertainment expense is not applicable in the case of tickets given to customers and clients when you do not attend the event. Instead, the cost is treated as a business gift, which is fully deductible up to $25 per recipient per year. This will work in your favor for inexpensive tickets but to your detriment for costly tickets.

Most club dues are not deductible, including dues for country, athletic, luncheon, and airline clubs. This prohibition does not apply to chambers of commerce, professional organizations, public service clubs, and similar organizations.

Tax Planning

If you entertain groups of customers or clients, it is best to plan a formal agenda for meetings. In 1992 the Tax Court ruled that a repossessor could not deduct the appropriate percentage of the cost of sending three busloads of referral sources to Las Vegas for a weekend of entertainment and general discussions despite a significant rise in business thereafter. Four years earlier, the same court had allowed a title company to deduct the appropriate percentage of the cost of flying lawyers, realtors, and bankers to Las Vegas for entertainment combined with limited formal meetings.

No formal agenda? Here is another idea—a court-created exception to the requirement of either a business setting or bona fide business discussions. Throw a party so big that the "clear purpose is to obtain publicity as opposed to maintaining goodwill." That is what a Virginia Federal District Court determined as it permitted a deduction for the annual party of a developer whose guests included all real estate agents who sold at least two of his homes during the previous year. The party for 1989 featured cocktails, a seated dinner, and entertainment by singer Barbara Mandrell. The cost of the party was $347,000.

Filing Pointer

Do not forget that entertaining at home may very well qualify as a deductible business meal subject to the percentage limitation so long as you meet the usual standards. Of course, the added cost of feeding spouses will not be deductible unless a business purpose for the spouses' attendance can be established.

Caution

Do you regularly have a legitimate business meal with an associate or colleague in which you and the other person pick up the check on an alternating basis? In a 1998 decision, the Tax Court determined that these meal costs are completely nondeductible. According to the Court, the reciprocity showed a well-established business relationship not requiring frequent meals for business purposes.

Question: I am a department head employed by a major corporation, and my annual bonus is based on our department's profitability. To improve morale among my staff of five, I wine and dine them a half dozen times a year. Can I deduct the cost?

Answer: The Tax Court says, at least in the absence of a company policy requiring the entertainment of employees under your direction, that entertainment of fellow employees is a personal and nondeductible expense.

Caution

After cutting the deduction for business meals and entertainment from 100 percent to 80 percent and subsequently to 50 percent, will there be a move in the opposite direction? Congress has periodically considered legislation that would restore the 80 percent deduction for business meals and entertainment.

Your Tax Home—Not Where the Heart Is

Many individuals work away from home, have two homes, or have two jobs. These situations generate unique problems.

Most of the litigation concerning tax homes has arisen when an individual is situated in one city and is assigned to another location for a lengthy period. If the assignment is *temporary* in nature rather than *indefinite*, lodging, 50 percent of food expense, and related costs at the temporary job location can be written off. Work away from home for more than one year will necessarily be considered as indefinite. Work away from home for one year or less will be considered as temporary only during such period as it was intended and realistically expected that the assignment not exceed one year. According to the Tax Court in a 1999 decision, the one-year limitation does not apply to intermittent work assignments away from home.

Tax Planning

An individual accepting an ongoing job or position away from his or her established home should have a contract tightly drawn in order that any obligation not extend into a second year.

Controversy

When an assignment is temporary and the tax home does not shift, transportation expenses incurred while traveling to the temporary site are deductible. What if an individual chooses to commute daily to the temporary work site? The IRS agrees with the Tax Court determination in 1993 that the transportation costs are still deductible, even if the work site is within the metropolitan area. However, the IRS issued a Revenue Ruling in 1999 that would deny a deduction for daily transportation costs to temporary work sites within the metropolitan area when the individual has an office at home (see "The Office-in-Home Deduction—A Wider Door" later in this chapter) that is not his or her principal office and has no regular work location away from the residence. The IRS continues to disagree with a 1993 Tax Court decision that allowed such a deduction.

Question: During the summer, I am president of a company that supplies lifeguards to swimming pools in New Jersey. During the winter, I manage a ski resort in Vermont. I own a home in each location, staying about six months at each place. My family lives year-round in Vermont. For which residence should I keep records and claim that I was away from home?

Answer: An individual's "tax home" is where that person's principal place of business is located regardless of where his or her family resides. For example, according to a 1993 Tax Court decision, a pilot's tax home is the airport city at which the pilot actually is based as opposed to where the pilot resides. When your family resides in the locale of your principal place of business, you will be "away from home" when you travel to your secondary place of business. When your family resides in the locale of your secondary place of business, you will find it harder to deduct expenses. Your tax home remains at your principal place of business and, as such, your expenses for lodging, food, and related expenses are not deductible there. Your family's expenses at your secondary place of business are not deductible; only your individual allocable share of deductible expenses in the location of your secondary employment properly attributable to your presence there for business can be written off.

It will be necessary in your case to determine whether New Jersey or Vermont is your tax home based upon the comparative time spent, business activity, and financial return at each of your locations. The First Circuit Court of Appeals recently ruled that an individual, who is not an itinerant, must have a single tax home; thus, you will be able to deduct appropriate costs related to the necessity of maintaining a place to live at a second location. However, you will fare better if you can show that your tax home is in Vermont.

Substantiating Your Travel, Meals, and Entertainment Expenses

Unless you comply with the strict substantiation requirements of the law, no deduction is allowed for the cost of business travel, meals, and entertainment. Although the substantiation requirements are strict, they are not so onerous as to be overwhelming. All that you need to do is to be organized. Your record of travel, meals, and entertainment expenses must reflect the amount of the expense, the time and place of the expense, the business purpose of the expense, and the business relationship to you of each person who was entertained.

You establish the elements of substantiation by maintaining a diary or log. You do not have to make entries in the diary immediately after an expenditure is made, but you must make entries at a time when you have present knowledge of expenditures. For example, once a week you could go and record the various elements of each of the expenses incurred during the preceding week. You may group incidental expenses together.

Receipts or other documentary evidence are not required to claim a deduction for all travel and entertainment expenses. Obviously, receipts or bills will concretely establish the amount of expenses and are therefore quite helpful. However, you need retain only the receipt or other bill in the case of lodging or in the case of any other expenditure of at least $75. Pursuant to a 1998 IRS letter ruling, facsimilies and e-tickets are acceptable.

Failure to keep sufficient records can be costly. A manufacturing company had season tickets for football and hockey games and gave them away liberally to customers, vendors, distributors, and employees. Although the company kept records of who used the tickets, the Tax Court in a 1994 decision denied a deduction because records did not indicate the business relationship of the recipients.

Tax Planning

In lieu of maintaining a diary of actual expenses and retaining receipts for out-of-town travel, employers who reimburse their employees and self-employed individuals can claim deductions for meals, lodging, and incidentals based on a *per diem* allowance. Under this *per diem* arrangement, the business person can treat between $36 and $46 per day depending on location as the cost of his or her meals and incidentals. If reimbursements are made for lodging as well as for meals and incidentals, the federal *per diem* rate for localities in the continental United States is set forth in tables issued by the IRS or, under a simplified method, reimbursements can be made at a standard maximum rate of $126 per day ($207 in high-cost areas) of which $36 per day ($46 per day in the high-cost areas) is considered meal and incidental reimbursements. Rates set forth are next scheduled to be adjusted effective October 1, 2004.

The *per diem* method should be used only where that method will provide the maximum allowable deduction.

The Office-in-Home Deduction—A Wider Door

If you operate your business from your home, you may be entitled to claim certain write-offs on IRS Form 8829 with respect to the ownership of the property as a business deduction (known in the aggregate as the office-in-home deduction). To qualify for the office-in-home deduction, the portion of your home, which need not be an entire room, that is used for business purposes must meet the following requirements:

- The business use of that portion of the home must be exclusive, and it must be used regularly for business purposes.
- The business use of that portion of the home must be the principal location of the business; a location in which you meet your patients, clients, or customers in the normal course of business; a storage place for inventory if the home is the sole location of the business (no exclusivity requirement in that case); or, in the case of a separate structure not attached to the home, must be used in connection with your business.

Most controversies arising from the office-in-home deduction have involved the definition of the *principal* location of the business. A home can be an individual's principal place of business if used for administrative or management activities and if no other fixed location exists where such activities are conducted.

The write-offs that you can claim for the office-in-home deduction cannot exceed the income generated by the business at the home reduced by the normal operating expenses of the business not associated with the home (for example, office supplies, salaries, and postage) and further reduced by the portion of interest and taxes allocable to the portion of the dwelling unit used for business purposes. In other words, the office-in-home deduction can never create or increase a loss.

Illustration

Assume the following facts:

Gross Income	$70,000
Business Expenses Unrelated to Business Use of Home	$60,000
Interest on Taxes on Home Allocable to Business Portion	$ 8,000
Expenses Related to Home Allocable to Business Portion (Insurance, Utilities, and so on)	$ 5,000
Depreciation on Home Allocable to Business Portion	$ 4,000

This individual's business expenses unrelated to the business use of the home and the interest and taxes on the home attributable to the portion used for business purposes totaled $68,000. Only $2,000 ($70,000 – $68,000) of the expenses related to the home that were allocable to the office use are deductible as the office-in-home deduction. The remaining $3,000 of these expenses plus $4,000 of depreciation is carried over to the subsequent year as a possible office-in-home deduction.

The courts have backed up the IRS position that the office-in-home deduction is unavailable to income-producing activities not constituting a business. A full-time investor consequently meeting other requirements will be denied the office-in-home deduction.

Question: I live in Topeka, Kansas, where I work as a salesman. My employer's home office is in New Orleans. Although I make occasional trips to New Orleans for management meetings, I spend 95 percent of my time working in my home in the Topeka regional area. My employer does not have a branch office in Topeka, so I need my home office. I even have customers come to my home every day. Can I claim the office-in-home deduction?

Answer: Yes, you can claim the office-in-home deduction if the area from which you operate is used only for business, and you are engaged in your sales activity on a regular basis.

Be sure that you get your employer to substantiate by contract or letter the requirement that you work at home, inasmuch as an employee can claim the office in-home deduction if the work away from the employer's office is for the convenience of the employer. Be as specific as possible in the job duties that are to be performed at home.

If you do qualify for the office-in-home deduction, as an employee you will be able to claim the deduction only if you itemize and only if the amount of the deduction, when combined with other miscellaneous itemized deductions, exceeds 2 percent of your AGI. It is then subject to the overall reduction in itemized deductions by high-income individuals (discussed in Chapter 1).

Question: I just had a baby, and I want to telecommute for a few years. I plan to go into the office a few hours per week and work at home the balance of the time. Do I have any problems in claiming the office-in-home deduction?

Answer: You will have a number of obstacles to overcome—the most difficult being your need to show that your work at home was for the convenience of the employer. You may be able to satisfy this requirement if your employer has no desk space for you and is willing to require you to work at home for a period of time. Second, you must avoid any personal use of your work area. Finally, although not as significant a problem for you as for the part-time telecommuter, your home must be the principal location of your business functions based on the "relative importance" of activities performed at each location and the "relative time" spent at each location. The IRS first examines the relative importance of the office-in-home versus other locations at which business is conducted. Only if that test is inconclusive does IRS consider the relevant time at various locations. (See Chapter 11, "Special Groups of Taxpayers," for a discussion of these tests in connection with a musician who rehearsed at home.)

Question: I run a day-care center out of my home and take care of three or four children each working day. My entire home, with the exception of two bedrooms and a bathroom, is occupied 10 hours a day, 250 days per year, by the kids. On evenings and weekends, all rooms are used by my family. Can I claim the office-in-home deduction?

Answer: A 1992 ruling by the IRS permits day-care providers to claim the office-in-home deduction through a multiple-step process for determining the percentage of interest and taxes, depreciation, and other expenses of the home that are allocable to its business use. To illustrate, if you use 1,500 square feet out of 2,000 square feet (75 percent) regularly for day care, multiply .75 times .2854.

This latter fraction is based on the fact that day-care use of the home is 2,500 hours out of 8,760 hours during the year. The result is that you can deduct 21.4 percent of the expenses related to your home, subject to the requirement that the office-in-home deduction not exceed business income less other operating expenses.

In other words, the portion of the home for which you claim the office-in-home deduction is broken out not only on the basis of space but also on the basis of time.

Caution

See Chapter 6, "Real Estate—the Most Tax-Favored Investment,"concerning the requirement of recapturing the depreciation claimed as part of the office-in-home deduction upon sale of your principal residence and the use of the $250,000/$500,000 exclusion of gain. Also see Chapter 6 concerning partial ineligibility for the exclusion if the office-in-home deduction is claimed for a separate structure over a period covering more than two of the five years preceding the sale of the property. Additionally, see Chapter 6 concerning leasing space to your C corporation as an alternative to the office-in-home deduction.

Working at Your Hobby—Is the Business for Real?

Here is a situation that may sound familiar to you. Tom has a regular job as an employee, but on nights, weekends, and any free time that he can find, he works on a sideline activity in antique sales. Or, perhaps Tom is not employed anywhere, and his antique business is a full-time endeavor. Even so, Tom must be careful of the hobby loss rules. If these rules are applied, Tom will be able to claim a deduction beyond taxes and allowable interest only to the extent that no loss is created from the activity. A taxpayer is not permitted to claim a net loss on any activity treated as a hobby to him. This rule applies regardless of whether Tom passes the material participation tests associated with limiting deductions for losses from passive activities (see Chapter 2) and regardless of the at-risk and basis rules (see Chapter 7, "Other Tax-Favored Investments").

A rebuttable presumption arises in the taxpayer's favor that an activity is not a hobby if the gross income derived from the endeavor exceeds the deductions in three out of five consecutive years. When the activity involves breeding, training, showing, or racing horses, the presumption will arise in favor of the taxpayer if a profit occurs in two out of seven years.

Even if you cannot meet the presumption, you may still be able to claim a deduction for losses sustained in the activity if you can establish that you are engaging in the activity for the purpose of making a profit. The following factors will be analyzed to determine your motivation:

- Is the activity conducted in a businesslike manner?
- What is your expertise or the expertise of those you engage? Do you know what you are doing, or do you hire somebody who is familiar with the operation that you are undertaking?
- How much time and effort do you spend on the activity?
- Will the assets used in the activity appreciate?
- How successful have you been in carrying on other business endeavors?
- What is your history of income and losses?
- What are your financial resources from other sources?
- What is the extent of personal pleasure obtained from your participation in the activity?

Just because a loss business is pleasurable does not mean that it is a hobby. It depends on the facts of each case. Noting that "suffering has never been a prerequisite to deductibility," the Tax Court ruled in 1992 that a manager of musical groups could deduct the nearly $140,000 spent in unsuccessfully promoting his wife's singing career. In the same year, the Tax Court permitted a struggling artist living off inherited money to claim large losses resulting from her unsuccessful career. Two years later the same court disallowed $60,000 worth of deductions to a father who sponsored his son's entry onto the professional golf tour. The son had won a total of $155 before Dad threw in the towel. In 1996 the Tax Court allowed a tuna boat operator to claim substantial losses. In one year he caught only one fish and lost $21,000. Later that year the Tax Court allowed a trash trucker to deduct more than $200,000 in losses arising from searching for gold. He found but a few coins and eventually gave up.

Lawyers themselves have been before the Tax Court. In a 1994 case, an attorney who had been raised on a farm sought to supplement his income by buying a farm. Instead, he lost $1.1 million over eight years. The Tax Court, however, permitted him to claim the losses inasmuch as he spent 500 to 700 hours per year running the farm in a "businesslike" manner. In another 1994 case, the IRS unsuccessfully sought to claim that an attorney was practicing law as a hobby.

The following are some of the other types of hobbies that can result in losses, with the presumption that they are hobbies:

- Freelance photographer
- Stamp, baseball card, or coin collector
- Comic book, print, or old postcard collector
- Antique or rare book collector

To avoid or minimize scrutiny of an activity under the hobby loss rules, be sure that your books and records are kept in a businesslike manner. Take every possible step to familiarize yourself with the whole operation from beginning to end. Hire individuals to work for you to add expertise if you cannot manage it all yourself. Most important, do not stick with a project if it proves to be a bad investment—do not throw good money after bad just to claim tax losses.

All may not be lost despite bad records over many years of losses. In a 1999 decision, the Sixth Circuit Court of Appeals allowed an individual to claim five years of farm losses. The Court found that his records were no worse than other farmers and that his continuing losses showed "commercial tenacity." However, in a 2000 decision, the First Circuit Court of Appeals denied a deduction to an individual with $6.6 million in horse racing and breeding losses over 37 years.

Year-End Reminder

If you use a cash basis of accounting to report income and expenses of an activity, you may be able to create a "profitable" year by delaying the payment of bills until after year-end.

Filing Pointer

You may want to elect permitted slower methods of depreciation in order to avoid a loss in the early years of a business.

Tax Planning

If your business is subject to the five-year or seven-year rules previously described, a special election might save your deductions. You can elect to suspend the application of the for-profit presumption until after the relevant period has lapsed. By giving a new business time to establish itself, you might be able to prove that the activity is conducted on a for-profit basis under the criteria listed previously. You also give the business two extra years to prove that the activity is conducted on a for-profit basis. After you make the election on IRS Form 5213, the statute of limitations for any deficiency during any year in the suspension period is extended to at least two years after the due date of the return for the last year in the five- or seven-year period.

Caution

The hobby loss rules apply beyond activities with an element of personal pleasure. The rules apply to any activity and require a profit-making intent. Consequently, to claim a loss related to real property not held for personal use, you must have a profit motive.

In a 1994 decision, the Tax Court struck a blow to individuals absorbing rental losses in the hopes of future property appreciation. The Court determined that the renting of a property and the holding of that property for appreciation are two separate activities. The decision appears to give a blank check to the IRS to disallow net rental losses when there exists little likelihood of net rental gains in the foreseeable future.

What Is an "Ordinary and Necessary" Business Expense?

Although certain business costs must meet specific requirements under the law to be deductible, most expenses must be only "ordinary and necessary."

What is an ordinary and necessary business expense must be determined on the facts of each case. In a 2001 case, the Tax Court allowed a business deduction for cat food. However, the taxpayer was a junkyard seeking to attract wild cats to keep out snakes and rats.

Harold L. Jenkins persuaded about 75 of his friends and associates to invest in a new burger chain. Three years later, the company failed and was shut down. Without a legal requirement, Mr. Jenkins repaid the investors every dollar of their investment plus an interest factor.

When Mr. Jenkins deducted the payments to the investors, the IRS disallowed the deduction. The Tax Court decided in favor of Mr. Jenkins, determining that, under the facts of the case, Mr. Jenkins repaid investors to protect his business reputation.

In country music, the Court observed, an entertainer must protect his reputation or suffer financially. Harold L. Jenkins was better known as the now deceased country singer Conway Twitty, and his burger was known as the Twitty Burger.

Breaking precedent, the Court put its decision to rhyme:

Twitty Burger went belly up
But Conway remained true
He repaid his investors, one and all
It was the moral thing to do.
His fans would not have liked it
It could have hurt his fame
Had any investors sued him

Like Merle Haggard or Sonny James.
When it was time to file taxes
Conway thought what he would do
Was deduct those payments as a business expense
Under section one-sixty-two.
In order to allow these deductions
Goes the argument of the Commissioner
The payments must be ordinary and necessary
To a business of the petitioner.
Had Conway not repaid the investors
His career would have been under a cloud,
Under the unique facts of the case
Held: The deductions are allowed.

Cynthia Hess, known professionally as Chesty Love, had her breasts enlarged in 1988 and again in 1991. Following the first implant, Ms. Hess, an exotic dancer, quadrupled her income.

When Ms. Hess claimed a depreciation deduction for her implants, the IRS disallowed the deduction. The Tax Court decided in favor of Ms. Hess, finding that, under the facts of the case, the costs were incurred solely in furtherance of business and that Ms. Hess derived no personal benefit from what she described as a necessary "stage prop."

CHAPTER 11

Special Groups of Taxpayers

Actors, Actresses, and Performing Artists

As previously discussed, employees are able to obtain a tax benefit from employee business expenses only to the extent that the aggregate expenses exceed 2 percent of AGI. Very often this means that employees will lose the tax benefit of most (if not all) of their employee business expenses. A special exception to the 2-percent floor is carved out for certain actors, actresses, and performing artists. Individuals who qualify under this special rule are entitled to claim a deduction for their employee business expenses in full regardless of the 2-percent floor (see Chapter 3, "Deductions and Credits—For Itemizers and Nonitemizers") or whether they itemize their deductions.

To qualify, the individual must have worked in the performing arts as an employee for at least two different employers during the year; the aggregate employee business expenses associated with this work must exceed 10 percent of gross income attributable to work as a performing artist; and the artist's AGI exclusive of the employee business expenses cannot exceed $16,000. If all of these conditions are met, the actor or other performing artist is entitled to claim all employee business expenses from the profession (not just those that exceed 10 percent of gross income) as a deduction in computing AGI.

For the purpose of determining whether the performing artist has worked for two different employers during the year, only those employers from whom the artist has received at least $200 in compensation are taken into account.

If the performer is married and has lived at any time during the year with his or her spouse, the couple must file a joint income tax return in order to be eligible for the special treatment. On the joint return, if both spouses qualify for the special rule, each will have to determine his or her own qualification for the special treatment by taking into account separate employment circumstances during the year and separate business expenses. However, the AGI ceiling of $16,000 remains the same regardless of whether one or both spouses is a performing artist.

For example, if Chad and Lisa are both performers, they will have to file a joint return for either one of them to be eligible for this special rule. Assuming that they file a joint return, either Chad, Lisa, or both of them may be able to claim employee business expenses as an adjustment to income (rather than as an itemized deduction subject to the 2-percent floor) if either or both of them meet the three conditions. If Chad were a struggling actor, but Lisa were a successful banker, Chad would be unable to use this special rule if the couple's AGI exceeded $16,000, even though his separate income from his acting jobs did not total $16,000.

If the special rule applicable to performing artists is unavailable, employee business expenses may be claimed as miscellaneous itemized deductions to the extent that they exceed 2 percent of AGI.

Controversy

Can valuable musical instruments be depreciated? In 1995, the Third Circuit Court of Appeals agreed with the Tax Court that a 17th-century bass viol was subject to wear and tear and was depreciable. The Court rejected the IRS argument that the viol was a treasured artwork without a useful life. The IRS has indicated that it will continue to litigate similar cases outside of the Third Circuit states of Pennsylvania, New Jersey, and Delaware.

Filing Pointer

Can a professional musician claim the office-in-home deduction (see Chapter 10, "Business Tax Planning")? The Ninth Circuit Court of Appeals said "yes" in a 2001 decision. Unable to determine the relevant importance of a violinist's home, where she rehearsed, versus the orchestra and recording studio where she performed, the Court looked to relative time spent in each location—an easy win for her living room studio.

Caution

As discussed later in this chapter, as in the case of athletes, states are aggressively pursuing actors, actresses, and others whose multistate performances allow states to tax *pro rata* shares of their income.

Alien Workers

An alien (a non-U.S. citizen), even an illegal alien, may be subject to U.S. income tax. The tax rules will vary depending upon whether the alien is a U.S. resident or a nonresident. Resident aliens are those who meet a green card test (they are lawful, permanent residents of the United States) or those who meet a substantial presence test.

An individual will be considered a resident alien under the substantial presence test if he or she is in the United States for at least 31 days during the current year and 183 days during the period consisting of the current year and the two preceding years, counting all of the days of physical presence in the current calendar year but only one-third of the days of physical presence in the first preceding year and only one-sixth of the days of physical presence in the second preceding calendar year.

For example, if a citizen of Japan were present in the United States for all of 2001, 260 days of 2002, and 40 days of 2003, the substantial presence test for 2002 will be satisfied.

	DAYS IN UNITED STATES	
2003	40 × 1	= 40
2002	260 × 1/3	= 87
2001	365 × 1/6	= 61
		188

Even though an individual may meet the 31-day/183-day substantial presence test, that person will not be considered a resident alien if temporarily present in the United States because of diplomatic status or employment with an international organization. Resident alien status will not arise in the case of a teacher present in the United States on a J visa, a student present on a temporary S or J visa, or a professional athlete here to compete in charitable sports events. Even though an individual may meet the substantial presence test, that person will not be considered a resident alien for tax purposes in a particular year if he or she is present in the United States for less than 183 days, has regular employment in a foreign country, and demonstrates closer ties to that country than to the United States.

Resident aliens usually are subject to the same income tax rules as those that govern U.S. citizens. The resident alien is taxed on worldwide income, not just income from U.S. sources. A resident alien is entitled to file a joint income tax return with a spouse only if the spouse is a U.S. citizen or resident alien. The resident alien may elect to treat a nonresident alien spouse as a U.S. resident. The effect of the election is to tax the couple on their worldwide sources of income. Without the election, the married resident alien must file using the higher married-filing-separately rates.

Resident aliens are entitled to claim a deduction for personal exemptions and are entitled to claim an exemption for a spouse even if a joint return is not filed, if the spouse has no income from U.S. sources. The resident alien may claim a deduction for personal exemptions of other individuals (for example, children and siblings) if the usual requirements for the dependency deduction are satisfied. One of the conditions is that the person to be claimed as a dependent must be a U.S. citizen, a U.S. national, or a resident of the United States, Canada, or Mexico.

Although resident aliens usually are taxed in the same manner as U.S. citizens, resident aliens who are employees of a foreign government, or of certain tax-exempt international organizations, such as the World Bank, are not taxed by the United States on their compensation received from the foreign government or international organization.

Any individual who is not a resident alien will be taxed under the rules governing the taxation of nonresident aliens. These individuals are subject to U.S. income tax on their income connected with a U.S. business (including most salary income) at the same rates at which U.S. citizens are taxed. Nonresident aliens who have income from the United States not connected with a U.S. business will be subject to tax on this income on a gross basis (no deductions) at a flat 30 percent rate or, as is often applicable, at a lower rate as a result of a treaty with the other nation.

A nonresident alien is required to pay tax at the regular U.S. income tax rates on gain derived from the sale of U.S. real property, regardless of the number of days of presence in the United States. To cover this liability, the buyer will be required to withhold 10 percent of the amount realized on the sale but no more than the seller's tax liability as determined by the IRS. Within 90 days of receipt of a request for tax determination, the IRS must act in order that the seller can claim a refund before the due date of his or her tax return if the tax liability is less than the amount withheld. In any event, no withholding is required if the buyer bought the property as a home and it cost no more than $300,000.

See Chapter 12, "Estate Planning Strategies," for a discussion of how aliens are treated differently under the estate and gift tax laws and Chapter 5, "Gains and Losses," for a discussion of how nonresident aliens would be treated differently under the carryover basis rules for inherited property, which are scheduled to commence on a limited basis in 2010.

An alien usually becomes a resident for tax purposes on January 1 of the year in which that person meets either of two residency tests. However, an alien usually ceases to be a resident for tax purposes upon "permanent" return to his or her home country.

Caution

The expatriation law applies to resident aliens. A resident alien in at least five of the most recent 15 years losing green card status or being treated as a resident of another country through treaty, like a departing citizen, is subject to U.S. income tax on U.S. source income for 10 years following expatriation if a principal purpose of the move was tax avoidance. An individual who had average tax liability for the most recent five years of more than $122,000 or a net worth on expatriation of at least $608,000 is presumed to have had a tax-avoidance purpose. These numbers for 2003 are indexed for cost of living in 2004 and succeeding years.

Caution

The United States has income, estate, and gift tax treaties with many foreign countries that may also impact on the tax rules governing alien workers in the United States. The applicability of a treaty to the particular situation must be considered before any final determination is made as to the liability of an alien worker for U.S. income taxes.

Athletes

Professional athletes require good tax planning to minimize tax liability for their high-income years. Nonqualified deferred compensation plans (see Chapter 2, "Taxable and Tax-Free Income and Benefits") are of particular interest to the highly paid professional athlete because the amount of employer contributions to qualified retirement plans is limited by law. Under a nonqualified deferred compensation plan, an athlete typically will receive payments after retirement. The obligation of the team or other payer to make these payments may not be secured, or it will cause the athlete to be taxed prior to receipt of the deferred compensation.

With the reduction in the highest marginal tax bracket from 70 percent to 31 percent during the 1980s, a lesser need existed for the athlete to seek to defer income. In most cases the athlete was better off paying taxes at yesterday's tax brackets rather than risk both higher brackets and possible default on the future obligation. With the 1993 increase in the highest marginal tax bracket to 39.6 percent, a resurgence in the use of nonqualified deferred compensation by athletes occurred. With the decline to a 35-percent maximum marginal tax bracket in 2003, this decade may see a decline in the use of nonqualified deferred compensation by athletes and other high-income individuals.

Filing Pointer

Fines imposed for rule breaking are deductible business expenses, distinguishable from fines assessed by federal, state, or local authorities for violations of law.

Tax Planning

Residency of an athlete in a state without an income tax, such as Florida or Texas, will minimize state income taxes. However, most athletes play in a number of states during the year, and states aggressively tax *pro rata* shares of athletes' income based on where the services were performed.

What services are counted in the proration? Is compensation earned only for game days or is compensation earned for exhibition games and practices as well? One multistate task force recommended a concept of "duty days" covering all days in which required services were performed. Many states have followed the recommendation.

The task force did not address issues related to athletes in nonteam sports, such as tennis and golf, who often practice in their home states between tournaments.

Clergy

Clergy (ministers, priests, and rabbis) are not taxed on the rental value of a home or on a rental or housing allowance provided to them. Even though a member of the clergy is entitled to this exemption when computing regular income tax liability, no similar exemption exists in the computation of the Social Security contribution through the self-employment tax.

For the purpose of this exclusion, furnishings for the home may be provided as part of the allowance. The allowance may include payments to purchase a home, including the principal and interest on a mortgage, as well as expenses directly related to maintaining a home, such as utilities, property taxes, insurance, and furnishings.

In connection with any such allowance paid to allow a member of the clergy to rent or provide himself or herself with a home, several limitations apply. First, the exclusion for a cash allowance or rental allowance may not exceed the fair rental value of the home, including furnishings, plus the cost of utilities. Second, the allowance actually must be used by the recipient to provide himself or herself with a residence (either by payment of rent or through payment of a mortgage), insurance, taxes, utilities, or furniture. Third, the rental allowance, when coupled with straight salary, may not exceed reasonable compensation. Fourth, the allowance officially must be designated by the ministry in an employment contract or in minutes as a housing or rental allowance prior to payment.

Even though clergy do not include the parsonage allowance in income, they are entitled to claim a deduction for interest and taxes paid on the residence as itemized deductions (see Chapter 4, "Deductions—For Itemizers Only").

For Social Security purposes, members of the clergy are considered self-employed and, therefore, generally are subject to the self-employment tax on their net earnings received from the religious organization. An automatic exemption from Social Security applies if the member of the clergy belongs to a religious order that has taken a vow of poverty. If that person is affiliated with a religion conscientiously opposed to public or private insurance, the clergy member may file Form 4361 with the IRS to elect out of coverage. A clergy member who opted out of coverage had a one-time opportunity to revoke the exemption by filing Form 2031 no later than the extended due date of the 2001 return.

Clergy who are not exempt compute net earnings from self-employment (see Chapter 10) in the same manner as a sole proprietor, meaning that this person deducts expenses incurred in generating income. The excluded housing allowance is added in to determine the basis on which the self-employment tax is computed.

For federal income tax withholding purposes, a minister is not considered an employee subject to income tax withholding. However, his or her income may be reported on a W-2, and he or she may voluntarily agree with the ministry to have income tax withheld in order to cover any potential income tax liability as well as self-employment tax liability. Without such withholding, a member of the clergy usually would make estimated tax payments on a quarterly basis to avoid penalty.

Caution

Systematic gifts by a congregation to clergy are attributable to services and taxable, according to a 1995 decision of the Eighth Circuit Court of Appeals. Payments to clergy for performing weddings, funerals, and similar functions are also taxable. However, individual gifts may on specific facts be tax-free to clergy as arising out of the disinterested generosity of parishoners. (See Chapter 2 for a discussion of when a gift is really a tax-free gift.)

Executives

Corporate executives will often be given some flexibility with respect to their compensation packages, including the ability to participate in cafeteria plans, qualified retirement plans, and nonqualified plans of deferred compensation. Start-up companies and well-established companies may offer their corporate executives the ultimate fringe benefit—the opportunity to acquire an equity interest in the company through restricted stock or stock options. Options to acquire the employer stock can be in the form of Incentive Stock Options or nonqualified options. Participation in these types of compensation plans require individual analysis and consideration of both the tax ramifications and the economic ramifications of the opportunity. Qualified retirement plans are discussed in Chapter 9, "Retirement Plans"; the other named benefits are discussed in Chapter 2.

Filing Pointer

Executives nearing retirement, who are in a 33 or 35 percent tax bracket, should give serious consideration to deferring income to post-retirement years, when they will often be in a lower tax bracket caused by both reduced income and the scheduled reduction of tax brackets.

Farmers

Farmers are required to capitalize, rather than deduct, the cost of raising plants and animals that have a pre-productive period of more than two years. If the crop's or animal's pre-productive period is two years or less and a farmer uses a cash method of accounting, the costs of growing the crop or raising the animal can be expensed.

As with other taxpayers, farmers are eligible to depreciate their equipment and other depreciable assets. Under this system of cost recovery, three-year property includes breeding hogs, tractor units, race horses that are more than two years old, and any other horse over 12 years old. Breeding and dairy cattle are included in the five-year property class. Breeding and workhorses 12 years old or younger, farm machinery, and equipment are among the kinds of property that fall within the seven-year class of property. Farm buildings fall into the 20-year class of property.

Rather than capitalize soil and water conservation expenditures, farmers can deduct such costs if they are made consistent with a plan approved by the Soil Conservation Service of the U.S. Department of Agriculture or similar state agency. The deduction for soil and water conservation expenditures cannot exceed 25 percent of the gross income, which is derived from the farming operation.

The types of expenses that can be the subject of this election are those that would otherwise be nondepreciable capital costs such as grading, terracing, contouring, or leveling land; constructing of drainage ditches, earthen dams, or ponds; removal of brush; planting of trees and other windbreaks to prevent erosion; or digging irrigation ditches.

If a farmer holds a full-time job but engages in farming as well, he must be particularly aware of the hobby loss rules (discussed in Chapter 10). These gentlemen farmers are often closely scrutinized by the IRS because their farming operations consistently report losses. If the farm operation is conducted with a profit motive, the losses will offset the farmer's salary income from the other job so long as the material participation and at-risk rules are met.

Such farming operations rarely will be able to show a profit in three out of five years (two out of seven years for horse breeders) so as to create a presumption under the hobby loss rules (see Chapter 10) that the farming activity was engaged in for profit. Even if the presumption cannot be created, gentlemen farmers should still be able to use the farm losses to offset their other income, assuming that they meet the material participation standards (see Chapter 2), satisfy the at-risk rules (see Chapter 7, "Other Tax-Favored Investments"), conduct their farming operations in a businesslike manner, educate themselves as to the latest farming techniques, and hire personnel with the appropriate expertise.

Filing Pointer

Farmers may carry back farm losses for five years instead of the usual two years (see Chapter 1, "Introduction to Personal Tax Planning"). Farmers may average income based on the sum of the tax on nonfarm income plus the tax computed by applying one-third of the farm income to the marginal tax bracket of each of the three prior years. Schedule J has been designed for eligible farmers. This income-averaging technique may not be used for the computation of AMT (see Chapter 1) or self-employment tax (see Chapter 10). IRS Regulations require that an income-averaging election be made on a timely filed return in the absence of IRS approval or adjustment to the return.

Filing Pointer

The IRS has done an about-face on the use of negative income numbers during the base years. After initially taking the position that a base year number could not be less than zero, the IRS has changed its mind. However, you must back out net operating losses that provide benefits in other years.

Filing Pointer

Individuals who derive at least two-thirds of their gross income from farming need not pay any estimated taxes if they file their return and pay the tax by March 1 (a month and a half early). If the farmer's return is not going to be filed by March 1, only one instead of the usual four estimated tax payments needs to be made, and that payment is due on January 15 following the close of the year. For example, a farmer can either file his or her 2003 tax return by March 1, 2004, or make an estimated tax payment by January 15, 2004. The amount of estimated taxes that must be paid if no return will be filed by March 1 is only two-thirds of the current year's tax (or 100 percent of the preceding year's tax, if that amount is less).

Handicapped Individuals

A handicapped individual, like all other taxpayers, must include amounts received from all sources, including salary, bonuses, and investment income, in his or her gross income. If a handicapped individual receives unemployment compensation, it will be fully taxable, but payments received under a worker's compensation act will be exempt from tax (see Chapter 2).

If a handicapped individual is under the age of 65, is permanently and totally disabled, and receives a taxable disability pension, that person may be entitled to a tax credit. An individual will be considered to be permanently and totally disabled if he or she cannot engage in any substantial gainful activity because of a physical or mental condition. A physician must certify that the condition has lasted or can be expected to last for a minimum of 12 months or that the condition can be expected to lead to death.

The credit amount for the disabled is 15 percent of a base amount, usually $5,000 (or, if less, 15 percent of the disability income). Before figuring the amount of the credit, the base amount is reduced by any nontaxable Social

Security benefits, nontaxable railroad retirement benefits, and the amount of any nontaxable pension or disability benefits paid by the Department of Veterans Affairs (VA). The base amount is also reduced by one-half of AGI to the extent that it exceeds $7,500. Thus, a single individual with nontaxable Social Security, VA, or other pension benefits of $5,000 or more, with AGI of $17,500 or more, or with a certain combination of both, will not be able to claim the credit.

Illustration

Ken is single and 40 years old. He is permanently disabled. He received $2,000 in Social Security benefits, $6,000 from a taxable disability pension, and $6,000 of interest and dividends.

$5,000	**Base Amount (lesser of $5,000 or disability income)**
(2,000)	**Nontaxable Social Security Benefits**
(2,250)	**One-Half Excess AGI ($12,000) greater than $7,500**
$750	**Credit Base**
$113	**Credit (15% × $750)**

If a permanently and totally disabled individual is married, a joint return must be filed to claim the credit, unless the couple did not live together at any time during the year. When a joint return is filed, the base amount is $5,000 if only one of the spouses is totally and permanently disabled or $7,500 if both spouses are so disabled. On a joint return, the base amount is reduced by one-half of the amount by which the couple's AGI exceeds $10,000. If a disabled person elects to file a separate return but is eligible for the credit because he or she lived apart from his or her spouse for the entire year, the base amount is $3,750 and is reduced by one-half of the amount by which AGI exceeds $5,000. This credit is calculated in conjunction with the credit for the elderly discussed in Chapter 3.

As discussed in Chapter 1, a blind individual is entitled to a higher standard deduction than other taxpayers. As discussed in Chapter 3, if an individual incurs expenses to care for a disabled spouse or dependent in order to work, a dependent care credit is available.

A handicapped employee who incurs employee business expenses, such as paying for an attendant in order to perform a job, is entitled to claim these kinds of expenses as miscellaneous itemized deductions regardless of whether they exceed 2 percent of AGI.

Filing Pointer

Small businesses, those with no more than 30 full-time employees or gross receipts of no more than $1 million in the previous year, can claim a tax credit equal to 50 percent of eligible expenditures in excess of $250 incurred for the purpose of complying with the Americans with Disabilities Act of 1990 by removing architectural, transportation, and other barriers for handicapped individuals. The maximum credit is $5,000. All businesses can expense up to $15,000 of the costs incurred to remove architectural and transportation barriers in order to make the business more accessible for use by handicapped people. Costs incurred that exceed $15,000 have to be capitalized and depreciated. The amount of any tax credit must be subtracted from costs eligible for expensing or depreciation.

Household Employers—The Nanny Tax

Responding to the avalanche of publicity regarding the failure of various candidates for public office and political appointees to comply with payroll tax requirements for household employers, Congress in 1994 passed the Social Security Domestic Employment Reform Act. In an effort to ease the tax reporting burden placed on employers of household workers, such as nannies and housekeepers, the legislation provides that household employers are not liable for Social Security taxes on small amounts of wages paid to their domestic workers. The threshold of $1,400 in 2003 and 2004 is indexed in 2005 and succeeding years for increases in average wages.

Household employers are no longer required to file federal quarterly payroll reports. Rather, Social Security, federal unemployment, and withheld federal income taxes are now paid with the employer's individual income tax return. However, the compliance rate remains low. Only about 260,000 returns acknowledge the use of household employees.

Question: I pay my 15-year-old babysitter about $25 per week throughout the year. Am I a household employer covered by these new rules?

Answer: Even though you might pay your baby-sitter more than $1,400 in a year, you are not a household employer. Specifically excluded from coverage by the new rules are individuals in your situation. So long as your sitter is under the age of 18 and domestic employment is not his or her principal job, you are not required to pay Social Security taxes. However, if your sitter is at least 18 years old or if baby-sitting is his or her principal occupation, you will be required to comply with the new rules.

Caution

Even though federal employment taxes on household employees are now paid annually on April 15, state law may still require that state unemployment taxes and withheld state income taxes be paid more frequently. Also, note the January 31 deadline for providing a household worker with a W-2.

Controversy

Lost in all of the hoopla surrounding payroll taxes on household workers is the possibility that certain domestic help may properly be classified as independent contractors. Although a 40-hour-per-week household worker is almost certainly an employee, the half-day-per-week cleaning person may be an independent contractor. See Chapter 10 as to the classification of workers as independent contractors or employees.

Insurance Agents

Insurance agents, like other workers, can be classified as employees whose compensation is subject to Social Security taxes, unemployment taxes, and income tax withholding, or as independent contractors whose net earnings from the business are subject to self-employment tax but not unemployment tax or income tax withholding. (See Chapter 10 for a discussion of the factors that are used to ascertain whether an employment relationship exists.)

If the agent is a full-time life insurance salesperson, a third classification applies. An insurance agent whose principal business activity is selling life insurance or annuity contracts is a statutory employee. As discussed in Chapter 4, such an agent will receive a W-2, and his or her compensation is subject to Social Security and Medicare withholding. However, no unemployment tax is paid on this compensation, and the compensation is not subject to any income tax withholding. For the purpose of deducting business expenses, he or she is an independent contractor.

An insurance agent will often have an agreement with the insurance company that will allow the agent to receive draws against commissions that the agent may earn in the future. According to a 1997 decision by the Tax Court, these advance commissions are not taxable if the advances are recognized as loans between the company and the agent and repayable on the company's demand after the agent's termination. In a 2001 Revenue Procedure, the IRS agreed—provided that written documentation exists for the loan, which must bear adequate interest and be repayable even if future commissions are insufficient offset to the debt.

Tax Planning

If you receive advance commissions, make sure that you have a written agreement to repay advances with interest, or you will be taxed on receipt of the advances instead of when the commissions are earned.

Controversy

Are payments received by a former self-employed agent from an insurance company after retirement subject to self-employment tax? The IRS insisted that they were, even though the Ninth and Federal Circuit Courts of Appeal disagreed. The Tenth Circuit Court of Appeals backed the IRS, and the Tax Court reached different results in different fact situations. Congress then got in the picture and legislated that payments are not subject to self-employment tax if received after the agent's employment termination; the agent performs no services thereafter until at least the end of the year of payment; the agent is bound by at least a one-year covenant not to compete; and the payment amount is tied to prior year sales and/or to policy renewals. Eligibility for payment but not the amount of payment can depend on length of service.

As to payments that do not meet the criteria of the new law, the controversy will probably continue. Retiring insurance agents are well advised to comply with the safe harbor in order to avoid being caught in the controversy.

Military Personnel and Victims of Terrorism

Military personnel are not taxed on the amount of housing allowances, costs of living allowances, and uniform allowances they receive. (According to the Court of Federal Claims in a 1999 decision, these types of excluded expenses are earned income for the purpose of the earned income credit discussed in Chapter 3.) Moving expenses paid by the military are not taxed, even though the time and mileage requirements applicable to other taxpayers are not satisfied. These expenses include dislocation allowances, temporary lodging expenses, and moving-in household allowances, all of which are taxable to civilians.

Although other military pay is generally taxable, the pay of U.S. military personnel with rank below noncommissioned officer serving in a combat zone or qualified hazardous duty area is exempt from federal income tax. This includes reenlistment pay whenever received if the reenlistment occurs in a combat zone or hazardous duty area. A commissioned officer's military pay up to the highest rate of pay of enlisted personnel is currently exempt. The President determines the existence of a combat zone or qualified hazardous duty area. President Bush declared service in Afghanistan starting September 19, 2001, to be in a combat zone with support service in certain nearby countries to be hazardous duty (the Persian Gulf area has been treated as a combat zone since 1991). The action permitted effected individuals to get an additional period without penalty or interest to file returns, pay taxes, and make qualified retirement plan and IRA contributions and rollovers. The period expires 180 days after the later of leaving the combat zone or, if wounded, 180 days after being released from continuous hospitalization. For hospitalization inside the United States, the extension period cannot exceed five years. Civilian personnel in affected areas under the direction of the military, Red Cross personnel, and accredited correspondents are eligible for the extensions. The IRS gets an equivalent extension for assessing and collecting tax liability. (See Chapter 13, "Dealing with the Internal Revenue Service," for these procedural topics.)

Military pay also receives an exemption from tax while an individual is hospitalized as a result of wounds, disease, or injury incurred in a combat zone, for up to two years after the termination of combat activities. A serviceperson's entire income is exempt from tax if the individual dies from injury or disease while serving in a combat zone, and the exemption is retroactive to the year in which service in a combat zone commenced. Other servicepersons or federal employees dying as the result of military or terroristic action outside of the United States receive the exemption for the year of death and the immediately preceding year.

A reduced estate tax liability applies to deaths arising from service in a combat zone.

The Victims of Terrorist Relief Act of 2001 gave retroactive relief to victims of the 1995 Oklahoma City bombing as well as to victims of the September 11, 2001 terrorist attacks and the Fall 2001 anthrax attacks. Their death benefits are tax-free if they would not have been payable on account of death from any other cause. An income tax (but not self-employment tax) exemption applies for the year of death and the immediately preceding year; a minimum tax benefit of $10,000 applies. Victims of these terrorist attacks receive the same reduced estate tax liability as military combat victims.

Tax Planning

A 401(k) or Simple retirement plan is permitted to offer a catch-up period on missed elective deferrals by military personnel returning to prior employers. Both types of retirement plans are discussed in Chapter 9.

Caution

Congress is considering legislation which, if enacted, would expand tax benefits to the military. Under one provision with broad applicability, the ownership and use periods required to calculate gain on disposition of a principal residence (see Chapter 6, "Real Estate—The Most Tax-Favored Investment") would be suspended at the option of the taxpayer for up to five years of military service. H.R. 1307, the Armed Forces Tax Fairness Act of 2003, passed the House unanimously on March 20, 2003 and the Senate unanimously on March 27, 2003 in different form requiring consideration by a conference committee.

Tax Planning

Service personnel often have the ability to reduce state taxes. They are not considered domiciles and residents of the state in which they are stationed but are deemed domiciles and residents of the state from which they entered the military. Entry into the armed services from Florida, Texas, or one of several other states without an individual income tax will minimize state income tax liability.

Overseas Workers

Although a U.S. citizen or resident is taxed on worldwide income and must file a tax return as any other individual, he or she can elect to exclude up to $80,000 of earned income (the amount is indexed for cost of living beginning in 2008) from the computation of federal gross income and may also elect to exclude (or deduct, in the case of a self-employed individual) a portion of foreign housing costs.

To be eligible for these benefits, the U.S. citizen or resident alien must have a principal place of work in a foreign country and not be a Federal Government employee. The worker must also establish bona fide residence in a foreign country for an entire year or must establish physical presence in a foreign country for at least 330 full days during a consecutive 12-month period.

The bona fide residence test involves a subjective analysis of your intention with respect to your stay abroad. If you tell the foreign authorities that you are a nonresident of that foreign country, you cannot claim that you are a bona fide resident of that country for U.S. income tax purposes. After you have established bona fide residence abroad for a period that includes one full calendar year, you can continue to qualify as a bona fide resident for future years until you abandon that foreign residence. Thus, even in your last year abroad, you would be considered a bona fide resident for that part of the year in which you were outside the United States.

The physical presence test requires that you be physically present in a foreign country for 330 days (approximately 11 months) during any 12-month period of time. It does not require that you be outside the United States for a full calendar year.

When you can satisfy the physical presence test or the bona fide residence test for only part of the year, the $80,000 ceiling on the foreign income exclusion is prorated based on the number of days during the year in which you meet the particular test. For example, if an individual qualifies as a bona fide resident in 2004 for only 90 days, the ceiling on the foreign income exclusion for the year would be 90/366 multiplied by $80,000 or $19,672. In a non-leap year, the proper fraction to use would be 90/365.

When proration is required under the physical presence test, you are entitled to count all days within a period of 12 months after you are physically present and have your tax home in a foreign country for the 330 days. You will want to select the 12-month period that allows for the largest exclusion.

Illustration

Assume that you worked in France from June 1, 2003, through September 30, 2004, when you left the country. During this period, you left France only for a 15-day vacation to the United States during December 2003. You earned $80,000 for your work in France during 2004. Your maximum 2004 exclusion is $64,262, figured as follows:

1. **Start with your last full day, September 30, 2004, and count back 330 full days during which you were abroad. Not counting the vacation days, the 330th day is October 22, 2003. This is the first day of your 12-month period.**
2. **From October 22, 2003, count forward 12 months, to October 21, 2004, which is the last day of your 12-month period.**
3. **Count the number of days in 2004 that fall within the 12-month period ending October 21, 2004. Here, the number of qualifying days is 294, from January 1 through October 21, 2004.**
4. **The maximum 2004 exclusion is $80,000 × 294/366 or $64,262. You may exclude $64,262, the lesser of the maximum exclusion or your actual earnings of $80,000.**

In addition to excluding up to $80,000 of income earned abroad, individuals who can establish a foreign tax home and pass either the bona fide residence or the physical presence test can also exclude certain employer-provided housing costs from their income or deduct their excess housing costs if the housing is not employer-provided.

continues

Illustration (cont.)

The maximum exclusion for foreign housing costs is the excess of the housing expenses greater than the amount equal to 16 percent of a U.S. government employee paid at the rate of a GS-14, Step 1 (in 2003, this rate was $72,381). In no event can the aggregate of the foreign income exclusion and the exclusion for excess housing costs exceed the taxpayer's foreign earned income.

For purposes of the foreign housing costs exclusion, housing expenses are the reasonable costs paid for housing abroad for the overseas worker and family if they reside with the worker. Utilities, insurance, and rent are examples of typical housing costs eligible for the exclusion. However, housing expenses do not include deductible interest and taxes or the purchase price of a house.

The income earned abroad exclusion is for each individual, permitting a married couple to claim twice the exclusion of a single individual. On a joint return, the housing costs exclusion may be computed jointly, in which case the exclusion may be claimed by only one spouse or separately, in which case housing costs may be allocated as desired.

To the extent that income earned abroad cannot be excluded, taxes on that foreign source income will be subject to credit on the U.S. tax return. The credit will be in an amount equal to the lesser of the foreign taxes paid or the U.S. tax liability attributable to the foreign income. If an individual elects either the foreign income exclusion or the excess housing exclusion, that person cannot claim the foreign tax credit or any deductions with respect to the income that has been excluded.

Caution

The IRS is scrutinizing the many Americans living abroad, believing that substantial noncompliance exists with the filing requirements. States are also active, searching for individuals who have not terminated their stateside *domicile*.

The IRS is also investigating large numbers of taxpayers, most living in the United States, who have overseas credit cards. Many of these individuals, according to the IRS, are hiding overseas income and drawing on cards against their credit balances. A three-month amnesty expired on April 15, 2003.

Real Estate Professionals

If you are in a real estate–related business, whether involved in development, construction, acquisition, rental, management, or brokering, your rental activities may not automatically be passive as they are for other individuals (see Chapter 2). To qualify under this special rule, you must work more than 750 hours during the year in real estate–related businesses in which you materially participate, and a majority of your time in all businesses in which you materially participate must be in real estate. If you work in real estate as a employee, you must be at least a 5-percent owner of the business. (See Chapter 2 for the definition of material participation.)

Caution

Excluded from the statutory list of real estate activities qualifying for the special rule are lending, consulting, and professional service (law and accounting) businesses that concentrate on real estate. Individual real estate agents probably qualify for the special rule under a broad definition of brokering.

Controversy

What does it mean if your rental activities are not automatically passive? Does it mean that you may use rental losses to offset all of your other income without limitation? Although this may have been the intent of Congress, IRS Regulations indicate that individuals who qualify under the special rule must still meet the tough material participation test (see Chapter 2) for the aggregate rental activities in order for rental losses to offset other income.

The hours spent on nonrental activities in real estate are ignored for this test, according to the IRS. And, if 10 percent or more of aggregate gross rental income is from limited partnership interests, the Regulations do not permit use of the 100-hour test or the "substantially all of the work" test to establish material participation.

Filing Pointer

A real estate professional capable of qualifying under the special rule, notwithstanding the tough standard set by the IRS, will need to remember to elect with an originally filed return to treat all rental real estate activities as though they were one. Without an election to aggregate, each activity is separately tested for material participation, and the special rule is less likely to apply. When made, the election is generally irrevocable.

Caution

If a real estate professional satisfies the material participation test under the special rule, losses from rentals will offset active, portfolio, and other passive income. However, not all individuals in real estate will benefit from the special rule for this profession.

continues

Caution (cont.)

Real estate professionals with passive losses from non-real estate activities and income from real estate rentals will want the rental income to be passive in nature to permit the use of these other passive losses. The election to aggregate each rental activity should be avoided. A real estate professional must look not only at the current year but also at the future, inasmuch as an election, when made, is binding on all future years.

Teachers and Other Educators

For 2002 and 2003, teachers, aides, counselors, and principals in grades kindergarten through 12 were permitted to deduct up to $250 each year for out-of-pocket classroom books, supplies, and equipment. The deduction was available whether or not you itemize.

Question: I work part-time as a substitute teacher and spend more than $250 on supplies. Am I eligible for the deduction on my 2003 return?

Answer: By law you must work in a school a minimum of 900 hours during the course of the school year to enjoy this special deduction.

Caution

The special deduction for teachers and educators was scheduled to expire after 2003 unless extended by a new statute.

Waitstaff, Casino Workers, and Other Tip-Earning Employees

Employees who receive tips from their customers must include the amount of the tips in their income. These tips cannot be considered as gifts.

Employees who receive $20 or more in tips during a month are required to report the amount of tips to their employers. The reported tips are subject to income tax and Social Security tax withholding.

The IRS used to believe that about one-half of tips paid at larger restaurants and two-thirds of those paid at smaller ones went unreported. In response, Congress enacted legislation that requires restaurants and other food and beverage establishments usually employing more than 10 workers on a typical day to allocate a deemed amount of tip income among the employees.

The amount that must be allocated among the employees is equal to the excess, if any, of 8 percent of the establishment's gross receipts over the amount of tips that the employees reported to the employer. For example, if all of the waiters and waitresses reported receiving tips amounting to 5 percent of the establishment's gross sales for the year, the employer would include an allocable share of the excess 3 percent on each employee's W-2. If the restaurant can establish that the average tips are less than 8 percent, the 8 percent figure can be reduced, but not below 2 percent. Now, following this law and stepped-up enforcement, the IRS believes that it has obtained more than 80 percent compliance from tipped restaurant workers but plans to continue strict scrutiny of them.

The Tax Court in 1996 determined that the gross income from tips of waiters and waitresses sharing tips with buspersons, bartenders, and others is determined after the sharing. The IRS had wanted the workers to deduct the offsets as miscellaneous itemized deductions only.

Caution

Tipped restaurant workers, particularly those who do not average 8 percent of receipts in tips, must accurately report tip income to their employers and keep their own records of tips to minimize the allocation of any deemed tipped income. Many employees of large food establishments may find themselves under audit as a result of an examination of the employer's tax records to make sure that the tipped employees are reporting all of their tip income. The IRS will look at the restaurant's gross receipts, analyze the geographic region's tip habits, and expect the tipped employee to have tip income based on this average. With the IRS buoyed by a 2002 decision of the U.S. Supreme Court sanctioning aggregate estimates of employer payroll tax liability for unreported tip income, both the numbers of audits and the extent of enforcement figure to rise.

Fresh from a study showing widespread noncompliance in the industry, the IRS compiled a training guide for its auditors setting forth examination techniques for barbers and beauticians. Shortly thereafter, the IRS announced a new tip compliance program for the gaming industry. These workers along with limousine and taxicab drivers, cosmetologists, and skycaps should expect widespread scrutiny of their tip income in upcoming years.

CHAPTER 12

Estate Planning Strategies

How the Federal Estate Tax System Works

Certain income tax decisions must be made in conjunction with estate planning decisions. For example, although it might make sense from an income tax perspective to title appreciated property in the name of the elderly husband in order to get a step up in the tax basis of the assets upon his death, estate tax needs may require that some of this property be titled exclusively in the name of the younger wife. It is wise to consider the estate tax consequences of many significant steps if any chance of a federal estate tax liability exists.

Basically, the federal estate tax system works as follows: On your death, if your federal *gross* estate exceeds a value of $1.5 million in 2004, your estate must file a tax return. If your federal *taxable* estate exceeds a value of $1.5 million in 2004, your estate will owe federal taxes. In 2001, the last year for which information is available, about 52,000 decedent estates owed taxes.

The marginal estate tax rates (the rates at which the next dollar of estate assets will be taxed) are 45 and 48 percent as applied against your federal taxable estate after the benefit of a *unified credit*. The taxable estate is basically the net value of all of the property that you own at the time of death (including often overlooked retirement plan benefits as well as most life insurance proceeds) reduced by various deductions. The most prominent deduction is the marital deduction. The full value of property transferred to a surviving spouse either outright or in certain types of trusts qualifies for the marital deduction and will reduce the gross estate.

The federal estate tax on your taxable estate is usually partially or totally offset by using a unified credit that eliminates tax liability on the first $1.5 million. However, to the extent that the credit was used to offset the tax on lifetime transfers, it is reduced and cannot offset the tax on death transfers.

Caution

The marital deduction usually is not available if the surviving spouse is not a U.S. citizen. The marital deduction is available in such cases, however, if the decedent's property is transferred to a qualified domestic trust, the terms of which provide that a trustee is a citizen of the United States, and the surviving spouse will be paid all of the income generated by the trust. By using a qualified domestic trust, the federal estate tax on the decedent's property is deferred until principal distributions from the trust are made to the surviving spouse or until the surviving spouse's death. Hardship distributions of principal to the surviving spouse, however, are exempt from tax.

Caution

For 2006–2008, the unified credit is scheduled to increase from a $1.5 million to a $2 million exclusion equivalent and to further rise to $3.5 million for 2009. Between 2004 and 2007, the highest marginal tax rate is scheduled to decline from 48 percent, creating a single tax rate of 45 percent. Then, under current law, the estate tax is schedule to be abolished for one year—2010. With the scheduled sunset of all of the provisions of the Economic Growth and Tax Relief Reconciliation Act of 2001 (EGTRRA) on December 31, 2010 (see Chapter 1, "Introduction to Personal Tax Planning"), the estate tax is scheduled to be restored in 2011 with a unified credit once again equivalent to an applicable exclusion of $1 million and a maximum marginal rate of 60 percent based on pre-EGTRRA law. Congress is considering legislation which, if enacted, would permanently repeal the estate tax. HR 8, the Death Tax Repeal Permanency Act, was approved by the House on June 18, 2003.

For 2003, the unified credit was a $1 million exclusion equivalent with an additional $200,000 deduction available to qualified family-owned business interests. Marginal tax rates ranged from 41 percent to 49 percent.

Question: My wife and I jointly own a great deal of stock. When I die, my wife will become the sole owner of the stock. Will this stock be included in my estate? If so, will the stock qualify for the marital deduction? Why do I need estate planning today, if the marital deduction can wipe out estate taxes when the first of us—my wife or I—dies? And, the chances are that one, if not both, of us will live until at least 2010.

Answer: Except for joint interests created before 1977 (see the discussion in Chapter 5 on "Computing Gain or Loss Correctly"), one-half of husband-wife jointly held property is includable in the estate of the first spouse to die. It does not matter that this property may pass automatically to the survivor under the law of your state and not be subject to local probate. It also makes no difference how the property is transferred to the surviving spouse to qualify for the unlimited marital deduction. It can be transferred to the spouse by operation of law where the decedent owns the property with the surviving spouse either as a tenant by the entirety with the right of survivorship or as community property. It can be transferred under the terms of a contract, where, for example, the spouse is the beneficiary of a life insurance contract on the deceased spouse's life. It can be transferred under the terms of a will or the laws of intestacy, which govern if there is no will. Because of the unlimited marital deduction, even if the value of your stock portfolio is in the millions of dollars, there need be no federal estate taxes due at the time of your death. The problem, of course, can arise upon the death of your spouse.

Illustration

Mr. Saveless died in 2004 owning a gross estate valued at $3 million, all of which was left to his wife. There were no federal estate taxes due at the time of his death. At the time of the death of Mrs. Saveless 12 months later (assuming that she lives off the income, does not consume the principal, and there is no appreciation or depreciation in the value of the property), her gross estate will be the same $3 million. Barring remarriage, she will not be entitled to a marital deduction, so her taxable estate will be $3 million. The precredit federal tax liability on a $3 million estate in 2005 is $1,250,800. If Mrs. Saveless has her full unified credit available to her in 2005 in the amount of $555,800, the federal tax liability at her death will be $695,000. The children of this marriage will inherit, after the death of their parents, $2,305,000 ($3 million less $695,000 in federal taxes) as shown here:

continues

Illustration (cont.)

On Death of First Spouse:		On Death of Second Spouse:	
$3,000,000	Gross Estate	$3,000,000	Gross Estate
(3,000,000)	Marital Deduction	($0)	Marital Deduction
$0	Taxable Estate	$3,000,000	Taxable Estate
$0	Federal Tax		
		$1,250,800	Tentative Federal Tax
		($555,800)	Unified Credit
		$695,000	Federal Tax
		$695,000	Combined Federal Estate Tax

Do your estate planning! It involves seeking to save taxes that will be due on the death of the second spouse. Not only can you not predict the timing of the second death, but also you cannot predict the estate tax law in that year. It is virtually certain that the estate tax will not be abolished just to be restored in the following year. It is at least as likely as not that the estate tax will not be abolished but that the applicable exclusion will be frozen at a higher level than today.

The Bypass Trust— The Best Single Step in Estate Planning

The $695,000 bite in the preceding illustration can be avoided with basic estate planning. The $695,000 liability is a result of the first spouse's failure to use his unified credit. Because the husband, as the first spouse to die, left his entire $3 million estate to his wife, no tentative federal tax existed against which to use the unified credit. The credit was wasted. The key to federal estate tax planning is to make use of the unified credit on the death of the first spouse and avoid overloading the estate of the second spouse. To use the unified credit, you cannot leave all property to your surviving spouse. Instead, you can transfer up to the exclusion equivalent ($1.5 million in 2004) to a qualifying trust established for the benefit of your spouse. Alternatively, you can transfer up to the exemption equivalent to your children, to a trust for your children, or to a trust for your spouse and children.

Illustration

When Mr. Savemore died in 2004, he left $1.5 million to his wife, but he provided for the remaining $1.5 million to be left in trust for the benefit of his wife and children. Unlike Mr. Saveless, the husband here has a tentative federal tax of $555,800. Assuming he has available to him a full unified credit of $555,800, no federal taxes will be due at the time of Mr. Savemore's death—the same result as in the first illustration. However, on the death of Mrs. Savemore in 2005, again assuming no consumption, appreciation, or depreciation, her gross estate will be equal to $1.5 million. Her taxable estate will be $1.5 million, but she will owe no federal estate taxes because of the availability of her unified credit. The remaining $1.5 million that was transferred to a trust for the benefit of Mrs. Savemore and the couple's children will not be part of her taxable estate because Mrs. Savemore will not be treated as having the equivalent of ownership of the trust property. As a result, the family's combined federal estate tax liability is $0, a savings of $695,000. The family is able to transfer the full $3 million estate to the children as shown here:

On Death of First Spouse:		On Death of Second Spouse:	
$3,000,000	Gross Estate	$1,500,000	Gross Estate
($1,500,000)	Marital Deduction	($0)	Marital Deduction
$1,500,000	Taxable Estate	$1,500,000	Taxable Estate
$555,800	Tentative Federal Tax	$555,800	Tentative Federal Tax
($555,800)	Unified Credit	($555,800)	Unified Credit
$0	Federal Tax	$0	Federal Tax
		$0	Combined Federal Estate Tax

Question: I want to save estate taxes because I do not want my hard-earned money going to the government and not to my children. However, my children are grown and doing well, and I am far more concerned now about my wife having enough money on which to live. How can I minimize or eliminate estate taxes and still not cause my wife to worry about money?

Answer: The typical estate plan, which uses a trust to keep some assets out of the estate of the surviving spouse, can distress people whose natural inclination is "I do not care about federal estate tax savings if it means that my spouse cannot get everything I own." However, a trust in the amount of the exemption equivalent for the benefit of your wife can be designed to give very close to outright ownership—but with the tax savings. The trust is often called a *bypass trust*, *unified credit trust*, *credit shelter trust*, or *family trust*. Property transferred to the trust will either not qualify for the marital deduction or, if eligible, no election should be made to have the property qualify. Consequently, a taxable estate is created at the time of your death. This is what you want because basic estate planning requires a tentative federal tax liability against which to use the unified credit.

The terms of the bypass trust can be quite broad. They can provide that your wife receive all of the income generated by the assets in the trust for her entire lifetime. They can provide that she receive up to the greater of $5,000 or 5 percent of principal each year without a showing of need. If an independent trustee has been named, the trust can provide for unlimited disbursement of principal to your wife within the discretion of the trustee. If you and your wife would rather not have an outsider, even another family member, as trustee, your wife can be trustee provided distributions of principal to her beyond the $5,000/5 percent figure are limited to disbursements for health, education, support, and maintenance.

Giving the spouse the right to receive annual distributions of $5,000/5 percent of principal will result in the greater of $5,000 or 5 percent of the value of the trust at the time of the spouse's death being included in the spouse's federal gross estate. If the bypass trust is worth $1 million when the spouse dies, this would mean that the spouse's federal gross estate would include $50,000 attributable to the $5,000/5 percent withdrawal right. However, this is often a small price to pay to give the surviving spouse the desired security.

The bypass trust is the best single step that a married couple anticipating likely federal estate taxes can take in planning to minimize these taxes and maximize the survivor's security. By using this trust, you have accomplished both of your goals—reducing the federal estate tax liability and providing security and protection for your spouse.

Question: My husband and I are not sure whether we will ultimately pay estate taxes. I do not want some of our assets going into a trust if it is not necessary. What can we do?

Answer: The best solution may be to use a *disclaimer trust*. Leave your entire estate to each other. However, provide that, if the surviving spouse executes a disclaimer within nine months of the first spouse's death, the disclaimed portion of the estate goes into the bypass trust. This enables you to make an intelligent planning decision based on the tax law and your family situation upon the death of one of you.

Caution

If the surviving spouse is to be the trustee (or a cotrustee unless the other trustees have interests that are deemed adversarial to the spouse), it is critical that proper language be used in setting an ascertainable standard for the surviving spouse to receive principal. The words "health, education, support, and maintenance" are time-proven terminology, and it is clear that such a right to receive principal in a trust will not cause inclusion of the remaining assets of the trust in the estate of the surviving spouse. However, if other words are used, the surviving spouse may be treated as having the equivalent of outright ownership, and a successful bypass of the trust amounts from the surviving spouse's estate will not be possible.

Controversy

Use of other words, such as comfort, when an ascertainable standard is required is risky and will invite challenge from the IRS. The courts look on a case-by-case basis as to whether this standard is met based on how the exact wording is interpreted under the law of the decedent's domicile. In 1993 the Tenth Circuit Court of Appeals, after analyzing Florida law, found that the terminology "continued comfort, support, maintenance, or education" created an ascertainable standard and reversed the pro-IRS decision of the Tax Court.

The Multipurpose Qualified Terminable Interest Property (QTIP) Trust

Many individuals do not want to leave all or part of their estate to their surviving spouse outright. They may be concerned about the surviving spouse's ability to manage a significant estate and may want the expertise of a professional manager. They may want to protect the estate from a new spouse. They may want to provide for the children of a prior marriage yet still offer the surviving spouse security during his or her lifetime. All of these concerns, as well as the elimination of estate taxes upon the death of the first spouse, can be alleviated through the use of a QTIP trust.

Property passing into a QTIP trust will qualify for the marital deduction if an appropriate election is made by the personal representative (executor) of the estate. If at the death of the surviving spouse any assets are remaining in the trust for which a QTIP election was made, their value will be includable in the estate of the surviving spouse just as though the property had been left to the surviving spouse outright.

To qualify property in the QTIP trust for the marital deduction, the surviving spouse must be the sole income beneficiary of the trust and must be paid all of the income generated by the QTIP trust at least annually. Distributions of principal follow the same rules as in the case of the bypass trust; they may be mandatory, nonexistent; discretionary without limitation where an independent trustee exists; or subject to such language as health, education, support, and maintenance if the surviving spouse will be the trustee. However, no distribution of the QTIP trust principal can be made to any individual other than the surviving spouse so long as he or she is alive.

The QTIP trust is an excellent vehicle to provide security and income to the surviving spouse during his or her lifetime yet ensure that, upon the surviving spouse's death, the trust principal, to the extent that it has not been used for the benefit of the surviving spouse, will pass to the beneficiaries designated in the will of the first spouse. For example, QTIP trust language can provide that upon the death of the surviving spouse the trust assets will be distributed among the children of the first spouse from a previous marriage. If the first spouse does not use a QTIP trust and leaves the property to the surviving spouse outright, there can be no assurance that the remaining estate would be left to the first spouse's children from the prior marriage upon the death of the surviving spouse.

Question: I like the idea of a QTIP trust. I am scared that my husband would remarry in the event of my death and could be influenced to divert funds away from our children upon his subsequent death. In fact, I like the idea of a QTIP so much that I would like to see all of my separately owned property go into this trust or into a trust in which my husband and children could both benefit. Are there any problems associated with this idea?

Answer: Two significant difficulties exist. First, if you want to avoid federal estate taxes upon your death, assuming your husband survives, you must limit the amount that goes into the bypass trust of which your children as well as your husband can be beneficiaries to the exclusion equivalent ($1.5 million in 2004 and 2005 before rising). This trust will not qualify for the marital deduction. The balance of your estate can go into the QTIP trust in which your husband must be the only beneficiary during his lifetime.

The second difficulty is that your husband may be able to object to the arrangement depending upon the law in your home state. Many states require that a certain fraction of an individual's probate estate (usually one-third or one-half) goes to the surviving spouse. A transfer to either type of trust is not the same as a bequest to the surviving spouse. Consequently, your husband may have the ability to challenge the disposition of at least a portion of the assets. However, if he insists on receiving a portion of the estate outright, state law may require him to give up any interest in the remainder of the estate.

Funding the Bypass or QTIP Trust

If a bypass or a QTIP trust is to be used, even if the result of disclaimer, sufficient separately owned assets must exist to fund the trust. If all assets are owned jointly with the spouse and a right of survivorship exists, usually called ownership by tenants by the entirety in noncommunity property states, the assets will all pass automatically to the surviving spouse, and there will be nothing left with which to fund the trust.

Life insurance is ideal for funding the bypass or QTIP trust through designation of the trust as beneficiary (or designation of the estate as beneficiary if the provisions of your will would have these assets going into either of these trusts). If insurance and other separate property are insufficient or if life insurance will be transferred to an irrevocable trust during your lifetime, it may be advisable to separate certain tenants by the entirety property into a tenancy in common in order to have assets to fund the trust upon the death of the first spouse. (See the discussion on life insurance trusts later in this chapter.)

Designation of the bypass or QTIP trust as beneficiary of qualified retirement plan benefits will result in the loss of the surviving spouse's ability to rollover the retirement proceeds to an IRA and name his or her own designated beneficiary (see Chapter 9, "Retirement Plans"). Thus, the income tax on the retirement benefits would continue to be deferred. Using qualified plan or IRA benefits to fund a bypass or QTIP trust should usually be avoided where the surviving spouse is not close to age 70 1/2 and avoided altogether in the case of a Roth IRA.

The best solution probably would be to name the surviving spouse as the primary beneficiary of the retirement benefits and the trust as the secondary beneficiary. Then the surviving spouse can, through the use of a disclaimer, direct some or all of the retirement benefits to the trust if needed to fully use the deceased spouse's unified credit. This technique affords the couple the flexibility of maximizing estate tax savings after taking into account the income tax consequences of the beneficiary designation.

Caution

IRS Regulations issued in 1997 permit the disclaimer of the one-half survivorship interest in tenants by the entireties property and in other husband-wife jointly held property. However, these regulations also state that in such cases the surviving spouse may not disclaim any portion of a joint bank, brokerage, or mutual fund account that is attributable to the survivor's contribution to the account if the account permits either co-owner to withdraw funds unilaterally. In that not all jointly held property may be disclaimed following death, planning to fund a disclaimer trust with interests in jointly held property should be used with care.

Caution

When tenants by the entirety property is converted into a tenancy in common or is transferred to one of the two spouses, the tenancy becomes attachable by the separate creditors of either spouse. The severing of a tenancy by the entirety should be accomplished only with a review of your casualty insurance situation to minimize the risk of loss of assets in the event of a suit arising from an accident in the home or on the road. Consideration also should be given to domestic relations questions under state law.

The Benefits of Lifetime Gifts

Each person can give $11,000 in cash or property to any person or any number of persons each year without any gift or estate tax implications. The historical $10,000 limitation was first adjusted for cost of living in 2002 and will continue to be indexed in 2004 and succeeding years in $1,000 increments. In order for the exclusion to apply, the recipient must receive a present interest in the property, meaning a right to enjoy the gift immediately.

Consequently, an individual with three children and five grandchildren can give a total of $88,000 in any single year to these close family members without any reduction of the unified credit. If the donor is married, and funds are coming from jointly held property, or if the spouse consents when the funds are coming from separately held assets of the donor, the $88,000 figure is effectively doubled to $176,000.

Thus, in the case of larger families particularly, it is possible to reduce the estate size significantly through a program of annual gifts to family members.

Even though the exclusion applies only to a gift of a present interest in the transferred property, control of transferred property can still be kept from a child or grandchild until age 21. Moreover, a contribution to a Coverdell Education Savings Account or to the acquisition of a tuition certificate (see Chapter 2, "Taxable and Tax-Free Income and Benefits," for information on both) in the name of another is considered to be a gift of a present interest at the time of the purchase qualifying for the annual exclusion on gifts. The donor may elect to treat a purchase of a tuition certificate as made ratably in the current year and in the four succeeding years in order to maximize use of the annual exclusion.

Sometimes it is advisable to make gifts in excess of the $11,000 per donor per donee annual exclusion. When an individual owns property and anticipates that it will go up significantly in value, it may be wise to use the unified credit for a lifetime gift in order to remove this appreciating asset from the estate before it goes up significantly in value.

To make lifetime gifts in excess of the annual exclusion, you can use a maximum of $1 million of your $1.5 million applicable exclusion equivalent otherwise available at death. Thus, a married couple can make $2 million in combined gifts greater than the annual exclusion.

However, you usually will not want to give property that has already appreciated significantly in value. It is better to let assets that have already gone up significantly in value remain with the original owner in order to pass them to the younger family members through inheritance after receiving a step-up in the income tax basis. The result is that the capital gain is forgiven. (See Chapter 5, "Gains and Losses," for a discussion of the planned partial elimination of basis step-up at death in 2010.)

Remember, in making gifts, you cannot effectively reduce the size of your estate by making a gift of property to another individual but retaining the right to live in the property or to receive income from the property for the remainder of your life or by transferring title to your name and that of another individual as joint owners with rights of survivorship. Property transferred in this manner is includable in the transferor's estate at its date-of-death value. If your goal is to reduce your federal taxable estate, you must relinquish not only legal title to the property but also any formal or informal understanding that you will receive benefits from the property in the form of a right to live in the property or the right to the income generated by the property.

Question: My wife and I inherited eight large tracts of land from my father two years ago. The real estate agent told me that I could sell the property for about $150,000. However, my wife and I would rather give the land to our four children so that they can develop it or hold on to it, at their option. If we do give the property to our children, what are the tax ramifications?

Answer: Assuming that you have made no other gifts to your children during the year, you can give $22,000 worth of the real estate to each of your four children without incurring a gift tax liability. Even more important is the fact that neither of you will have used any of your unified credit. Next year, the remaining real estate can be given to the four children using most of the next year's $11,000/$22,000 annual gift tax exclusion. The benefit to you is that you remove the $150,000 from your current estate and also ensure that the potential appreciation escapes federal estate taxes. You can accomplish your goal by gifts of entire tracts, of fractional interests in all tracts, or of interests in a real estate entity formed to hold the property, choosing the approach that minimizes state and local transfer taxes.

Caution

Use of an entity such as a limited partnership or limited liability company may facilitate the use of minority and lack of marketability discounts in valuing the gifts. However, the IRS has stepped up its scrutiny of large discounts. Additionally, the IRS stated in a 1997 letter ruling that an unduly restrictive governing document of an entity, causing the donees to lack immediate tangible benefit, may cause transfers of interests not to qualify for the exclusion as present interests. In a July 11, 2003 decision, the Seventh Circuit Court of Appeals affirmed a prior determination of the Tax Court, which had backed up this view of the IRS.

Year-End Reminder

Older individuals facing estate tax liability upon death, particularly individuals whose spouses have predeceased or who are otherwise unmarried, should determine the advisability of year-end estate reduction through gifts within the $11,000 annual exclusion. When a quick need exists for estate reduction, consider the spouses of children and grandchildren as possible recipients, further increasing the number of possible beneficiaries for the purpose of maximizing the annual exclusion in the aggregate. Remember also that this $11,000 exclusion per donor per donee is computed on a calendar year basis. Consequently, when the initial round of gift-giving to family members in order to reduce estate size occurs late in the year, a second round of gifts in the following January can be accomplished. Remember that such a program in certain estate tax situations will save at least $4,950 in estate taxes for each $11,000 annual exclusion used.

The donee must present a year-end check to his or her bank by December 31, or the gift will be considered as made in the following year. The IRS has dropped its prior position that the check needed to clear by year-end.

Year-End Reminder

Gifts of other assets raise similar issues as to the year in which they are completed, requiring care on the part of the taxpayer. A father who wrote a letter to his son in 1974 giving him stock in a family business, but who did not endorse the stock certificate to his son until 1988, survived IRS scrutiny only when the Fifth Circuit Court of Appeals reversed the Tax Court in 1997 and determined that the gift occurred in 1974.

Caution

Although the applicable exclusion equivalent for estates rose in 2004 from $1 million to $1.5 million as the next stage toward scheduled abolition of the estate tax in 2010, the applicable exclusion equivalent for gifts remained at $1 million. No further increase is planned in order to limit lifetime gifts to individuals in lower-income tax brackets. Between 2004 and 2007, the highest marginal gift tax rate declines from 48 percent to 45 percent. When the estate tax is abolished in 2010 as scheduled under current law, the gift tax rate declines to the highest individual income tax rate (35 percent if the law is unchanged). With the scheduled sunset of all of the provisions of the Economic Growth and Tax Relief Reconciliation Act of 2001 on December 31, 2010 (see Chapter 1), the maximum marginal gift tax returns to the 60 percent pre-EGTRRA level.

Caution

Gifts by someone who holds a power of attorney on behalf of another individual pose other problems. Any gift made by the attorney must be authorized under the document or by state law. Any deathbed gift by check must be presented and paid prior to death, according to the Second Court of Appeals, agreeing with the Tax Court, in a 2001 decision which the U.S. Supreme Court declined to review.

Tax Planning

Gifts between spouses not only allow the creation of a spouse's separate estate in order to fund a bypass or QTIP trust, but also permit a couple to place the most highly appreciated property in the name of the older spouse or the spouse with health problems in order to obtain the largest possible step-up in the tax basis of the property at death. (See Chapter 5 for a discussion of the increased basis at death.) However, a spouse who receives a gift from the other spouse must survive more than one year for a bequest back to the donor spouse to enjoy the basis step-up.

These interspousal transfers usually can be made freely, inasmuch as gifts between spouses qualify for the unlimited marital deduction.

If the recipient spouse is not a U.S. citizen, no marital deduction is available for gifts. Rather, the first $112,000 of gifts each year to a non-U.S. citizen spouse is excluded from the federal gift tax. This maximum for 2003 will be indexed for cost of living in 2004 and succeeding years.

The Benefits of Revocable Trusts

You establish and fund a *revocable trust* during your lifetime, and you retain the power to terminate the trust at any time. No federal income, gift, or estate taxes are saved by using a revocable trust. Any income generated by the assets held in a revocable trust will be included on the trust creator's income tax return. No gift of property is placed in a revocable trust, because the creator can always change his or her mind and get the property back. Legislation in 1997 clarified prospectively that gifts from a revocable trust are treated in the same manner as direct gifts from the trust's creator. Furthermore, any assets remaining in a revocable trust at the time of the creator's death will be included in the federal gross estate so that the creator will not have diminished the size of the estate.

Why use a revocable trust? Revocable trusts are useful tools to provide professional lifetime management for an estate. For example, you may be considering a particular financial institution to manage your estate after your death, and you want to test the institution's management skills and investment return.

A second use of a revocable trust is to guard against the potential disability of its creator. By having a trustee as the legal owner of investment assets, there will be no gap in management of assets should you become disabled. The management of your assets will continue following your disability just as the trustee had managed your assets before your disability. Without a revocable trust, upon your incapacity, your family might have to get the courts to name a formal guardian of your assets. Thus, potentially expensive guardianship proceedings are avoided by using a revocable trust.

A third use of a revocable trust is to save on probate costs. Depending upon the jurisdiction, the size of your estate, the composition of your estate, and the size of your family, the probate process may be complicated and costly. By using a revocable trust you avoid the probate concerns. The assets of the revocable trust are often not subject to public disclosure as would be the assets that pass under the terms of your will. No delay exists in having your heirs benefit from your estate as there might be if they had to wait for the probate of your estate to be completed.

Caution

Whether using a revocable trust will save any state inheritance taxes for you will vary from jurisdiction to jurisdiction. Many states subject revocable trusts to inheritance tax, although they are exempt from the probate process.

Careful thought should go into the use of a revocable trust. Unless all separately titled assets are transferred into the trust, the probate process is not avoided. The transfer of most assets will require retitling of property. The transfer of certain assets (real estate, stocks, and automobiles, for example) will require

Caution (cont.)

the recording of the legal change in ownership. Many individuals find both the transfer process and the subsequent handling of the trust to be a nuisance.

Consequently, many individuals prefer to delay using a revocable trust for all assets until they no longer want to administer their assets. During the interim, a revocable trust may be the best suited for separately titled real property and personal effects located outside of the state of domicile. An ancillary probate in the second state can be avoided by transferring those assets to a living trust.

The Benefits of Irrevocable Trusts

An *irrevocable trust* is formed during the creator's lifetime, and the creator retains no power to revoke the terms of the trust. Once signed, the terms of such an instrument cannot be modified or revoked. The creator of the irrevocable trust is not taxed on the income generated by the trust assets so long as he or she does not retain control over the trust assets and receives no benefit from the trust. Rather, the trust or the income beneficiaries of the trust pay tax on the income generated by the trust's investments.

What are some of the uses of irrevocable trusts? Many individuals use an irrevocable trust for the same reason that they make outright gifts of property—they want to reduce the size of their estate. However, they form trusts instead of making outright gifts because they do not want the recipients to have outright ownership of the gift property either because of age or other circumstances. Perhaps the creator of a trust may want to provide one person with the benefit of the gift property for a period of time and then transfer the enjoyment to another party. For example, a father may want to provide financial security for his daughter for her lifetime, and upon her death have the assets transferred to his grandchildren.

Caution

A completed gift occurs upon creation and funding of most irrevocable trusts. Therefore, the federal gift tax laws (and, to the extent applicable, state gift tax laws) must be considered. The annual gift tax exclusion may not apply to gifts transferred by means of an irrevocable trust, because such gifts often do not involve a present interest. This means that a gift by means of an irrevocable trust will often use some or all of the creator's unified credit. However, with careful drafting of the irrevocable trust instrument, gifts made through the irrevocable trust can qualify in many cases for the annual exclusion and, therefore, minimize or perhaps eliminate use of the creator's unified credit.

Life Insurance as Part of the Estate Plan

Individuals often overlook the amount of insurance that they are carrying on their life when undertaking an estate analysis. For federal estate tax purposes, if you are the owner of a life insurance policy, its value is includable in your federal estate and can very well throw you over the threshold at which estate tax liability exists. Life insurance, together with retirement plan benefits and appreciating real estate, will often create a taxable estate in excess of this figure in the case of many middle-class Americans.

Life insurance is an excellent candidate for lifetime gifts. It usually has only a nominal value, or its cash surrender value is much smaller than its face value so that the cost of making a lifetime gift of an insurance policy is minimal compared to the cost of having to include the death benefit proceeds in one's gross estate. So long as the transfer of complete ownership of a policy occurs more than three years prior to death, the insurance proceeds payable to the beneficiary are not includable in the estate of the deceased individual.

A gift of the life insurance policy can be made either outright or, more often, to an irrevocable trust under which the surviving spouse can receive a lifetime income interest with the principal passing to the children without inclusion of the proceeds in either spouse's estate.

Caution

Life insurance trusts should be considered especially by couples facing likely estate tax liabilities upon the second death, even with the use of bypass trusts. Congress has periodically considered legislation that would restrict or eliminate the ability to remove life insurance from an estate by transferring the incidents of ownership.

Generation Skipping to Avoid Tax Piggybacks

If you start with $1 and lose 45 percent in taxes and then lose 45 percent of the remainder in taxes, you have kept just 30 cents. The estate and gift tax structure was designed to do just that, generation after generation.

Many wealthy families were able to avoid the cumulative effect of estate and gift taxes by retaining assets in trust for generations. The assets were not included in the estate of descendants for a number of generations because those heirs were not outright owners of the property. The only restriction on these trusts was one from the English common law—that outright title had to vest within 21 years following the death of the last descendant of the creator who was alive when the trust came into existence. This Rule Against Perpetuities, now abolished in a number of states, still allowed a trust to hold assets for as long as 100 years or more without added taxes at each generation level.

The generation-skipping tax assessed at a flat 48-percent rate in 2004 is designed to ensure that even transfers in trust are taxed at each generation level. However, each individual has a $1.5 million exemption for generation skipping transfers, allowing a couple with a large estate to leave $3 million in trust for grandchildren, with their children enjoying rights to income and certain rights to principal during their lives.

Caution

Effective 2004, the generation-skipping tax exemption is the same amount as the estate tax applicable exclusion equivalent. The exemption was $1,120,000 for 2003. Between 2005 and 2007, the tax rate declines with the highest marginal estate tax rate from 48 percent to 45 percent. Under current law, the generation-skipping tax, like the estate tax, is abolished for 2010. With the scheduled sunset of all of the provisions of the Economic Growth and Tax Reconciliation Act of 2001 on December 31, 2010 (see Chapter 1), the estate tax will be restored in 2011 with the 2003 exemption indexed for cost of living over the seven intervening years and the pre-EGTRRA tax rate of 55 percent.

Tax Planning

Bypass trusts, QTIP trusts, lifetime gifts, and irrevocable trusts are techniques to be considered for estate tax savings by individuals whose federal gross estates exceed the threshold for tax liability. The generation-skipping trust is one of many techniques best suited as a tax planning mechanism for much larger estates. Other tax-saving strategies for much larger estates include charitable lead and remainder trusts as well as trusts (GRATs, GRUTs, and QPRTs) in which the creator retains an interest for a period of years. Each of these techniques saves taxes by reducing the gift tax value of the transferred property.

CHAPTER 13

Dealing with the Internal Revenue Service

Always File Your Tax Return on Time

Tax filing time is stressful for many Americans. In fact, one in five individuals declared in a recent survey that the period around April 15 is the most stressful time of year. Many of these individuals owe money to the IRS and do not have it. Unfortunately, a large percentage believes that the proper method of dealing with a tax liability, which cannot be paid by the due date, is to send in the return late. This is the wrong decision.

In the case of an individual return, you will be facing a 5 percent per month combined late filing/late payment penalty for the first five months of tardiness (15 percent per month if willful). This penalty will usually be difficult to abate, because lack of funds is not reasonable cause for late filing. Penalties taper off after five months to 1/2 percent per month. In addition, you will be paying interest at prescribed rates, which are adjusted every quarter.

But, if you file the tax return and fail to enclose a check, you will be billed for any liability plus interest plus 1/2 percent per month late payment penalty doubling only ten days after the IRS has issued a Notice of Intent to Levy (lowered to 1/4 percent when an installment agreement to pay, discussed later in this chapter, is in effect). Consequently, if you owe the IRS $5,000 and pay five months late, your penalty will be $125. However, if you do not file the return on time, your penalty will be $1,250—ten times as much.

Caution

If you fail to file a return, not only do you face the steep failure-to-file penalty, but the IRS may also file a "substitute return" for you based on the limited information in its file. You face a hassle to get the IRS to accept the information shown on your subsequently filed return. As discussed later in this chapter, such a late-filed return may preclude you from discharging the tax liability in bankruptcy.

Filing Pointer

If you request an extension of the April 15 filing deadline (about 6.5 percent of individual filers get an automatic four-month extension to August 15 by filing IRS Form 4868), you will not be subject to the late filing penalty. However, the filing extension does not extend the time for payment of your tax bill beyond April 15; thus the lesser late payment penalty will apply.

Controversy

For a further extension request to as late as October 15 to be valid, it is unclear whether you must make a bona fide and reasonable estimate of your tax liability and pay the unpaid portion of the estimated liability with the second extension request. Regulations issued in 1996 are silent on the issue, although the IRS appears to be handling the issue in the same manner as the first extension. About 2 percent of individual filers get a second extension.

Nonfilers and Other Troubled Taxpayers—Coming Forward

For a decade, the IRS has focused on bringing what was an estimated 7 1/2 to 10 million nonfilers (including accountants and lawyers), mostly self-employed, back into the tax system.

To facilitate bringing nonfilers into compliance, as a general rule, the IRS does not recommend that the Justice Department prosecute individuals who come forward on their own and file back returns. If there are more than six unfiled years, it may be possible to negotiate filing only for those most recent years, particularly if the individual is without means of full payment of all of the tax, penalties, and interest on all of the back returns.

In 1992, an "informal amnesty" program began for individual income tax nonfilers who came forward with a "voluntary disclosure" so called because only the Justice Department can decide whether or not to prosecute. The program was extended in the following year to corporate and other taxpayers as well as to payroll and other types of taxes. However, by 1999, the IRS had revised its manual to state that a voluntary disclosure will be "considered with all other factors" in determining whether to recommend prosecution by the Justice Department.

Guidelines for making a voluntary disclosure were issued in 2002. The IRS must not have commenced any inquiry, audit, or investigation of the taxpayer and, in the case of income tax returns, income must have been from legal sources. The taxpayer must cooperate in determining tax liability as accurately as possible and in paying any delinquency to the extent of the ability to pay. Voluntary disclosure applies not only to unfiled returns but also to unreported income.

Caution

Nonfilers and others with criminal exposure should consult with an attorney versed in criminal tax matters. Despite the 1999 revision, the IRS in practice concentrates its efforts in seeking prosecution of violators who have not come forward and are caught. If you are contacted by a representative of the Criminal Investigation Division (CID) of the IRS (they will identify themselves as such), or if an examiner indicates that he or she may turn the case over to the CID, run—do not walk—to that attorney. Pending the advice of counsel, make no statements and turn over no more records to the IRS. Almost always, there is no benefit in making further statements to the IRS or in turning over privileged materials.

The IRS commences about 5,000 criminal investigations each year, seven percent of which are against auto dealers and five percent of which are against the preparers. A criminal investigation should be taken seriously from the beginning. Historically, statistics show that 50 to 60 percent of criminal inquiries have led to prosecutions, of which more than 90 percent are successful. More than 70 percent of convictions and guilty pleas result in jail time or other detention. About 3,000 individuals are convicted each year. Football great Lawrence Taylor and baseball greats Pete Rose, Darryl Strawberry, Duke Snider, and Willie McCovey have been among these recent numbers. Between 1997 and 1999 seven National Basketball Association referees pleaded guilty to tax evasion. Staffing declines that led to a reduced number of prosecutions in recent years, have been reversed, and CID remains very active in its search for intentional violations of the tax law.

Cut Your Chances of Being Audited

The best step that you can take to minimize your chances of audit is to avoid outlandish and unreasonable positions, particularly those that are conspicuous on a tax return. For example, a couple in a reported case some years ago was purportedly engaged in home sales for profit. However, the couple reported only $526 in gross income and $18,538 in expenses including a business meeting in Hawaii. The return was understandably pulled for examination and the taxpayer was unable to prove a profit-making intent.

About 56 percent of audits arise from one or more conspicuous line items on the tax return; these tax returns are selected for examination by computer formula although they are thereafter screened to determine the likelihood that errors exist. Those items which cause a return to be selected may relate to factual or legal issues. This is not to recommend that you abstain from taking positions that might be at odds with the IRS. There are many unclear or unanswered questions within the tax law, and you have the right to take a legally justifiable position even if it may counter the IRS view on the matter. The IRS position on issues may have been (or may be) declared incorrect by the Tax Court or other judicial forum. However, positions without significant basis in law or fact often stand out and increase your chances of audit.

A return that says too much (or too little) can generate an audit. If you own a roofing business in Boston and attend the trade convention in St. Thomas, do not state "Virgin Islands trip" under "Other Expenses" on Schedule C. Determine the proper portion allocable to travel, seminars, and business meals. Classify the component parts accordingly. On the other hand, do not group most of your business expenses into a mass category called "Miscellaneous." Group the costs under properly deductible headings.

Be certain that you include all required forms and supplemental documents with your tax return. For example, if you claim depreciation on an automobile or other asset used in a business or investment, you must attach IRS Form 4562 to the tax return. Failure to include this necessary form could alone trigger an audit.

Some individuals face likely audit in any event. One study of individual returns selected for audit showed that the common link among a high percentage of these returns was itemized deductions in excess of 35 percent of AGI. Among the many other entries or situations that can be audit-triggering by themselves or in conjunction with others are the following:

- Claiming persons other than children, grandchildren, or parents as dependents or two persons claiming the same dependent
- Schedule C losses from a business or profession on modest gross income (intended to avoid the employee business expense limitation)
- Travel, meals, and entertainment expenses on Schedule C disproportionate to the income
- The office-in-home deduction
- Substantial employee business expenses
- High medical expenses well over the 7 1/2 percent of AGI floor

- Substantial points deducted as interest expense when there has been no change in a taxpayer's address
- Significant charitable contributions of property
- High interest deductions
- High rental losses
- Bad debts
- A high percentage of business use of a vehicle in an occupation not historically associated with extensive automobile usage
- Casualty losses
- Earned income credit (which due to its refundable nature has become a major source of fraud)
- Obvious inaccurate depreciation
- Claiming material participation in activities with losses (especially with high W-2 income)
- Little or no tip income in a business that receives gratuities
- Reporting gross income less than shown on information returns or reporting deductions greater than those shown
- Providing inaccurate Social Security numbers
- Acknowledging a foreign bank account

About 12 percent of audits arise from IRS activity targeted at specific industries, particularly those which deal in cash. To assist auditors, the IRS is designing guidelines in at least 75 industries under its new Market Segment Specialization Program (MSSP).

About 10 percent of audits are generated from other audits and by information provided by tipsters such as neighbors and ex-spouses, who received collective rewards of $10.8 million in fiscal 2000 but only $3.3 million in the following year. A tipster can even be an IRS agent, as a New Hampshire couple found out several years ago after they parked their Rolls Royce outside a restaurant in a small town. The IRS employee made note of the license number, and the ensuing audit led to a referral to the CID and a conviction.

About 8 percent of audits arise from scrutiny of unreputable tax return preparers, about 65 of whom are convicted each year of tax offenses. If your return is so complex that you require a tax preparer or if you simply choose to pay someone else for the trouble of preparing your return (about 53 percent of individuals use a paid preparer), the best single step you can take to minimize your chances of an audit is to obtain the services of a competent preparer. A paid preparer must place an identification number on your tax return, and this can be used to screen all returns prepared by less than scrupulous preparers.

With 2001 individual returns, the IRS resumed random audits which were halted in 1994. The IRS uses the results for determining its computer formula for selecting most of the audited returns. With a lapse of many years in random audits, about one-fourth of examinations resulted in no change. Under the new National Research Program (NRP), the IRS was looking at about 47,000 returns, about 39,000 in face-to-face meetings. In about 1,700 of those returns, the IRS planned to audit every line with "reasonable" substantiation required in contrast with the strict substantiation rules of the predecessor Taxpayer Compliance Measurement Program (TCMP).

With a decline in the number of examiners, the IRS audited just over 1/2 percent of individual income tax returns in fiscal 2001 and 2002, down from just over 1.67 percent in fiscal 1995, but up from fiscal 2000. More than 70 percent of audits are by correspondence. The IRS promises that the percentage of returns audited will take an upward turn as it seeks to raise tax-compliance levels from the current 87 percent to at least 90 percent of reportable liability. Each 1 percent rise in the compliance level for any year raises billions of dollars. Consequently, the IRS has expanded its matching of information returns to include more than 23 million K-1s with income information reported by partnerships, LLCs, S corporations, estates, and trusts. The IRS believes that 71 percent of noncompliance is from unreported income and the balance is from overstated deductions. It believes that only two-thirds of Schedule C income is being reported—and only 19 percent by Schedule C cash businesses, such as street vendors and child-care providers.

The IRS may have a difficult time raising the current level of compliance. In a 2001 survey by the IRS Oversight Board (see "The IRS in the 21st Century" later in this chapter), only 76 percent of taxpayers said that cheating on taxes was unacceptable; five percent said that it was okay to cheat "as much as possible."

The IRS expects to increase its focus on upper income taxpayers, particularly those using complex tax shelters, abusive trust schemes, or offshore bank accounts. Beginning in 2000, the IRS issued summons to the major credit card companies to obtain information on Americans with foreign credit and debit cards.

Caution

The IRS is also looking for scams to obtain refunds. In 2001 it received almost 80,000 returns claiming a credit or deduction for "slavery reparations" and about 200 for "Native American reparations."

Tax Planning

When you know that an incorrect information return has been filed with the IRS, submit an explanatory statement with the tax return if the provider of the information return will not make a correction. This may (but will not always) keep you from being among the millions of taxpayers contacted by the IRS each year for discrepancies as determined by computer reporting.

Caution

Although you can take any legally justifiable position, your tax return preparer can be penalized for taking a position that does not have a "realistic possibility" of being sustained. Under IRS Regulations, a position has a realistic possibility of success if it has at least approximately a one-in-three chance or better of prevailing on the merits. If a position is not "frivolous" but has longer odds of winning, the preparer may take that position if adequately disclosed on the return.

Audits, Appeals, and Litigation

The time and effort required in preparing for a meeting with an IRS examiner and ease in which the audit will be conducted is dependent upon a number of factors, including:

- The nature of the audit
- The shape of your records
- The knowledge and experience of your Taxpayer Representative (or your knowledge if you are going to the meeting alone)
- The knowledge and experience of the IRS examiner (training has been reduced and turnover has increased)
- Whether the IRS conducts an economic reality check to examine whether the income reported on your return is commensurate with your lifestyle (these are prohibited by law in the absence of other indications of unreported income)

One of the first decisions you must make if you receive an audit notice is whether to go to the examination alone, bring your tax preparer or other professional along, or stay at home and let your attorney, CPA, or agent enrolled to practice before the IRS go to the meeting in your place. The last approach is usually the best one, unless your presence is needed to establish credibility or is required by the IRS.

Most individuals have a tendency to say too much rather than just answer the examiner's questions. This can open up new points for examination or can complicate ones being scrutinized. Additionally, most individuals will act emotionally and defensively when meeting with an examiner.

When a matter cannot be resolved with the examiner, an examination report will be prepared. If not accepted by the taxpayer, a 30-day letter (so-called because you have 30 days to respond; 60 days if sent to you outside the United States) will be issued and the next step is an Appeals Office Conference. The conference is obtained by making a written request to the local district director pursuant to instructions in the 30-day letter. A formal written *protest* may be required in order to obtain the conference when the total amount of proposed additional tax exceeds $10,000 for any taxable period. Instructions concerning the content of the protest are contained in the 30-day letter.

At the Appeals Conference, a taxpayer will have a greater opportunity to resolve a controversy than existed with the examiner. Appeals officers will consider court decisions that have been contrary to the IRS as well as the hazards of litigation. A particular issue may also be settled at a certain number of cents on the dollar based on the risks of litigation.

Most tax matters are resolved at the Appeals Conference along the lines that they would be resolved by a court. If a case cannot be resolved with Appeals (as they are about 90 percent of the time), the IRS will issue a *statutory notice of deficiency,* also known as a 90-day letter because the taxpayer has 90 days from the mailing date of the letter (150 days if sent to an address outside the United States) to forestall assessment of the tax and subsequent collection by filing a *petition* with the Tax Court.

The time period for filing a Tax Court petition is statutory and cannot be extended, even if an individual is improperly advised by the IRS. Note that 90 days is generally less than three months. For example, if a notice of deficiency is issued on June 23, your Tax Court petition is due on September 21 (which is the 90th day). Notices of deficiency are now supposed to show the exact due date for you. The failure of the IRS to state the 90th day on the notice of deficiency does not make the notice invalid, at least when this late filing was not the result of a miscalculation of the due date, ruled a divided Tax Court in a 2001 decision.

Instead of filing a petition with the Tax Court, you can pay the full liability, file a claim for refund with the IRS (which will, in all likelihood, be denied), and then sue the IRS for a refund in U.S. District Court or in the Court of Federal Claims.

Payroll tax matters such as the Trust Fund Recovery Penalty (discussed in Chapter 10, "Business Tax Planning") are not within the jurisdiction of the Tax Court and, accordingly, special rules apply. If the payroll matter cannot be resolved, the IRS will make an assessment and provide notice and demand for payment. You commence the steps toward litigation by paying a certain portion of the liability, filing a claim for refund with the IRS (which in such cases will normally also be denied), and suing the IRS for a refund in U.S. District Court or in the Court of Federal Claims. The IRS may not seize assets for the remaining liability during the pendency of the litigation unless collection is in jeopardy.

The hard facts are that taxpayers rarely win their cases in court. Recent statistics indicate that taxpayers win outright only 4 percent of the time in Tax Court, faring a bit better in District Court and the Court of Federal Claims. Absent clear error on the part of the IRS, a taxpayer with an attractive settlement offer must realistically look at his or her chance of success upon proceeding to court, particularly in light of legal fees and other costs of litigation. Alternate dispute resolution (ADR) may facilitate settlement. As mandated by law, the IRS is establishing a broad-based mediation program if requested by one party and a binding arbitration program if requested by both the taxpayer and the IRS.

Caution

The Tax Court will not hear the case of a business entity not in good standing under state law on the date it files its Tax Court petition. Corporations, limited liability companies, and limited partnerships (see Chapter 10) must pay heed to this 2000 decision.

Controversy

The Second Circuit Court of Appeals and several federal district courts interpret the "full payment rule" for litigation in District Court and the Court of Federal Claims as requiring a taxpayer to pay the entire amount of assessed tax, assessed penalties, and assessed interest before jurisdiction is conferred on the court. In contrast, the United States Court of Appeals for the Federal Circuit (the court that hears appeals from the Court of Federal Claims) has ruled that the full payment rule requires the taxpayer to pay only the assessed tax liability and not the assessed penalties and interest when the taxpayer is not making a substantive claim regarding the penalties and interest. The Federal Circuit would require full payment of assessed penalties and/or interest, as the case may be, if the taxpayer raises substantive arguments beyond the automatic reduction or elimination of penalties and interest when the tax liability is reduced or eliminated as a result of the court's decision.

Caution

Proposed regulations would require a written protest only where the proposed additional tax liability exceeds $25,000. This change will be effective 60 days after the regulations become final. In the meantime, follow the instructions in the 30-day letter.

Moving—Let the IRS Know

Failure to actually receive correspondence from the IRS will generally be no excuse for missing a deadline if the notice was sent to your "last known address." Because the IRS historically used the address shown on your most recently filed tax return as the address of record for purposes of sending audit, deficiency, and levy notices, it is important to keep the IRS informed of any change in address by "clear and concise notice." Once a tax return has been filed, the IRS will be considered to have received a notice of the address reported on that return 45 days after receipt. However, as a result of the high volume of returns filed between February 14 and June 1, addresses shown on tax returns filed during that period will not be considered as received for this purpose until July 16.

If you move after filing your tax return, the "clear and concise" notice requirement can be met by filing Form 8822 with the service center where you filed your last tax return. If you do not notify the IRS of your move until it processes your next return, the IRS may get your new address anyway. Effective 2001, the IRS began receiving weekly address changes from the Post Office. If you are on the list, this address becomes your last-known address.

In any event, make sure the post office forwards your mail. The IRS was initally unable to deliver $176 million in advance 2001 refunds to more than 555,000 taxpayers because of erroneous addresses. After the returns were filed, the IRS was still holding $80 million in refunds for 97,000 taxpayers. About 12 percent of taxpayers are unable to contest proposed tax assessments because they do not receive the 90-day letters sent to their last known addresses.

Controversy

Before the IRS adopted the 45-day rule in 1990, the courts on numerous occasions scrutinized the issue of what constitutes a taxpayer's last known address. While most decisions favored the IRS, the courts did not universally accept the time period that the IRS claimed was needed for processing address changes. It is unclear whether the current rule will survive the scrutiny of the courts.

Form **8822** (Rev. December 2002) Department of the Treasury Internal Revenue Service

Change of Address

▶ Please type or print.

▶ See instructions. ▶ Do not attach this form to your return.

OMB No. 1545-1163

Part I Complete This Part To Change Your Home Mailing Address

Check **all** boxes this change affects:

1 ☐ Individual income tax returns (Forms 1040, 1040A, 1040EZ, TeleFile, 1040NR, etc.)

▶ If your last return was a joint return and you are now establishing a residence separate from the spouse with whom you filed that return, check here . . . . ▶ ☐

2 ☐ Gift, estate, or generation-skipping transfer tax returns (Forms 706, 709, etc.)

▶ For Forms 706 and 706-NA, enter the decedent's name and social security number below.

▶ Decedent's name ▶ Social security number

3a **Your name** (first name, initial, and last name) | 3b **Your social security number**

4a **Spouse's name** (first name, initial, and last name) | 4b **Spouse's social security number**

5 **Prior name(s).** See instructions.

6a **Old address** (no., street, city or town, state, and ZIP code). If a P.O. box or foreign address, see instructions. | Apt. no.

6b **Spouse's old address,** if different from line 6a (no., street, city or town, state, and ZIP code). If a P.O. box or foreign address, see instructions. | Apt. no.

7 **New address** (no., street, city or town, state, and ZIP code). If a P.O. box or foreign address, see instructions. | Apt. no.

Part II Complete This Part To Change Your Business Mailing Address or Business Location

Check **all** boxes this change affects:

8 ☐ Employment, excise, income, and other business returns (Forms 720, 940, 940-EZ, 941, 990, 1041, 1065, 1120, etc.)

9 ☐ Employee plan returns (Forms 5500, 5500-EZ, etc.).

10 ☐ Business location

11a **Business name** | 11b **Employer identification number**

12 **Old mailing address** (no., street, city or town, state, and ZIP code). If a P.O. box or foreign address, see instructions. | Room or suite no.

13 **New mailing address** (no., street, city or town, state, and ZIP code). If a P.O. box or foreign address, see instructions. | Room or suite no.

14 **New business location** (no., street, city or town, state, and ZIP code). If a foreign address, see instructions. | Room or suite no.

Part III Signature

Daytime telephone number of person to contact (optional) ▶ ____________

Sign Here

▶ Your signature | Date

▶ If joint return, spouse's signature | Date

▶ If Part II completed, signature of owner, officer, or representative | Date

▶ Title

For Privacy Act and Paperwork Reduction Act Notice, see back of form. Form **8822** (Rev. 12-2002)

ISA
STF FED7154F

Form 8822, Change of Address

Abating Penalties and Interest

All but a few of the more than 150 types of civil penalties in the tax law will either not be assessed or are abatable in the event that reasonable cause can be shown. However, the IRS has drastically slashed its penalty abatements. For fiscal 1990, the IRS abated almost one-half of the billions of dollars in assessed penalties.

During the following year, less than 10 percent of penalties were abated. Today, the abatement rate remains low and the penalty structure remains so complicated that then IRS Commissioner Margaret Richardson in 1997 called for an "urgent overhaul." In 1999, then IRS National Taxpayer Advocate, W. Val Oveson called the penalty structure one of the most serious problems facing the agency.

Both Treasury and the Congressional Joint Committee on Taxation agree, and in 1999 each made specific recommendations for simplification while seeking to maintain fair and effective sanctions.

Pending any overhaul, legislation in 1998 provided some relief. The accrual of certain time-measured penalties (except failure to file) and interest is suspended until 21 days after IRS notice if the IRS has not sent a notice specifically stating the amount and reason for a post-filing adjustment for 12 months (18 months before 2004) after the later of the original due date of the return or the actual filing date. This automatic abatement provision is only for individuals and is not applicable to those who file beyond the extended return due date or in the case of fraud. Additionally, penalty assessment (other than late filing, late payment, and underpayment of estimated taxes) now requires written supervisory review.

As previously discussed, it is often difficult to show reasonable cause in connection with the late filing of an income tax return. Among examples of reasonable cause are death or serious illness of the taxpayer or a member of his or her immediate family, unavoidable absence of the taxpayer, or destruction of business records. Illness may be either physical or psychological. In the latter case, a good affidavit from the taxpayer's psychiatrist or psychologist is essential but is no guarantee of success.

Fortunately, the courts are more sympathetic than the IRS to penalty abatement. A Kentucky man several years ago filed a return three years late during a period in which he became totally paralyzed from a degenerative disease. The IRS refused to abate the late filing penalty, but a federal district court was more sympathetic. To its credit, the IRS did not appeal the decision. However, see Chapter 1, "Introduction to Personal Tax Planning," concerning how the courts would not abate penalties assessed against actress Skye Bassett for her parents' failure to file returns on her behalf when she was a youngster.

One of the most popular defenses to the late filing penalty is to blame the tardiness on a tax professional. The U.S. Supreme Court in 1985 resolved this formerly controversial area, determining that reliance on a professional to file a tax return does not take the taxpayer off the hook. However, if the professional gives improper tax advice, good faith reliance on the substantive guidance should suffice to make the penalty inapplicable.

Other penalties are much easier to abate. More than a quarter century after ERISA (technically the Employee Retirement Income Security Act of 1974, but popularly known in the tax profession as Every Rotten Idea Since Adam) overhauled the retirement plan laws, they remain such a source of confusion to taxpayers, practitioners, and the IRS itself that virtually every request to abate penalties for late filing of the 5500 series information return is granted.

The most severe penalties (excluding the Trust Fund Recovery Penalty discussed in Chapter 10, which is really a transfer of portions of corporate or limited liability company payroll tax liability to responsible individuals) are the civil fraud penalty and the negligence penalty. In the case of civil fraud, a taxpayer will pay, in addition to principal and interest, an amount equal to 75 percent of the portion of the liability that is attributable to fraud. Short of civil fraud is negligence, with a 20 percent penalty on the portion of the liability that is attributable to negligence. Interest will be imposed on the fraud or negligence penalty amount as well as on the tax deficiency.

Interest, which is imposed on tax and certain penalties, can be dropped to the extent attributable to ministerial (procedural) or managerial (substantive) error. Pending more expansive language in future legislation, interest abatements are relatively uncommon. In 1999, the Tax Court agreed with the IRS that a delay of 14 years before resolving issues related to a timely filed 1980 return is not in itself "grossly unfair" so as to require abatement. However, during the same year, the Tax Court required the IRS to abate interest accruing after an incorrect payoff amount was provided to the taxpayer.

Tax Planning

Keep records of all telephone contact with IRS staffers. Record their names and telephone numbers along with the dates of contact. These records may be useful in abating penalties and interest.

Caution

Because the IRS has been so unwilling to abate penalties even for first-time inadvertent errors, Congress was considering legislation which, if enacted, would require the IRS to abate first-time penalties for individuals in cases when minor negligence results in a liability that is "disproportionate and unreasonable." H.R. 1528, the Taxpayer Protection and IRS Accountability Act of 2003, passed the House on June 19, 2003.

Filing Pointer

When a tax matter is pending for a long period of time, interest can approach or exceed the principal amount of tax liability, particularly during periods of high rates.

The interest rate taxpayers pay to the IRS is adjusted quarterly, with the new rate three points above the short-term rate on federal obligations during the first

continues

Filing Pointer (cont.)

month of the preceding quarter, rounded to the nearest full percent. Between July 1, 1985, and December 31, 2003, interest rates on obligations to the IRS ranged between 4 percent and 11 percent, though they have been much higher in the past. A special interest rate of 120 percent of the regular rate applies to certain tax-motivated transactions. In either event, interest is compounded daily on the unpaid balance.

When it is clear that you may owe some liability but settlement of other issues will be drawn out or difficult, it often makes sense to cut the interest amount by paying undisputed principal and the interest on that principal. If you prevail on the remaining issues, you should owe nothing more. Under certain circumstances it is possible to designate payments as interest only.

Statute of Limitations—Sometimes They Benefit You, Sometimes They Do Not

Suppose that you had more gains on commodities trading one year than you reported to the IRS. Suppose your inadvertent error is discovered many years later.

In this case, the statute of limitations would have expired long ago and is a bar to imposition of a tax deficiency. Nonetheless, on these facts, former President and Mrs. Clinton made a voluntary payment of $14,615 tax and interest (no penalty) in 1994.

The normal statute of limitations during which the IRS can assess a deficiency is three years from the later of the due date or the filing date of the tax return. However, the statute is six years rather than three if over 25 percent of gross income is omitted. There is an unlimited statute of limitations in the case of nonfilers or in the event of civil fraud.

Not only may a statute of limitations bar imposition of a tax deficiency, but it also may bar collection on an outstanding deficiency. The IRS has normally ten years from the date of assessment of a deficiency to take collection action or to sue for a judgment (upon which case the time period for collection is determined under state law). Exceptions include an extension of the time period on your part (which under the law is valid only when executed in connection with an installment agreement), the submission of a request for an installment agreement which extends the time period during the pendency of the request, the rejection or termination of an installment agreement which extends the time period during any appeal but for no less than 30 days, the submission of an Offer in Compromise which extends the time period for its pendency plus one year, or the filing of a bankruptcy or other court proceeding which extends the time period for its pendency plus six months. Offers in Compromise, installment agreements, and bankruptcies are discussed later in this chapter.

A statute of limitations can work to your disadvantage as well. A claim for refund (usually on Form 1040-X in the case of an individual income tax refund or on Form 843 for employment taxes, penalties, and certain other matters) must generally be filed by the later of three years from the due date of the tax return, or two years from the date of payment. Consequently, if you filed your 2000 tax return on time and made full payment, a refund claim must be filed by April 15, 2004. And, if you never filed your 2000 tax return, but you are due a refund, you will never see your check unless the return is filed by that date.

For refund claims that were not barred by the statute of limitations on July 22, 1998, the time period for filing does not run during an individual's physical or mental impairment that can be expected to result in death or to last continuously for at least one year. There is no suspension when another individual has legal authority to act such as through court appointment or power of attorney.

Caution

Pursuant to a 1993 decision of the U.S. Supreme Court, even though the IRS missed a statute of limitations against an S corporation, it may still come after the shareholder for his or her share of taxes on the entity income until the expiration of the individual assessment period. Later that year the Ninth Circuit Court of Appeals determined that the same reasoning applied in the case of a partner as to taxes on his or her share of partnership income.

Always Pay the IRS If You Can—

Although the IRS interest rate may appear lower than some other creditors, it will often be higher than credit card rates when coupled with the usual 1/2 percent-per-month failure to pay penalty, when applicable. In 1999, the IRS began to accept credit cards to pay your tax bill and over 200,000 taxpayers have taken advantage of the opportunity to use plastic each year (and to pay a convenience fee"). The record charge was one of $7.2 million (think of the frequent flier miles) in 2000.

Given any choice, owe on your credit cards, owe the bank, or owe your in-laws. Their collection remedies pale compared to those available to the IRS, which is America's largest collection agency. And their collection departments are usually more responsive and more sympathetic to your telephone calls and letters.

When you owe money to the IRS, you are negotiating with a powerful counterpart, wounded by recent legislation such that the numbers of enforcement actions have dropped, but one that is still very much alive. The IRS can force you as a debtor to provide a financial statement to learn of the whereabouts of your assets (existing bank accounts seem to have very little money and new bank accounts seem to be opened in many cases within a day or two of the financial statement).

While a federal tax lien exists on all property of a taxpayer as of the date of assessment, there is no public knowledge of the lien unless and until the revenue officer files a Notice of Federal Tax Lien. This Notice is filed in locations as provided by state law. A Notice of Federal Tax Lien affects an individual's credit standing (including his or her ability to borrow to pay off the IRS) as well as restricts disposition of certain property.

Without filing a Notice of Federal Tax Lien, the IRS can levy and seize the property of a taxpayer. Under federal law, only the following property is totally exempt from levy:

- Wearing apparel and school books necessary to the taxpayer or family members
- If the taxpayer is the head of a family, fuel, provisions, furniture, personal effects, firearms, livestock, and poultry to a collective maximum of $6,890 in value prior to indexing for cost of living in 2004
- Books and tools necessary in a trade, business, or profession to a maximum in the aggregate of $3,440 in value prior to indexing for cost of living in 2004
- Undelivered mail
- Certain payments to Congressional Medal of Honor winners
- So much of salary, wages, or other income necessary to comply with court-ordered child support (not applicable to support provided in a voluntary separation agreement not incorporated in a court decree)
- Military service-connected disability payments
- Payments under the Job Training Partnership Act

Under a continuing levy, wages and other compensation are reachable subject to an exemption computed by formula. Also, under a continuing levy, 15 percent of unemployment compensation, Social Security benefits, worker's compensation, and public assistance payments are reachable.

A levy on nonrental residential real estate of an individual is prohibited in the case of tax liability of $5,000 or less and is otherwise permitted only if approved by a U.S. District Court. A levy on tangible property "used in the business of an individual taxpayer" requires approval of the district director or his assistant unless collection of the tax is in jeopardy.

The most frequently reached assets by the IRS are wages and bank accounts, both because of the simplicity in levying as well as the ease in obtaining information. Without resorting to obtaining a financial statement from you, the IRS can often locate your sources of wages from the W-2s attached to your most recently filed tax return and your bank accounts from the sources of interest income shown on that return. However, the IRS can seize a variety of assets. In 1994, it levied on a second-place purse awarded in a stakes race at Saratoga Race Track (the horse was reported to have nipped the revenue officer).

While the larger and more complex collection cases are assigned to a particular revenue officer, most collection matters are handled by the Automated Telephone Collection System (ACS). If your delinquent account is assigned to ACS, your telephone number will be dialed periodically and automatically between the permitted hours of 8 A.M. and 9 P.M. until you are reached. The telephones are manned by less experienced personnel, and you normally cannot arrange to deal a second time with the person initially handling your matter. ACS will not hesitate to garnish or attach if it knows where you work or have bank accounts. However, payment arrangements can most often be worked out over the telephone.

While ACS often offers a quick ability to resolve simpler collection matters, it has major problems in handling more complex matters such as unapplied payments, requests for substantiation, and requests for penalty abatement.

Tax delinquents owe collectively more than $200 billion according to the IRS. However, a General Accounting Office audit indicated that less than 14 percent of this amount will be recovered. The balance represents liabilities that are either disputed, duplicated (such as multiple assessments of the Trust Fund Recovery Penalty discussed in Chapter 10), or uncollectible. Tax delinquents include hundreds of thousands of federal workers (including IRS and Tax Court employees) as well as retirees.

The General Accounting Office is critical of IRS collection efforts and, most specifically, the amount of uncollectible debt. However, the work of the IRS is made more difficult by taxpayer protections included in 1998 legislation following days of hearings by the Senate Finance Committee during which taxpayers told of IRS abuses. Accordingly, the number of liens and levies dropped from a high of about 4.2 million in fiscal 1997 to about 500,000 in fiscal 2000. The number rose to about 1.16 million by fiscal 2002.

Now the imposition of a lien or levy, except by ACS, must be approved by a supervisor. The IRS must give written notice no later than five days after filing a notice of lien. The taxpayer has a 30-day period to request a hearing with Appeals.

Also, the IRS must now generally give written notice of an intent to levy no sooner than 30 days before the levy. The taxpayer again has a 30-day appeal period. Appeals may consider challenges to the tax liability, spousal defenses (see Chapter 8, "Marriage and Divorce"), the propriety of the collection action, and alternatives to the proposed action. The IRS may not levy during a bankruptcy and is generally prohibited from levy during the pendency of an installment agreement or Offer in Compromise or while either is being sought. These three topics are discussed later in this chapter.

Unfavorable decisions on liens and levies may be taken to the Tax Court (or, instead, in the case of payroll taxes, a federal district court) within 30 days but only if, according to the Tax Court in a 2000 decision, the taxpayer previously requested an Appeals hearing. In some cases the court may hear challenges to the tax liability itself. The statute of limitations is suspended during a levy appeal, with at least 90 days to remain after final determination.

Question: I owe money to the IRS and I am expecting an inheritance. Can I disclaim the bequest and let it pass to other family members in order to keep it out of the hands of the IRS?

Answer: In 1999 the U.S. Supreme Court determined that an IRS lien attaches to bequests even prior to their receipt, so that they may not be disclaimed to defeat IRS collection.

Question: I am delinquent in paying my taxes but my wife is current; she files a separate return. Can the IRS levy on our joint bank and brokerage accounts?

Answer: Yes, at least if only one of your signatures is required to remove funds. The IRS stands *at least* in the shoes of the debtor. See the Controversy that follows if the account requires two signatures for a withdrawal.

Caution

The IRS can seize a federal or state tax refund and apply it against another year's delinquent tax liability. Can the IRS seize a joint tax refund and apply it against the back tax liability owed by only one spouse? It does and shifts the burden to the couple to get back part of the refund by filing a claim for refund on IRS Form 843 and attaching Form 8379, which computes the portion of the refund not attributable to the debtor spouse.

Controversy

To what extent can the IRS seize property that other creditors cannot? This important question remains largely unanswered despite a 2002 decision of the U.S. Supreme Court, determining that an IRS lien attaches to the interest of the debtor spouse in tenants by the entirety property when the other spouse has no debt to the IRS. Reversing the Sixth Circuit Court of Appeals, the Supreme Court went the opposite direction from six federal courts of appeal that had ruled on the issue.

continues

Form **8379**
(Rev. December 2002)
Department of the Treasury
Internal Revenue Service

Injured Spouse Claim and Allocation

OMB No. 1545-1210
Attachment Sequence No. **104**

Are You an Injured Spouse?

You are an injured spouse if you file a joint return and all or part of your share of the overpayment was, or is expected to be, applied (offset) against your spouse's past-due Federal tax, child or spousal support, Federal nontax debt (such as a student loan) or state income tax. Complete Form 8379 if **all three** of the following apply and you want your share of the overpayment shown on the joint return refunded to you. **But** if your main home was in a community property state (see line 6 below), you may file Form 8379 if only item **1** below applies.

1. You are not required to pay the past-due amount.

2. You reported income such as wages, taxable interest, etc. on the joint return.

3. You made and reported payments such as Federal income tax withheld from your wages or estimated tax payments, or you claimed the earned income credit or other refundable credit, on the joint return.

Do not use this form if you are requesting relief from liability for tax that you believe should be paid only by your spouse (or former spouse). Instead, file **Form 8857,** Request for Innocent Spouse Relief.

How Do You File Form 8379?

• If you have not filed your joint return, attach Form 8379 to your return in the order of the attachment sequence number. **Enter "Injured Spouse" in the upper left corner of the return.** Because the IRS will process your claim before an offset occurs, filing Form 8379 with your original return may delay your refund by 6 to 8 weeks.

• If you have already filed the joint tax return, mail Form 8379 by itself to the Internal Revenue Service Center for the place where you lived when you filed the joint return. See your tax return instruction booklet for the address. **Be sure** to include copies of all W-2 and W-2G forms of both spouses and any Forms 1099-R showing income tax withheld. The processing of your claim may be delayed if you do not include these copies. Please allow at least 8 weeks for the IRS to process your claim.

• If you later file **Form 1040X,** Amended U.S. Individual Income Tax Return, requesting an additional refund, you should attach a revised Form 8379 if you want the refund allocated between you and your spouse.

Note: *The Treasury Department's Financial Management Service (FMS), not the IRS, is authorized to apply (offset) all or part of the joint refund to past-due child or spousal support, Federal nontax debt, or state income tax. If you also owe past-due child or spousal support, Federal nontax debt, or state income tax, the FMS will apply all or part of your share of the refund to the debt. If an offset occurs, you will receive a notice from the FMS.*

Part I **Information About the Joint Tax Return for Which This Claim Is Filed**

1 **Enter the following information exactly as it is shown on the tax return for which you are filing this claim. The spouse's name and social security number shown first on that tax return must also be shown first below.**

First name, initial, and last name shown first on the return	Social security number shown first	**If Injured Spouse, check here ▶** ☐
First name, initial, and last name shown second on the return	Social security number shown second	**If Injured Spouse, check here ▶** ☐

Note: *If you are filing Form 8379 with your tax return, skip to line 5.*

2 **Enter the tax year for which you are filing this claim (for example, 2002) ▶** ________

3 ________

Current home address	City	State	ZIP code

4 Is the address on your joint return different from the address shown above? . . . . . ☐ **Yes** ☐ **No**

5 Check this box only if you are divorced or separated from the spouse with whom you filed the joint return and you want your refund issued in your name only . . . . . ☐

6 Was your main home in a community property state (Arizona, California, Idaho, Louisiana, Nevada, New Mexico, Texas, Washington, or Wisconsin) at any time during the year entered on line 2? . . . . . ☐ **Yes** ☐ **No**
If "Yes," which community property state(s)? ________
Note: *Overpayments involving community property states will be allocated by the IRS according to state law.*

Go to Part II on the back.

Privacy Act and Paperwork Reduction Act Notice. Our legal right to ask for the information on this form is Internal Revenue Code sections 6001, 6011, 6109, and 6402 and their regulations. You are required to give us the information so that we can process your claim for refund of your share of an overpayment shown on the joint return with your spouse. We need it to ensure that you are allocating items correctly and to allow us to figure the correct amount of your claim for refund. If you do not provide all of the information, we may not be able to process your claim. We may give this information to the Department of Justice for civil and criminal litigation, and to cities, states, and the District of Columbia to carry out their tax laws. We may also disclose this information to other countries under a tax treaty or to Federal and state agencies to enforce Federal nontax criminal laws and to combat terrorism.

You are not required to provide the information requested on a form that is subject to the Paperwork Reduction Act unless the form displays a valid OMB control number. Books or records relating to a form or its instructions must be retained as long as their contents may become material in the administration of any Internal Revenue law. Generally, tax returns and return information are confidential, as required by Code section 6103.

The time needed to complete and file this form will vary depending on individual circumstances. The estimated average time is: **Recordkeeping,** 13 min.; **Learning about the law or the form,** 10 min.; **Preparing the form,** 59 min.; and **Copying, assembling, and sending the form to the IRS,** 25 min.

If you have comments concerning the accuracy of these time estimates or suggestions for making this form simpler, we would be happy to hear from you. You can write to the Tax Forms Committee, Western Area Distribution Center, Rancho Cordova, CA 95743-0001. **Do not** send the form to this address. Instead, see **How Do You File Form 8379?** above.

ISA
STF FED6632F.1

Form **8379** (Rev. 12-2002)

Form 8379, Injured Spouse Claim and Allocation (page 1)

Form 8379 (Rev. 12-2002) Page 2

Part II Allocation Between Spouses of Items on the Joint Tax Return

Allocated Items	(a) Amount shown on joint return	(b) Allocated to injured spouse	(c) Allocated to other spouse
7 **Income.** Enter the separate income that each spouse earned. Allocate joint income, such as interest earned on a joint bank account, as you determine. But be sure to allocate **all** income shown on the joint return. a Wages			
b All other income. Identify the type and amount ▶			
8 **Adjustments to income.** Enter each spouse's separate adjustments, such as an IRA deduction. Allocate other adjustments as you determine			
9 **Standard deduction.** If you itemized your deductions, go to line 10. Otherwise, enter in both columns **(b)** and **(c)** 1/2 of the amount shown in column **(a)** and go to line 11			
10 **Itemized deductions.** Enter each spouse's separate deductions, such as employee business expenses. Allocate other deductions as you determine			
11 **Number of exemptions.** Allocate the exemptions claimed on the joint return to the spouse who would have claimed them if separate returns had been filed. Enter whole numbers only (for example, you **cannot** allocate 3 exemptions by giving 1.5 exemptions to each spouse)			
12 **Credits.** Allocate any child tax credit, child and dependent care credit, and additional child tax credit to the spouse who was allocated the dependent's exemption. **Do not** include any earned income credit here; the IRS will allocate it based on each spouse's income. Allocate business credits based on each spouse's interest in the business. Allocate any other credits as you determine. .			
13 **Other taxes.** Allocate self-employment tax to the spouse who earned the self-employment income. Allocate any alternative minimum tax as you determine			
14 **Federal income tax withheld.** Enter Federal income tax withheld from each spouse's income as shown on Forms W-2, W-2G, and 1099-R. **Be sure to attach copies of these forms to your tax return or to Form 8379 if you are filing it by itself.** (Also include on this line any tax withheld on any other Form 1099 or any excess social security or tier 1 RRTA tax withheld.)			
15 **Payments.** Allocate joint estimated tax payments as you determine.			

Note: *The IRS will figure the amount of any refund due the injured spouse.*

Part III **Signature.** Complete this part only if you are filing Form 8379 by itself and not with your tax return.

Under penalties of perjury, I declare that I have examined this form and any accompanying schedules or statements and to the best of my knowledge and belief, they are true, correct, and complete. Declaration of preparer (other than taxpayer) is based on all information of which preparer has any knowledge.

Keep a copy of this form for your records	Injured spouse's signature		Date	Phone number (optional)
Paid Preparer's Use Only	Preparer's signature ▶	Date	Check if self-employed ☐	Preparer's SSN or PTIN
	Firm's name (or yours if self-employed), address, and ZIP code ▶			EIN Phone no.

Form **8379** (Rev. 12-2002)

STF FED6632F.2

Form 8379, Injured Spouse Claim and Allocation (page 2)

—But Installment Payments Are Available If You Cannot Pay Now

Not only are installment payments available in the event you cannot pay the IRS in full, but also the procedure for obtaining a payment plan has been simplified recently. About 3 million installment agreements are outstanding.

If you are unable to pay your tax bill now, but you can pay it off in the future, attach IRS Form 9465 to your return and indicate the monthly amount you can pay and the date each month that you want to pay. For smaller amounts, your

Controversy (cont.)

However, the Supreme Court did not look at issues arising from its decision. Does its decision apply retroactively? The Sixth Circuit Court of Appeals said "yes" in a June 4, 2003 decision. With a lien attached to the interest of the debtor spouse in tenants by the entirety property, can the IRS force its sale? Both the Sixth Circuit and Pennsylvania Bankruptcy Court in a March 28, 2003 decision have allowed the IRS to order sale. If there is a forced sale, does the IRS get up to one-half of the proceeds or are the interests of spouses with different life expectancies valued unequally? The Pennsylvania Bankruptcy Court required consideration of different life expectancies. What happens if the spouses divorce? A New Jersey Federal District Court in an August 18, 2003 decision held that a non-liable transferee spouse takes the property subject to the debt of the liable transferor spouse. The decision of the Supreme Court related to a house; would any issues be resolved differently if the asset in issue were an installment note, a two-signature bank account or, a brokerage account, for example? The Sixth Circuit treated an installment note no differently from real property.

Broader issues have not even been looked at by the courts. What happens if the debtor spouse dies? Must the IRS be paid off or is the lien extinguished by death? Principal residences are entirely exempt from seizure in a few states, and wages cannot be garnished in several others. Do these exemptions still stand to restrict the collection ability of the IRS? And what about the nine community property states (listed in Chapter 1) which differ among themselves as to the extent that community assets and community income can be reached by a creditor of one spouse but not the other. What is the interaction between federal lien law and state community property law?

On September 29, 2003, the IRS published its answers to some of the issues. According to the IRS, although the decision applies retroactively, it will normally not seize property when acquired as tenants by the entireties before the Supreme Court decision. In the case of a forced sales, however, the IRS will value the interests of each spouse equally. Although a non-liable transferee spouse in a divorce takes property subject to the transferor spouse's debt, a non-liable widow takes property free and clear.

proposal normally will be accepted, no financial statement will be required, and no tax lien will be filed.

A large debt will normally require more effort to obtain a payment plan and will necessitate a detailed financial statement including a balance sheet and cash flow statement (which should support the requested monthly installments). A one-page form 433-F is often used, but the six-page 433-A may be required for larger liabilities or more complex situations.

If the case is assigned to a revenue officer, a meeting may be required and an installment agreement becomes far more difficult to negotiate as the IRS

Form **9465**
(Rev. December 2002)
Department of the Treasury
Internal Revenue Service (99)

Installment Agreement Request

▶ **If you are filing this form with your tax return, attach it to the front of the return. Otherwise, see instructions.**

OMB No. 1545-1350

Caution: *Do not file this form if you are currently making payments on an installment agreement. Instead, call 1-800-829-1040.*

1 Your first name and initial | Last name | **Your social security number**

If a joint return, spouse's first name and initial | Last name | **Spouse's social security number**

Your current address (number and street). If you have a P.O. box and no home delivery, enter your box number. | Apt. number

City, town or post office, state, and ZIP code. If a foreign address, enter city, province or state, and country. Follow the country's practice for entering the postal code.

2 If this address is new since you filed your last tax return, check here . . . . . ▶ ☐

3 Your home phone number | Best time for us to call

4 Your work phone number | Ext. | Best time for us to call

5 Name of your bank or other financial institution:
Address
City, state, and ZIP code

6 Your employer's name:
Address
City, state, and ZIP code

TIP *If you are filing this form in response to a notice, do not complete lines 7 through 9. Instead, attach the bottom section of the notice to this form and go to line 10.*

7 Enter the tax return for which you are making this request (for example, Form 1040) . . . . . ▶ 7

8 Enter the tax year for which you are making this request (for example, 2002) . . . . . ▶ 8

9 Enter the total amount you owe as shown on your tax return 9

10 Enter the amount of any payment you are making with your tax return (or notice). See instructions . . . 10

11 Enter the amount you can pay each month. **Make your payments as large as possible to limit interest and penalty charges.** The charges will continue until you pay in full 11

12 Enter the date you want to make your payment each month. **Do not** enter a date later than the 28th . ▶ 12

13 If you want to make your payments by electronic funds withdrawal, see the instructions and fill in lines 13a, 13b, and 13c.

▶ a Routing number ☐☐☐☐☐☐☐☐☐ ▶ c Type: ☐ Checking ☐ Savings

▶ b Account number ☐☐☐☐☐☐☐☐☐☐☐☐☐☐☐☐☐

I authorize the U.S. Treasury and its designated Financial Agent to initiate a monthly ACH electronic funds withdrawal entry to the financial institution account indicated for payments of my Federal taxes owed, and the financial institution to debit the entry to this account. This authorization is to remain in full force and effect until I notify the U.S. Treasury Financial Agent to terminate the authorization. To revoke payment, I must contact the U.S. Treasury Financial Agent at **1-800-829-1040** no later than 7 business days prior to the payment (settlement) date. I also authorize the financial institutions involved in the processing of the electronic payments of taxes to receive confidential information necessary to answer inquiries and resolve issues related to the payments.

Your signature | Date | Spouse's signature. If a joint return, **both** must sign. | Date

General Instructions

Section references are to the Internal Revenue Code.

Purpose of Form

Use Form 9465 to request a monthly installment plan if you cannot pay the full amount you owe shown on your tax return (or on a notice we sent you). Generally, you may have up to 60 months to pay. But before requesting an installment agreement, you should consider other less costly alternatives, such as a bank loan. If you have any questions about this request, call 1-800-829-1040.

Guaranteed Installment Agreement. Your request for an installment agreement cannot be turned down if the tax you owe is not more than $10,000 and **all three** of the following apply.

1. During the past 5 tax years, you (and your spouse if you are making a request for a joint tax return) have timely filed all income tax returns and paid any income tax due, and have not entered into an installment agreement for payment of income tax.
2. The IRS determines that you cannot pay the tax owed in full when it is due and you give the IRS any information needed to make that determination.
3. You agree to pay the full amount you owe within 3 years and to comply with the tax laws while the agreement is in effect.

CAUTION *A Notice of Federal Tax Lien may be filed to protect the government's interest until you pay in full.*

Bankruptcy or Offer-in-Compromise. If you are in bankruptcy or we have accepted your offer-in-compromise, **do not** file this form. Instead, call 1-800-829-1040 to get the number of your local IRS Insolvency function for bankruptcy or Technical Support function for offer-in-compromise.

For Privacy Act and Paperwork Reduction Act Notice, see back of form. Form **9465** (Rev. 12-2002)

ISA
STF FED7259F.1

Form 9465, Installment Agreement Request (page 1)

scrutinizes the necessity of expenses and the ability to liquidate assets. In the process, certain actual expenses are discarded in favor of national or local standards. The result is that an installment arrangement may be difficult if you have higher-than-average expenses for basic needs such as housing, food, and transportation. If you have a high income, an installment arrangement may be

Form **433-F** (Rev. 12-1999) | Department of the Treasury — Internal Revenue Service

Collection Information Statement

Your name(s) and address	Your Social Security Number Your Spouse's Social Security Number
	Area Code and Phone Number Home: Your Work: Your Spouse's Work:
Your Employer or Business (name and address)	Your Spouse's Employer or Business (name and address)

A. ACCOUNTS: (include Banks, Savings and Loans, Credit Union, Certificates of Deposits, Individual Retirement Arrangements (IRAs), Roth Individual Retirement Arrangements (IRAs), Keogh Plans, Simplified Employee Pensions, Mutual Funds, and Stock Brokerage Accounts)

Name of Institution	Address	Type of Account	Balance

B. REAL ESTATE: (home and other real estate)

County/Description	Value	Balance Owed	Equity	Monthly Payment

C. OTHER ASSETS: (cars, boats, recreational vehicles, whole life policies, etc.)

County/Description	Value	Balance Owed	Equity	Monthly Payment

D. CREDIT CARDS:

Type (e.g., VISA/Nations Bank)	Credit Limit	Balance Owed	Minimum Monthly Payment

E. MONTHLY INCOME:

Your Gross Pay: ______
Federal Tax Withholding: ______
State and Local Taxes: ______
Social Security Taxes: ______
Retirement/Medicare: ______
Court Ordered Payments: ______
Your Net Pay: ______
Other Income: ______
Your Available Income: ______

Spouse's Gross Pay: ______
Federal Tax Withholding: ______
State and Local Taxes: ______
Social Security Taxes: ______
Retirement/Medicare: ______
Court Ordered Payments: ______
Spouse's Net Pay: ______
Other Income: ______
Spouse's Available Income: ______

Your Available Income: ______
Spouse's Available Income: ______
Total Available Income: ______

F. MONTHLY EXPENSES

	Amount	IRS USE
Rent: (don't show mortgage here)		
NATIONAL STANDARDS: food, household/ personal needs, miscellaneous *(See Instructions)*		
Utilities (electric, water, heat, telephone)		
Transportation (gas, bus fare, car insurance, etc.)		
Medicine (health insurance, drugs, doctor bills)		
Child /Dependent Care Costs		
Quarterly Payment of Estimated Taxes (Form 1040ES)		
Life Insurance (if NOT listed in Section C)		
Other Deductions or Expenses NOT Listed		
1.		
2.		
3.		
TOTAL EXPENSES		

G. ADDITIONAL INFORMATION

Total Number of Dependents (include yourself and spouse):	
Expected Change To Income, Health Expenses, ETC.	
MONTHLY AMOUNT YOU PROPOSE TO PAY THE INTERNAL REVENUE SERVICE FOR YOUR ACCOUNT:	$

FOR IRS USE ONLY (Sections B, C, D, and F)
TOTAL ALLOWABLE EXPENSES:
MONTHLY PAYMENT AMOUNT:

Under penalties of perjury, I declare to the best of my knowledge and belief this statement of assets, liabilities, and other information is true, correct, and complete.

Your Signature	Spouse's Signature	Date

ISA
STF FED1079F

Form **433-F** (Rev. 12-99)

Form 433-F, Collection Information Statement

next to impossible to achieve inasmuch as the guidelines consider all after-tax income as "disposable" once you make upper five figures.

In contrast to an audit situation, when it is usually better to let the taxpayer representative handle the matter while the taxpayer stays at home, it is often advisable even for a taxpayer represented professionally (as he or she should be before the Collection Division) to be present at the meeting with the revenue officer. The face-to-face relationship allows a rapport to be created and the situation to be personalized. Sheer human nature makes it more difficult to say no when the affected person is sitting across the table from you. But if the revenue officer still says no, ask to meet with the supervisor (and perhaps, if needed, the supervisor's supervisor).

Under IRS Regulations issued in 2002, the IRS is normally barred from levying on assets while an installment agreement is in place or is being sought and for 30 days thereafter. The restriction does not apply if the IRS determines that collection of tax is in jeopardy or if it believes that a request for an installment agreement was submitted only for purpose of delay.

Given all of its remedies, why would the IRS even agree to a payment plan? First, it cuts the number of cases that must be actively worked; second, the IRS may seize a paycheck or some cash in the bank account, but most taxpayers in that situation who have options of mobility in their jobs and accounts are going to take whatever steps are necessary to be able to pay the rent or mortgage and to put food on the table; and third, if the taxpayer defaults, the same harsher remedies are available later.

The IRS charges a user fee of $43 for installment agreements, payable with the first installment.

Caution

Even though an installment plan may be available, it should not be used when alternatives exist such as private financing. Taxpayers making timely payments often must deal with improper application of funds or installment agreements ignored by the IRS computer system.

—But an Offer in Compromise Is Available If You Can Never Pay

Do you owe the IRS more money than you can ever reasonably expect to pay? After years of routine rejection of most taxpayer settlement offers, the IRS several years ago changed its official policy and claimed to be favorably disposed to accepting partial payment in full satisfaction of a tax debt that would otherwise probably be uncollectible. For its 2002 fiscal year, the IRS received 124,033 Offers in Compromise. Many of them were bounced in early processing on account of unfiled returns, other tax delinquencies, incomplete forms or attachments (in only 22 percent of offers are all required attachments submitted), or insufficient amounts offered based on quick analysis. Nonetheless, it accepted 29,140 offers, many for higher amounts than originally proposed by the taxpayer. Still the average payment on an accepted offer was only 12 cents on the dollar.

To get your offer even processed, you must have filed all back returns and have offered the IRS a minimum amount equal to the sum of the "quick-sale" value of your assets (in some cases net of taxes) plus a multiple of your monthly cash flow after "necessary" living expenses. If you will pay the offered amount within 90 days of acceptance of the offer, the multiple is 48 times the deemed monthly cash flow. If you will pay the offered amount in more than 90 days but within two years, the multiple is 60 times the deemed monthly cash flow. If you will pay the offered amount over more than two years, the multiple is the remaining number of months before expiration of the statute of limitations times the deemed monthly cash flow.

Unless the facts of the particular case indicate they should be disregarded, national and local standards determine many of your necessary living expenses. Usually, they total far less than actual living expenses within those categories.

Joint offers from husband and wife consider the assets and cash flow of both spouses. When only one of a married couple owes taxes, IRS Regulations require that the IRS consider only the assets and cash flow of the individual who is liable, although the IRS will request income and expense information on both spouses (or on any other adult living in the home) to determine who should be responsible for paying which expenses.

Even if your offer is processible, it will still be rejected if you are unable to convince the IRS that it would not likely ever collect the amount of your offer. Notwithstanding that singer Willie Nelson had an offer accepted in 1984, most individuals who currently have or who previously had high incomes are unable to convince the IRS to settle for a portion of the liability.

If you do decide to submit an offer, you generally file IRS Form 656 along with a financial statement on IRS Form 433A and/or 433B. Be sure that you can come up from the amount you promise on acceptance. Even better, submit the offered amount with your compromise proposal. If the IRS rejects your offer, it must return the money. The source of funds for most offers is borrowed amounts from family and friends.

Although most offers are submitted based on doubt as to collectibility, an offer may be based on doubt as to liability. In such cases, tax and legal issues rather than financial issues are examined by the IRS. Offers also may now be submitted based on economic hardship (by individuals only) or special circumstances in which collection of the full liability will be detrimental to voluntary compliance by taxpayers. Examples of the latter under IRS Regulations illustrate an individual who ignored financial matters during years of bad health and an individual who received incorrect advice from the IRS.

IRS
Department of the Treasury
Internal Revenue Service
www.irs.gov
Form 656 (Rev. 5-2001)

Form 656
Offer in Compromise

IRS RECEIVED DATE

Item 1 — Taxpayer's Name and Home or Business Address

Name ______________________

Name ______________________

Street Address ______________________

City ______ State ______ ZIP Code ______

Mailing Address *(if different from above)*

Street Address ______________________

City ______ State ______ ZIP Code ______

DATE RETURNED

Item 2 — Social Security Numbers

(a) Primary ______________________

(b) Secondary ______________________

Item 3 — Employer Identification Number *(included in offer)*

____

Item 4 — Other Employer Identification Numbers *(not included in offer)*

____

Item 5 — To: Commissioner of Internal Revenue Service

I/We (includes all types of taxpayers) submit this offer to compromise the tax liabilities plus any interest, penalties, additions to tax, and additional amounts required by law (tax liability) for the tax type and period marked below: (Please mark an "X" in the box for the correct description and fill-in the correct tax period(s), adding additional periods if needed).

☐ **1040/1120 Income Tax** — Year(s) ______________________

☐ **941 Employer's Quarterly Federal Tax Return** — Quarterly period(s) ______________________

☐ **940 Employer's Annual Federal Unemployment (FUTA) Tax Return** — Year(s) ______________________

☐ **Trust Fund Recovery Penalty** as a responsible person of (enter corporation name) ______________________

for failure to pay withholding and Federal Insurance Contributions Act Taxes (Social Security taxes), for period(s) ending ______________________.

☐ **Other Federal Tax(es)** [specify type(s) and period(s)] ______________________

***Note:** If you need more space, use another sheet titled "Attachment to Form 656 Dated ______________." Sign and date the attachment following the listing of the tax periods.*

Item 6 — I/We submit this offer for the reason(s) checked below:

☐ **Doubt as to Liability** — "I do not believe I owe this amount." You must include a detailed explanation of the reason(s) why you believe you do not owe the tax in Item 9.

☐ **Doubt as to Collectibility** — "I have insufficient assets and income to pay the full amount." You must include a complete Collection Information Statement, Form 433-A and/or Form 433-B.

☐ **Effective Tax Administration** — "I owe this amount and have sufficient assets to pay the full amount, but due to my exceptional circumstances, requiring full payment would cause an economic hardship or would be unfair and inequitable." You must include a complete Collection Information Statement, Form 433-A and/or Form 433B **and** complete Item 9.

Item 7

I/We offer to pay $______________ (must be more than zero). Complete item 10 to explain where you will obtain the funds to make this offer.

Check one of the following:

☐ **Cash Offer (Offered amount will be paid in 90 days or less.)**

Balance to be paid in: ☐ 10; ☐ 30; ☐ 60; or ☐ 90 days from written notice of acceptance of the offer.

☐ **Short-Term Deferred Payment Offer (Offered amount will be paid in MORE than 90 days but within 24 months from written notice of acceptance of the offer.)**

$______________ within ______________ days (not more than 90 — See Instructions Section, **Determine Your Payment Terms**) from written notice of acceptance of the offer; and

beginning in the ______________ month after written notice of acceptance of the offer, $______________ on the ______________ day of each month for a total of ______________ months. (Cannot extend more than 24 months from written notice of acceptance of the offer.)

☐ **Deferred Payment Offer (Offered amount will be paid over the life of the collection statute.)**

$______________ within ______________ days (not more than 90 — See Instructions Section, **Determine Your Payment Terms**) from written notice of acceptance of the offer; and

beginning in the first month after written notice of acceptance of the offer, $______________ on the ______________ day of each month for a total of ______________ months.

ISA
STF FED1106F 1

NOTE: Signature(s) of taxpayer required on last page of Form 656

Form 656, Offer in Compromise (page 1)

Under IRS Regulations issued in 2002, the IRS is normally barred from levying on assets while an offer is pending and for 30 days thereafter. This restriction does not apply if the IRS determines that collection of the tax is in jeopardy or if it believes that an offer was submitted only for purpose of delay.

Effective November 1, 2003, a user fee of $150 applies to offer submissions except in hardship cases or when relief is sought on account of doubt as to liability.

Item 9 — Explanation of Circumstances

I am requesting an offer in compromise for the reason(s) listed below:

Note: *If you are requesting compromise based on doubt as to liability, explain why you don't believe you owe the tax.*
If you believe you have special circumstances affecting your ability to fully pay the amount due, explain your situation.
You may attach additional sheets if necessary.

Item 10 — Source of Funds

I/We shall obtain the funds to make this offer from the following source(s):

Item 11

If I/we submit this offer on a substitute form, I/we affirm that this form is a verbatim duplicate of the official Form 656, and I/we agree to be bound by all the terms and conditions set forth in the official Form 656.

Under penalties of perjury, I declare that I have examined this offer, including accompanying schedules and statements, and to the best of my knowledge and belief, it is true, correct and complete

11(a) Signature of Taxpayer

Date

11(b) Signature of Taxpayer

Date

For Official Use Only

I accept the waiver of the statutory period of limitations for the Internal Revenue Service.

Signature of Authorized Internal Revenue Service Official

Title

Date

NOTE: Signature(s) of taxpayer required on last page of Form 656

STF FED1106F.4

Form 656, Offer in Compromise (page 4)

Tax Planning

An Offer in Compromise should be submitted with the recognition that the IRS may counter with a larger dollar amount.

Caution

Changes in the offer program may be in the works. Many members of both Congress and the IRS Oversight Board have criticized the current system, most particularly the length of time that it takes the IRS to process an offer. The IRS has acted quickly in response. The processing of offers from non-business taxpayers has been consolidated in two service centers, one in Holtsville (New York) and the other in Memphis.

Controversy

Can you file an Offer in Compromise while you are in bankruptcy? Although the IRS guidelines prohibit the processing of offers during such a period, Bankruptcy Courts in Virginia and Georgia disagreed in two 2003 decisions. Why would you want to file an offer while in bankruptcy? Some bankruptcy proceedings involve only a reorganization and not a liquidation. Additionally, some taxes will not be discharged in a liquidation bankruptcy. Read on!

—But Bankruptcy Is Generally Available as a Last Resort

If the IRS rejects your Offer in Compromise, if you have no means with which to make an offer, or if you are overwhelmed by other debts, you may wish to file bankruptcy in the event that the IRS is continuing collection actions. However, the trust portion of employment taxes (including the Trust Fund Recovery Penalty discussed in Chapter 10) is nondischargeable, eliminating bankruptcy as an available option when sizable withholdings have gone unpaid

Most taxes are dischargeable in bankruptcy, assuming that they involve the "mere nonpayment" of taxes and not willful evasion by the taxpayer and provided more than three years have passed from the original or extended due date of the return and more than two years have passed from the date the return was actually filed (or more than 240 days have passed from the date of an additional IRS assessment not reflected on a return).

Caution

If you intend to discharge tax debt in bankruptcy, you'd better file the return by the original due date if you want to declare bankruptcy on the earliest possible date—three years and one day later.

Controversy

If you wait to file until the IRS has prepared a substitute return (discussed earlier in this chapter) for you, the tax liability may become nondischargeable. While it is

Controversy (cont.)

clear that a substitute return is not a "return" for purpose of discharge, some courts have determined that a subsequently filed return by the taxpayer is automatically without tax purpose and, accordingly, is not a "return" under the bankruptcy statutes. Other courts disagree and allow a taxpayer to show that a late submission was a "reasonable attempt to comply with the tax law." Even the courts adopting this standard disagree as to this application, most particularly as to whether it suffices to allow discharge simply by showing that the subsequently filed return reduced the tax liability shown by the IRS on the substitute return.

Caution

Congress is considering legislation that, if enacted, would force higher income individuals to pay a portion of all debts, including taxes, over time in order to receive a discharge. H.R. 975, the Bankruptcy Abuse and Consumer Protection Act was passed by the House on March 19, 2003.

Caution

The bankruptcy laws affecting the discharge of taxes and the retention of assets are complex and face major change. Counsel should be consulted as soon as the option of bankruptcy becomes a viable choice to a taxpayer, even if only in the future. The IRS is challenging more and more bankruptcies on grounds that the taxpayer went beyond mere nonpayment.

For example, in 1996 an Indiana Federal District Court denied a debtor's discharge of income tax liability because he overstated withholding allowances on Form W-4 (see Chapter 1) to increase his take-home pay. In 2000 both the 11th Circuit Court of Appeals and a Missouri Federal District Court denied discharge to debtors who had transferred assets to their spouses to avoid payment. A New York Bankruptcy Court denied discharge to a self-employed law firm partner who helped his wife pay her separate taxes and borrowed $60,000 for his daughter's college. The 11th Circuit Court of Appeals reversed a decision of an Alabama Federal District Court that would have allowed an alcoholic physician with three divorces to discharge his tax liability with his third bankruptcy. In 2002, a New York Bankruptcy Court denied discharge to an attorney with a masters degree in taxation who had paid for the private school education of all four of his children and who had made significant gifts to his former wife and friends. In 2003, a Florida District Court denied discharge to a physician and a New York Bankruptcy Court denied discharge to a bond trader. Each case involved a lavish lifestyle of travel and extensive gifts.

continues

Caution (cont.)

However, a Virginia Federal District Court in a June 23, 2003 decision reached an opposite result although the debtor earned in excess of $450,000 and incurred private schooling costs of $68,000 per year. Because his tax liability to the IRS in excess of $5.1 million arose from forgiveness of indebtedness income (see Chapter 2, "Taxable and Tax-Free Income and Benefits") related to a decline in the real estate market and not from "misconduct, fraud, or gross negligence," he was granted a discharge after being denied an Offer in Compromise.

Controversy

Although the U.S. Supreme Court determined in 1992 that qualified retirement plans (see Chapter 9, "Retirement Plans") are protected under federal law from creditors in a bankruptcy proceeding, certain lower courts have subsequently determined that this decision does not extend to plans of unincorporated business owners in which the only participants are owners and their spouses as well as to other retirement plans such as IRAs. These issues remain unsettled. The proposed bankruptcy legislation, if enacted, would expand bankruptcy protection to cover all employer-sponsored retirement plans and would offer protection for up to $1 million in IRAs. Currently, state law may grant additional bankruptcy exemptions beyond those provided under federal law. In any event, most courts have not exempted retirement plans including IRAs from the reach of the IRS upon bankruptcy.

Communicating with the IRS

The greatest frustration of taxpayers and professionals alike in dealing with the IRS is the failure of the IRS to process correspondence quickly or in many cases to process it at all. Nothing is more frustrating than to respond to a letter and then receive follow-up correspondence that says, "We have not heard from you."

In 1990 then IRS Commissioner Fred Goldberg told members of the Commissioner's Advisory Group that correspondence with taxpayers was the IRS's biggest problem but that a new automatic correspondence system should result in a "dramatic improvement." Nonetheless, a 1994 General Accounting Office survey of two IRS service centers found that 15 percent of IRS correspondence was "incorrect, unclear, incomplete, or nonresponsive." There appears to be little improvement today. In his 1999 report to Congress, then IRS Taxpayer Advocate W. Val Oveson, listed the clarity and tone of IRS correspondence as one of the biggest problems facing taxpayers, second only to the complexity of the tax law itself. The IRS acknowledged in 2001 that the number two problem in our tax system was communication, second only to the complexity of the law.

Unless the matter has been turned over to a particular individual or office, communicating by telephone has often produced comparable results to written communication. At a 1989 town meeting in which the IRS heard complaints by the public, taxpayers claimed to be unable to reach the Kansas City Service Center after two or three days of constant dialing. The IRS began 24 hours a day, seven days per week, telephone service in 1999 following reports that still only about one-half of all calls were going through. This was eventually discontinued although the IRS claims an 83 percent connection rate for the 2003 filing season.

The error rate of the IRS on those making contact and seeking substantial guidance was as high as 27 percent according to a 2000 survey by the General Accounting Office. A 2002 survey by the Treasury Inspector General for Tax Administration showed a reduced error rate of 20 percent. The IRS claimed an error rate of 12 percent for the 2003 filing season. One 1996 blunder made national news when a Washington, D.C., accountant called the IRS about an estate tax issue and was asked whether he was the decedent. Recent years, however, have seen an improved ability of the IRS to resolve most uncomplicated collection cases over the telephone.

When the matter is urgent and you wish to visit an IRS office, this is no guarantee of proper handling, as a Rockville, Maryland, eight year old and his father found out in 1989, in another nationally reported blunder. The eight-year-old first grade student had reported a tax liability of $152 on interest and dividend income but received a refund check from Philadelphia in the amount of $39,541.55. When his father visited the nearest IRS office in Wheaton, Maryland, the next day, the receptionist listened to his story and told him to take a number and wait. After an hour and 15 minutes, Dad's turn came but he ended up walking out of the office describing IRS personnel as "confused." The check did get returned the next day. A similar error occurred in 1996 when a three-year-old Pittsburgh boy received a $219,495 improper refund check from the IRS. By 2002, the IRS discontinued Saturday "Problem-Solving Days," open houses held in a number of locations on the same day. Its rationale was that every day is a problem-solving day.

Walk-ins who ask substantive tax questions face an even higher error rate than telephone callers. A 2001 report of the Treasury Inspector General for Tax Administration (TIGTA) found that 73 percent of walk-ins received incorrect or insufficient answers. One year later that number was reduced to 46 percent. However, the number climbed again the following year to 55 percent.

Caution

Send all important documents to the IRS by registered or certified U.S. mail. Many documents, particularly those sent to service centers, end up lost or misplaced. Although certain services of Airborne Express, DHL Worldwide, FedEx, and United Parcel Service are now treated similarly to the U.S. Postal Service for purpose of determining whether a document was timely mailed, only registered or certified U.S. mail enjoys prima facie proof that a document was delivered.

Controversy

The Courts of Appeals are divided as to whether a taxpayer not using registered or certified mail can prove mailing of a form or document by proving that it was placed in a mailbox. The Eighth and Ninth Circuit Courts of Appeals as well as a Colorado Federal District Court have backed taxpayers while the Second and Sixth Circuit Courts of Appeals have backed the IRS. The U.S. Supreme Court declined to review the issue in 1996.

Tax Planning

IRS offices and service centers have Taxpayer Advocates to deal with procedural problems meeting select criteria that are not handled properly through regular channels. In hardship cases, use of IRS Form 911 should get immediate attention from the Taxpayer Advocate in the office who can issue a Taxpayer Assistance Order (TAO) in the event of immediate threat of adverse action, irrevocable injury, long-term adverse impact, or substantial costs if relief is not granted, or upon the passage of more than 30 days in seeking resolution through normal channels.

The IRS and the Double Standard

Mail your tax return on the last day with insufficient postage; it will be returned and you will be considered as filing late. Address your Tax Court petition to the wrong address and miss the deadline; you will be permanently barred from Tax Court.

What if the IRS makes a mistake? In 1990, the IRS admitted that about 550,000 tax packets contained filing envelopes for the incorrect service center. In 1991, the IRS indicated that it lost in excess of $22 million as a result of its failure to sign necessary forms prior to the expiration of statutes of limitation. In 1992, at a cost of more than $175 million, the IRS sent refund checks arising from the earned income credit to 270,000 ineligible individuals. In 1993, the IRS sent huge erroneous tax bills out of its Kansas City Service Center; a Centerville, Virginia, man was dunned for back taxes in excess of $68 million. In 1994, the GAO reported that it could not audit the IRS in that it could not account for $2.1 billion of expenses.

In 1995, the IRS sent about 43,000 improper bills to high-income individuals who had elected under a transition rule to spread their retroactive tax increase in 1993 over three years. In 1996, a former IRS historian called the agency a "black hole" of history, claiming that the IRS routinely throws away documents. In 1997, the IRS sent about 90,000 notices to household employers charging them with failure to file and pay unemployment taxes, ignoring that these taxes are now paid with Schedule H of the individual income tax return. In 1998, a Chattanooga, Tennessee, man got a bill from the IRS for more than $300 million; he got off easy compared to the Wynnewood, Pennsylvania, woman who got a bill for $40 billion. The IRS blamed programming errors. In 1999, the IRS jumped the gun on Y2K and sent notices to hundreds of taxpayers that their May 1999 tax deposits were being applied to the January 31, 1900, tax period.

In 2000, a private vendor retained by the IRS "flipped" some of the names on estimated payment vouchers and sent them to the wrong taxpayers. In 2001, 523,000 households received letters from the IRS promising rebates of more than their entitlements under the Economic Growth and Tax Reconciliation Act of 2001, and 71,000 taxpayers who sent in more than $1.2 billion found that their payments were "lost" by workers at an outserviced lockbox facility. In 2002, the Treasury Department Inspector General was asked to investigate the loss of 6,600 computers and several firearms by the IRS. In 2003, a GAO report cited inadequate controls over taxpayer payments in cash to the IRS.

So only taxpayers have to be perfect—and keep all of their records.

The Taxpayer Bill of Rights—Parts 1, 2, and 3

Concern about taxpayer problems with the IRS caused enactment in 1988 of a Taxpayer Bill of Rights, which provided taxpayers with many specific rights including the following rights, not previously discussed, which are still in force today:

- The IRS must provide taxpayers with a written explanation of their rights.
- On prior notice to the IRS, a taxpayer is permitted to make an audio recording of an interview. The IRS may also choose to record the interview, in which case a taxpayer is entitled to a copy or transcript upon request and payment of costs.
- The IRS must abate any penalty attributable to erroneous written advice by an IRS employee when the advice was specifically requested and was reasonably relied upon.
- The IRS is prohibited from using tax enforcement records to evaluate the collection performance of revenue officers and their supervisors.
- If the IRS wishes to modify or terminate an existing agreement for the payment of an outstanding tax liability in installments, it must provide the taxpayer with 30 days' notice setting forth a reason for the proposed modification.
- Taxpayers have the right to sue in Federal District Court if any IRS employee knowingly or negligently fails to release an IRS lien when required or if an IRS employee acts in reckless or intentional disregard of a law or regulation in connection with collection of a tax.

- A taxpayer may be awarded reasonable litigation costs if he or she "substantially prevails" in the matter. In the case of an examination, expenses of the administrative appeal may also be awarded.

The belief of continuing unfairness by the IRS led to enactment of a Taxpayer Bill of Rights—Part 2 in 1996. Senate Finance Committee Chairman William Roth praised the legislation as "a victory for every taxpayer who has ever been intimidated, bullied, browbeaten, threatened, harassed, or unjustly accused or investigated by the IRS." Among the taxpayer benefits and rights included in Part 2 are the following rights, not previously discussed, which are still in force today:

- An individual is entitled to an appeals process in the event of modification or termination of an installment agreement.
- The IRS is given expanded authority to abate interest, and the Tax Court, as in the case of penalties, is given authority to review most failures of the IRS to abate interest.
- A separated or divorced individual who filed a joint return is entitled to information as to collection activity against and recovery from the spouse.
- The IRS may withdraw a tax lien without full payment if the withdrawal is in the best interests of both the taxpayer and the IRS.
- The IRS may return levied property if the levy was not in accordance with administrative procedures or return is in the best interests of both the taxpayer and the IRS.

In 1998, 10 years after the first Taxpayer Bill of Rights, Taxpayer Bill of Rights—Part 3 was enacted. Among its provisions not previously discussed are the following:

- CPAs, enrolled agents, and enrolled actuaries enjoy confidentiality in IRS proceedings and in tax litigation (except in criminal and certain tax shelter matters) in regard to tax advice provided to clients.
- The IRS is prohibited from using the "illegal tax protester" designation and must remove a "nonfiler" designation when a taxpayer has filed and paid taxes for two consecutive years.
- No third-party contacts are permitted in determining or collecting tax liability without providing reasonable notice to the taxpayer (except in criminal cases or when collection is in jeopardy).
- Effective for court proceedings arising in connection with audits, adjustments and review of refund claims, the burden of proof in court on any factual issue is with the IRS if the taxpayer maintains records, complies with substantiation requirements, introduces credible evidence, and cooperates with reasonable requests by the IRS.

The three Taxpayer Bill of Rights laws are the first steps toward establishing the principle that an agency of almost 100,000 employees charged each year with reviewing the personal tax strategies reflected on more than 130 million individual tax returns, more than 227 million total returns, and collecting almost $2 trillion must be based upon clear and equitable procedures.

The IRS in the 21st Century

"Provide America's taxpayers with top quality service by helping them to understand and meet their tax responsibilities and by applying the tax law with integrity and fairness to all."

Such is the new mission statement of the IRS. To carry out its mission, the IRS declared in 1998 that modernization had begun. To replace its geographical structure, the IRS has converted to four operating divisions based on "market segments." Governance of the tax filings by most individuals is by the Wage and Investment Income Operating Division with about 90 million filers. The Small Business & Self-Employed Operating Division handles most other individual filers. The remaining two divisions regulate larger business and tax-exempt organizations.

Charles Rossotti, a business executive with a background in technology rather than in tax led the IRS into the 21st Century with assistance from a nine-member oversight board including five members from the private sector. His successor, Mark Everson, also recruited from outside the tax community, does not have an easy task. A rating several years ago of 200 companies and government agencies by 46,000 people in a survey cosponsored by the University of Michigan showed the IRS finishing dead last—just after the post office. However, in a 2002 survey of "customer" satisfaction of federal agencies, also conducted by the University of Michigan, the IRS had advanced to third to last with a score of 62 on a scale from 1–100. The IRS has conducted its own surveys including a 1998 "customer satisfaction survey" of 150 taxpayers whose property was seized. Only nine questionnaires were returned.

The natural tendency of individuals to dislike bill collectors has been inflamed by bad press. For example, when the IRS threatened to seize balls, bats, and uniforms of a California girls' preteen softball league, front page stories across the country helped cause the IRS to relent. Following congressional pressure, then Commissioner Rossotti had to personally intervene in September 1998 to assure fans returning home run balls to record-breakers Mark McGwire and Sammy Sosa that they would not face adverse tax consequences.

The press has also reported the disciplining of IRS employees for their own tax violations and for incidents of intentional unauthorized access to taxpayer records. Between July 1998 and September 2002 the Treasury Inspector General for Tax Administration substantiated 419 employee violations resulting in 71 firings.

Meanwhile, after $4 billion of costs, the IRS is attempting to bring its aging telephone infrastructure and its 1960s-like computer system into the 21st century. Part way into the computer upgrades, one assistant commissioner recommended that the IRS start all over again.

In testimony before a House Subcommittee in 1999, then Commissioner Rossotti conceded that modernization "requires almost a complete replacement of IRS information technology systems, which are built on a 30-year-old fundamentally deficient foundation." The IRS has started by constructing a popular Web site which receives millions of "hits" daily during filing season.

There has been some good press too for the IRS. Employees have raised money for charity in several cities by allowing the public a chance to throw pies in their faces or to dunk them under water. Ask any two people whether the IRS is fair and you will probably get two different answers.

For example, ask the man who hitchhiked several years ago to the Ogden, Utah, service center to pick up a badly needed tax refund. Ogden informed him that refund checks were issued by another IRS office; however, employees verified his refund, ordered the check sent to Ogden, and collected food and cash to hold him over until the refund check arrived.

Then ask the Tulsa, Oklahoma, man who drove naked to the post office a couple of years ago just before midnight on April 15 to file his tax return. He complained that the IRS had taken the shirt off his back—to say nothing about the pants off his seat.

Index

A

B

C

D

E

J

K

L

M

N

O

P

Q

R

S